Frank Stewart's Nexus

AN AMERICAN PHOTOGRAPHER'S JOURNEY, 1960s TO THE PRESENT

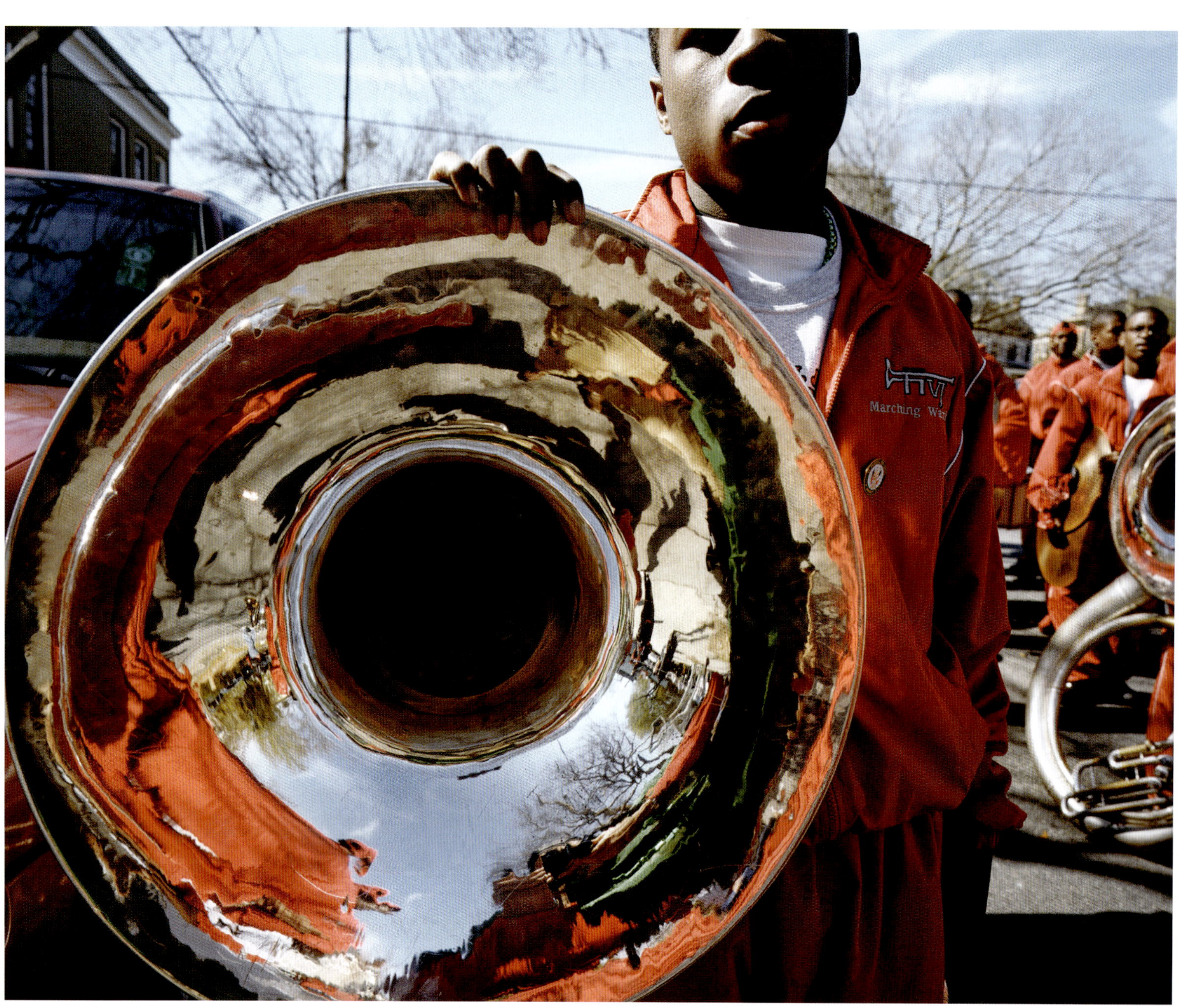
Marching

Frank Stewart's Nexus

AN AMERICAN PHOTOGRAPHER'S JOURNEY, 1960s TO THE PRESENT

Ruth Fine and Fred Moten

With contributions by
Wynton Marsalis
Mary Schmidt Campbell
Frank Stewart
Cheryl Finley

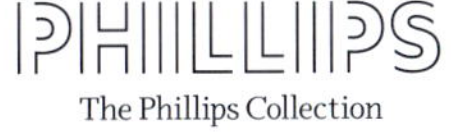

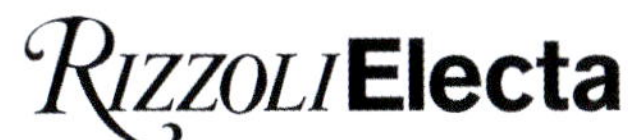

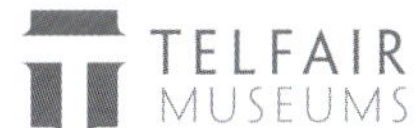

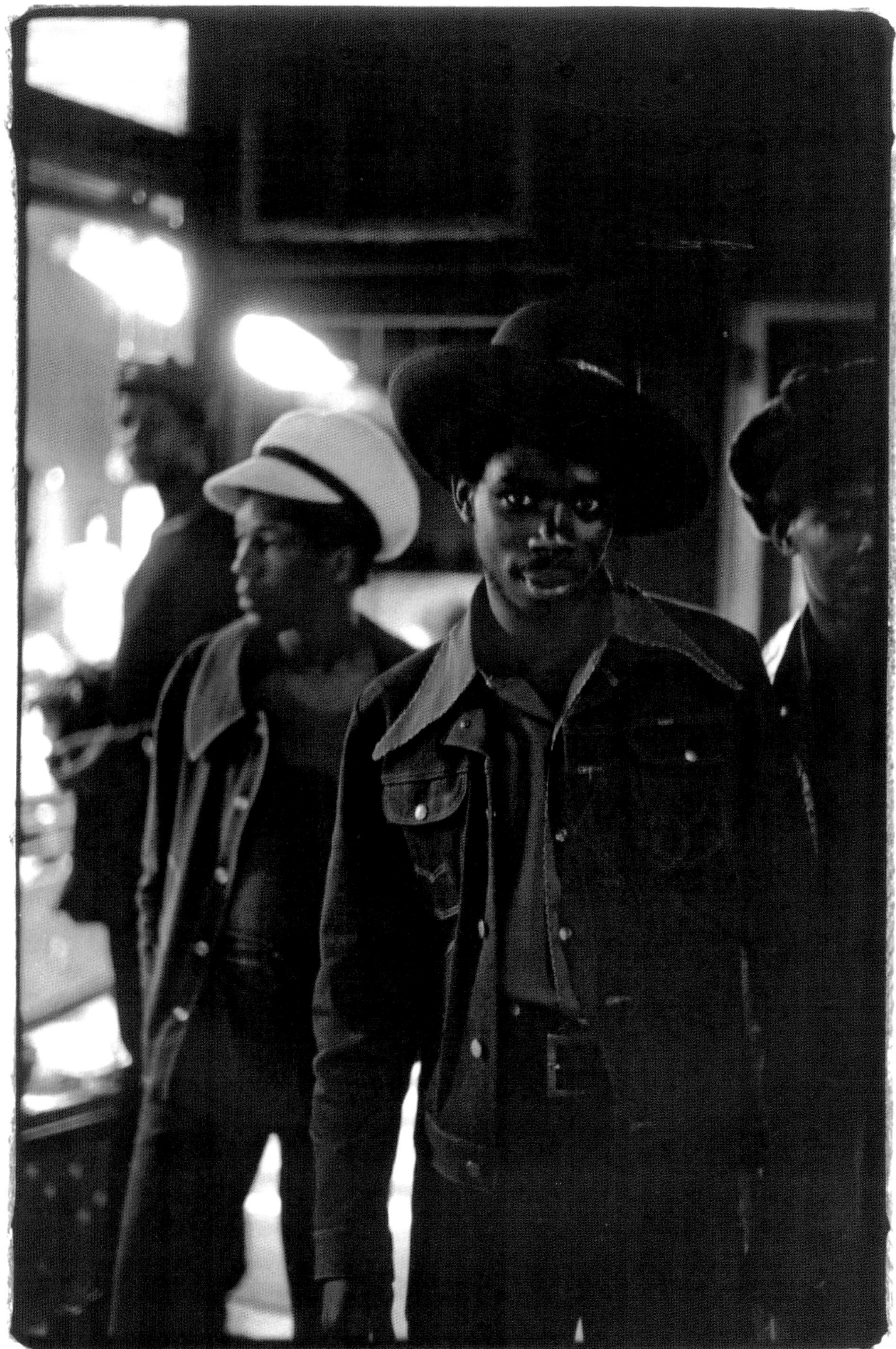

CONTENTS

George in the Doorway, 1969

Previous spread: *Circle in the Square, Savannah*, 2007

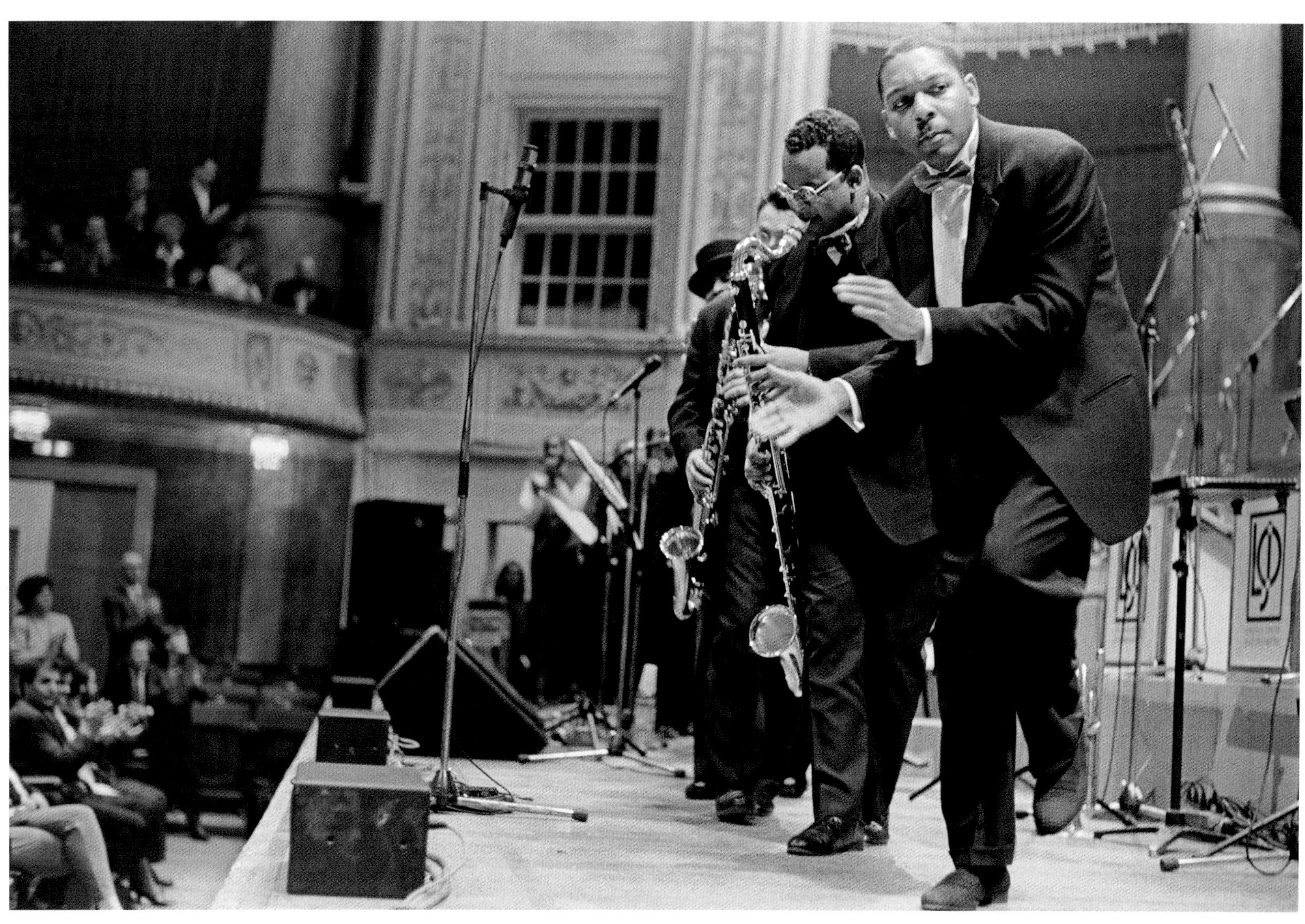

Stomping the Blues, 1997

SOME FEW CHORUSES FOR THE EXCELLENT FRANK STEWART

Wynton Marsalis

May 9, 2022

High Point on the court with the ball in his hand,
Pit Boss smoke ribs in the fire can

Up in the mornin' at the crack of dawn,
Close down clubs when the bourbon gone

Pour Southern gravy on gritty Northern streets,
train-track traveler with track-star feats

Born Nashville country
raised Memphis blues,
South Side Chicago
paid New York City dues

Knows all the hustlers and the high priest too,
Pit Boss flick his shutter quick
when Boozie stumble through

Khaki jacket Borsilaano
early to the field,
Solitary maan e mano
seek his daily yield

Watch him walking ginger
down a never trodden trail,
He snatched a song the mockingbird
stole from a nightingale

Crisp and cool, searing hot
like Ahmad's piano sound,
High Point take that perfect shot
'fore the fleeting truth go down

Eagle-eyed ninja up a tricky mountain pass,
Drive down easy—twice as fast

Pit Boss read the changing seasons
in the bowels of the land.
He Shawnee, Pawnee, Navajo
with High John in his hand

He step in stony silence,
He a Singapura cat,
Ol' – Silver – Fox
just – be – like – that.

Largest living palette,
(He from Bearden's pedigree).
Raise himself up on Carolina shine,
eat the fruit of the baobab tree

Go 'head Glorious Griot with your Leica ready set,
He line up all the angles (ain't a gesture he don't get)

He tears from blackest shadows
their contrapuntal light,
Lester Young and Lady Day when the Basie band is right

High Point hit nine jumpers,
"'fore his feet was even set,"
Print kaleidoscopic pulsing
of a Mandelbrot set

Master, student, pastor—
of the black, the brown, the beige,
him red, him white, him yellow—
Him yin/yang Eastern sage

He squeeze the spaces forward
He pull the faces back
He balance on the razor rim
and shimmy down the crack
Tells tallest smallest flawless tales
of deeds that needs be told,
Silver cloaks our cosmic consciousness in a double-quilted fold

"Imageus Capturus!"
shout his name outright
as K burns midnight road,
Hundred-miles-an-hour-speak in
magic mystic mode

Dress up new mythologies
in shin'est pearl white silk,
He slow-bathe our culture,
in first-time-mother's milk

High Point the One Who Cracked the Holy Code (of purest modern jazz),
He mopped a crowded subway floor
with three dumb thugs' young ass.

He pot a gumbo file' yumbo
Crescent City stove,
dark room brim with jumbo files:
him tintype treasure trove

When a soul at last is free
and in its final rattle,
Franklin snap the tambourine agleam
to trap the tale it tattle

Be ye foreign or of native born,
a fan or "just don't care,"
If you have the eyes to see
the Silver Fox is there.

If you have the heart to be,
On land, on sea, on air

If you mind your mind set free,
"He out here" . . . (everywhere)

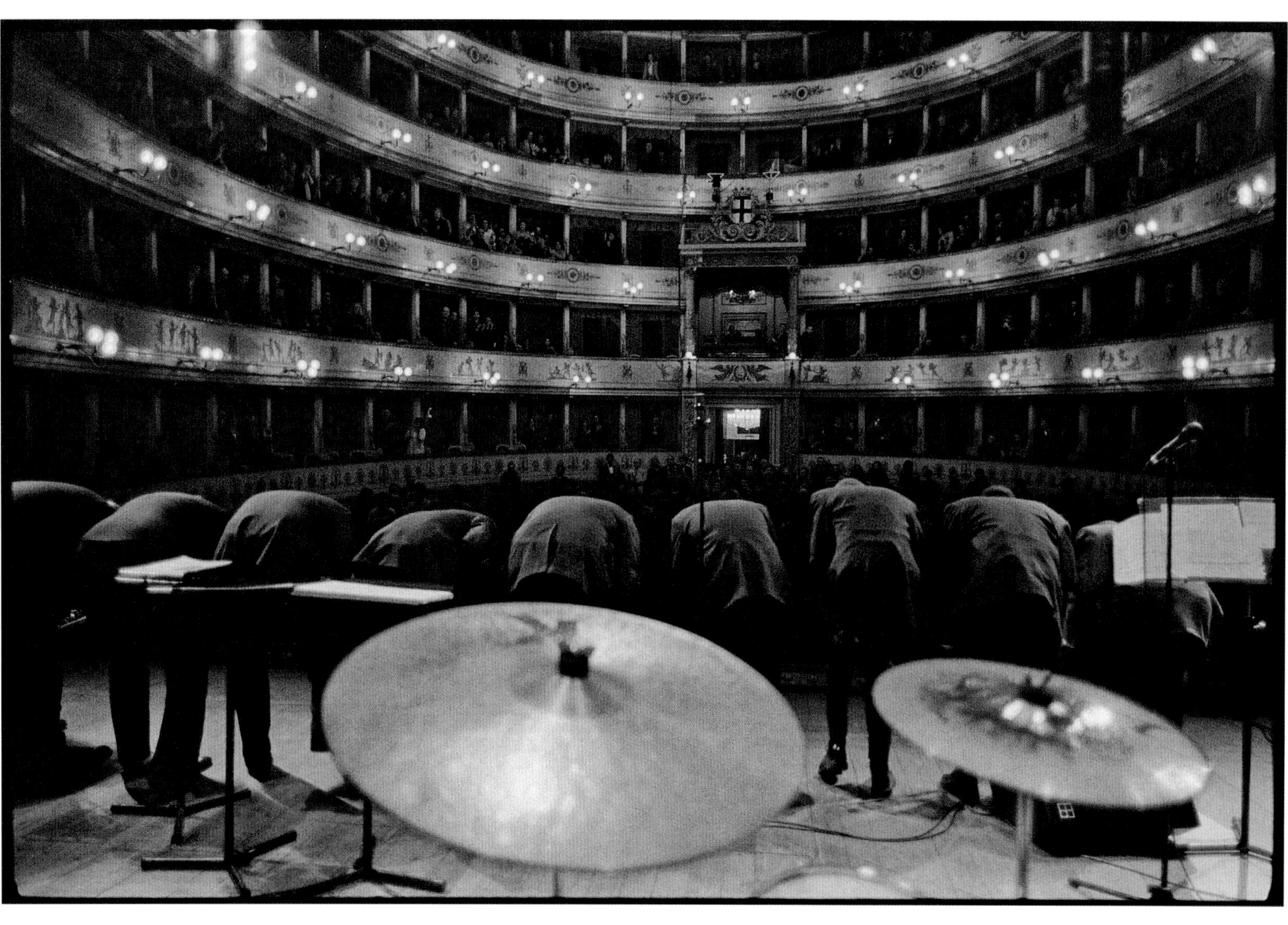

DIRECTORS' FOREWORD

Over the past six decades, Frank Stewart has emerged as an expressive, individual voice who has engaged in spontaneous and sensitive portrayals of world culture and Black life. His emotionally charged photographs—immersive investigations of art, food, dance, music, and the environment—show Stewart at the cultural vanguard, a creative visionary for our time. *Frank Stewart's Nexus: An American Photographer's Journey, 1960s to the Present* is the first major museum retrospective of this artist's career; it highlights Stewart's range of interests and practices as he embraces the world around him, often working from the road. Co-organized by The Phillips Collection and Telfair Museums, this exhibition and publication offer a comprehensive visual biography of 103 photographs from the 1960s to the present day.

We would first and foremost like to thank Frank Stewart, whose extraordinary photographs are the impetus for this collaboration. Stewart's vision, creative spirit, kindness, and generosity of time and energy propelled this project to the finish line. As co-organizers of this important project, it has been a joy for us to connect with this remarkable artist in so many ways.

Frank Stewart's ties to Washington, DC, coincide with his first significant interaction with the camera. At the age of fourteen, he traveled to the nation's capital to participate in the 1963 March on Washington for Jobs and Freedom, and he used his mother's Brownie to record the events of the day. Already then, Stewart showed intuitive compositional sophistication and determination. In the 1970s, with David C. Driskell, Stewart visited and photographed artists in their DC studios, including Alma W. Thomas and Loïs Mailou Jones. He returned to the city in the 1980s to photograph its landmarks. These works call to mind several examples of documentary and street photography in The Phillips Collection, including images by Joel Meyerowitz, one of Stewart's teachers.

The Bow, Modena, Italy, 1996

Photography is the Phillips's fastest growing area of collecting, approaching 1,600 objects. The first gift of photography to the collection came in 1949, when Georgia O'Keeffe gave nineteen cloud images by Alfred Stieglitz. In the 1960s, the museum purchased five photographs by Henri Cartier-Bresson and held an exhibition of his work. Stewart has long been influenced by Cartier-Bresson's concept of the "decisive moment." His intimate, candid images of African American artists in their homes and studios, where he has captured their artistic environment and spirit, shows his synthesis of this modernist aesthetic. The Phillips exhibited artist portraits by Stewart and Cartier-Bresson in the seminal *Riffs and Relations: African American Artists and the European Modernist Tradition* (2020). *Frank Stewart's Nexus* reexamines these intimate portraits and a variety of important photographs by Stewart, and places them within the larger context of his life and career. We are pleased to premier Stewart's art in the city that inspired him, and the project also fosters the institutional efforts of the Phillips as we continue to enrich our photography collection with Stewart's impressive works.

Frank Stewart grew up in the South and has made trips to New Orleans and to Jackson, Mississippi, among his many returns to the region. Savannah, Georgia, has been part of his experience for over twenty years, since he was hired as a staff photographer for the Savannah Music Festival (SMF), an annual cross-genre musical event that occurs in early spring. Telfair is grateful to SMF for first bringing Stewart to Savannah. SMF and other spring events, such as the Savannah Saint Patrick's Day parade (one of the largest in the country), offered compelling material for Stewart's lens. Telfair Museums currently holds two photographs by Stewart in the collection, both of which formally explore the abstracting and painterly effect of reflection and consider Savannah's environment. Taken in 2006, *Savannah Tour Bus* shows a passing trolley of smiling tourists, whose faces are slightly distorted by the vinyl bus window coverings that reflect the bright red marquee signs in front of Paula Deen's signature restaurant. *Circle in the Square, Savannah* features a tuba player in the H. V. Jenkins High School marching band, known as the "Marching Warriors," taken during preparation for the Saint Patrick's Day parade in 2007. The energy of the parade and the bold colors of the bright spring day and red uniforms are captured in the reflective surface of the round tuba. In 2020, Telfair hosted Stewart as a speaker for the annual Lawrence Lecture as *Circle in the Square, Savannah* was featured in an exhibition exploring youth in photography. His representation in the collection and his strong ties to the community reinforce Telfair's excitement about bringing a wide-ranging collection of his work to audiences in the spring of 2024 for further discovery and understanding.

It has truly been a pleasure to collaborate across the board on *Frank Stewart's Nexus*. We are thrilled that Artis—Naples, The Baker Museum signed on as a venue for the exhibition. Artis—Naples is a multidisciplinary organization that encourages appreciation of art in all forms, a belief that aligns with the intersectional art forms in Stewart's photographs. We wish to thank the museum staff, especially Courtney McNeil, museum director and chief curator, for recognizing the importance of this exhibition and sharing it with the museum's audience.

Producing an exhibition and publication requires the dedication of many individuals. We wholeheartedly thank guest curators Ruth Fine and Fred Moten. Ruth Fine, former curator at the National Gallery of Art, has known Frank Stewart for over two decades and is a consummate professional who has been an unwavering source of enthusiasm, assistance, and knowledge. Poet, professor, and critic Fred Moten has been an active supporter of the project since the beginning and has been instrumental in bringing the exhibition and publication to fruition.

The publication features a sweeping survey of Stewart's black-and-white and color images, and includes an interview with the artist and texts by significant voices. We fervently thank the contributors to the publication, whose investment in and friendship with Stewart have helped to illuminate his remarkable career. Thank you to Wynton Marsalis for his poetic chorus that pays homage to Stewart's engaging life and character; to Mary Schmidt Campbell for her perceptive introduction; to Ruth Fine for her keen insights and probing questions; to Fred Moten for exploring the mutability of the medium of photography through Stewart's mastery of light; and to Cheryl Finley for broadening our international perspectives.

The beautiful design of this catalogue was conceived and executed by Phil Kovacevich, whose astute visual eye proved indispensable. We wish to thank Margaret Rennolds Chace, associate publisher, and Andrea Danese, senior editor, of Rizzoli Electa for their firm management and stewardship of the publication that complements the exhibition but also offers insight beyond the museum walls into the life and career of Stewart.

Renée Maurer and Erin Dunn, the lead curators at our respective institutions, are to be commended for their tireless spearheading of the exhibition and publication, which required exceptional feats of organization, foresight, and enthusiasm.

An exhibition of the scope and complexity would not be possible without the participation of numerous national lenders, including museums, galleries, and private collectors. We would like to thank directors and curators at the following museums and institutions: Bowdoin College Museum of Art, Anne Collins Goodyear and Frank Goodyear, codirectors; Gallery Neptune & Brown, Christine Neptune and Robert Brown, codirectors; Kenkeleba House, Corrine Jennings, director; Memphis

Brooks Museum of Art, Mark Resnik, interim director, and Jennifer Draffen, director of collections, exhibitions, and publications; Museum of Art and Origins, George Nelson Preston, founder; Museum of Modern Art, Glenn D. Lowry, the David Rockefeller Director; National Museum of African American Art and Culture, Kevin Young, the Andrew W. Mellon Director; Philadelphia Museum of Art, Sasha Sudo, George D. Widener Director and CEO, Hyunsoo Woo, the Pappas-Sarbanes Deputy Director for Collections and Exhibitions, and Peter Barberie, curator of photography; and The Studio Museum in Harlem, Thelma Golden, director and chief curator, and Connie Choi, associate curator of the permanent collection. We offer gratitude to the following private collectors: Fay and Blake Boswell, Collection of a Friend of the Memphis Brooks Museum of Art, Manny's Bistro, Elizabeth Cooper Davis, Gordon and Peggy Cooper Davis, Walter O. Evans, Rob Gibson, Sandra Grymes, Andre Kimo Stone Guess and Cheryl Peterson Guess, Sing Lathan and Bining Taylor, Rodney M. Miller, Jeanne Moutoussamy-Ashe, Robert O'Meally, The Medium Group, LLC, courtesy of Larry Ossel-Mensah, Adam A. Rose and Peter R. McQuillan, Greg Scholl, John Simmons, Beuford Smith, John-Conrad Ste Marthe, Frank Stewart, Marquise Stillwell, Eileen and Major E. Thomas Jr., and those who wish to remain anonymous. The extraordinary commitment of our lenders has led to the successful realization of *Frank Stewart's Nexus*.

We also want to thank the staffs at both museums whose professionalism and effort all played a role in making the publication and exhibition a tremendous success. At The Phillips Collection, the project received direction and counsel from Elsa Smithgall, chief curator, and Yuma Tomes, the Horning Chair for Diversity, Equity, Accessibility, and Inclusion. Trish Waters and Sarah Perdue, associate registrars for exhibitions, diligently and with great effort coordinated the crating and shipping arrangements and managed the insurance negotiations; Cherie Nichols, chief financial officer, oversaw costs; Michele DeShazo, assistant registrar, handled key visual resource requests; and Elizabeth Steele, head of conservation, and Patricia Favero, associate conservator, provided the necessary examinations of these important loans. Additional thanks go to other essential museum staff, including Kathryn Rogge, manager of exhibitions; Renée Littleton, chief communications officer and director of marketing; Vivian Djen, head of editorial and design services; Anne Taylor Brittingham, deputy director for education and responsive learning spaces; Nehemiah Dixon III, director of community engagement; Ashley Whitfield, head of public programs; Wendy Ponvert, director of development; Elizabeth Temme, director of major gifts; Bridget Zangueneh, director of institutional giving; Victoria Potucek, grants manager; Micha Winkler Thomas, director of strategy and operations; Pete Bernal, museum shop manager; Robert Harris, security operations manager; and Huy Huynh, chief engineer. We would also like to acknowledge the industrious efforts of the installation team of Alec MacKaye, Taryn Harris, and Carson Garhart. At Telfair Museums, the project was supported by Crawford Alexander Mann III, chief curator and director of curatorial affairs; Anne-Solène Bayan, assistant curator; Jennifer Levy, chief registrar, and Margaret von Spreecken, associate registrar, adeptly facilitated shipping; Beth Moore, rights and reproduction assistant curator, was ever helpful in obtaining image credit lines and rights for usage; Harry DeLorme Jr., director of education and senior curator, led the important educational components of the exhibition; Rana Edgar, director of development, Lauren Grant, director of corporate and foundation relations, and Jason Kendall, senior grant and communications writer, supported the exhibition and publication through rigorous fundraising; Joey Rudder, chief financial officer, kept the budget and accounting in line for a complicated project. In addition, thanks are due to staff who have played a role, big or small, in bringing this project to Telfair and ensuring its resounding success, including Brittany Salley, director of marketing and communications; Melissa Hill, creative director; and David Reinerth, director of visitor and retail operations. Finally, thanks to the preparators and designers of the exhibition, Heath Ritch and Andrew Gatti.

DOROTHY KOSINSKI, PHD
Vradenburg Director and CEO of The Phillips Collection

BENJAMIN T. SIMONS
Executive Director and CEO of Telfair Museums

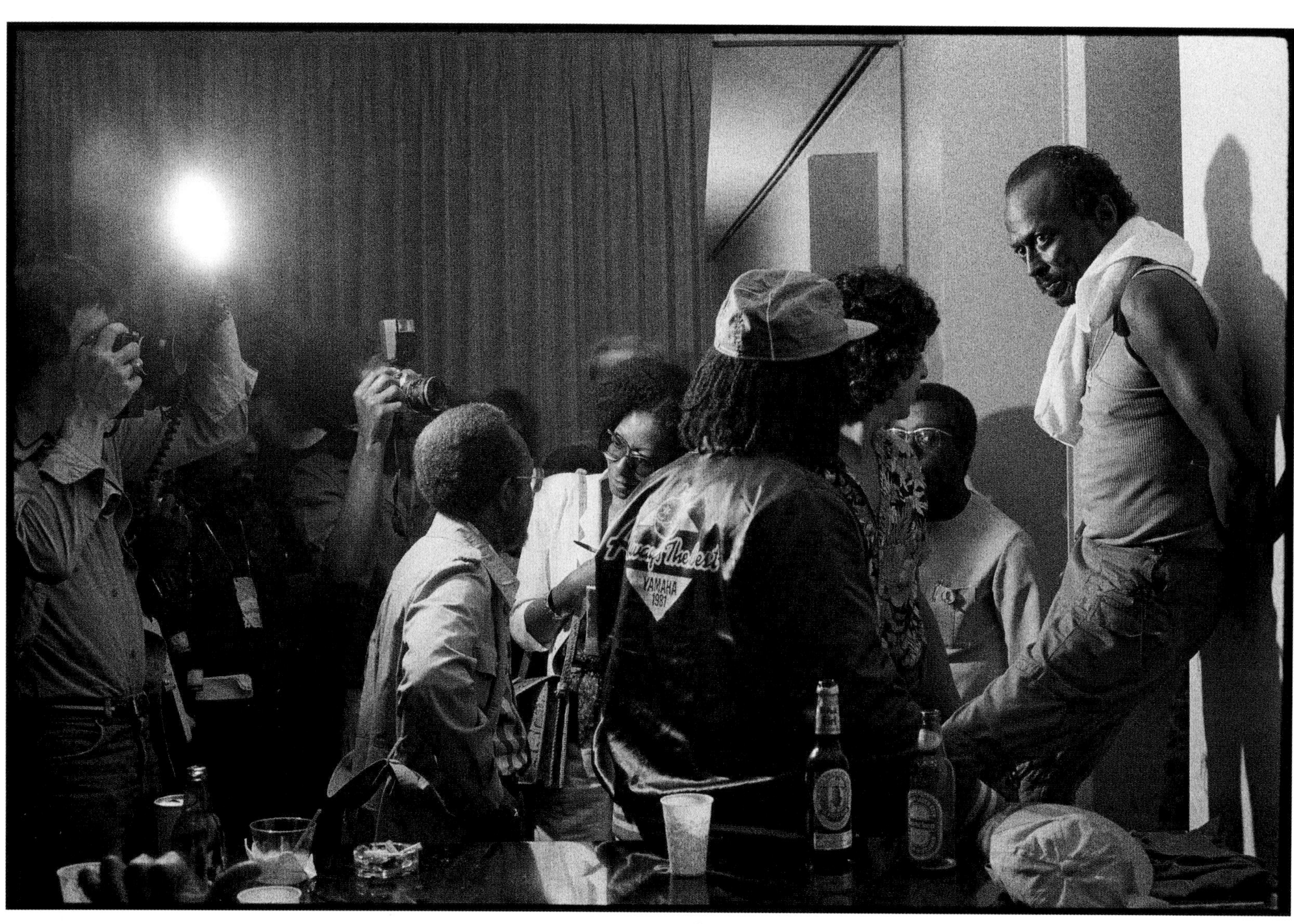
YAMAHA
1981

INTRODUCTION

Mary Schmidt Campbell

To look at a photograph by Frank Stewart is to look at an image that feels familiar. Like his teacher and mentor Roy DeCarava, Stewart creates a sense of intimacy and familiarity, a feeling of *I know these people. I have been there. They resemble my family.* No matter what subject matter Stewart is capturing, whether it is the itinerant life of the Jazz at Lincoln Center musicians, a family reunion, or the grief amid the losses of Katrina, Stewart beckons the viewer to join him in getting to know the place and people who inhabit his photographs.

Bearing witness is a phrase that is often used to describe photography as a testimonial artifact. But, in the case of Stewart's photographs, no one is on trial. There is no moral judgment or indictment or effort to evoke a stand for or against the subjects captured. By contrast, when shooting for *LIFE* magazine, superb photographer and journalist Gordon Parks often issued a moral challenge to his audience. Stewart's photographs are never evidence; rather they are invitations to remember time, places, people—whether those are circumstances in which people are trapped, liberated, or alone. In extending the invitation, he is inviting us to know these people, places, and situations. We travel with him and trust the honesty of a portal that opens onto life unposed and unstaged.

Guest curators Ruth Fine and Fred Moten's retrospective exhibition of Frank Stewart's life, subtitled *An American Photographer's Journey, 1960s to the Present*, captures in an array of thematic groupings the restlessness that has moved Stewart's work from one subject to another and from one city and one country to another. To name the American cities, count the number of countries, identify the rites and rituals he photographs—a formidable theme throughout this project—is to feel his fascination with both rootedness and uprootedness. As nomadic as his eye might be, in the most pedestrian detail, his images often portray both continuity and connection, as those seen in an exhibition grouping, *The Culture: Rituals*: an interment service in a St. Louis cemetery; Black women proud in the ceremonial wearing of Easter hats in Harlem; a wedding reception in Chicago; a street performer on Bourbon Street in New Orleans; and, as despicable as they may be, Klansmen in a ritualistic gathering in Mississippi—each, in its way, is about affirming some form of community. Like his domestic roaming, his photographs of his global travels, included in the grouping *Ancestors*, are the setting for those established ways that shape lives as well: women carrying water in Ghana; drummers in Côte d'Ivoire; the Door of No Return on Gorée Island, Senegal. His images feature the small and large rites of passage that celebrate milestones in our lives or in the history of our shared heritage.

He is a photographer of the famous as well. Yet, when Stewart captures them, he is adept at avoiding the crown of celebrity, locating them, instead, inside of their

Miles in the Green Room, 1981

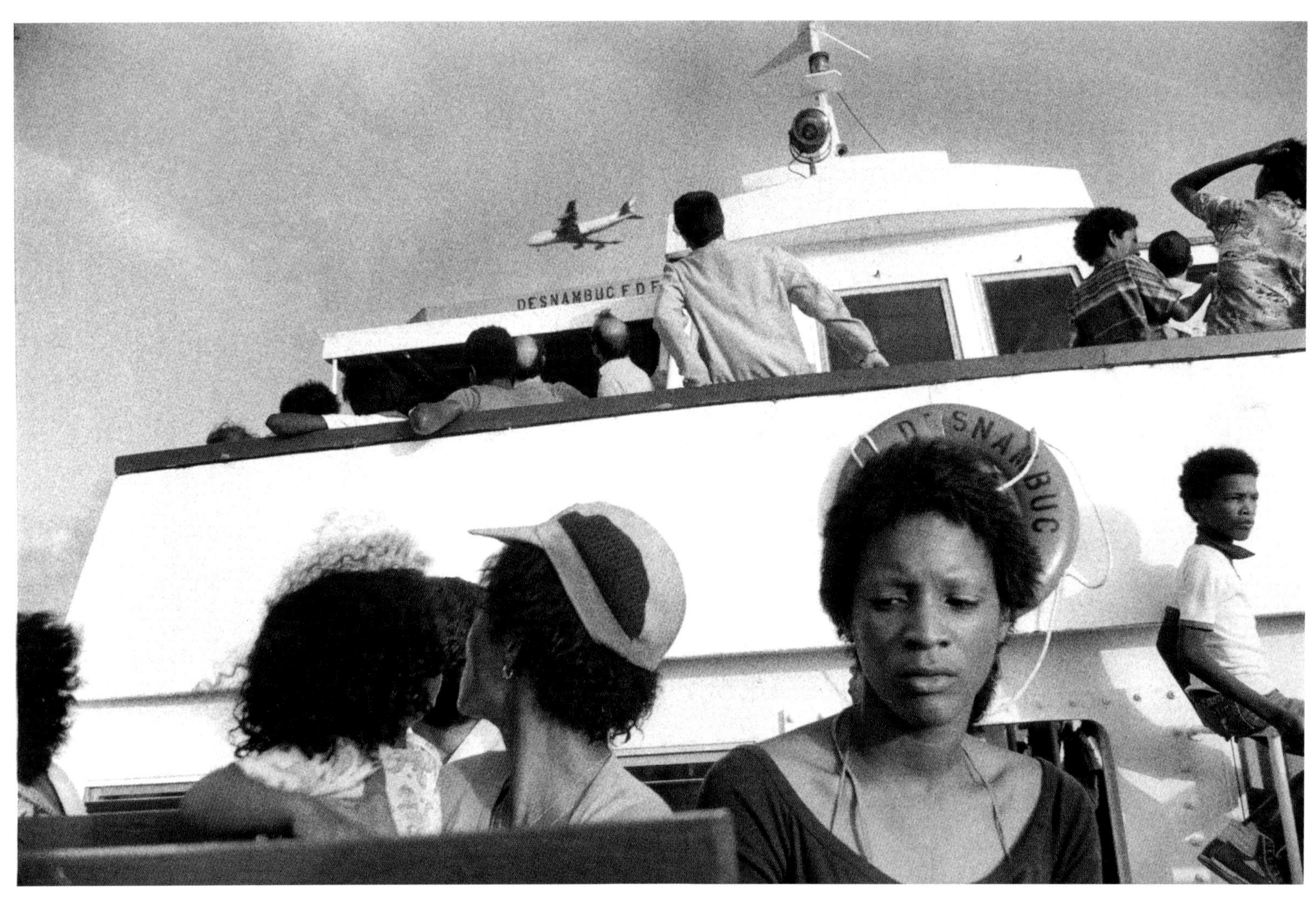

Desnambuc, 1975

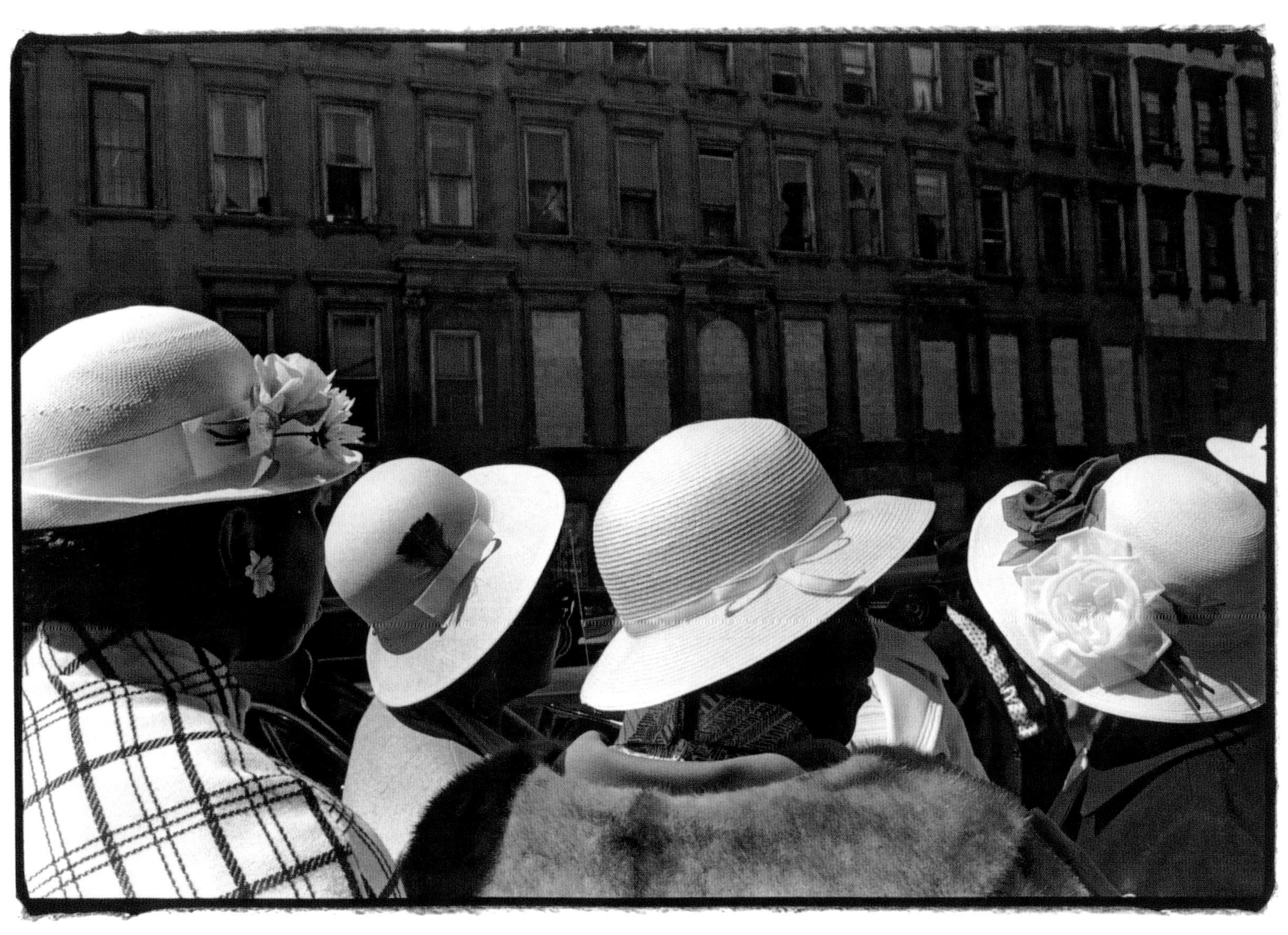

Easter Sunday, Harlem, 1976

defining habits: Miles Davis, caught unaware in the greenroom; Fidel Castro pontificating at the microphone. In *Artists and Workplaces*, candid shots reveal well-known Black visual artists and musicians socializing, especially: Romare Bearden, Alma W. Thomas, David C. Driskell, and Cassandra Wilson. Stewart's photographs of fellow artists are a cornerstone of his oeuvre. His most noteworthy endeavor in this category of pursuits was his thirty years with the Jazz at Lincoln Center Orchestra, seen in *Around the World: Chromatic Music*. He traveled with them everywhere and got to know the individual musicians and the repertoire of the orchestra. As a result, he highlights everything from public performances to personal moments, creating a portrait of the culture of the ensemble, as well as individually private and intimate images.

Stewart never permitted his creativity to be limited, and the exhibition and publication demonstrate not only his geographic and exploratory subject matter but also his stylistic journey. Fine and Moten include a series of photographs we might not readily associate with Stewart. Self-proclaimed *Drawings*, these fast confrontations on the street veer at times toward abstraction and reveal an eye keenly attuned to the painterly qualities of photography. The influence of Stewart's mentor, DeCarava, whose black-and-white photographs are often described as painterly, is again apparent. But Stewart's color photographs evoke something different: the collages of Romare Bearden or the audacity of Sam Gilliam's drape paintings. Bearden is a particularly apt comparison, since Stewart, in addition to photographing Bearden, often played the role of driver for the older non-driving artist. An astute selection of color photos adds an unexpected dimension to the work of an artist whose long-standing affiliation with Jazz at Lincoln Center might lead us to put him into a box with a label, thinking we know him, only to discover we don't know him at all.

Unlike his black-and-white images, Stewart's color photography often contains no people. People, nonetheless, are the subject. In their absence, he has conveyed what has been torn and decimated in their lives. *Environmental Catastrophe,* his portrait of New Orleans in the wake of Katrina's devastation, brings the subjects of destruction, loss, and pain into sharp focus without a single person in the frame. Juxtaposing images and words, Stewart adopts a muted color palette that conveys the energy drained from a once vibrant city. He titles each scene as something that Hurricane Katrina owns. *Katrina's Houses I* (page 157)*,* for example, is a shot of a car trapped with water up to its windows, surrounded by houses. *Katrina's Parlor* (page 19) is the wrecked interior of a once lovely living room; the keys of a piano jumble with a pile of rubble in *Katrina: Hammond B-3, 9th Ward, New Orleans* (page 159). Color is not reserved for the catastrophic only. A group of photographs assembled under the heading *Around the World: Cultures in Color* demonstrates a subtle use of color to display a dazzling emotional range.

Ruth Fine's distinguished, forty-year career at the National Gallery of Art has given her an impeccable eye, a quality shared by the esteemed poet/critic Fred Moten. Their selection of photographs from the 1963 March on Washington to 2020 betrays a patience and attentiveness that has enabled them to assemble a penetrating portrait of Frank Stewart's art. Though his long career as the official photographer of Jazz at Lincoln Center has made his work widely visible, until now the depth and breadth of it has not been well known. We owe a debt of gratitude to The Phillips Collection and Telfair Museums for their wisdom and judgment in revealing the artistry of an important American photographer.

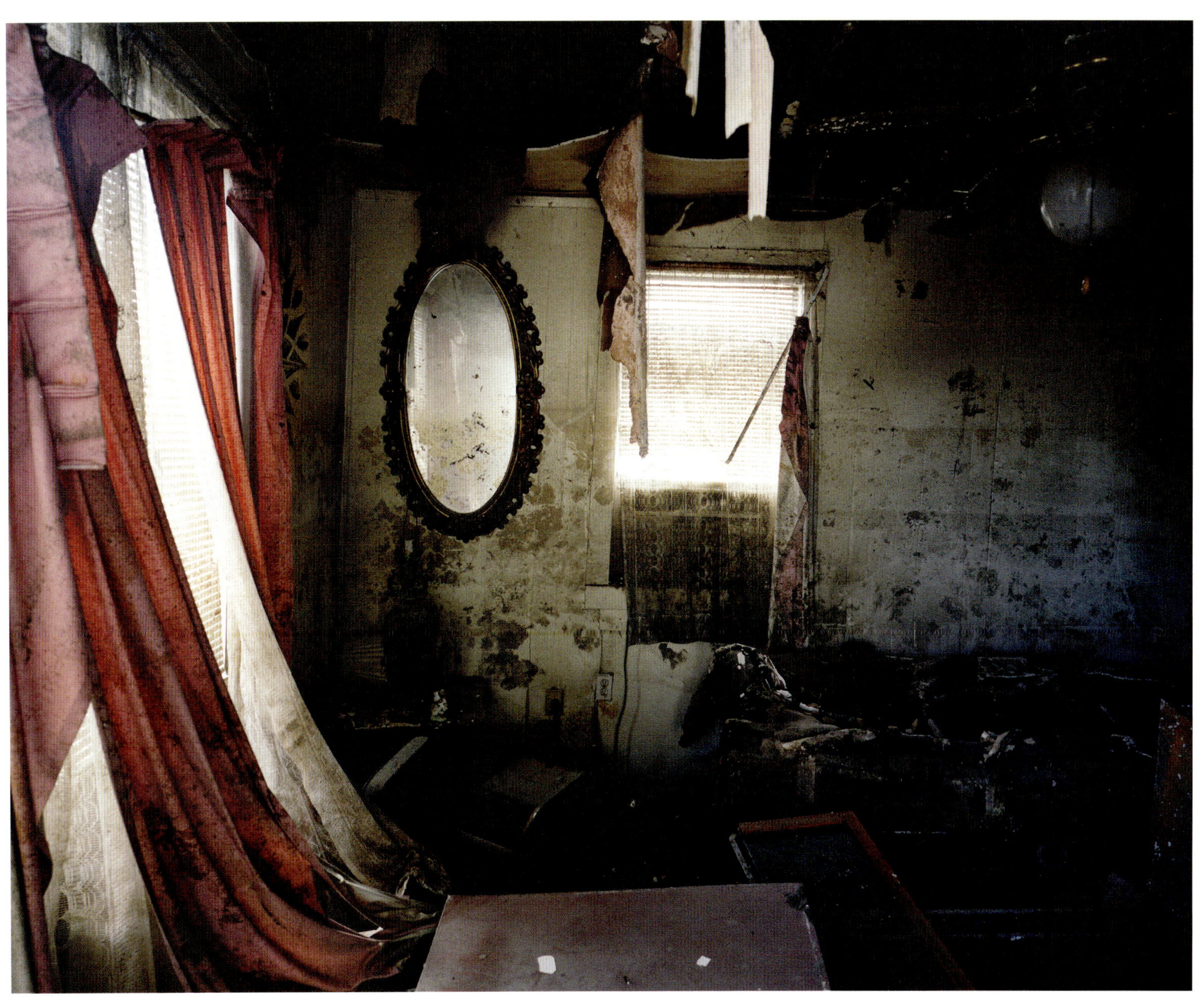

Katrina's Parlor, 2006

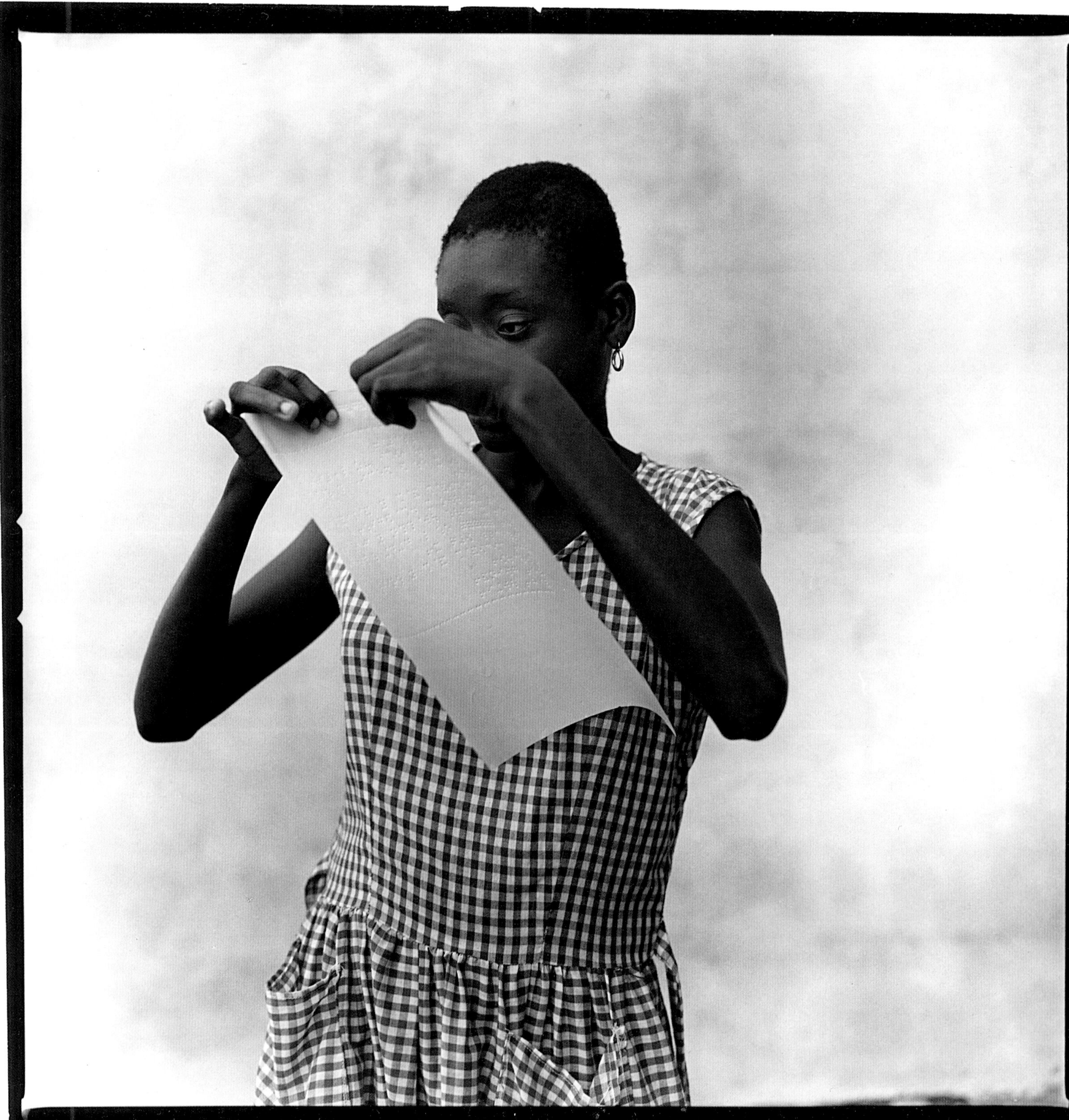

HAUNTED BY THE MEDIUM

Ruth Fine and Fred Moten

Frank Stewart often speaks of being haunted by the medium of photography, specifically by the intelligence of the medium. Thoughts centered on this compulsive passion are always with Stewart, regardless of whatever else he is engaging. This is a pervasive subject of the exhibition, with calls and responses threaded throughout. Because if photography is intelligent, if it has something to say and to withhold, then Stewart is its medium, its sounding board and confidant, its familiar interlocutor.

Stewart's ongoing conversation with and in photography is a careful, everyday affair. All the perennial concerns are met with gentle severity: light on surface; organization of the printed plane with attention to every inch; issues of implied space and emphatic pulse; an engagement with the past, with the present, and with the future, aware that the ensemble of the tenses must be held in generative tension if the art is to live and, therefore, be genuinely and ecstatically historical.

The entirety of the cultural field informs Stewart's photographic journey, which touches upon as much of the universe as he encounters and imagines. While many different subjects addressed over several years may be seen as work in series, this is not highlighted here. Emphasis, instead, is placed on the range of subjects that have captivated Stewart's imagination, the consistency with which he presents them as art experiences, and the intensity with which he keeps faith with the very ground of the various and the numerous. An autobiographical calling is likewise apparent throughout this exhibition, in both its subjects and its contributing lenders. What emerges can be considered serial only insofar as what is revealed is the aspect—the internal temporal constituency—of a long pilgrimage of seeing, an extended practice of vision, an accompaniment of photography on and in the way of things.

Girl Reading, Mamfe, Ghana, 1997

Stewart's earliest subjects are rooted in a range of ancestral experiences, both African American and more broadly Afro-diasporic in their content. Later work encompasses this exploration as well. However, Stewart further layers his visual encounters with many other cultures. He seeks to discover what makes each of them unique, but he also uncovers those elements that are shared between these initially unfamiliar cultures and his roots.

At the same time, being uprooted is an essential part of this story, beginning with Stewart's transient childhood and early years and continuing throughout his life, especially during the decades when he was the senior staff photographer for the always-on-the-move Jazz at Lincoln Center Orchestra. Travel continues now for his increasingly independent projects, which confront issues of, for instance, the climate change destroying our world for future generations. This virulent uprooting of our planet, so urgently studied by a child of the uprooted, is the primary concern that keeps Stewart on the road today. It can't be resisted by settling, by merely and brutally digging in. Always in motion, Stewart has been at home in and all over the world. His work constantly shows the necessity of this convivial, cosmopolitan imperative of human differences; and the human differences are to survive and keep time and step with the planet.

Abiding friendships and professional relationships are documented in the names of the lenders to this exhibition. They include friends from Stewart's childhood. A potent inscription on *Girl Reading, Mamfe, Ghana* (page 20), borrowed from John Simmons, says it all: "From the womb to the tomb." But many other lenders are longtime associates of the photographer as well, a tribute to the power of Stewart's photography—how his being haunted by the medium communicates the intellectual and emotional content of the world around him to all with whom he widely and closely shares.

The Culture: Rituals

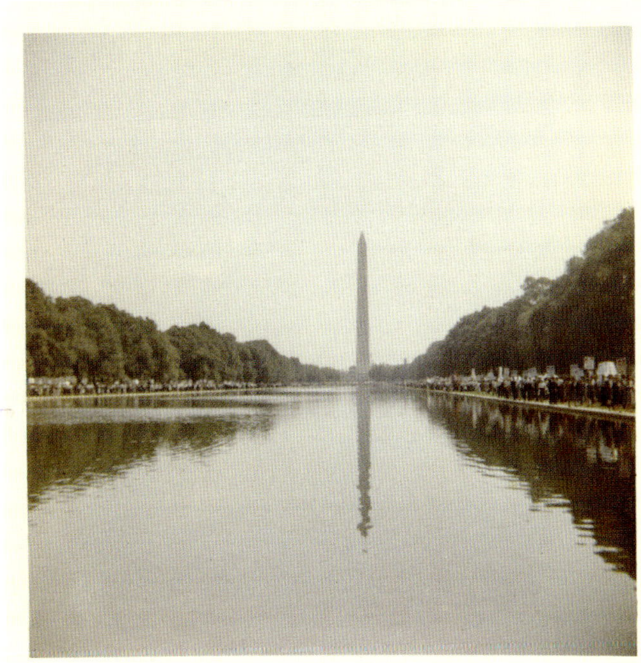

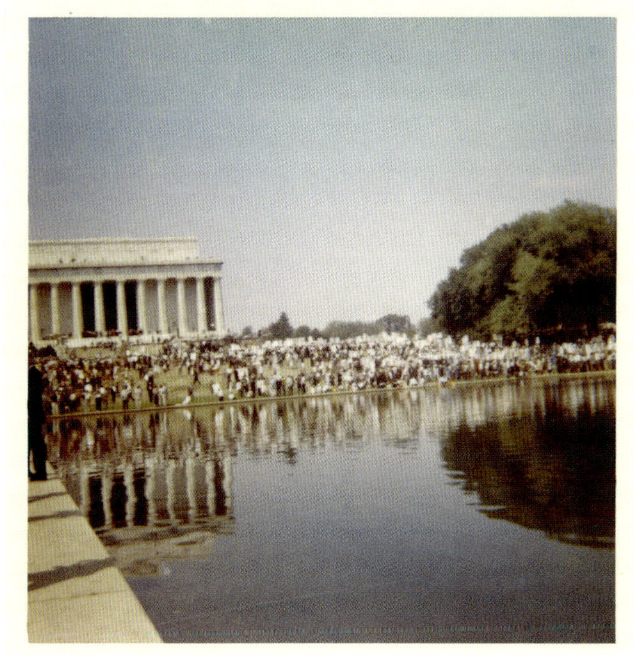

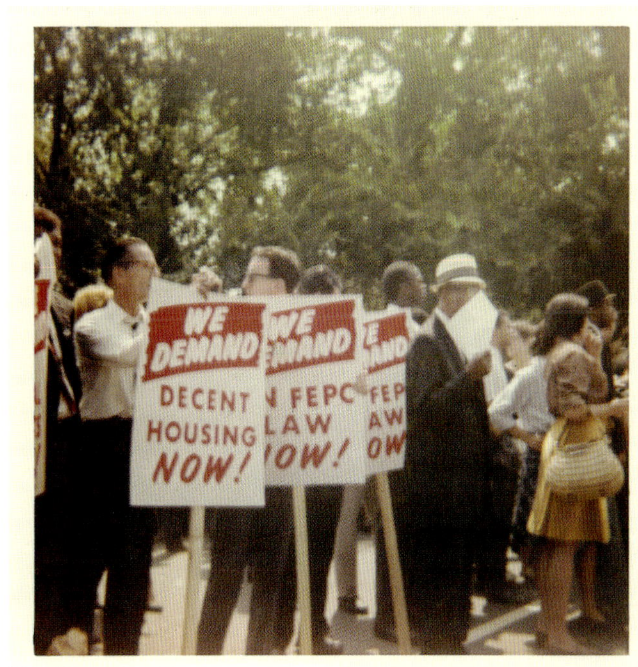

This page and the following spread:
Nine Snapshots from March on Washington for Jobs and Freedom, 1963

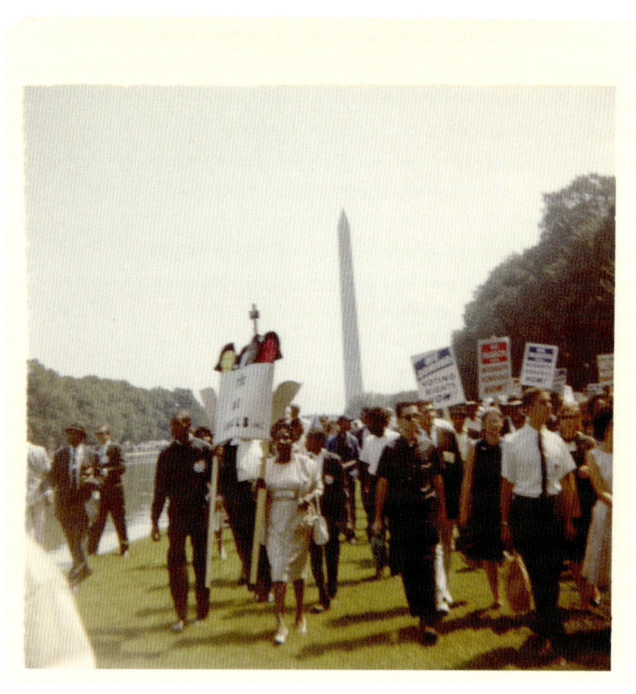

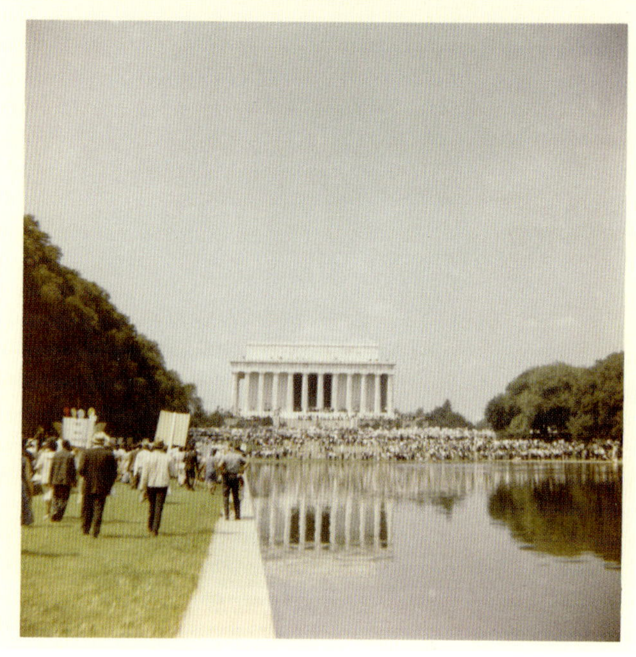

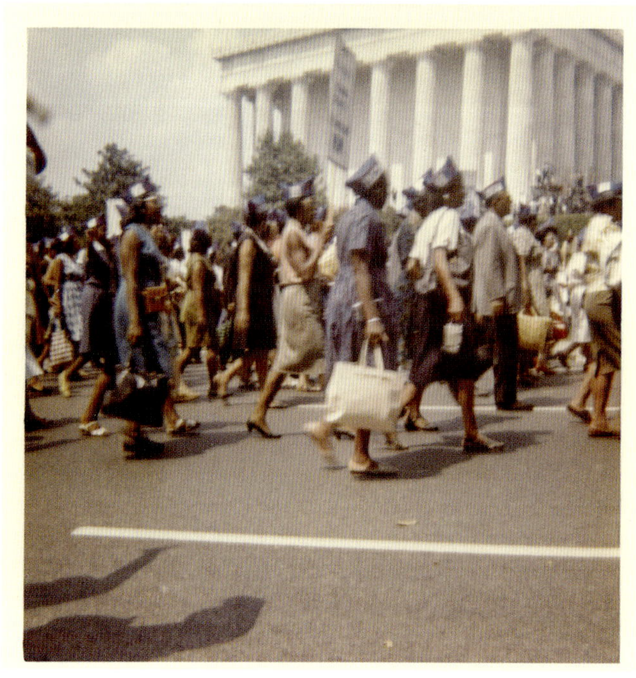

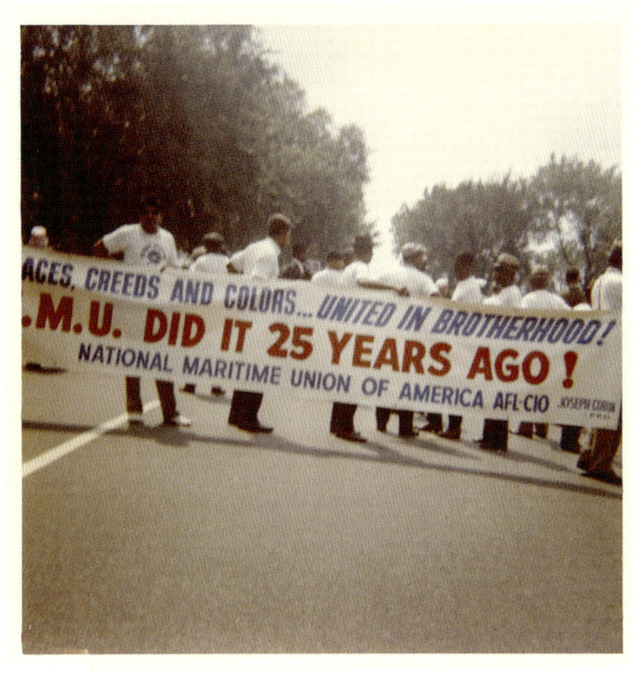
ACES, CREEDS AND COLORS... UNITED IN BROTHERHOOD!
.M.U. DID IT 25 YEARS AGO!
NATIONAL MARITIME UNION OF AMERICA AFL-CIO
JOSEPH CURRAN

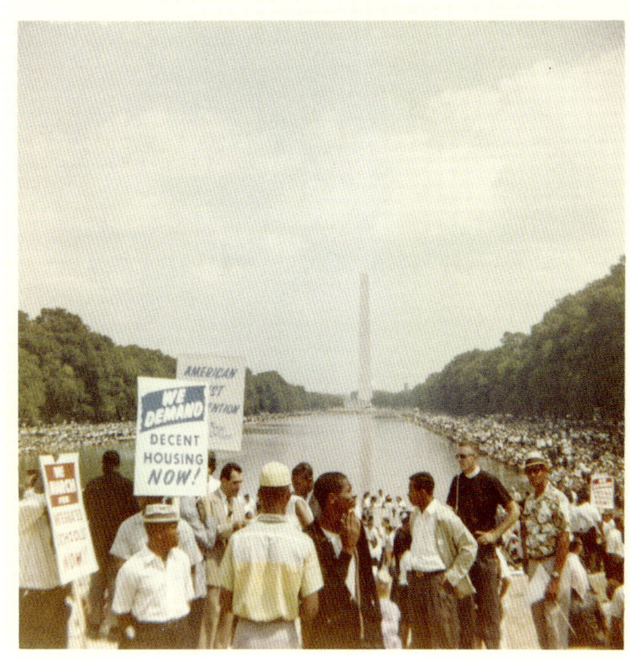
AMERICAN
WE DEMAND
DECENT
HOUSING
NOW!

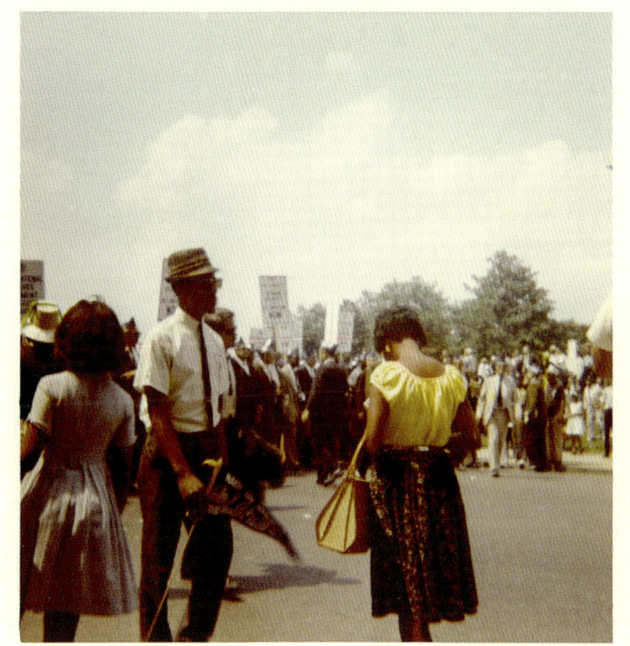

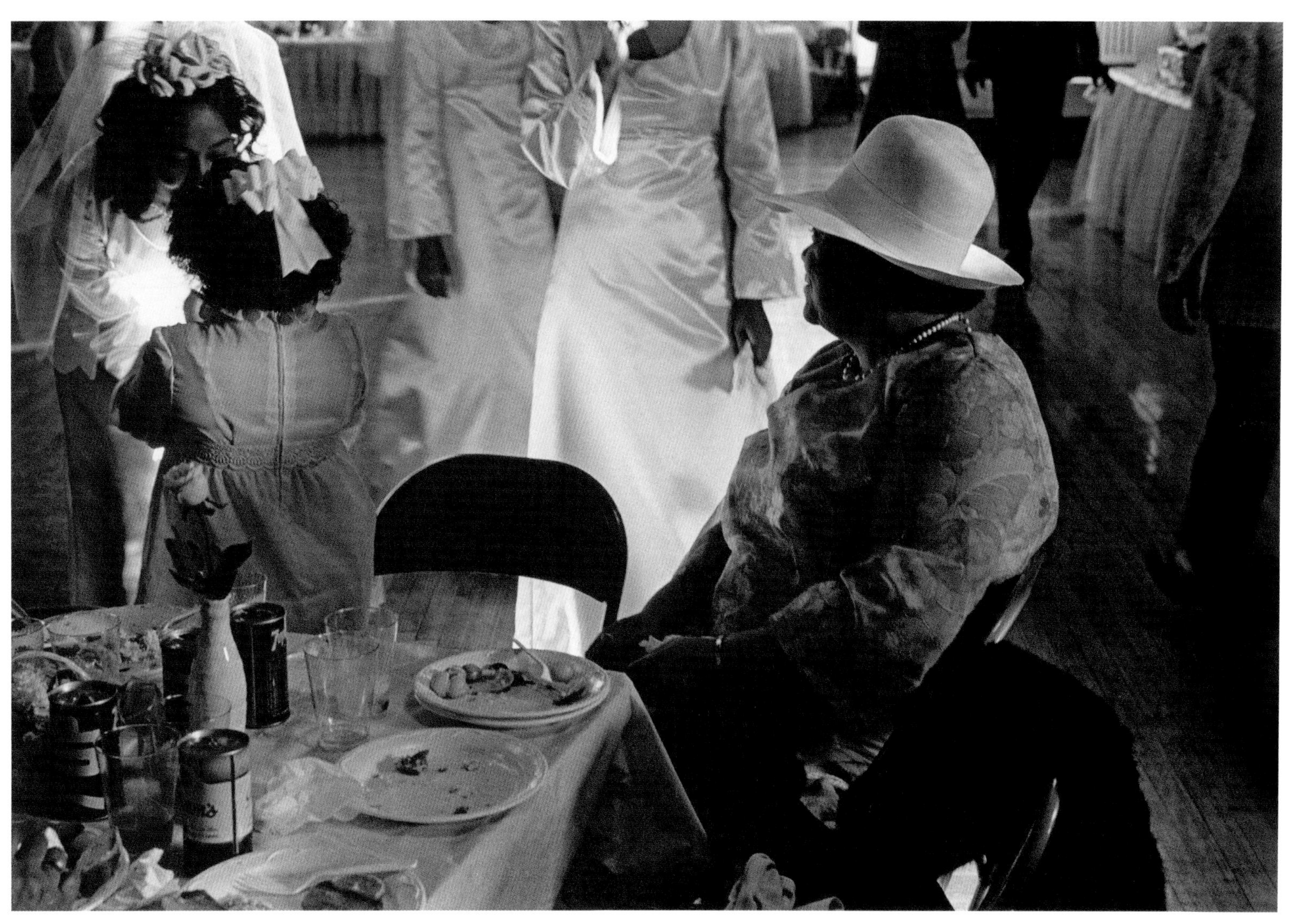

Frank Stewart cropped the image above most significantly along the left edge, emphasizing the secret being shared between the bride and a young guest. It acts as a contrast to the version on the opposite page, showing the full frame.

Chicago Wedding Reception (The Secret), 1972 (image cropped by the artist)

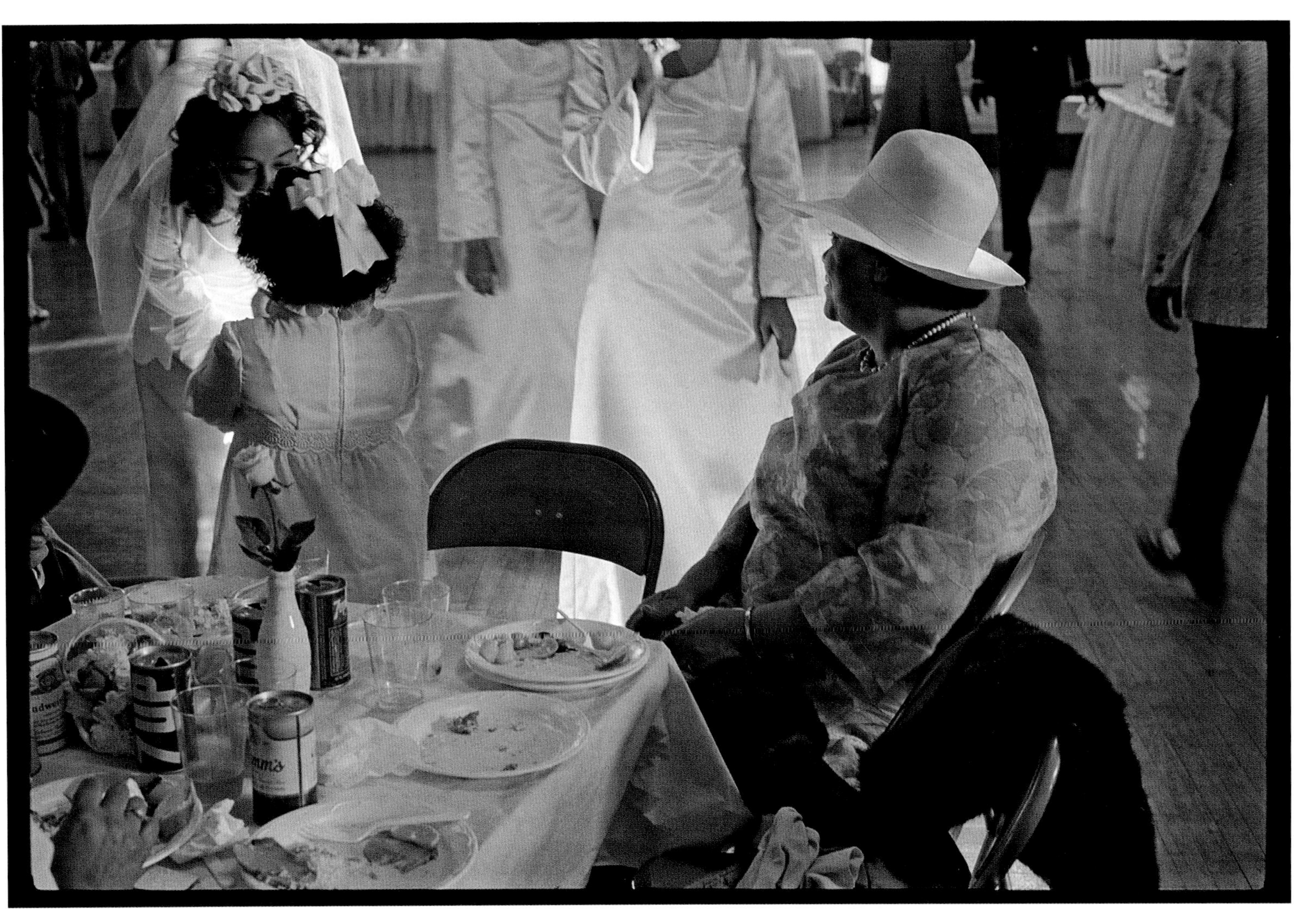

Chicago Wedding Reception (The Secret), 1972

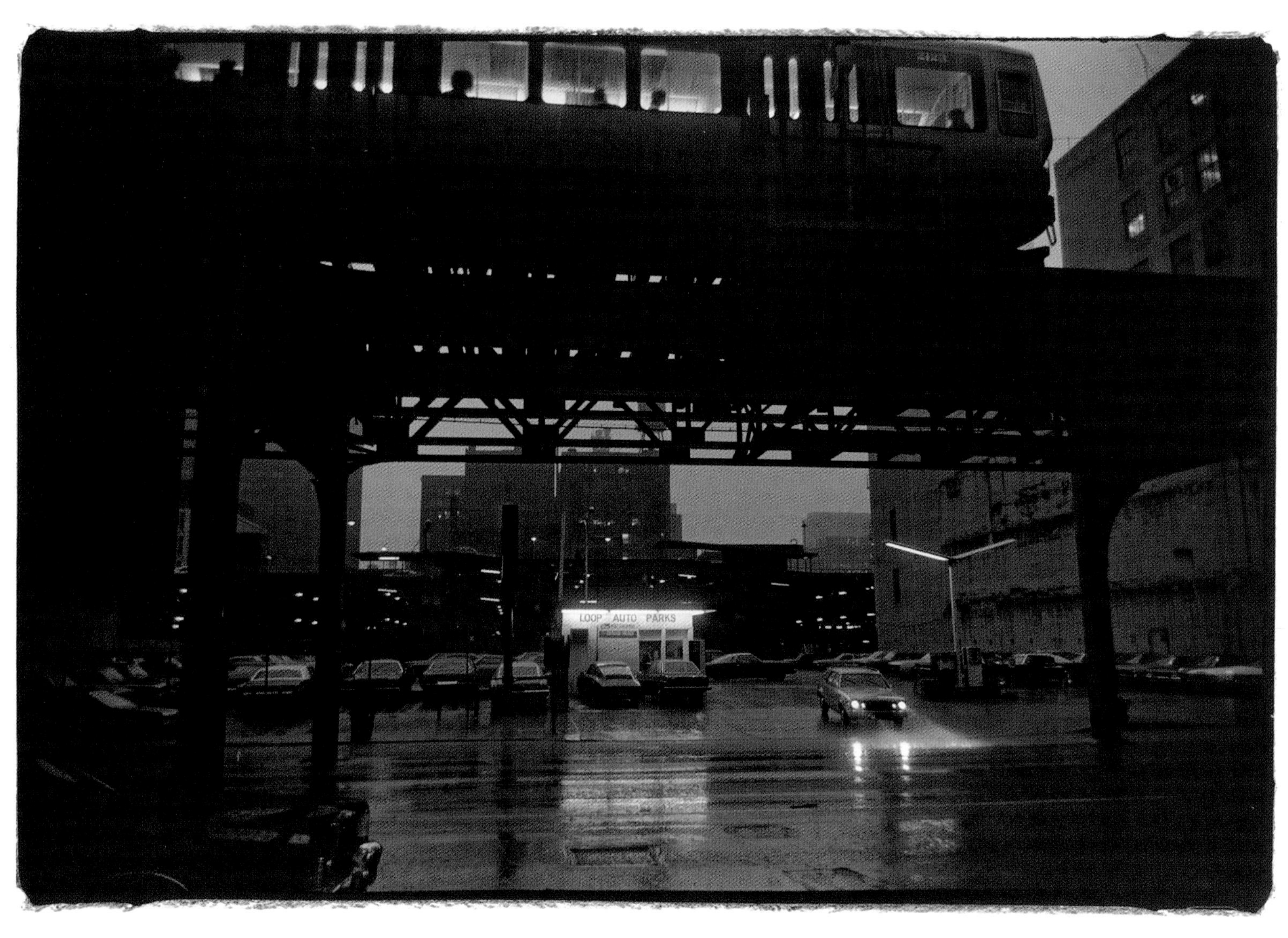

Loop Auto Park, Chicago, 1976

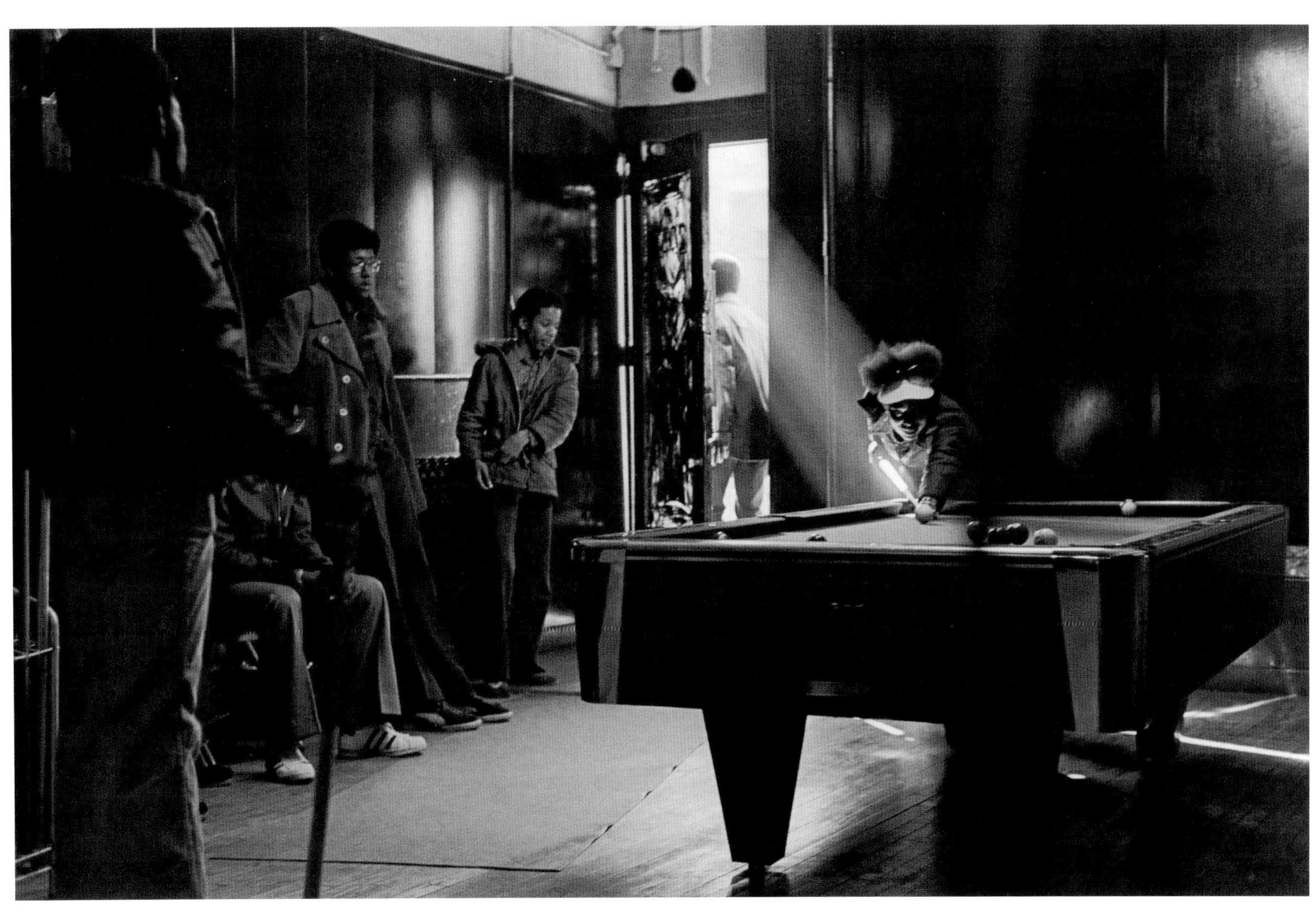

Neon Pool Cue, Harlem, 1975

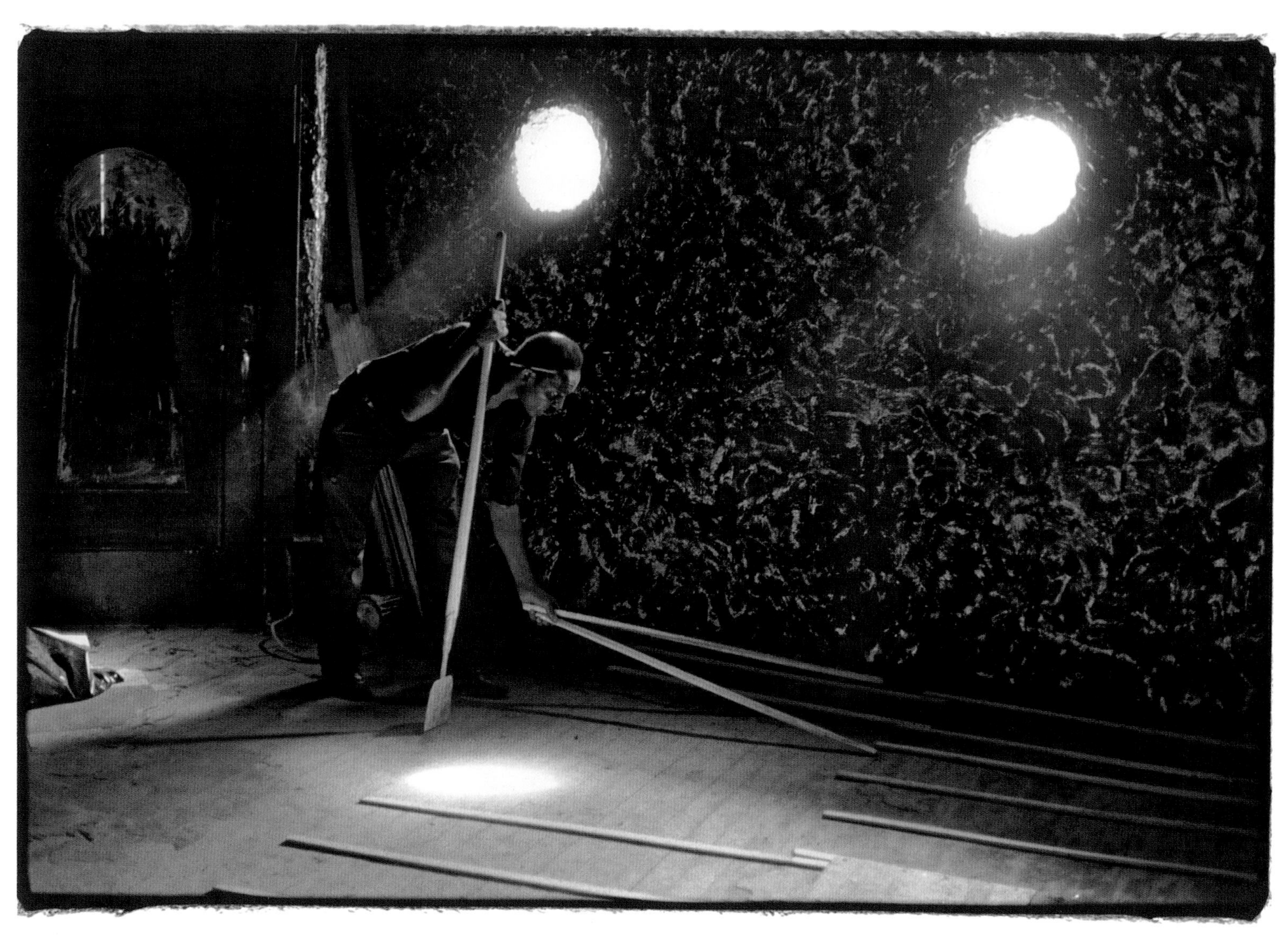

Alex in the Keyhole, 1975

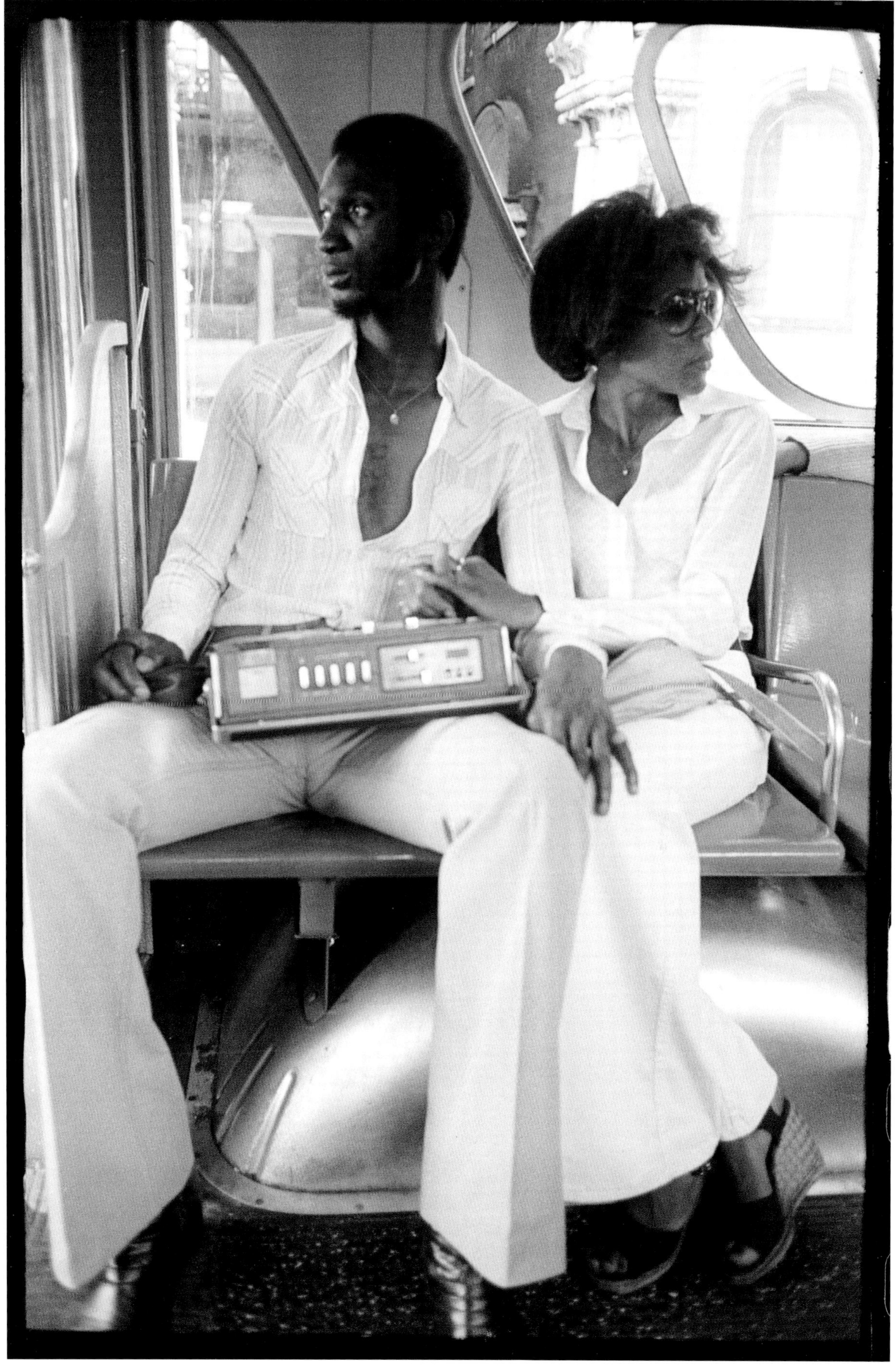

Radio Players Series, 1978

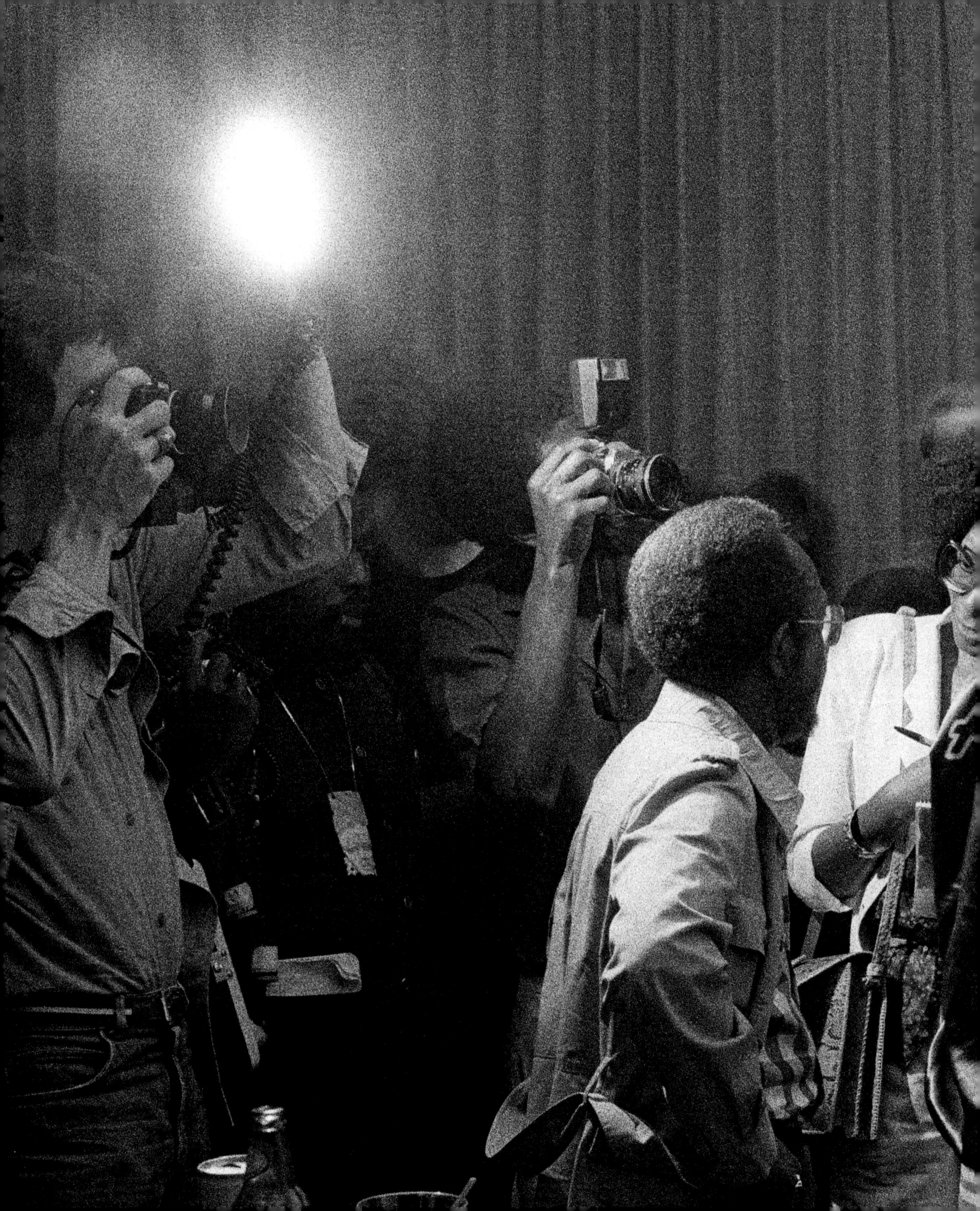

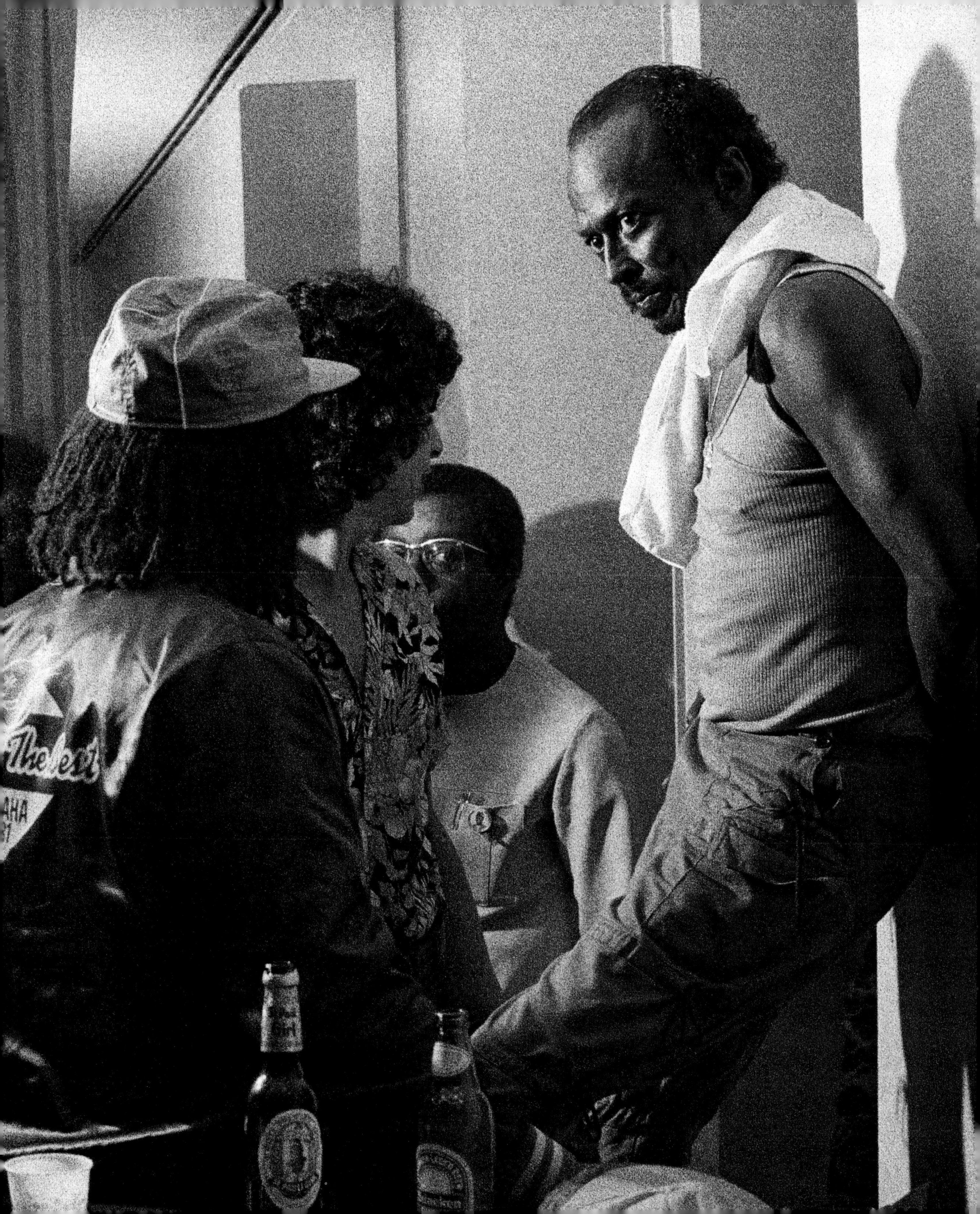

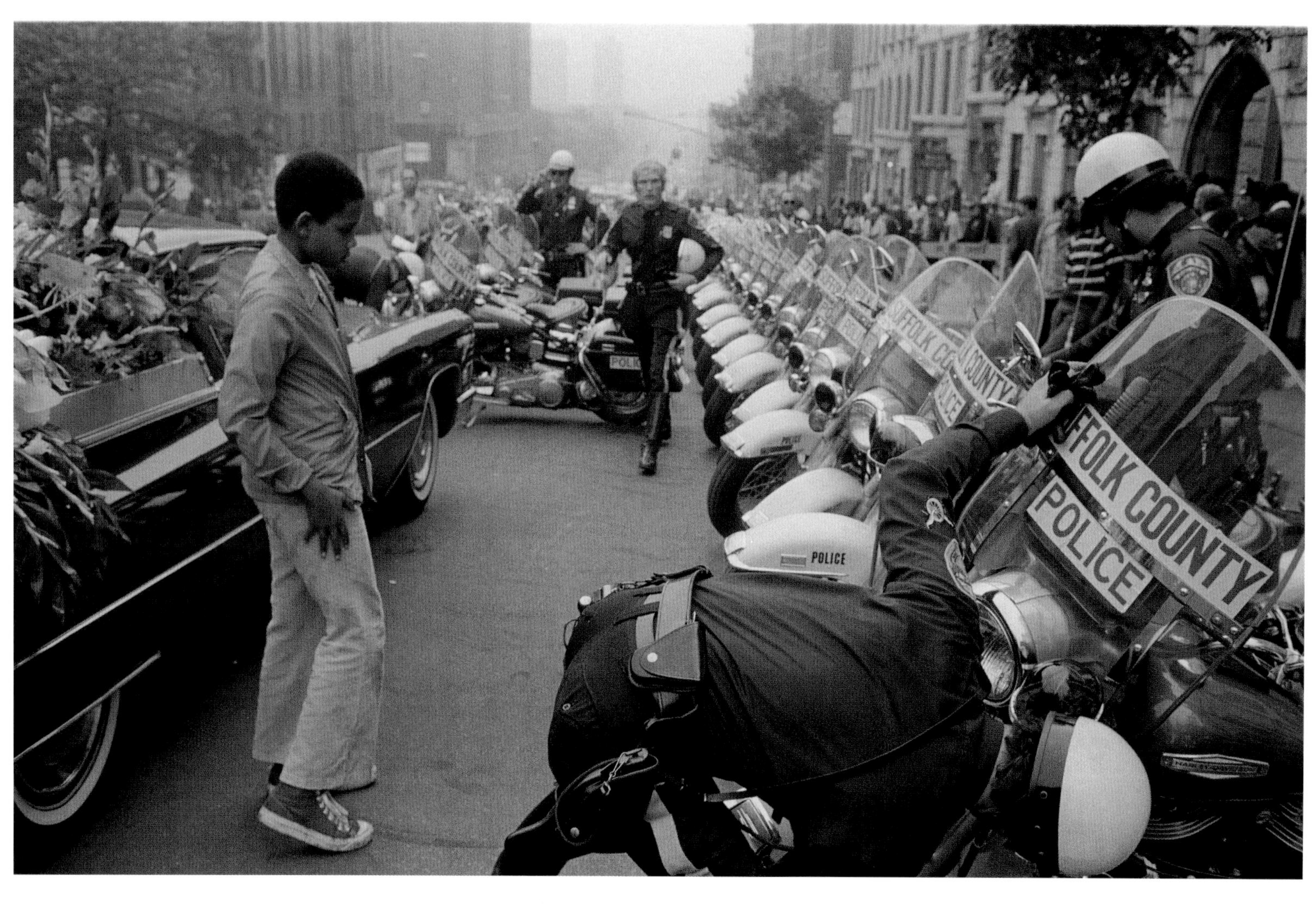

Boy and Motorcycles, 1976

Previous spread: *Miles in the Green Room* (detail), see page 14

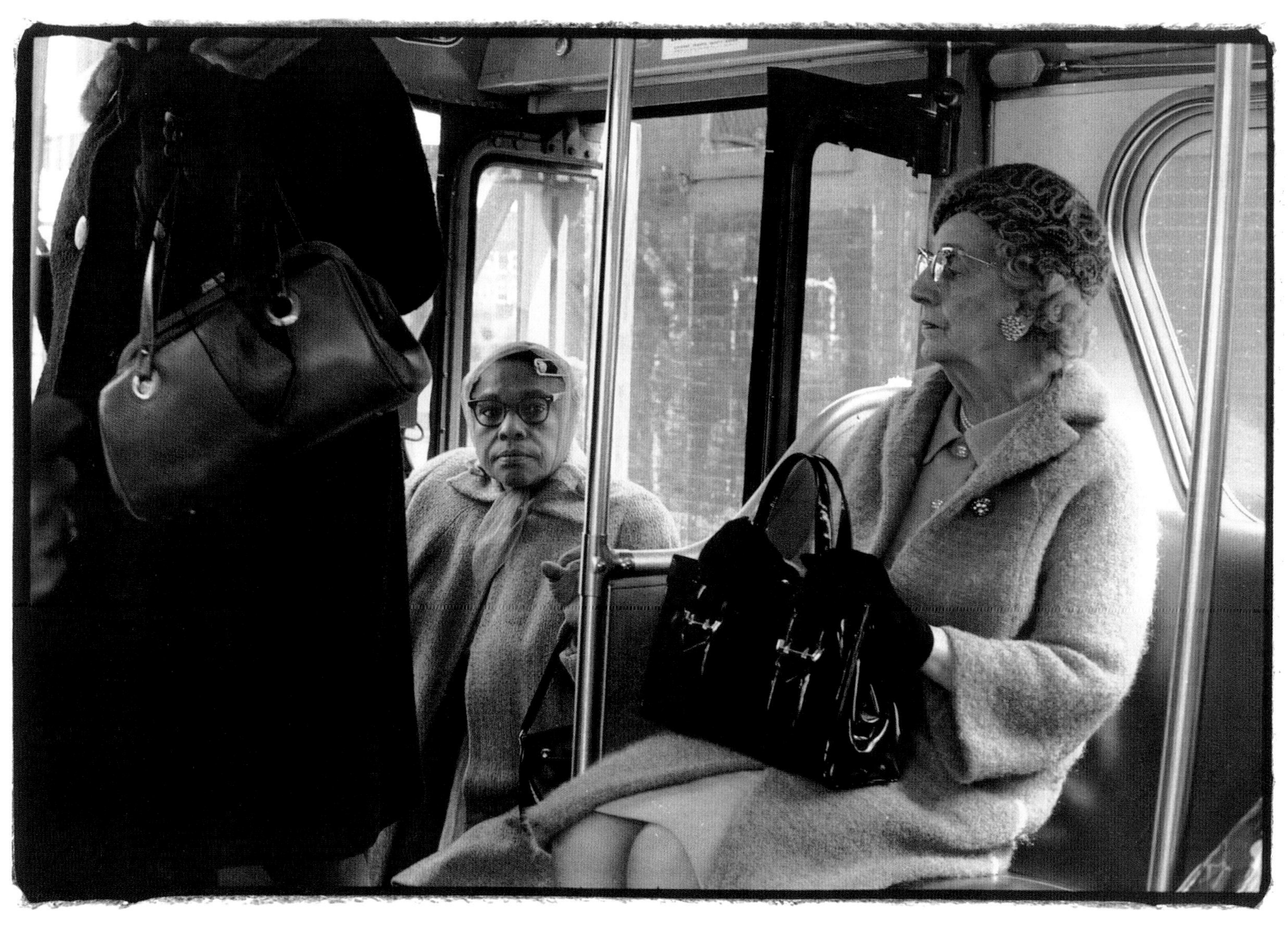

Contrast in Black and White, 1972

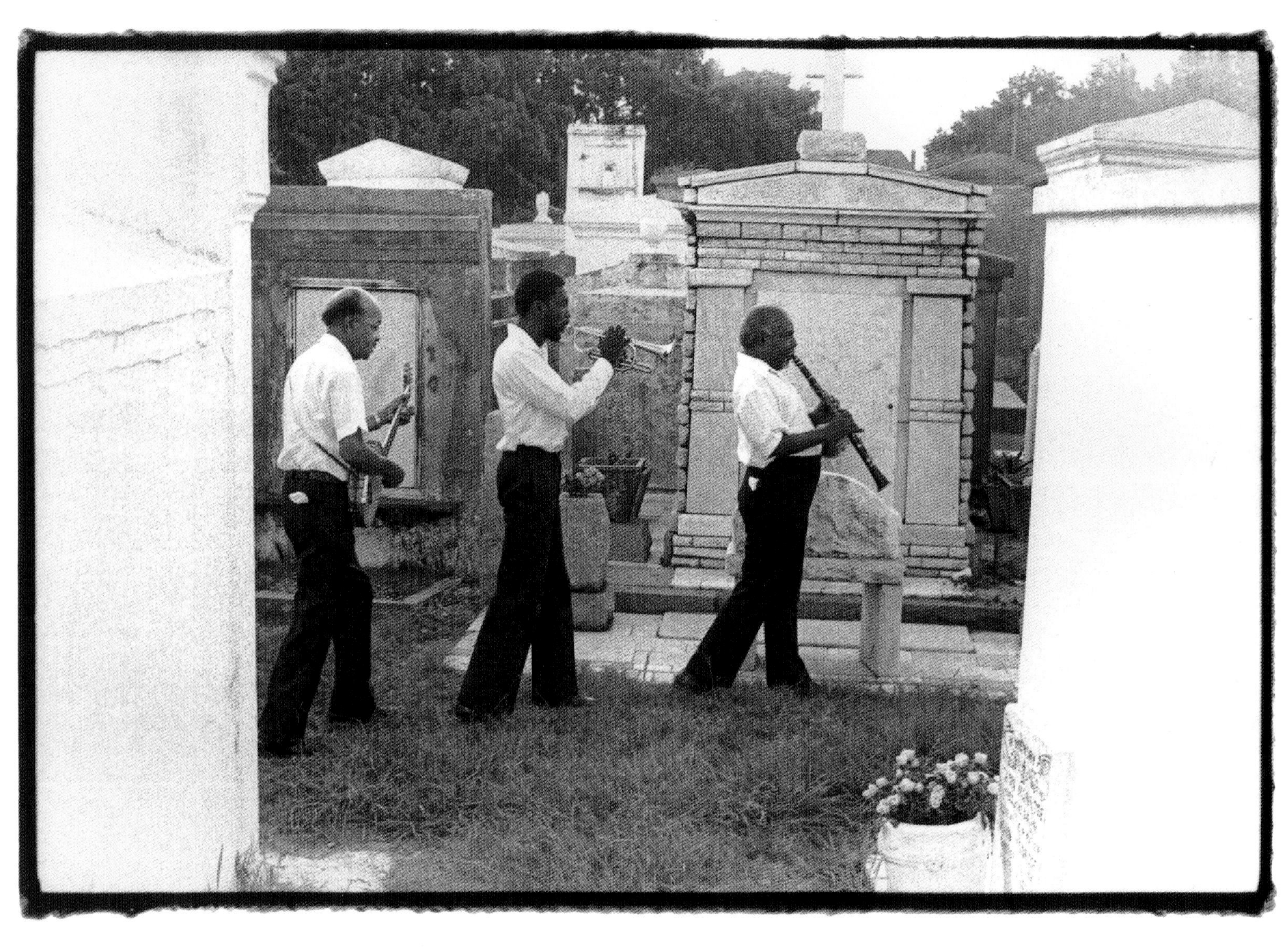

St. Louis Cemetery II, 1980

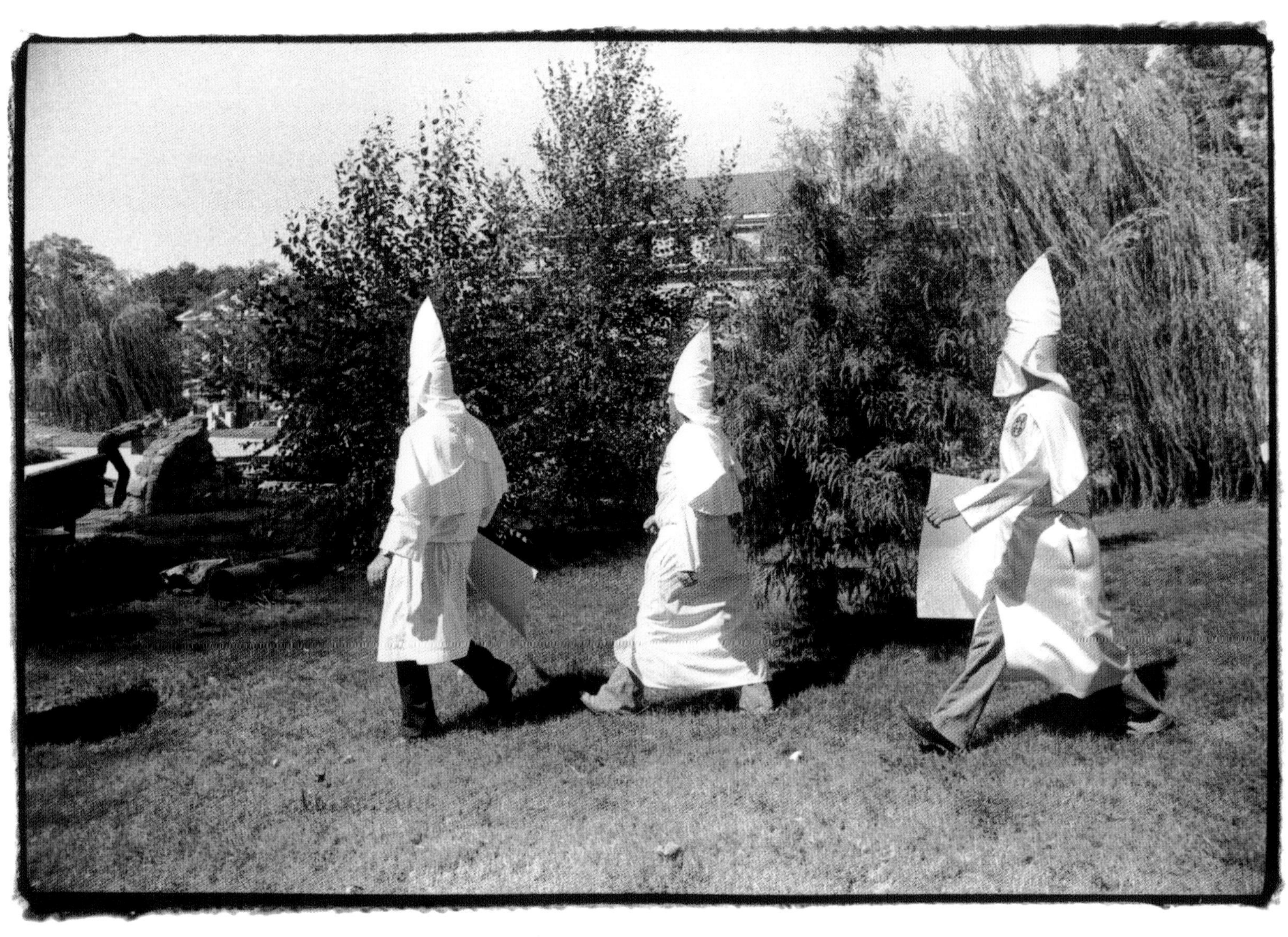

Klan Rally, Jackson, Mississippi, 1981

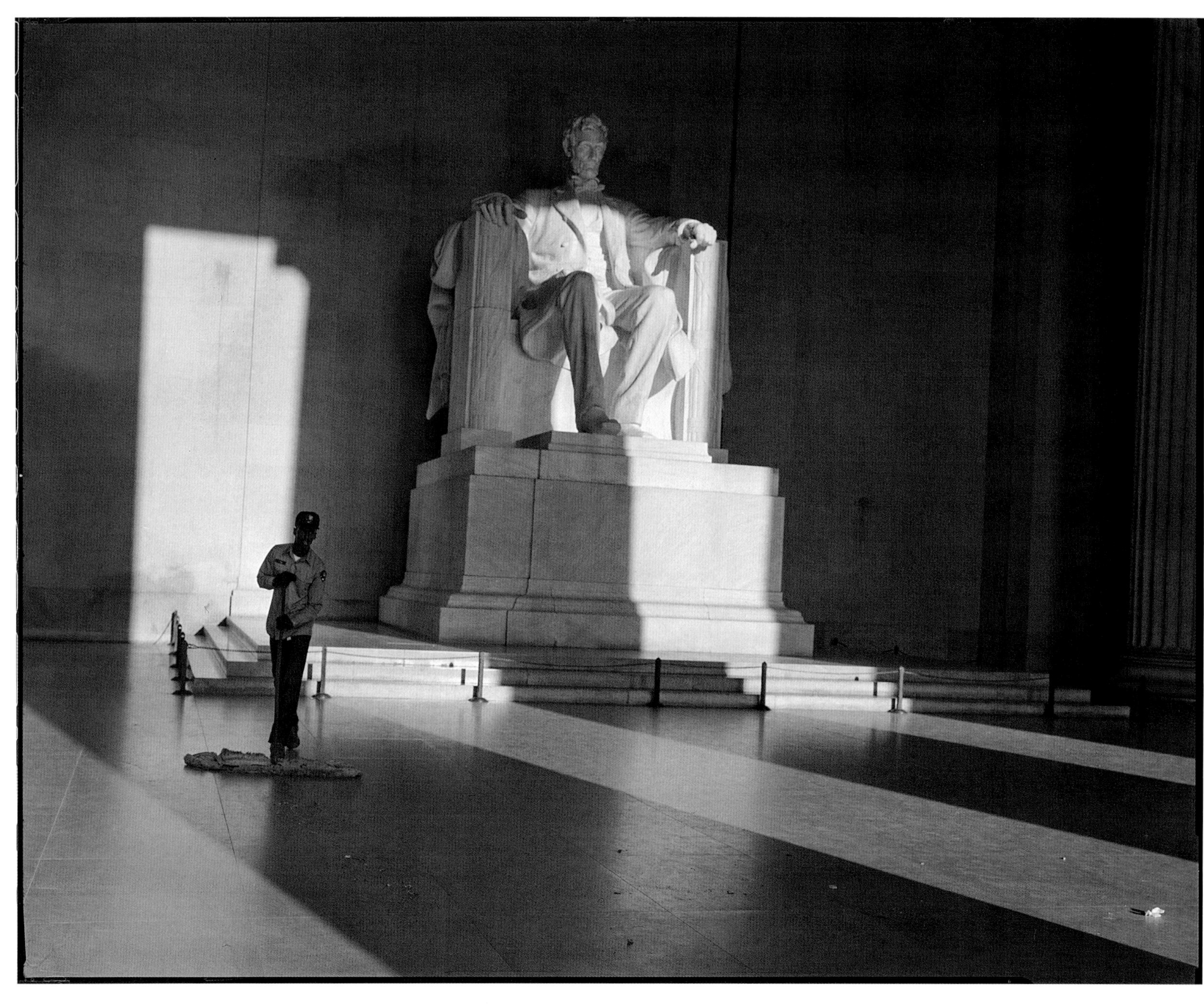

The Clean Up, 1988

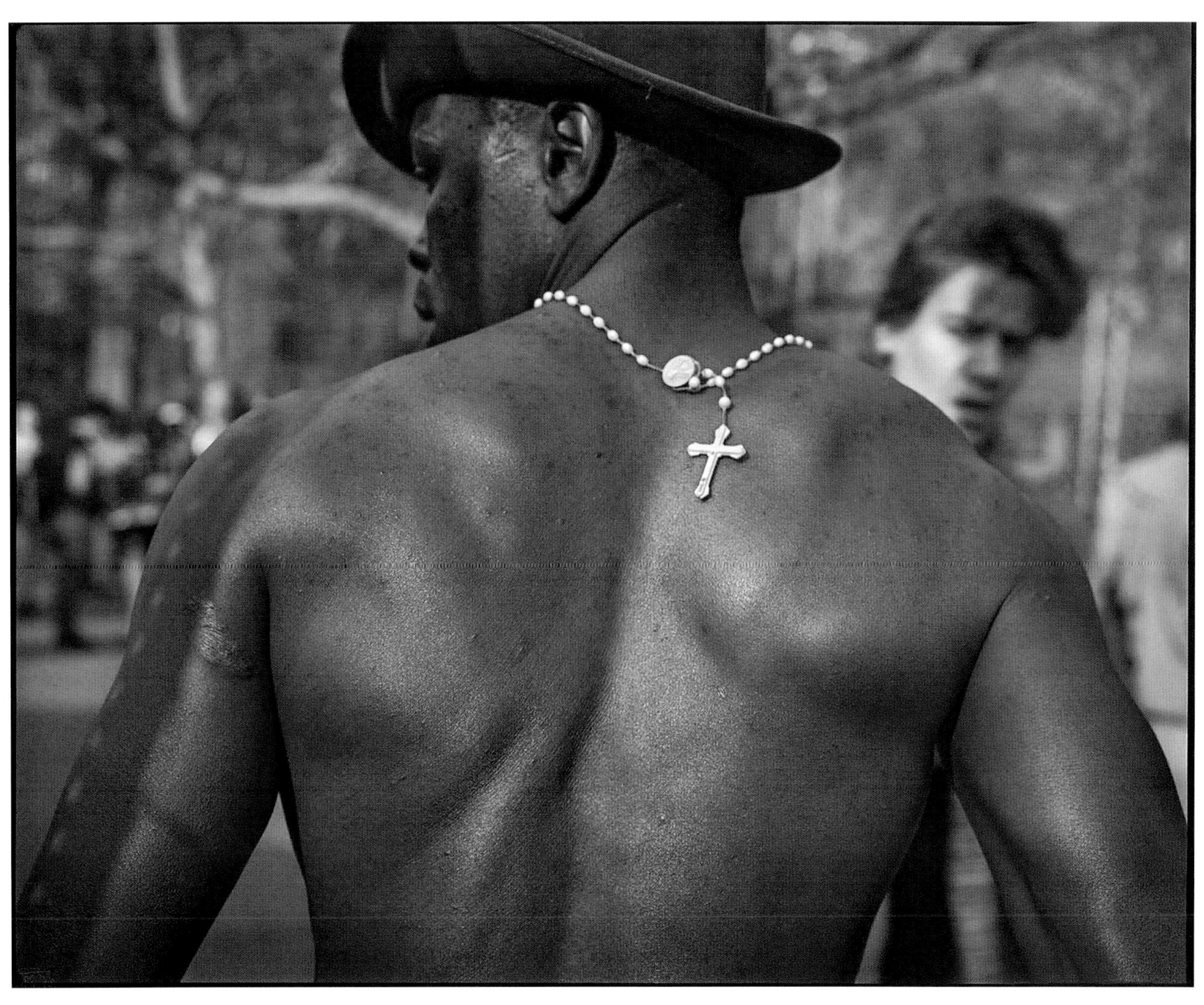

Only God to Watch My Back,
N.Y., 1987

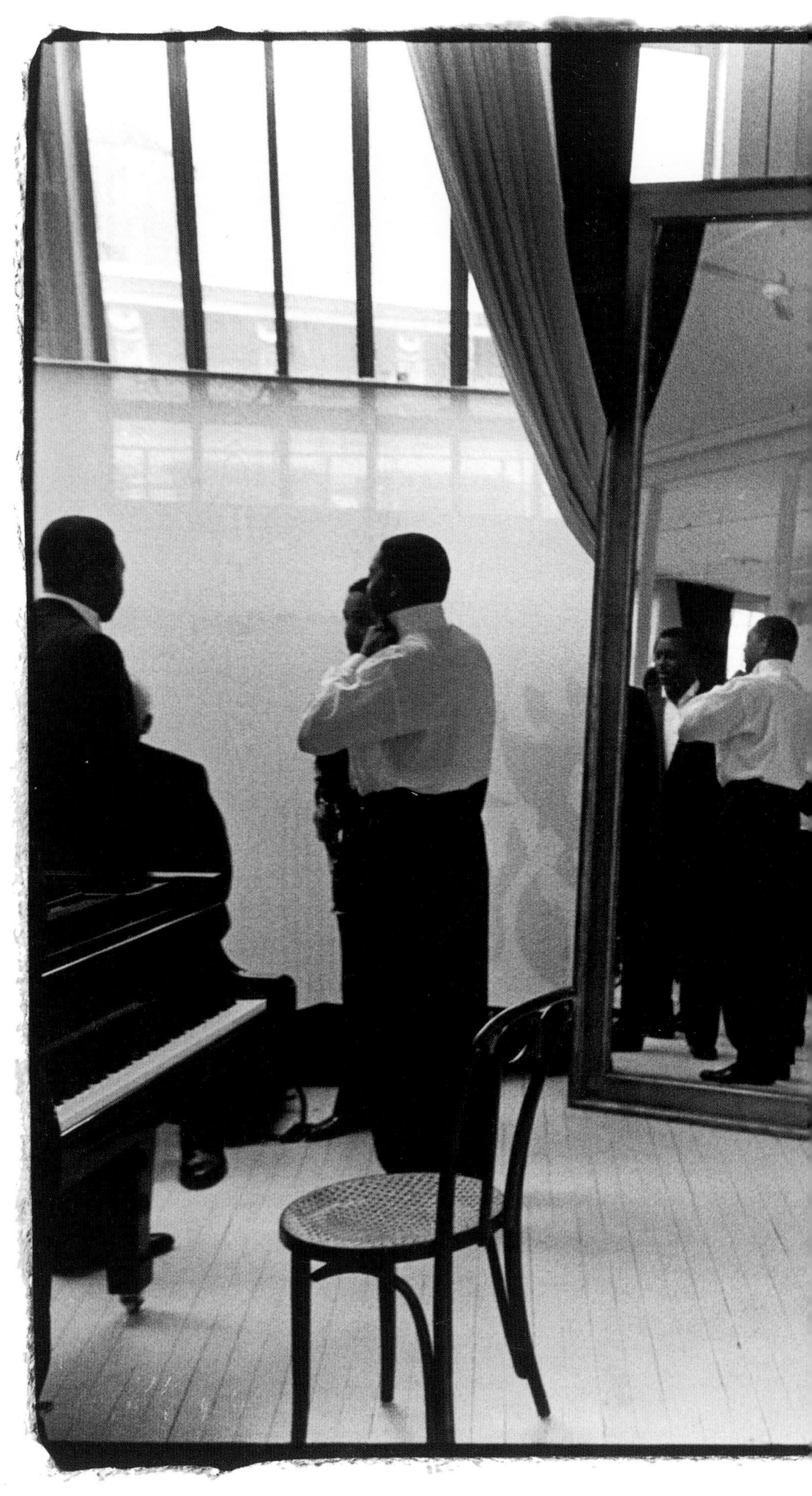

Blues and Abstract Reality, 1990

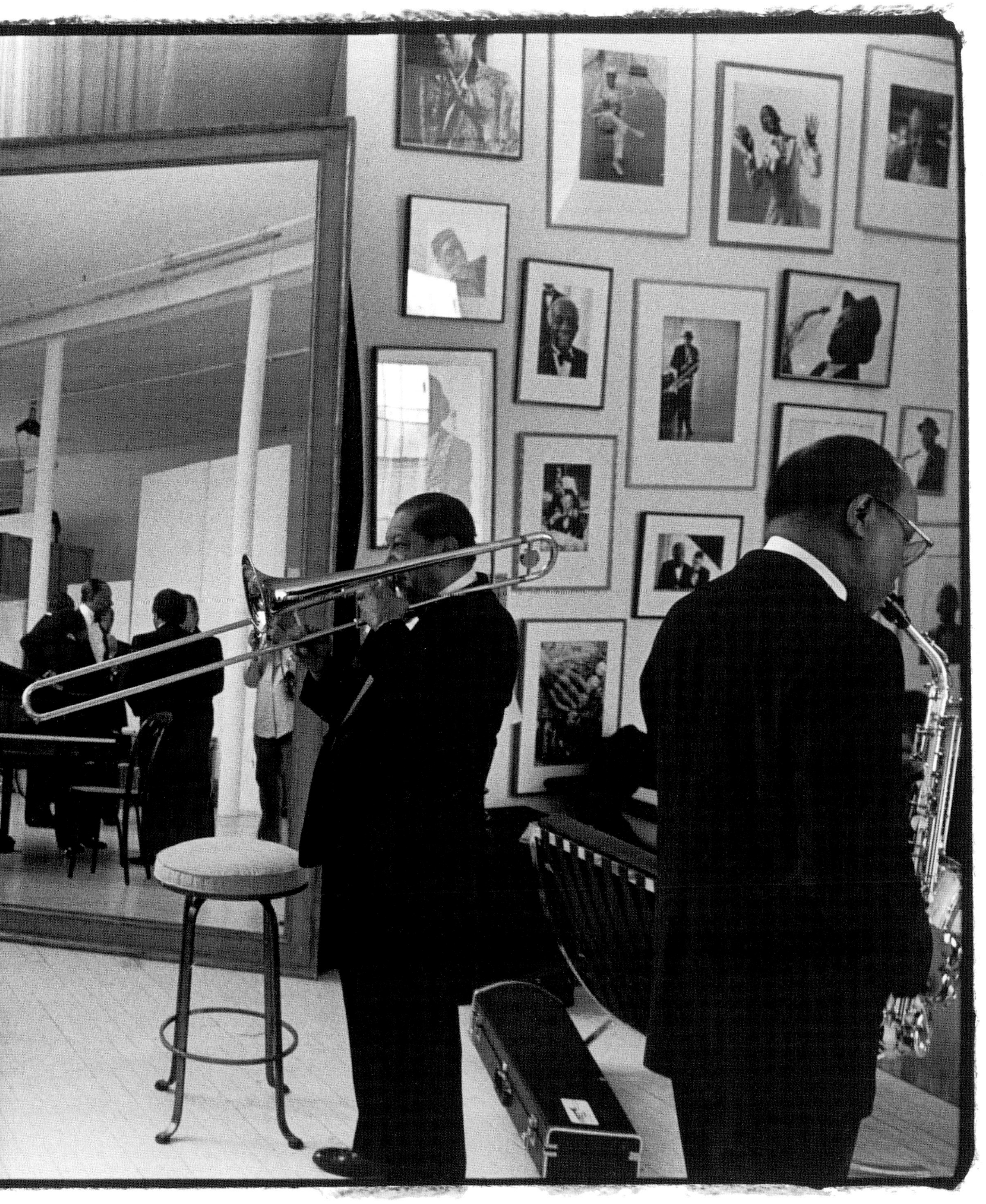

The Culture: Sound, Taste, Touch

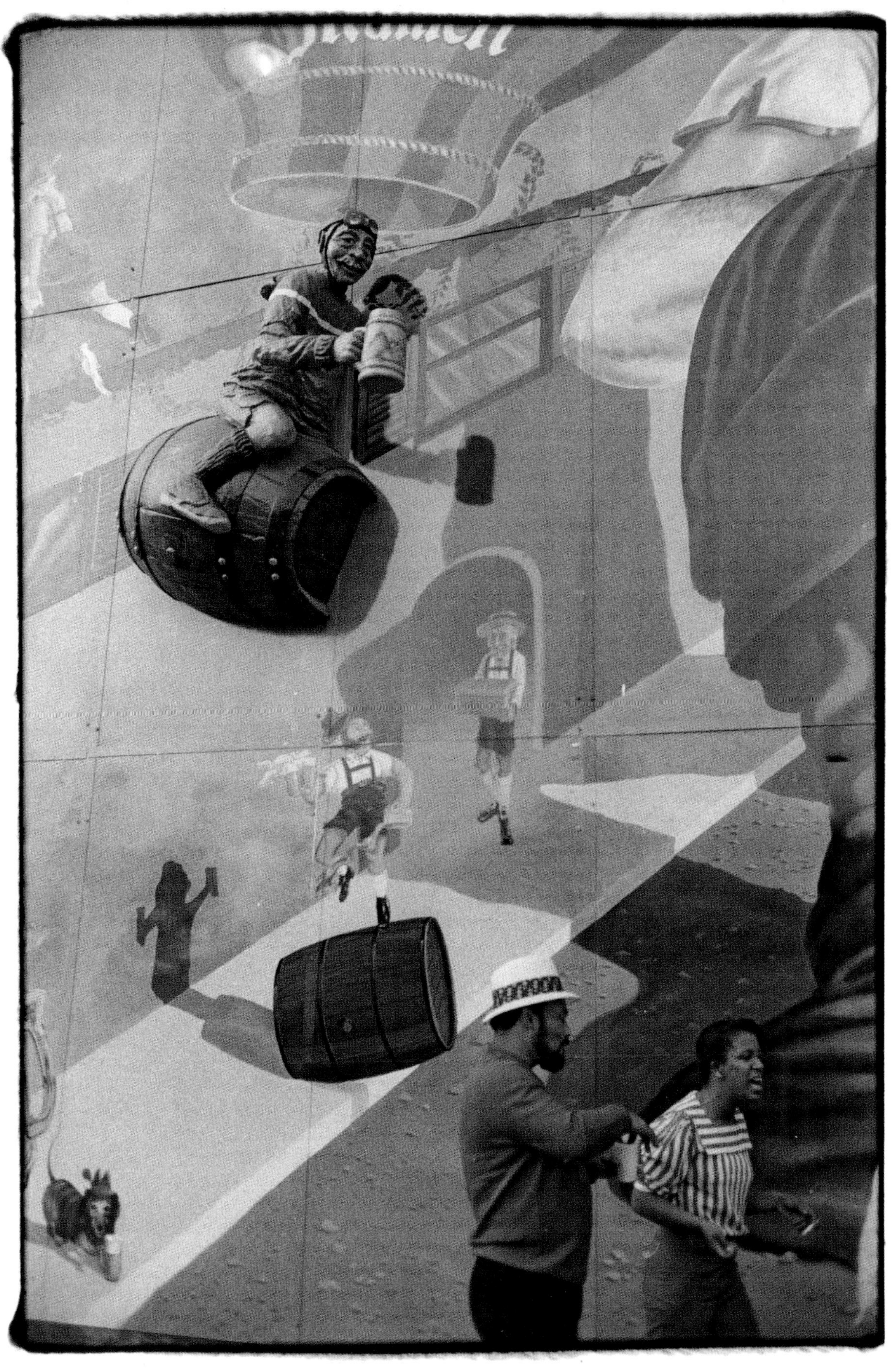

Beer Garden, Yonkers, 1982

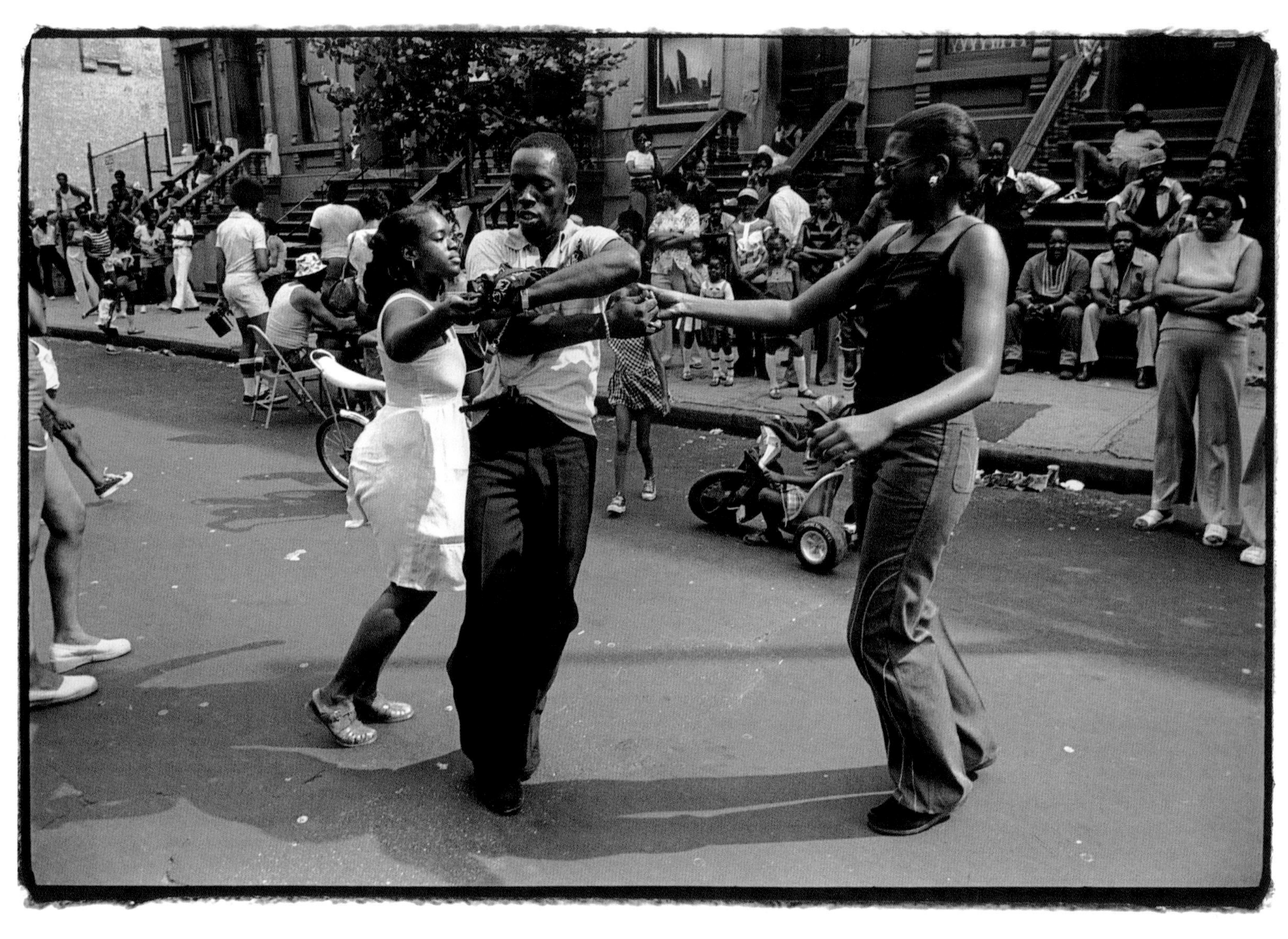

Youth in Harlem Series: Man Dancing with Two Girls, 1976

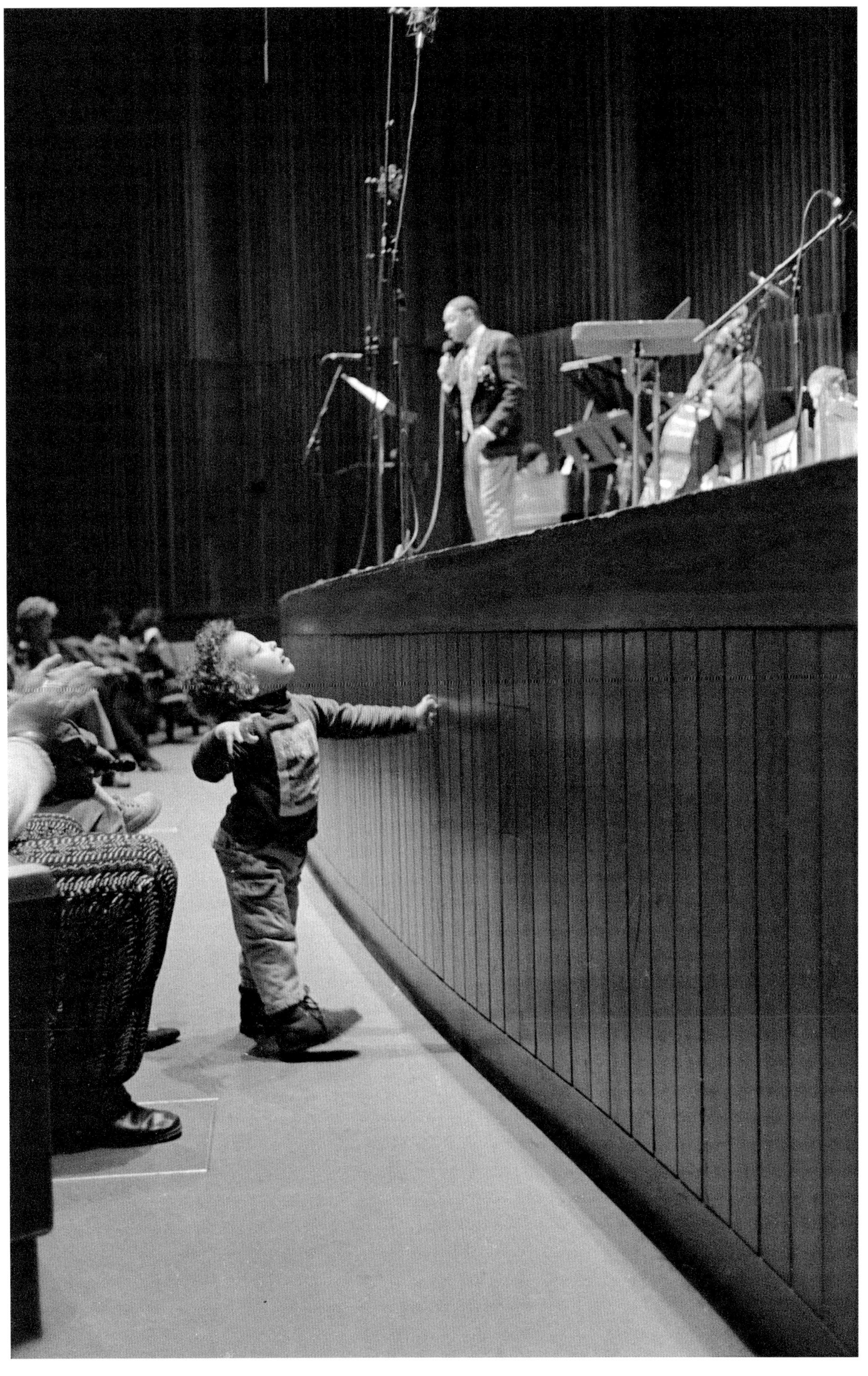

J4YP, 1996

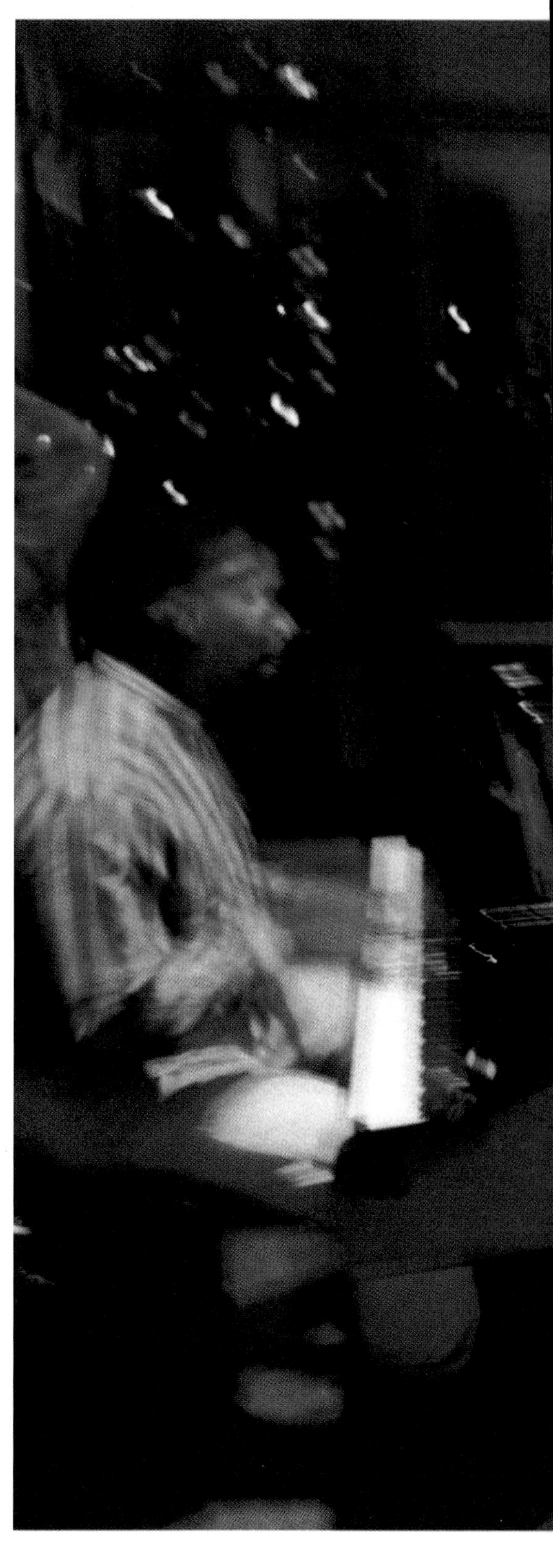

Warmdaddy in the House of Swing, New York, 1996

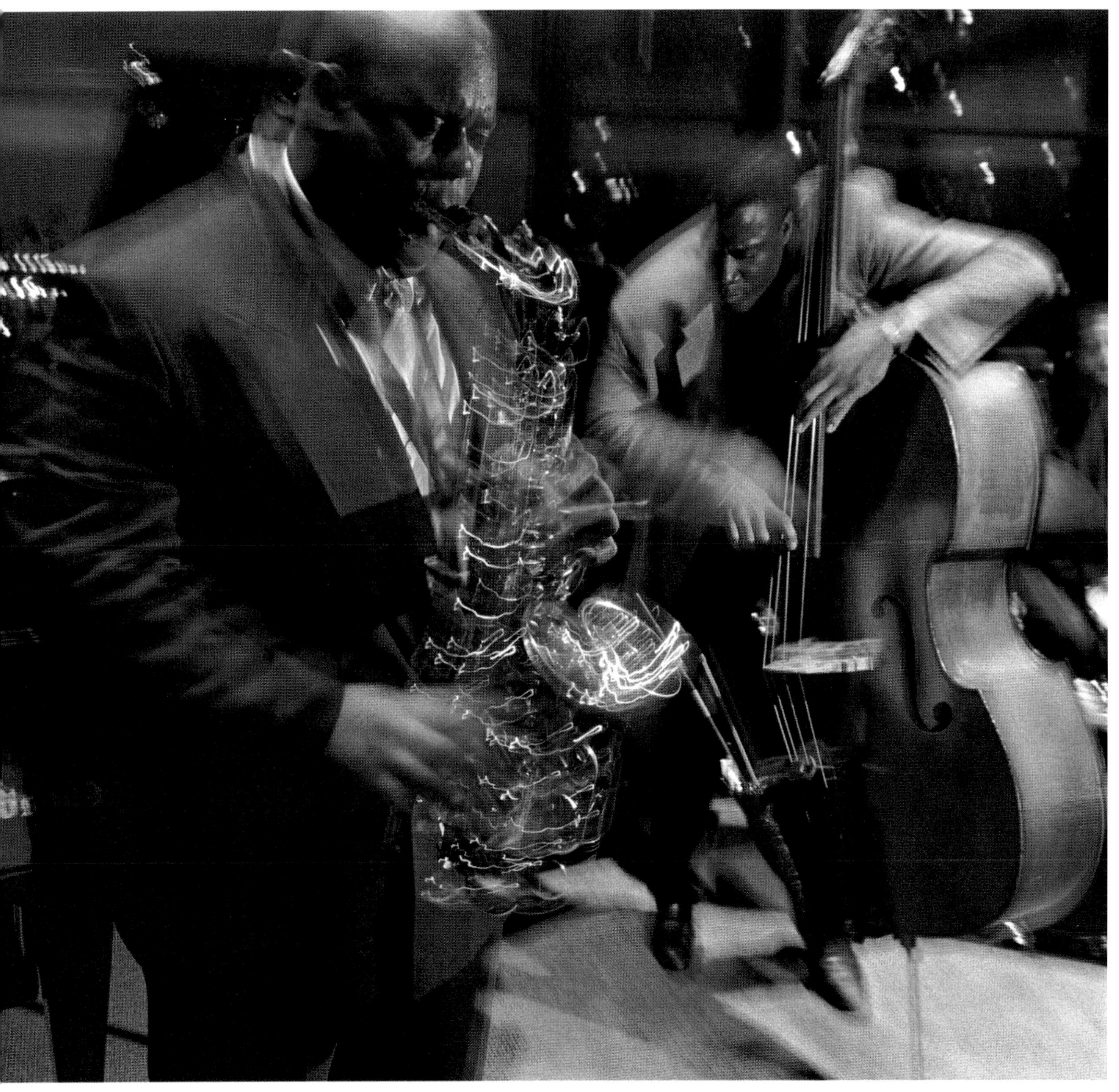

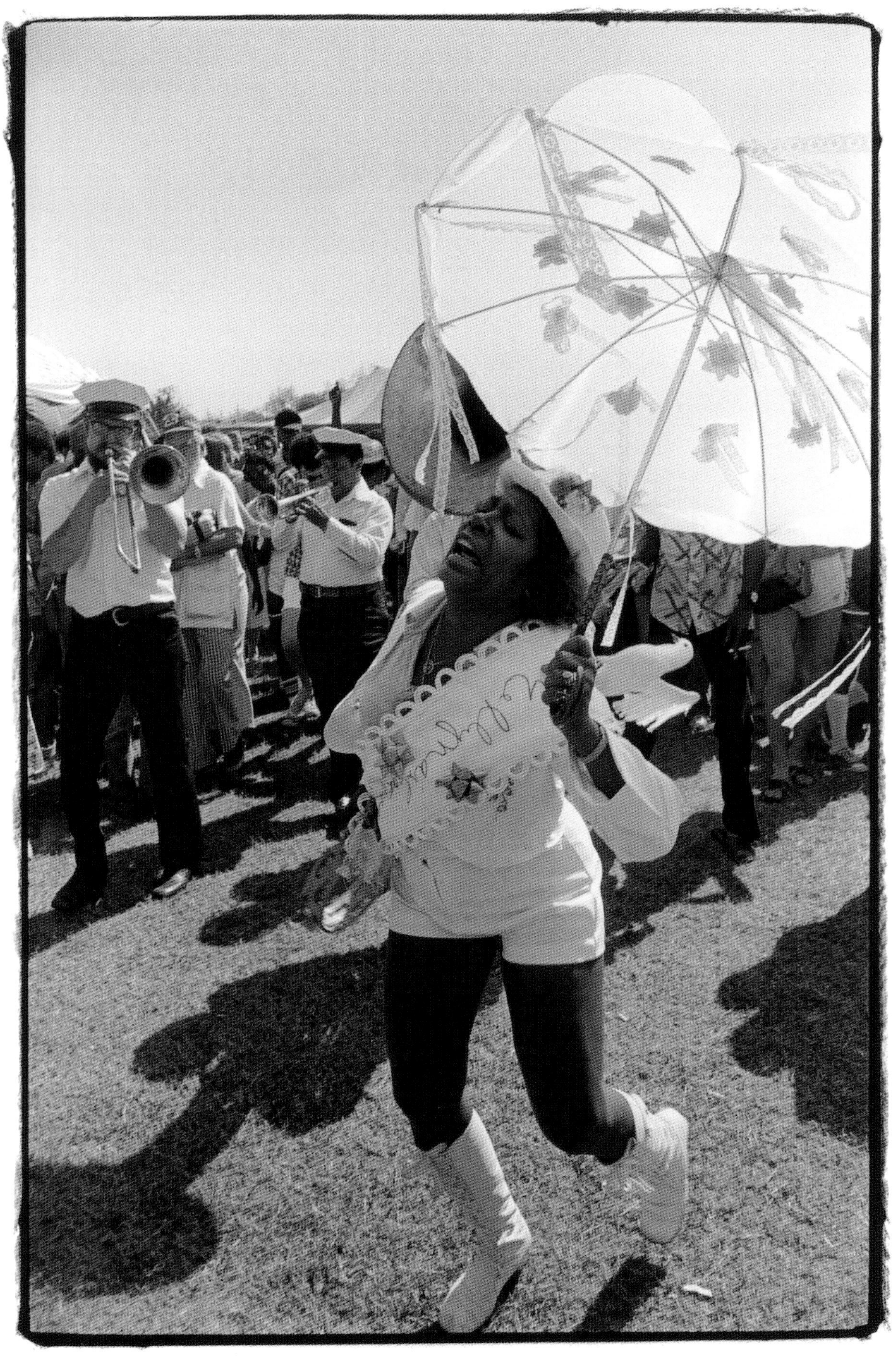

Untitled (from the *Second Line* series), 1976

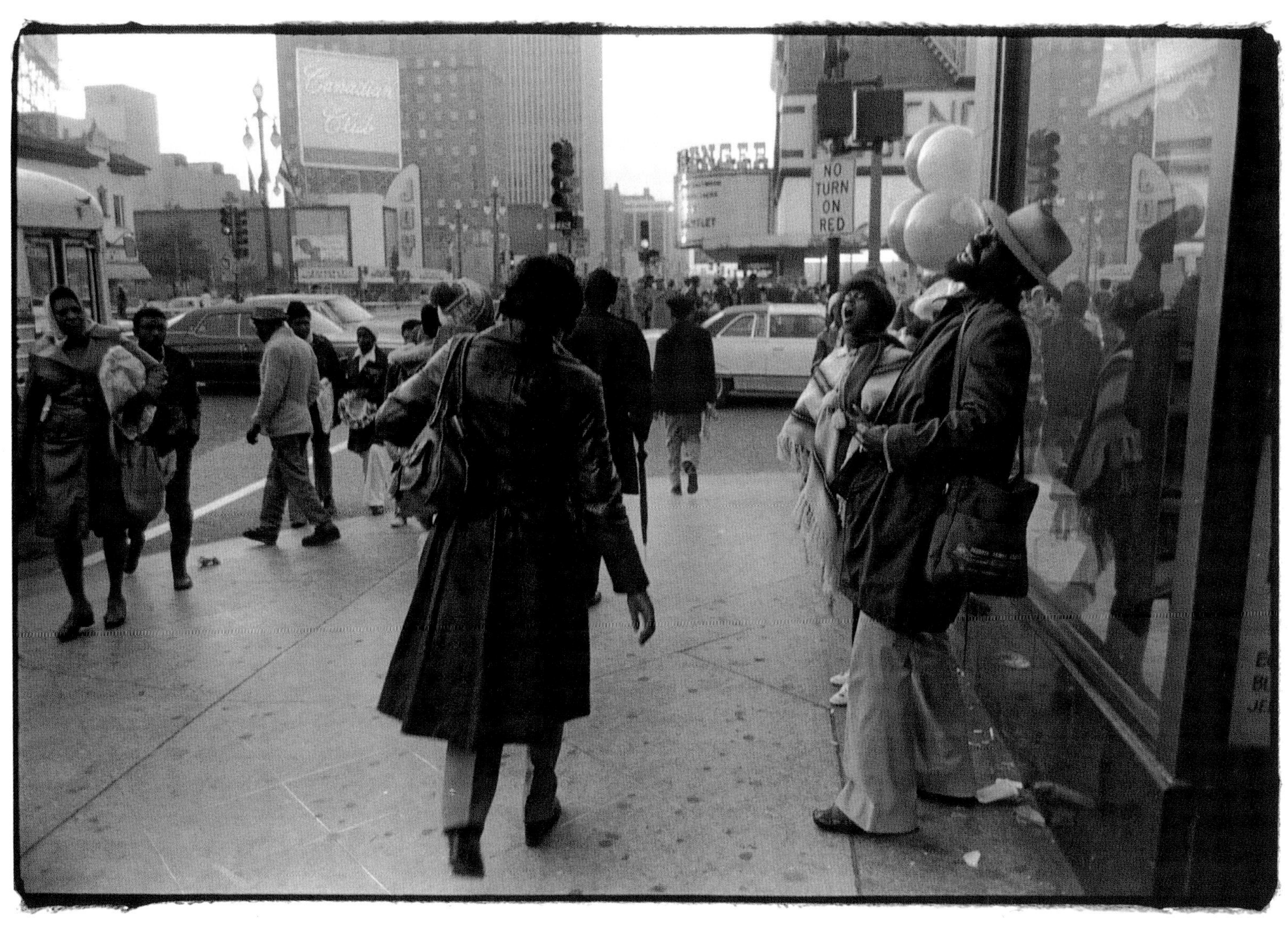

Canal Street Shout, New Orleans, 1978

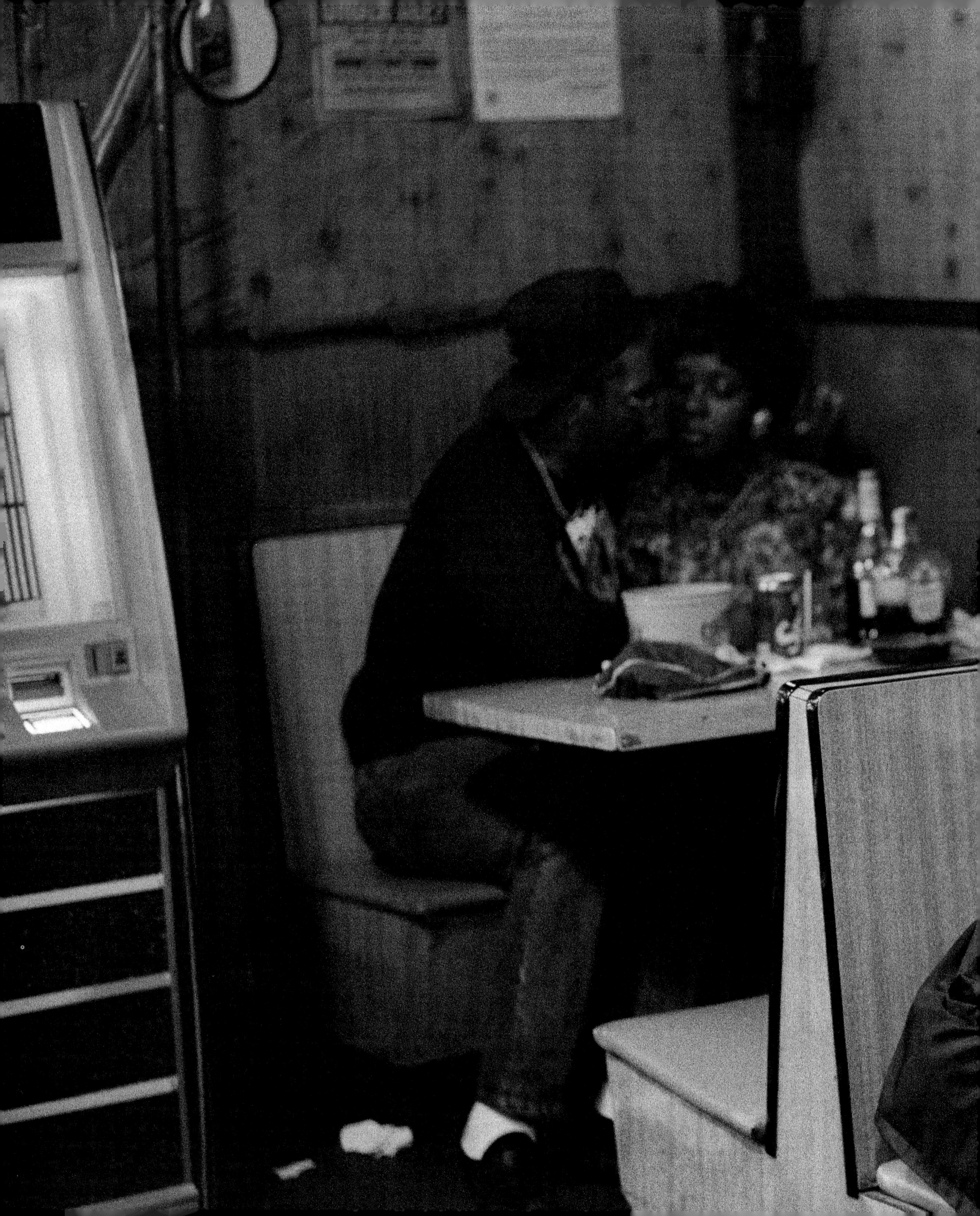

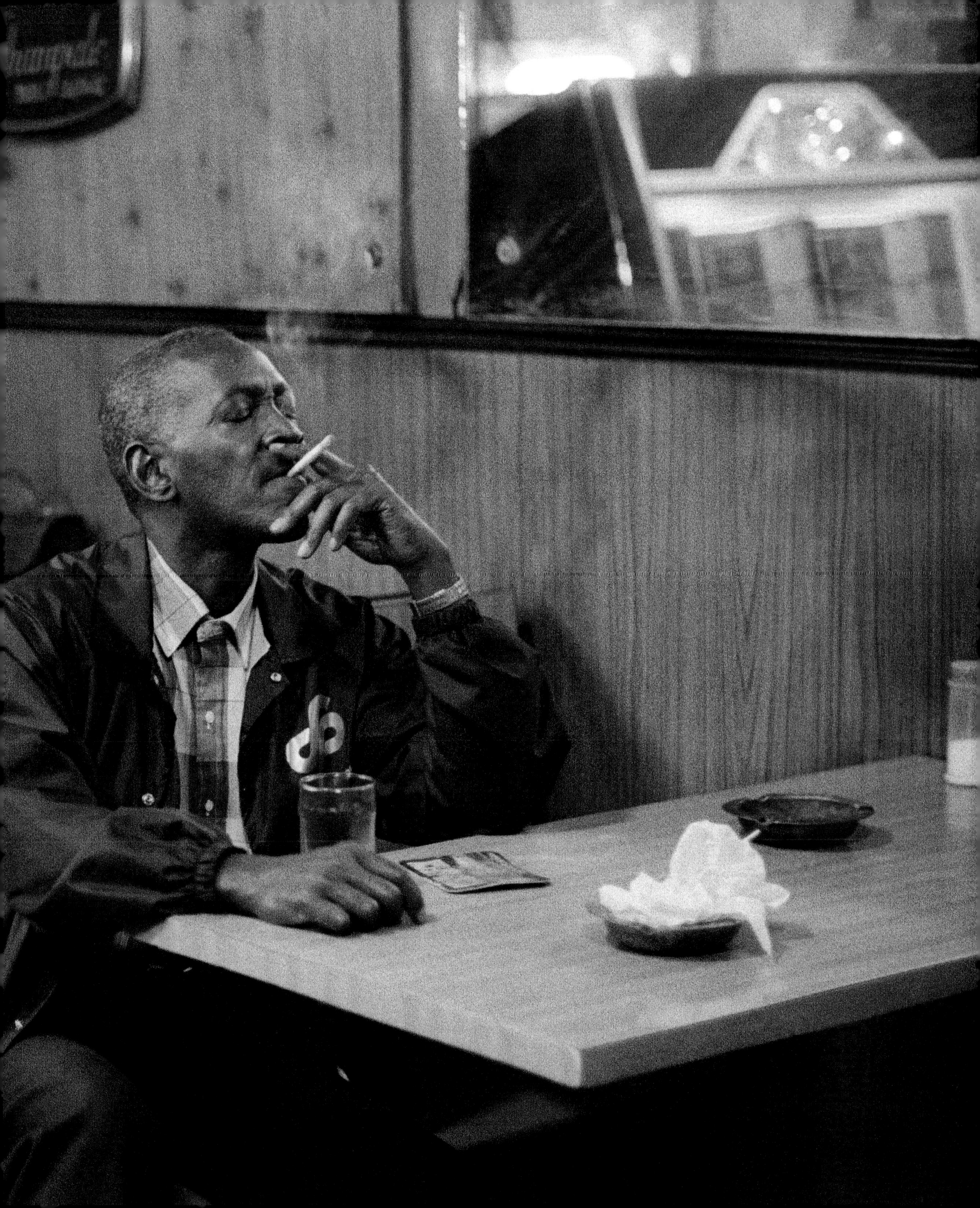

The Culture: Artists and Workplaces

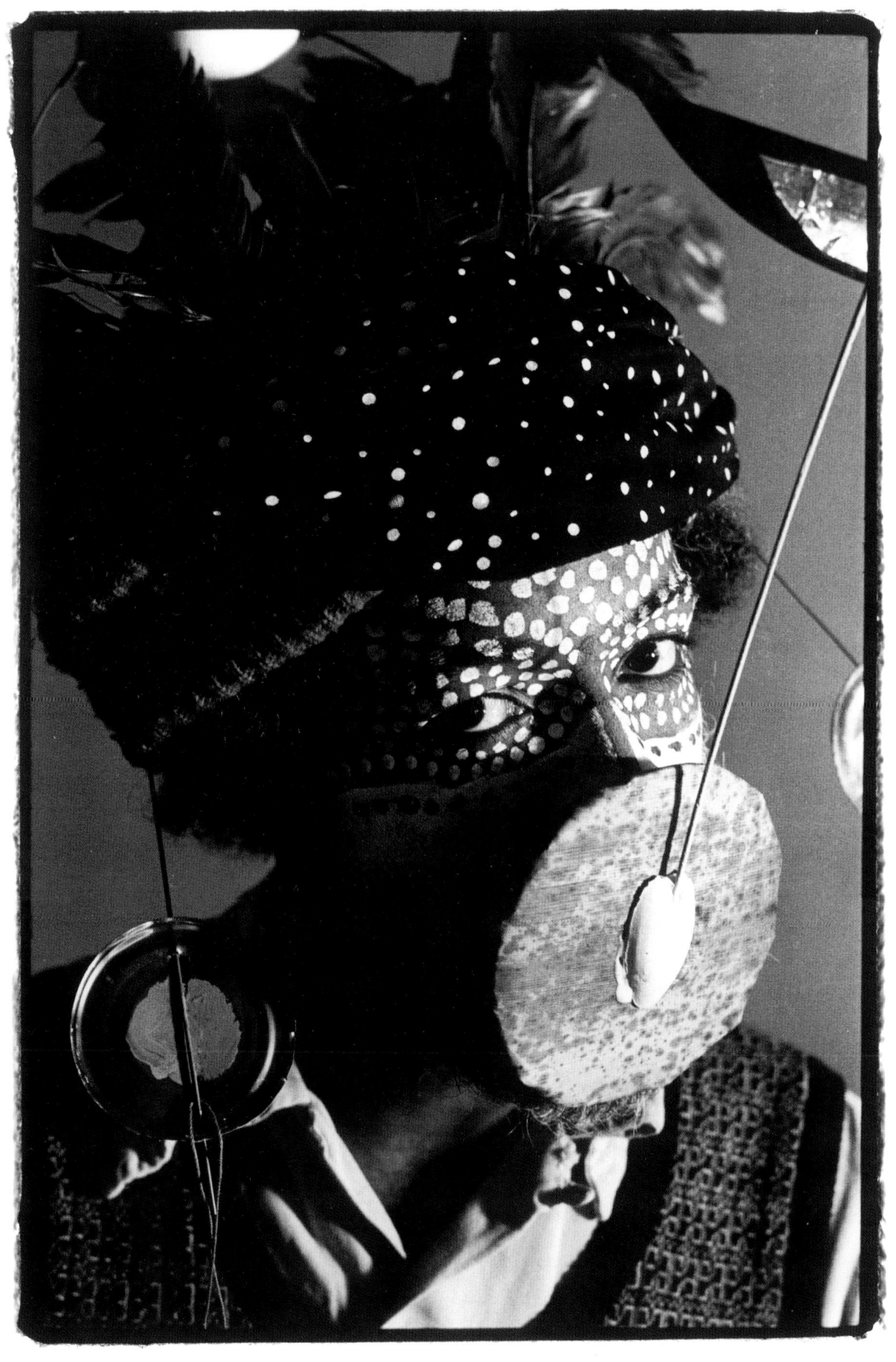

Endangered Species: David Hammons, 1981

Previous spread: *Smoke and the Lovers* (detail), see page 102

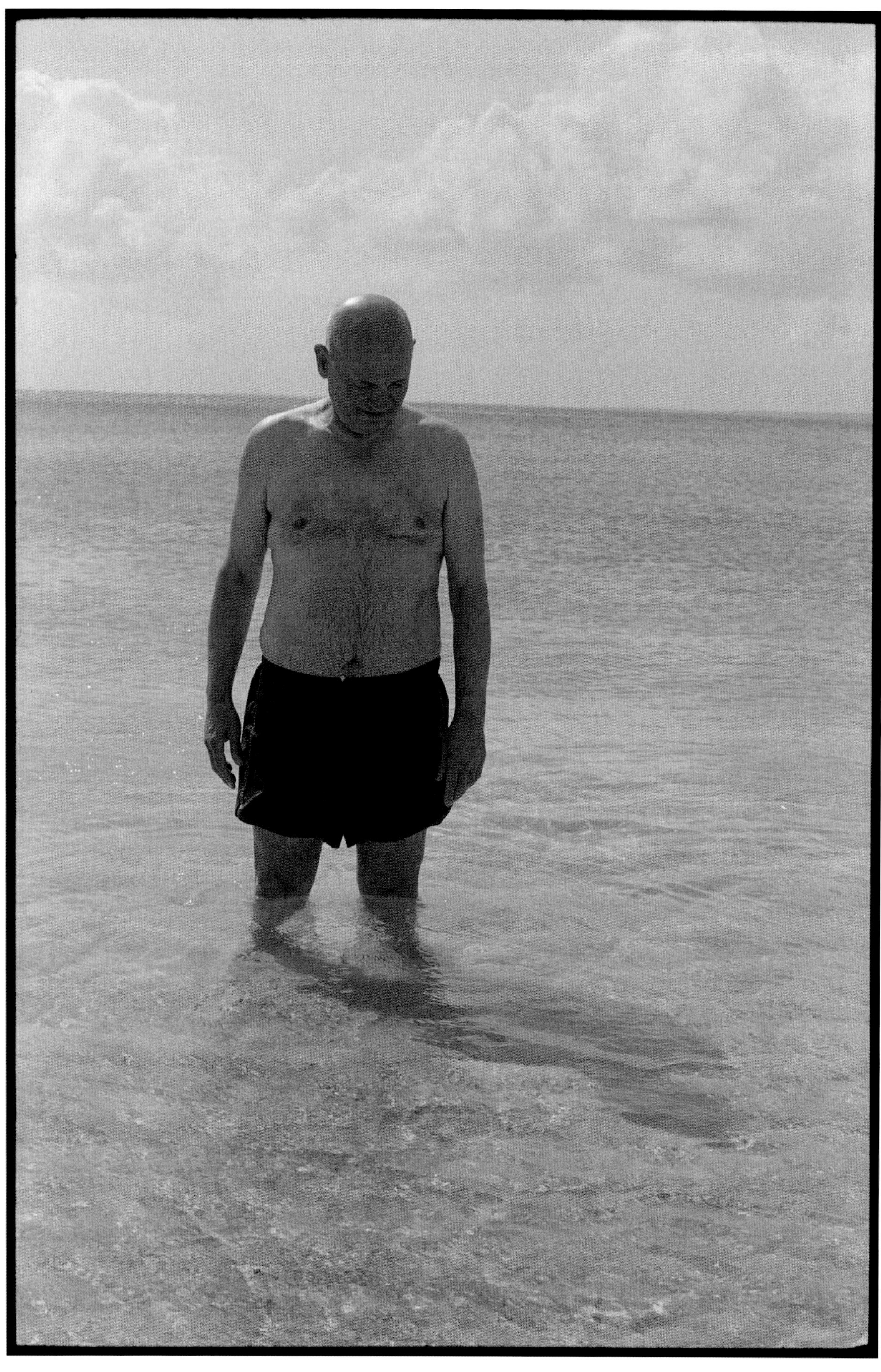

Romie in the Ocean, St. Martin, c. 1977

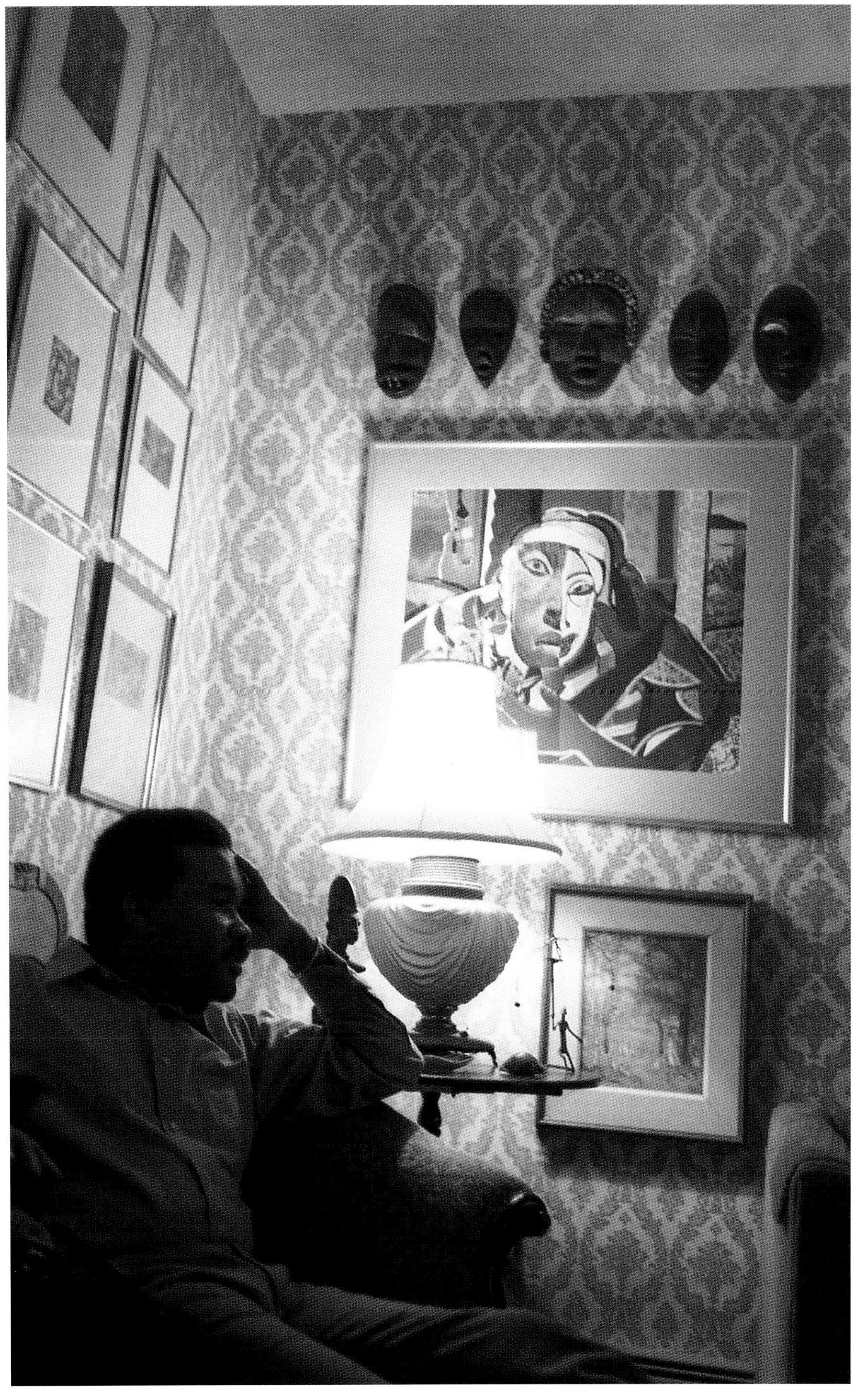

David C. Driskell, 1978

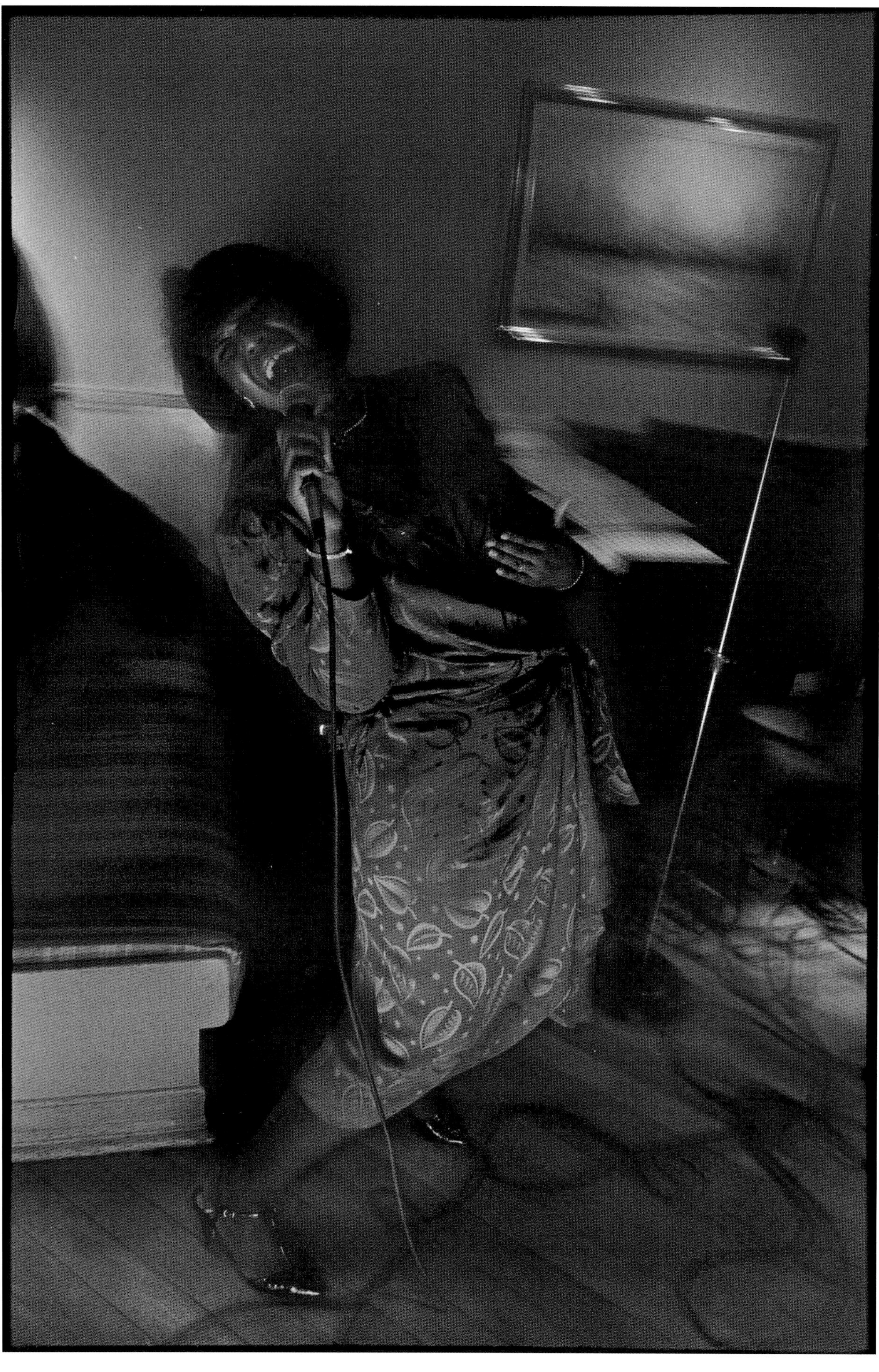

Keisha at Lola's, 1986

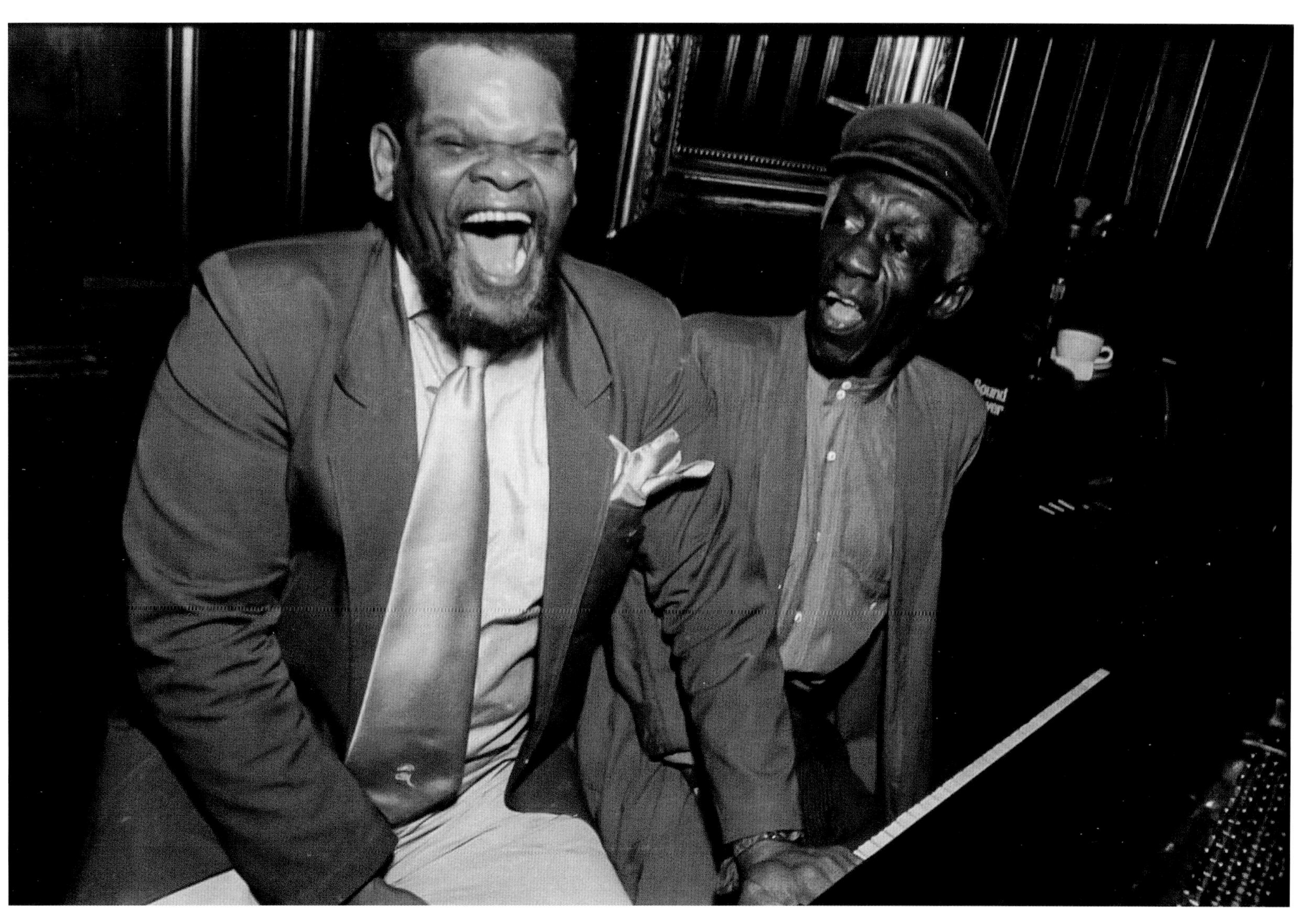

Boo and Humphrey, 1989

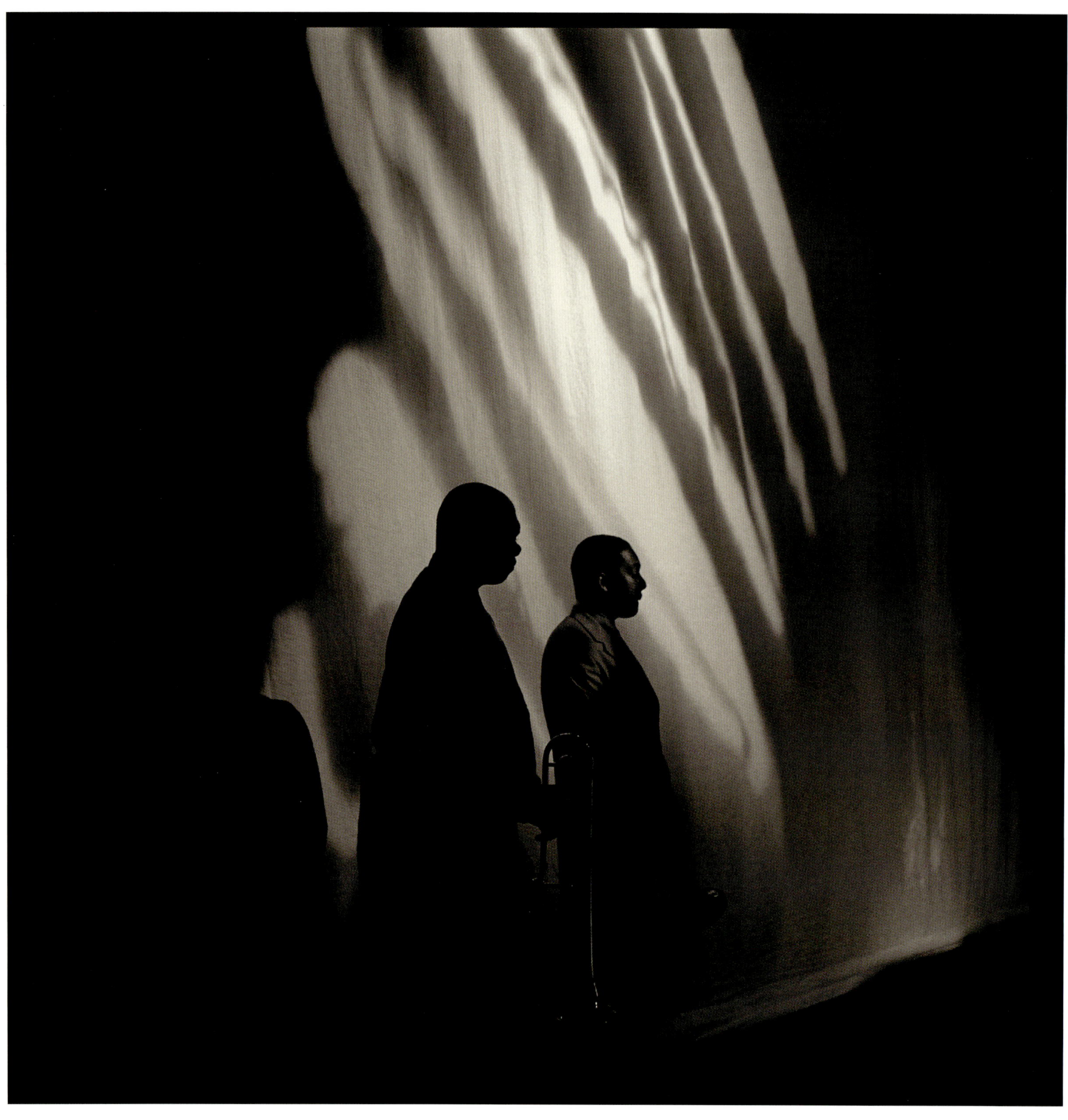

Skaine and Coopty, Palm Beach, Florida, 1992

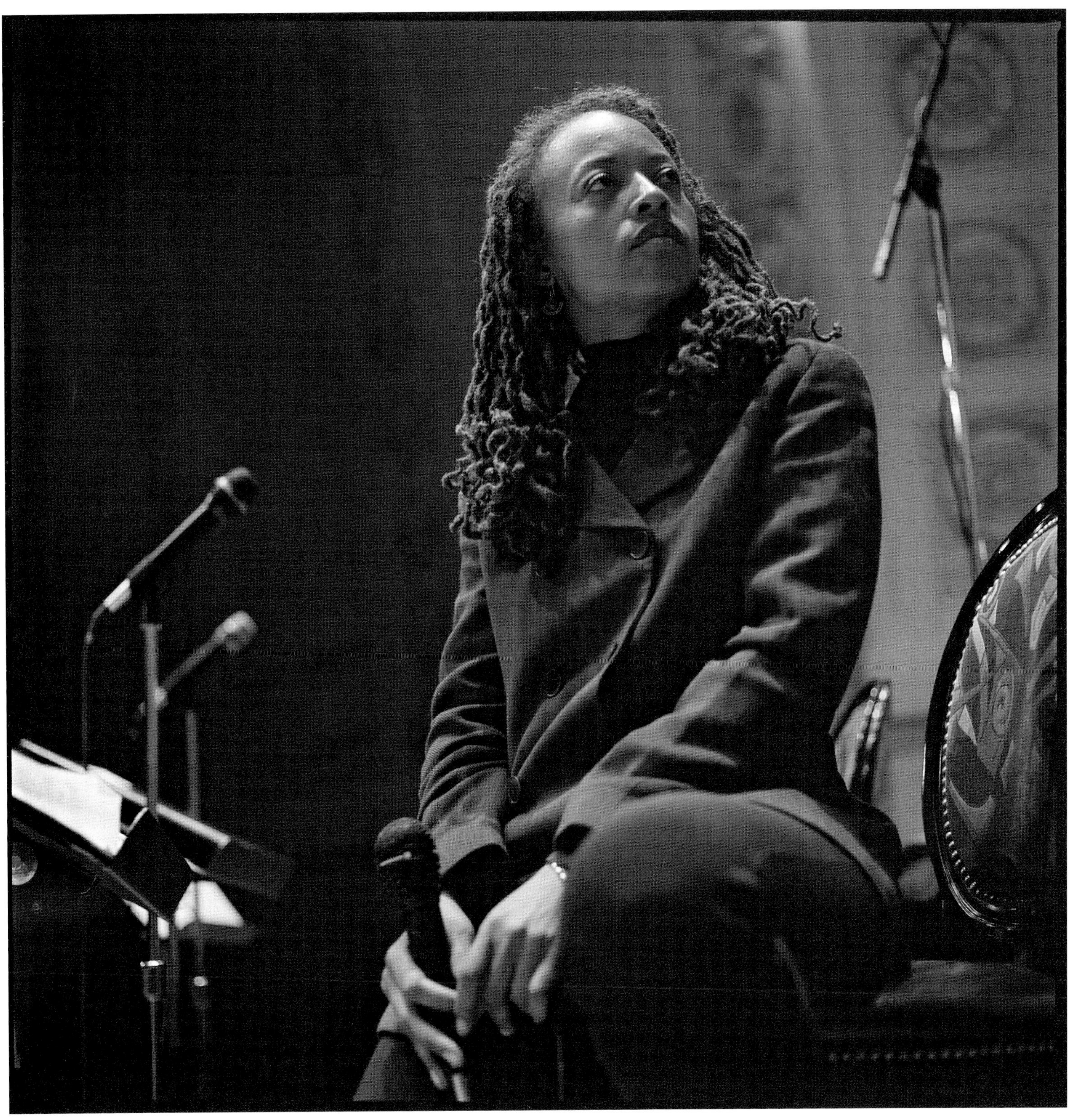

Cassandra Wilson, 1994

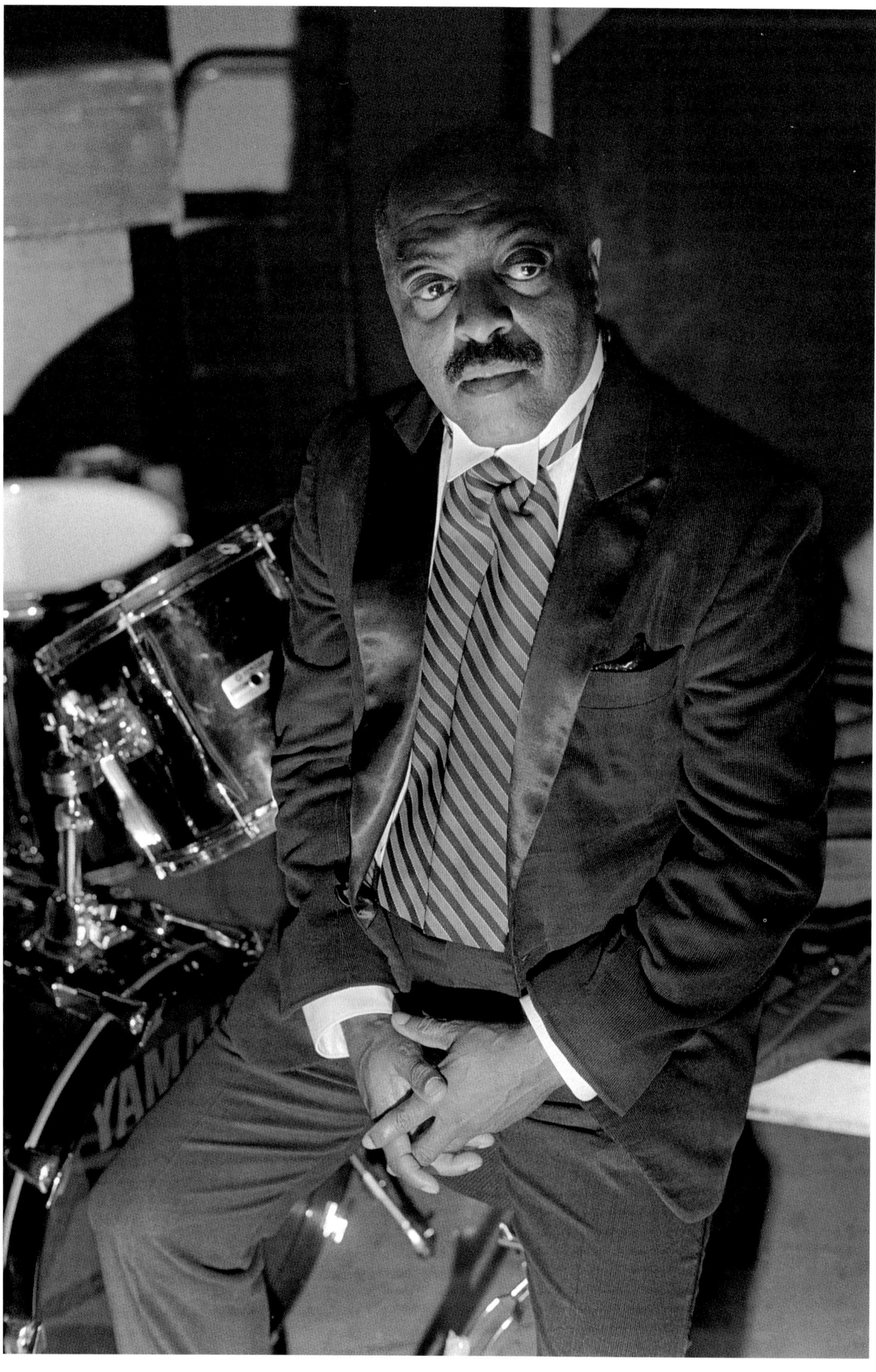

Roy Haynes, Alice Tully Hall, 2002

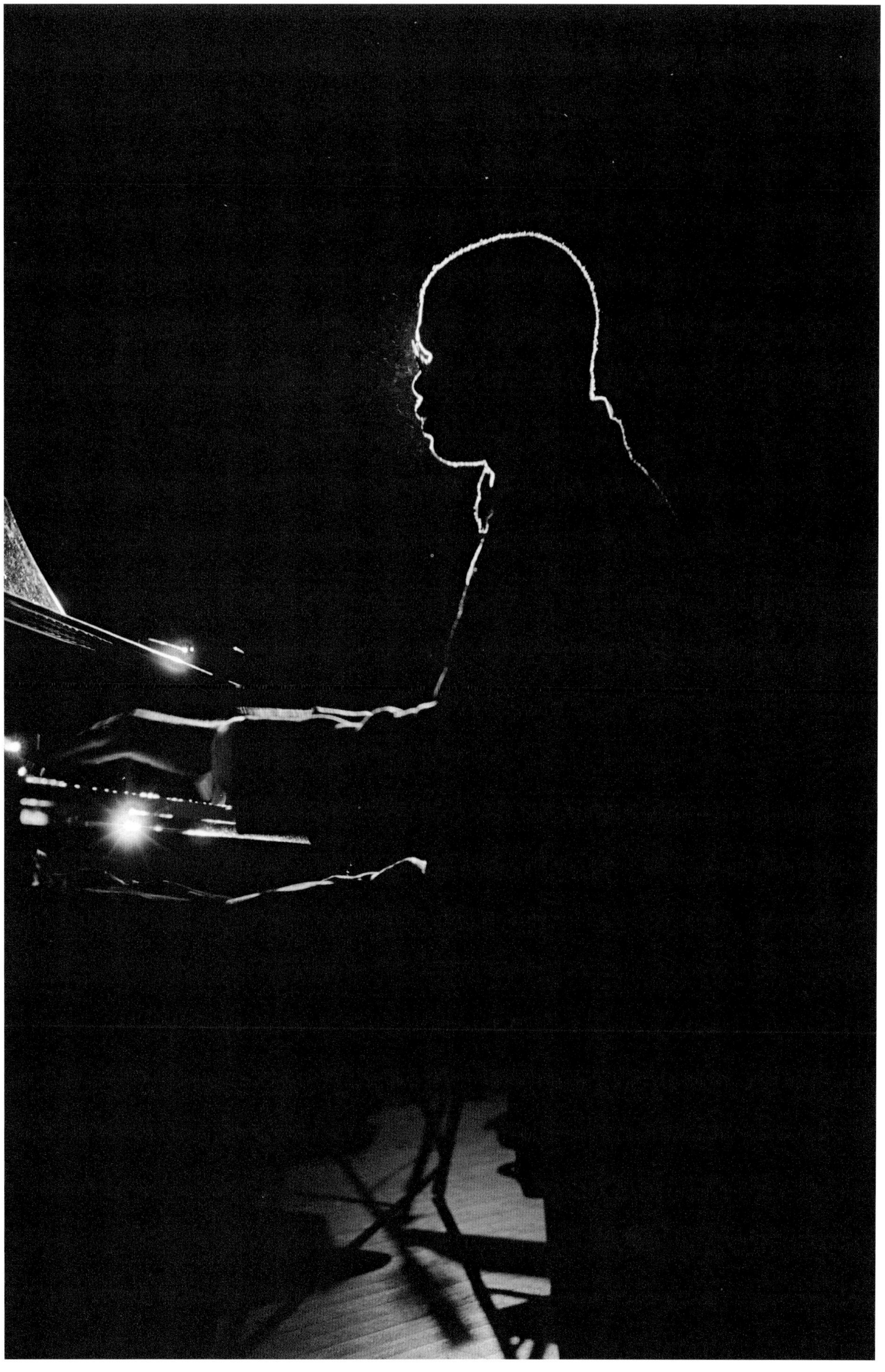

Marcus Roberts, 1994

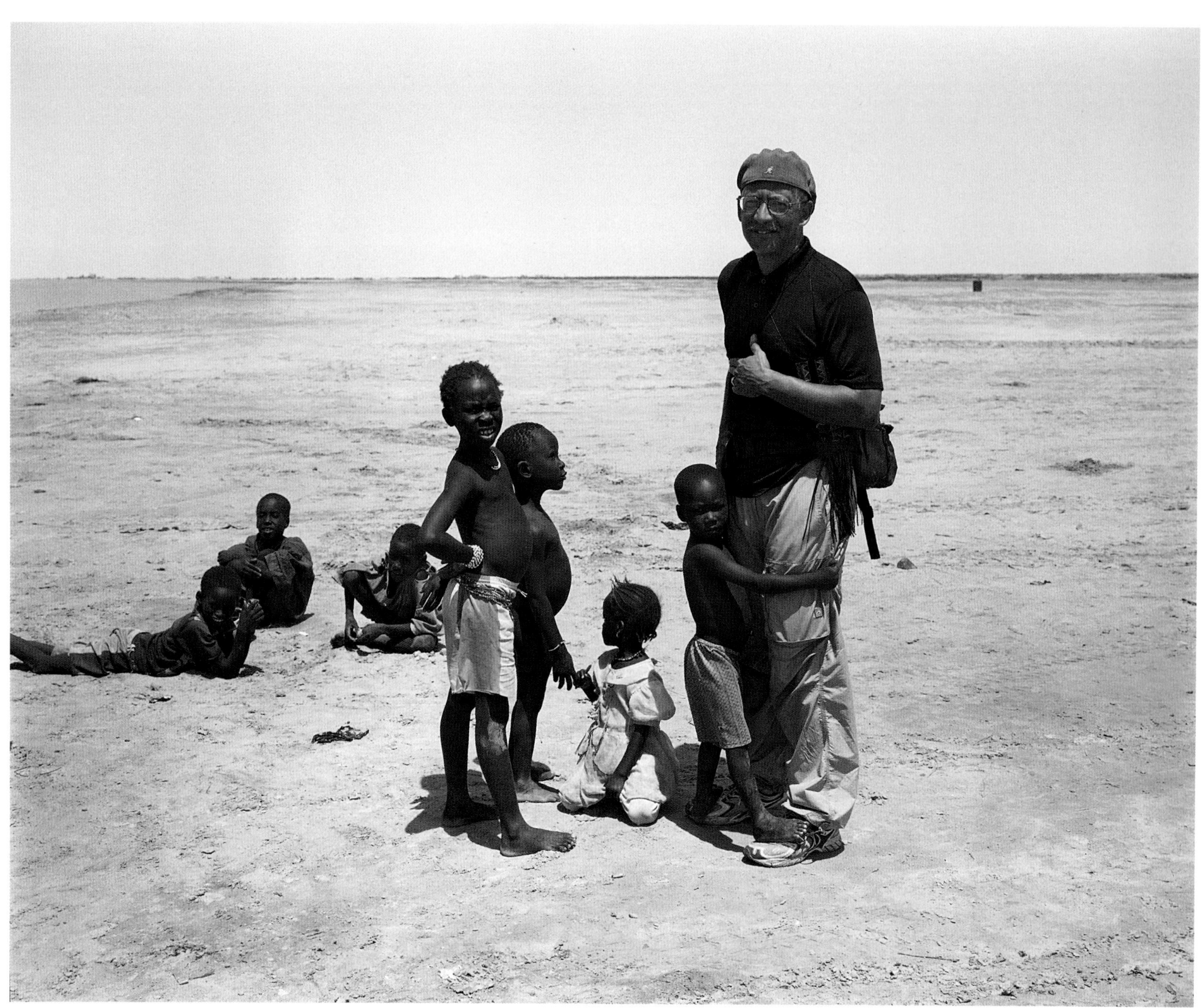

IMPROVISING ON A RIFF: A CONVERSATION WITH FRANK STEWART

Ruth Fine and Frank Stewart

RUTH FINE: You often talk about growing up in Memphis, but you have said very little about your earliest years, which were spent in Nashville, where you were born. Please talk about what you remember about your time there as a very young boy.[1]

FRANK STEWART: I was in Nashville with my mother for the first five years of my life. We lived in the projects, a community on the outskirts of town built for the underclass of the Black folk who lived in the city. It was the Deep South before the 1964 and 1965 Civil Rights Acts, complete with stores you couldn't go into if you were the wrong shade. My mother and I were part of the in-between race that was seldom talked about—light-skinned Negroes, the brown bag society measure, apart from the rank-and-file poor Black man and woman.

I can remember the kids would get a box of Niagara starch, open it, and pour the contents onto a plate of water to dissolve it, then place it in the sun to dry it out. It would then be broken up and chewed on. Well, it was starch—nourishing.

There was a creek in the back of our block of houses. I was banned from going there alone, but one hot day I happened to find myself at the creek alone, nobody around but me. The creek was running and it was cool. I took my shoes and socks off and got in. There were crayfish I played with, and I had a good time. Coming home, I was asked where I had been. Not knowing how to make up a lie plausible enough to believe, I told the truth. Believe it or not I got a whipping for that, because I'd been told by her not to go down to the creek.

My mother had a '53 Pontiac that a benefactor bought her. Black and white with a white interior. I loved that car. Nobody on our block had such a car. My mother was attending school at this time, Tennessee State A & I [Agriculture and Industry], on scholarship for winning a beauty pageant, as was my father, on an athletic scholarship.

I didn't know my father, or that I even had one. Except one day as we were riding in the Pontiac, my mother turns to me and tells me, "See that man over there, that's your father." There were three men walking. I tried to pick out who this man could have been, but hard as I tried, recognition didn't come to me. Then one of the three broke away and came toward the car with a big smile on his face. He seemed happy to see me. For the rest of our time in Nashville I would see him sporadically from time to time.

RF: Talk about leaving Nashville and living in what also were segregated communities, both in Memphis and Chicago. New York, I know, presented a different situation.

Petra Richterová, *Waiting to cross the Niger River, Northern Mali*, 2006

FS: You can't talk about Memphis without talking about colored and White. White water, colored water; White bathrooms, colored bathrooms. Front of the bus, back of the bus. One pool in the city for colored, later there came to be two more. The guy that was running the pool closest to where I lived went to school with my father at Tennessee State. We didn't even know where the White pools were. We could go to the zoo one day a week when they cleaned the cages. You could go into the shops, but if you touched something or put it on, you had to walk out with it. Whether shoes fit or not you had to buy them. So, we ended up buying at Goodwill when I would be with my grandmother and great-grandmother, Mudear and Mama.

RF: Wasn't music already important to you during your childhood?

FS: Oh yeah, especially blues and gospel. There was Martha Jean, the Country Queen, on WDIA Memphis radio. She was one of the first Black women disc jockeys in the United States. I went to first, second, and third grade with her daughter, Dianne, who was a piano player. Dianne's father, Luther Steinberg, started and was the head of the territory band called the Luther Steinberg Orchestra. Martha Jean's daughter just found me on Facebook, wanting to know if I was the guy she went to school with. It was like finding a long-lost sister.

RF: Family was hugely important for you, once you became connected to your mother Dotty's multi-generational group in Memphis. I recall you talking about when your two uncles, your mother's two younger brothers, came back from the Korean War.

FS: It was an evening like most evenings: the sun was already golden and it hit the stained-glass window in the front door. Yellow, red, blue, and green patterns lit the floor and made it like a large sundial marking the passing of time. Evening chimes had already started from the Ebenezer Baptist Church with the A.M.E. Zion rounding off a two-part harmony—"Rock of Ages" and "Shall We Gather at the River." The bus, named the Four Walker, pulls up to the corner of Mississippi and Wicks, and the day laborers exit along with two men in soldier uniforms with large duffel bags over their shoulders, walking toward our house. Janet sees them first and shouts, "Hey y'all, Zoog and Robert are home." The words echo through the house, which produces a stampede to the front door and onto the porch: Mama, Mudear, Janet, Harold, and myself.[2] Two of our dogs, after hearing the commotion, get caught up in the excitement and start barking. Tears of joy start to flow. This is the first time I remember meeting these two uncles. I was too young to be aware of knowing them before they went off to war. I was content to keep my distance and watch how the others greeted these larger-than-life war heroes. Zoog looks at me and says, "Is that Lee? When I left you were just a baby."[3] Zoog got shot doing maneuvers, and Robert had lots of stories to tell about that. It was great that the two of them came back together.

RF: And what about your time as a child in New York?

FS: I'm in Memphis, living with my grandmother and great-grandmother. I was about to do the fourth grade, but my mother had married the jazz piano player Phineas Newborn Jr., and they wanted me to come and live with them, to make a family. So, I came up from Memphis. Phineas was playing opposite Count Basie at Birdland, so I got to hang out at Birdland, and Phineas and I hung out at the Vanguard and the Five Spot, too. He also got me into photography. Phineas was fascinated by photography, so he bought himself a small Minox camera that he used whenever he went on the road. He would hook it up somehow to binoculars and it worked like a telephoto lens. He would come back from being on the road with color slides and he had a small projector. We would sit up and he would project the color images. This was before color TV. I remember vividly these pictures he shot in Vatican City, showing the saints all in a row around Vatican square. And he had an enlarger that he never used. It was on top of the dresser in my bedroom, the last thing I saw at night before I went to sleep. It looked like something that a dentist would use, and it always intrigued me, wondering, how does that work? Art Farmer's ex-wife, Renee Farmer, who was a photographer, was getting rid of her darkroom and she gave me my first enlarger. It was about 1968 or 1969. It was a big thing when I learned to use it, even before I went to Cooper [Union]. I learned how to print on it and get a portfolio together to apply at Cooper.

RF: What else was important about New York?

FS: When I went to live with my mother and Phineas, that was the first time I saw a Black person speaking Spanish. It was also the first time I saw a Black man cursing out a White policeman. He was on a horse, up in Harlem, and I thought that Black man was surely going to get his ass whipped then and there, taken to the police station.

In New York, there were influences from around the world. It was very different from Chicago, which was more like Memphis. All the Black people were from the South. Apart from the music, we had our own culture—food, dress, language. I spoke a Southern dialect when I first came North, and my mother was upset with my grandmother for not correcting me.

In New York, the community had immediate roots in Africa, the Caribbean, South America, [there were those] who could be speaking Portuguese or Spanish, Latin Americans with origins in Spain. People in New Orleans, the most northern Caribbean city, had French and Spanish influences. People there would be talking a different dialect than in Memphis, putting positives or negatives at the end of sentences, like "You tickle me, yeah" to mean "You're funny." In New Orleans, an auntie is a *marraine*; an uncle is a *parrain*.

RF: You are used to living on the road, and it seems to me that you were pretty rootless and nomadic by the time you were in high school, having lived in multiple cities with different family members and friends. How do you think that has impacted your life overall?

FS: All I needed was a bed and something to eat. The whole thing was to get me to a point where I could be on my own. The reason I'm comfortable on the road now is because of that peripatetic childhood. Both my mother and father had multiple partners and were shifting their lives all the time. As a result, my life got shifted, not with them but apart from them, from foster homes to different family members to friends and strangers. Once I was out of school, I got a job on the road with Ahmad Jamal, which was just a further exploration of different cities. It took me out to the West Coast and points in between.

I love being on the road. My home became the car from the time I got a license. That's where I was most comfortable.

Wynton [Marsalis] didn't like to fly, so I drove him all around America. With two drivers we could do New York to the West Coast in forty-four hours. This had an impact on my photography because the way I take pictures is that I have to be in the place that the photograph is taken; I have to be in the moment.

RF: So, how did this play a role in the subjects that have called out to you?

FS: When you first start taking pictures, you document the most familiar things to you, like friends and family members. By traveling so much, I moved from familiar subjects to branch out into the abstract. Each negative is a problem to be solved—first how to make your subject matter make sense, and then how to print it. The way you grow is by looking at how other photographers solve their problems. You think about how they have done it and you apply that to what you do. That's what Picasso said, and I had long conversations with the painter Raphael Soyer, who said that he would go to the Metropolitan Museum [of Art] every day and copy the masters.

RF: Let's shift to talking specifically about photography. How did you decide what to shoot at the 1963 March on Washington, when you took Dotty's camera from her? What got you to do that?

FS: Even then, I thought that was a heavy, important moment that should be documented. That I should document it. I wasn't near the stage, but off to the left, and the crowd was euphoric. The atmosphere was filled with possibility, and that became interesting to me. So, I started photographing what was going on, the crowd of euphoric people, the good feeling in the humanity that was around me: people carrying signs, a lot of singing (pages 23–25). It was the first time I had seen that big of an interracial crowd—White and Black people together—and I thought that was interesting. The euphoria was like when Barack Obama became president, you thought everything was going to change. Back in 1963, before the march, there was no way that you could imagine there'd be no segregation in America.

RF: What about the importance of your trips to Fisk University when you were enrolled at Middle Tennessee State, how that impacted your decision to focus life on photography?

FS: I didn't like Middle Tennessee that much, so I would go to Fisk almost every day. I had a cousin Adrienne who was a painter and in the art program, and she was in a class with a teacher named David Driskell. I would practice in the morning, and then go to Nashville and audit classes at Fisk, which was about twenty-five miles away from my school.

My best friend at the time was John Simmons. He was at Fisk as an assistant to Bobby Sengstacke, who was the photography teacher, who I knew from Chicago. At Fisk, I saw working with Bobby and Johnny as a way to learn more about a passion I already had. But it really started as a hobby for me, I majored in political science before I started studying photography as a serious profession. A long time before that, about 1964 or '65, visiting the Sengstacke home with Johnny, I saw Bobby's photographs enlarged to 11 by 14 inches and mounted on cardboard. They were very different from what I was used to, which were photographs that were developed through the local Walgreens drugstore, like those I took at the March on Washington.

RF: In the past you have told me how the idea of true integration had not seriously taken hold at Middle Tennessee State when you were there for that one semester. Can you say more?

FS: If you were a state school, you had to admit Black students, or the state wouldn't be giving you money. All the Black students at Middle Tennessee were on either an athletic or an academic scholarship. Mine was for track and field. I was running track at a very racist school, so whenever we would go to a meet we had to eat in the kitchen. Sometimes we couldn't even go into the restaurant. We're talking about 1967 to 1968, in the South. For many classes, those that had physical contact, such as dancing or CPR, Black students could only touch Black students, so the process of integration was extremely limited.

Going over to Fisk, Bobby Sengstacke was my first informal teacher in photography, because he let me watch him in the darkroom and he talked about photography.

RF: Isn't that when you learned about filmmaking also?

FS: Yeah. We learned film through a guy from California named Carlton Moss. He would come in once a month and he would teach 16mm film, shooting, editing, lighting, so forth and so on.

RF: But after a semester, didn't you go back to Chicago?

FS: Yes, and soon after that Bobby showed me the Roy DeCarava and Langston Hughes collaboration, *The Sweet Flypaper of Life,* and I decided I wanted to meet this guy, to study with him. So I went to New York. But I was still working with Johnny and Carlton on films. I hadn't seen anybody show Black people like DeCarava did. The love and compassion he had for his subject matter came out in the book.

RF: What other photography books influenced you early on?

FS: There were only a handful of Black photography books when I was coming along, and I knew every one of them like the Bible. One was by Ernest Cole, called *House of Bondage: A South African Black Man Exposes in His Own Pictures and Words the Bitter Life of His Homeland Today*. Another one was *In Our Terribleness*

Garry Winogrand, *Klamath River, California*, 1964. © Estate of Garry Winogrand, courtesy Fraenkel Gallery, San Francisco

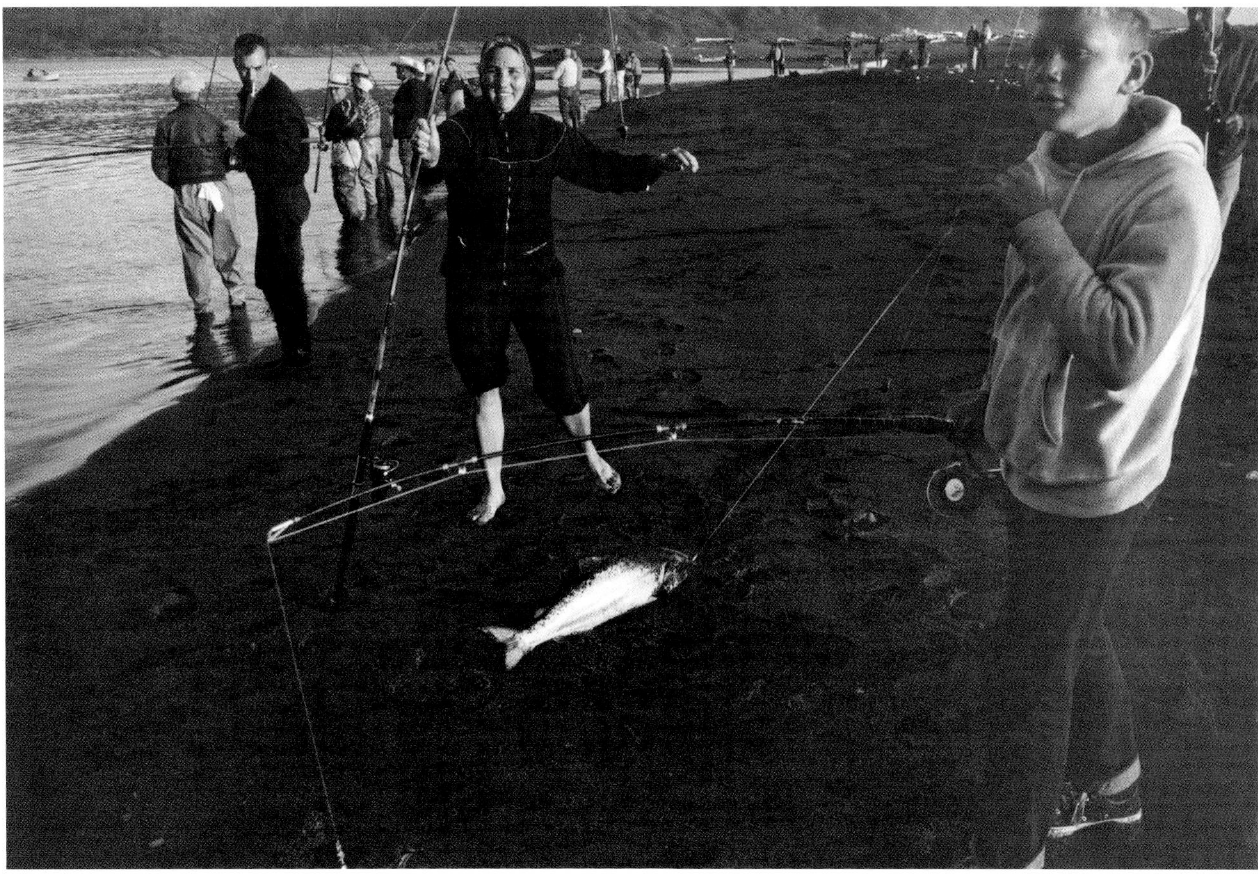

by [Imamu] Amiri Baraka with Billy Abernathy, who was called Fundi, and that was about Chicago.

RF: Did you see, or know about, the *Harlem on My Mind* show at the Metropolitan Museum of Art?

FS: I didn't see it but knew about it from [James] Van Der Zee. He was getting evicted from his house in Harlem when a researcher for the Met for the show found him and included his images in the show. Van Der Zee told me when he went to the opening, he was surprised to see life-size images he had photographed featured.

RF: What about the importance of Garry Winogrand? You first studied with him during a summer course at the Art Institute of Chicago in 1972, while you were at Cooper.

FS: Winogrand showed us that there is no way a photograph has to look, and that anything can be photographed. He had done a shot of a boy who had just caught a fish, and the fishing line he'd used was on the ground. The subject of the photograph was as much the line on the ground as the fish, or the boy who caught it. After that summer he started teaching at Cooper Union, and I got to know him better there. His work opened up a whole new world of prospects to me—the way he told stories; how he shot with a wide-angle lens; the way he broke up space.

RF: You generally have used a variety of cameras, and you still do. Can you talk about the specific cameras you have used, and what you like about working with each of them?

FS: I started with a Pentax camera, with a screw mount for the lens, which is less efficient than a bayonet mount for the lens, which clicks in quicker. Then I got a Leica, and fell in love with the one body and one 50mm lens, which gives a 35mm negative—the image is more of a rectangle. I think young photographers, when they're starting out, should shoot with one body and one hard lens, 50mm, to learn how to see. Then I added a Hasselblad, which is a two-and-a-quarter by two-and-a-quarter negative and is one and a half times larger than the 35mm, so you get a tighter grain and it is square. After that I went to a 4 by 5-inch negative, which requires sheet film rather than a roll of film. I used that while shooting on the street, so people know that you're there, and that you have a big-ass camera, and they want their picture taken with it.

When I was at The Studio Museum in Harlem [starting in the mid-1970s], I used an 8 by 10–inch negative to copy art, which is how I got used to this format. Later I added a 6 by 7 format camera, which is a rectangle, but larger than 2¼, and still uses roll film. Roll film came as 120, which had ten frames, and 220, which had twenty frames, but you can't find that anymore.

RF: What about different lenses?

FS: A telephoto lens flattens out the perspective; a wide-angle lens elongates the perspective.

RF: And your use of color?

FS: I started out with color prints from Walgreens, then shooting black-and-white film photography, and every once in a while, I shot color. My first color class was at Cooper with Joel Meyerowitz and Jay Maisel. Using Kodachrome was like painting, like digital, raw, luscious color. The difference was with black and white, gelatin silver, you are dealing with tone, silver particles in gelatin emulsion; with color you are dealing with pigment. The color of the form, of the shape. Kodachrome was developed in the form of a 35mm slide, which is a positive image, not a negative. It could then be printed with a positive-to-positive process known as Cibachrome. Those prints are archival and meant to last forever. Maisel gave me Kodachrome film when I went to Africa in 1974, and the Cibachrome prints I made when I got back look precisely as they did when they were made.

RF: What about the differences among various films and why they matter?

FS: You have fast films and slow films. A fast film gives you more grain, but less emulsion; the slow film has more emulsion and tightens the grain up. So, it needs more light to make it saturated. Tri-X was my main film. What happened with the digital world is you got much more flexibility.

RF: Is it fair to say you tried everything?

FS: I shoot in many formats, and I have tried everything from 35mm to 8 by 10 format and many digital processes as they developed. The paper and the chemistry evolved. It is hard to find paper with silver in it.

RF: You have had several important grants and commissions over the years. We can talk about only a few of them. Let's start with your 1977 trip to Cuba.

FS: The trip was sponsored by the Center for Cuban Studies. They sent seven photographers down there. I roomed with Rene Gelpi. I haven't seen him in years, and just read that he died in 2018. Rene had a grandfather who lived in Cuba, and Rene found him while we were there.

To get there, we went first to Canada, and from Canada we went on a Russian military plane to Cuba, and they didn't stamp our passports. I think we were the first American journalists to be there in almost two decades.

We were there for a month. We went all over—from Havana to Santiago and all in-between, and we really got to see the island. We traveled in a van, and each day would be a different city, or sometimes we'd spend a couple of days in the same city. We hit two or three different places in a day, like schools, hospitals, factories, day care centers, housing projects.

RF: And what were you trying to capture in your photographs?

FS: I was trying to capture as much as I could. My whole thing for going was to see if this revolution was working and how African Americans could apply the benefits of the revolution to our plight in America.

RF: And what did you learn?

FS: I learned that I could probably run a Black American country if I got five million dollars a day in money and technical help, like they were getting then from the Russians. There was 99 percent literacy; everybody had shoes; health care was among the best in the world. There was music all around. They subsidized musicians and athletes. It was an interesting and energetic time. The revolution seemed to be working.

RF: And what about your photography when you were there?

FS: I shot color and black-and-white film. Had two Leicas, one with color film, one with black-and-white. What I found was that it was such a vibrant place and it was so closed, and they weren't familiar with people taking pictures. So, they would want their picture taken. They only spoke Russian and Spanish, no English, and I only spoke English. Most of the time I was walking around by myself, finding what was there. Looking to put the people into the places. Like *Communist Windows, Havana* (page 147) was Cuban people existing inside the Communist regime. I was doing what I generally do, following what I learned from shooting in the streets while at Cooper Union, and a further extension from Africa to Cuba. Starting to put it all together. Learning how to put people in spaces. It was about the people, especially in Cuba. In Africa, it was about whatever I could find; in Cuba it was about the people and their living conditions. They would ask where I was from and I would say, "Estados Unidos," and they would say, "Cuba sí, Yankee no." They thought I was Spanish. In Havana we met Huey Newton and a few other Panthers. On the way home, we went through Mexico City, and we met photographer Manuel Álvarez Bravo, went to his house. He was an old man at that time, and I was just in awe.

RF: Let's move on to another project. You were one of ten photographers invited to photograph the 1984 Summer Olympics in Los Angeles. Your proposal was to shoot the crowds as they interacted with the athletes. How did you arrive at that idea, rather than shooting the sports events themselves?

FS: We had to submit a proposal, and the journalists were shooting the athletes. What I wanted to do was to show that the crowds had influence over the participants, how they fed off each other. This went on for thirteen days, and I tried to shoot everything that moved. The Olympics were completely overwhelming. I shot black-and-white and color, and you would have to change the color film because of the light. There was incandescent light, sunlight, mercury vapor light, and you would need different film for each of them. This was before the digital age. So, I was shooting four or five different color films a day in addition to black and white. I never even showed any of the black-and-white stuff. I had three Leicas: one with black-and-white film and two with color film. Each kind of color film is exposed at a different temperature—daylight is 6500 kelvin; incandescent is 3200 kelvin; and so on.

RF: Talk about your imagery.

FS: I tried to shoot as much of the crowds as possible, and as much of the crowds with the athletic participants as possible, with emphasis on the crowds, who were from all over the world. Basketball, boxing, track and field, and then I would go to gymnastics. One day I went and shot the equestrian, and the crowd there was so subdued you wouldn't think anything was happening. It was so quiet there.

RF: Did your own life as an athlete make this a special gig?

FS: It did, and I was keen to shoot my own events. There were only three events where people fell out at the end, they would be so exhausted: the marathon and the 440-yard dash and the mile relay. And the 440-yard dash was my race, what they used to call a "man's race."

RF: Fascinating. Let's talk about your thirty years shooting with the Jazz at Lincoln Center Orchestra and shooting whatever else came to your attention when you were on your own between concerts. Talk about that life on the road.

FS: I started out with Wynton to do a book—*Sweet Swing Blues on the Road*—about what it's like being on the road with a jazz band. That band got absorbed by the Jazz at Lincoln Center Orchestra. After I did the book, I got absorbed into Jazz at Lincoln Center as well. And I saw from the beginning that it wasn't just going to be about photography for me if I wanted to stay with the band. 'Cause you're living with these guys more than you're living with your family. You're eating with them, working with them, traveling with them.

I saw they needed help in this area, that area—like getting the equipment from one place to another, setting up the stage, somebody to drive the truck, to drive cars. So, I saw ways to fill in, in addition to taking pictures.

I also could see that my scenery was going to change every day, so I saw the opportunity to take pictures every day in different cities. I got to the point where Wynton would ask me, "Are you getting your pictures?" He meant the pictures on the street that I'm taking for myself.

The stuff I take out there on the street influences the stuff I'm taking for Jazz at Lincoln Center—how I am balancing the form with the space, what I'm learning in the street as opposed to on the stage and behind stage, with the guys that I know so well because I'm with them every day and every night. It becomes a family, a functional/dysfunctional family, like most families are to a point. If someone in the family throws the whole chemistry off, they get replaced.

I'm looking for harmony, just like what they're playing, harmony that I haven't shot before, heads, hands, arms in different positions than I shot before. I'm looking for different ways to apply what I already know. Every night they're in a different space; I'm in a different space. I never take the same picture over and over again. I'm always trying to improve so it's always different and challenging.

RF: How does the music itself impact your art?

FS: I'm trying to do in photography what they're doing on the instruments, in terms of improvisation. You have notes they have to read and breaks where you have your own individual input as a soloist. That's where you put your stamp on the music that's being played. Like, with his trumpet, Louis Armstrong playing improvisation to whatever has been played and what's going to be played. Like [Thelonious] Monk and his piano, what's not played is just as important as what is played. The space in between objects in a photograph is just as important as the objects themselves.

What I'm trying to say is that the photograph is always changing, just like the music is always changing. It can be rhythmic, it can be harmonious, have open spaces, repetition of form, forms turned around, inverted.

RF: You mentioned *Sweet Swing Blues on the Road*, with Wynton, but you have completed several other compelling books. I would appreciate your talking about the 2004 Kamoinge-based project, for which you edited the selection of photographs that were accompanied by a text by Ntozake Shange, *The Sweet Breath of Life: A Poetic Narrative of the African-American Family*. Its title suggests an homage to *The Sweet Flypaper of Life*, the Roy DeCarava and Langston Hughes collaboration of 1955 that helped to set the course for your life in photography.

FS: The larger reference of the "African-American Family" is to all Black families, or for that matter, all families in general. The thrust of the book is to portray a positive image of African American people, with style, dignity, humanity, and integrity. Characters are leading their everyday lives, except that the cameras preserve particular moments. Men, women, young and old, will participate in a dance of life caught on the sweet breath of it. Ntozake provides the mortar, words, the poetry, and Kamoinge provides the bricks and photos to construct what is a lasting work of art.

We hoped to reach an audience of photography lovers worldwide. In the midst of seeing Black people portrayed as victims or, worse, as perpetrators, of crime, *The Sweet Breath of Life* is a breath of fresh air in an otherwise

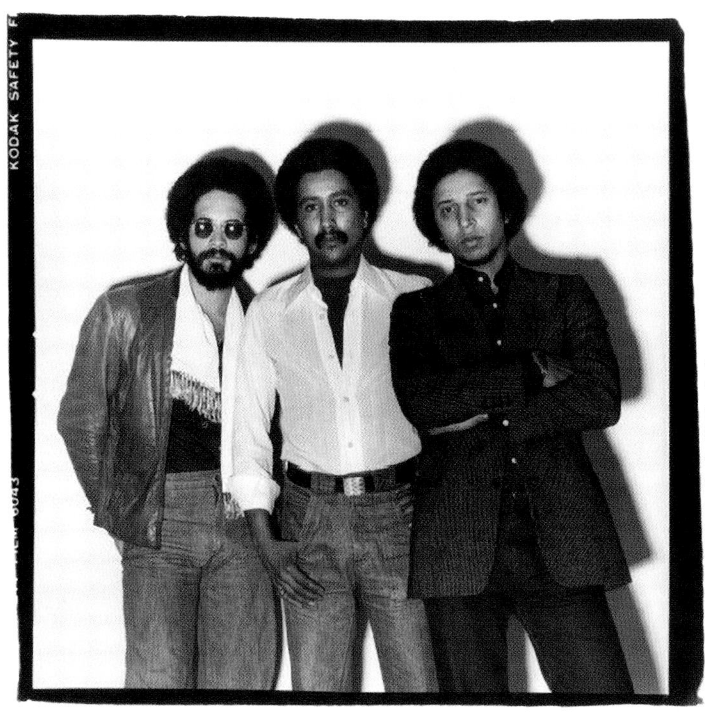

Anthony Barboza, *Untitled* (Frank Stewart, John Pinderhughes, Anthony Barboza), 1978

barren market starved for positive imagery. The endeavor of the book was for the Kamoinge Workshop to further the conversation that Roy DeCarava started in the 1950s. It took eight years for somebody to pick up *The Sweet Breath of Life* and publish it.

RF: You have always been committed to African American culture at the center of your work. And you have said to me at various times, "I'm a photographer who happens to be Black." But you also have said that while you essentially work for yourself, you are eager to connect with the largest possible network of appreciative viewers. Can you expand on that?

FS: The thing is, and this is what I tell all my students, you're not making art for people who don't like it. You are making art for yourself, and strangers that like it, whatever time or place they are living in—now, and somebody fifty years from now, in China or Russia, as well as New York or Savannah. Art is a universal language. It's like math—two plus two is four at the beginning of the century; it's four at the end of the century. Great art is going to be great art, whenever it's made, by whomever it's made. To think about it any other way is insulting to the art. People come to art from the sum of their own experience. You come to it with the sum of your experience by making it; the people who look at it come to it with the sum of their experience, to appreciate it—or not. The richer the experience that is brought, the richer the experience that is taken away. Not only experience in art; it can be experience in living, and that's what you do. You come to the art with the sum total of all of your experience.

RF: You talk about painting often, and ideas of painterly structure being important to you. In 2000, a reviewer in a Miami newspaper, Alfredo Triff, compared your photograph of *Wynton's Mutes* to the paintings of Giorgio Morandi. Does that make sense to you? If so, with what other painters would you think your work might be compared?

FS: I never thought about Morandi, but there's a bunch of painters that I got a lot from—Daumier, Goya, Van Gogh, Pollock, Gorky, Bearden—their use of line, color, modeling of form, political overtones, satire. If we add photographers, among those I didn't study but that matter a lot to me are Frank Sutcliffe, Atget, Cartier-Bresson, Walker Evans, Kertész, and Robert Frank.[4]

RF: A while ago you said that as a young man you didn't want to teach photography, that it took too much out of you and that you preferred doing jobs such as photographing art as a way to make ends meet. But now you seem to enjoy teaching. What changed for you?

FS: I am older now, and photography is backbreaking, walking around with all the heavy equipment all the time. I always liked teaching. I just didn't want to do it full-time. Also, I have more to say now in terms of teaching. I bring more to the subject matter than I had when I was younger, and I have a little bit more patience now than when I was younger.

RF: Since Hurricane Katrina, you have been committed to exploring the results of climate change on our environment, first in New Orleans, then the resettlement of residents of Isle de Jean Charles, also in Louisiana, the lands of the Biloxi Choctaw Indigenous communities, and, lastly, the aftermath of the wildfires that have consumed much of the Pacific Coast. Can you speak about your intentions in these projects?

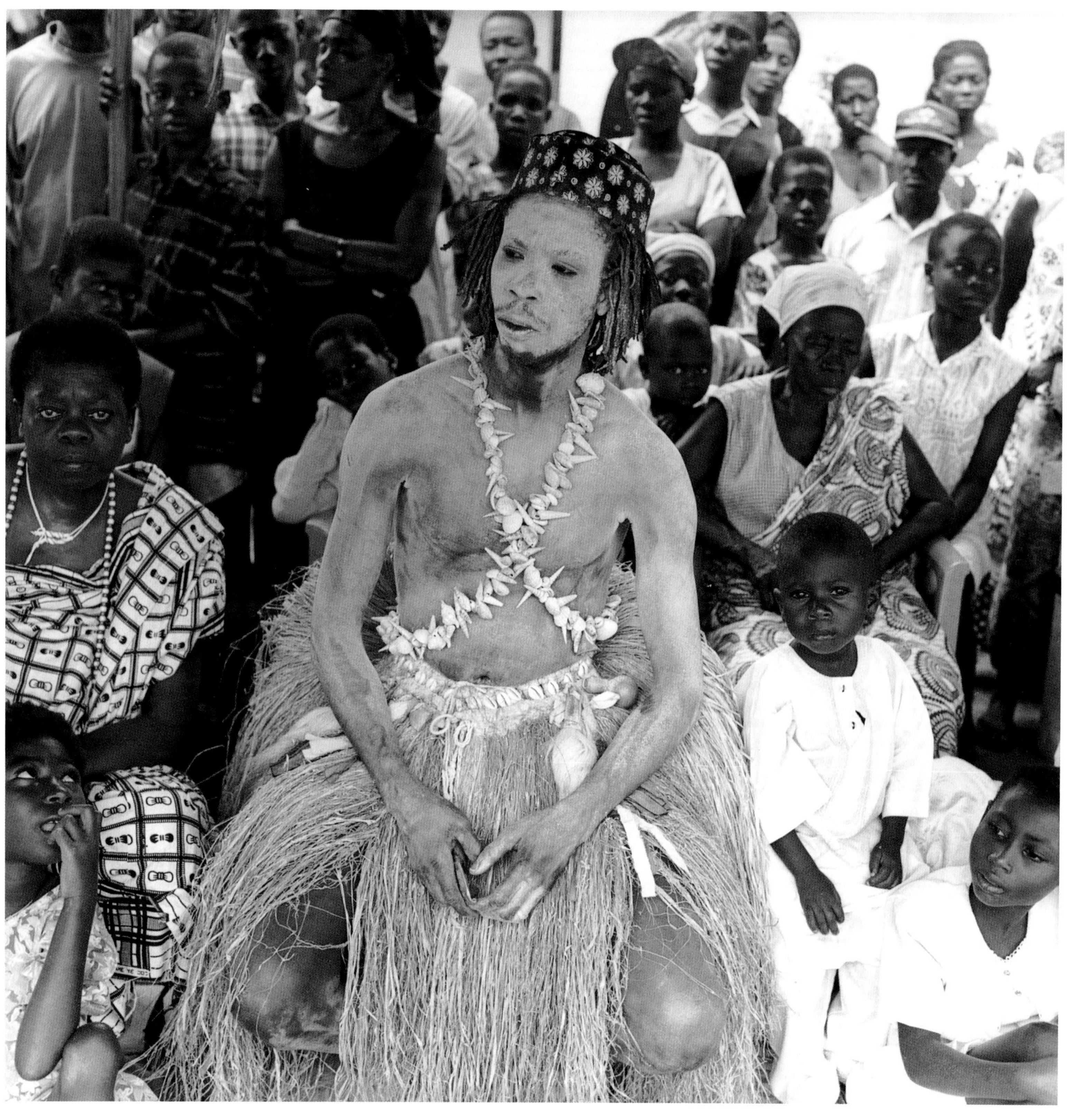

Medicine Man, 2002

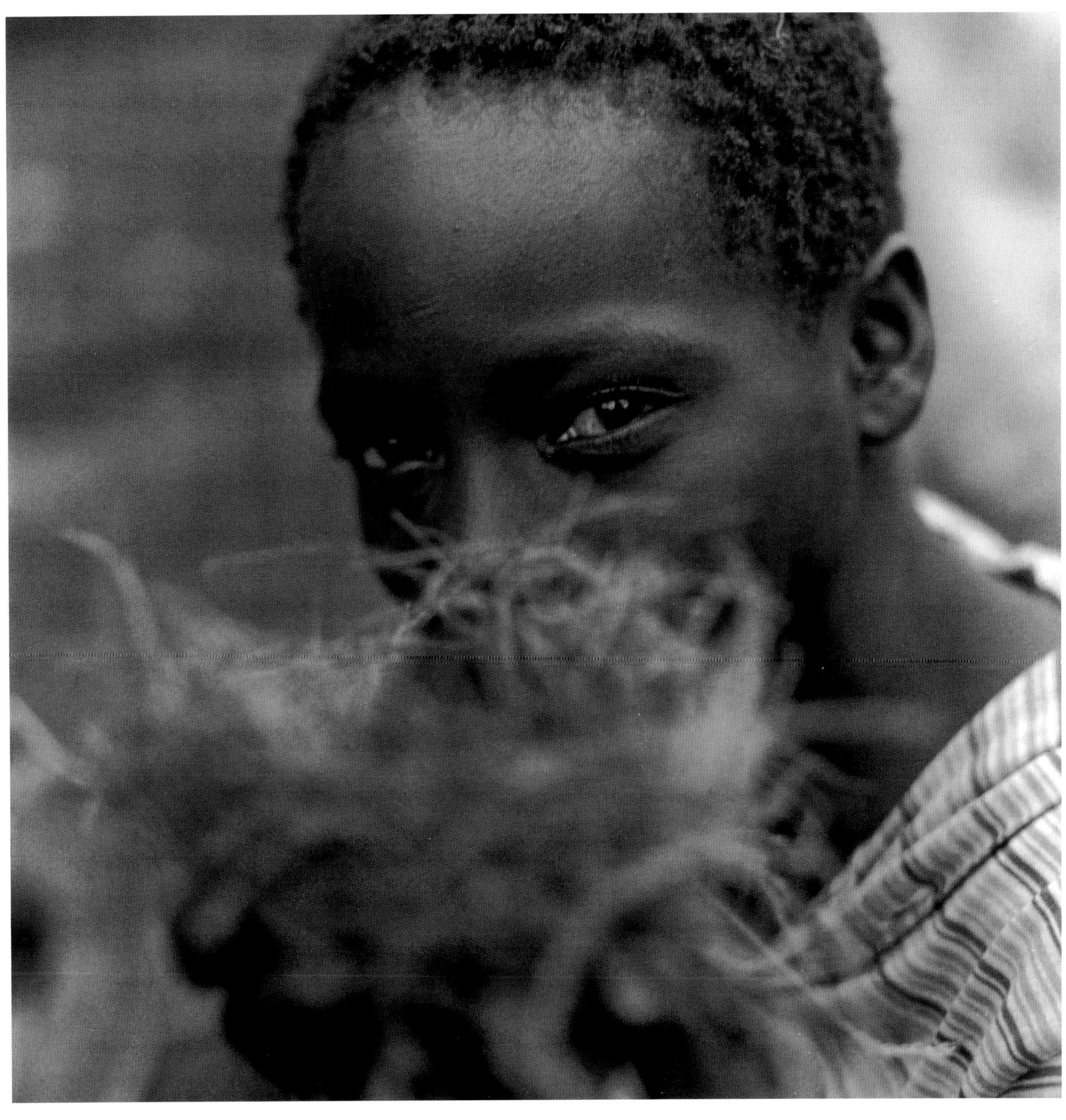

Boy with Bird's Nest, Mamfe, Ghana, 1998

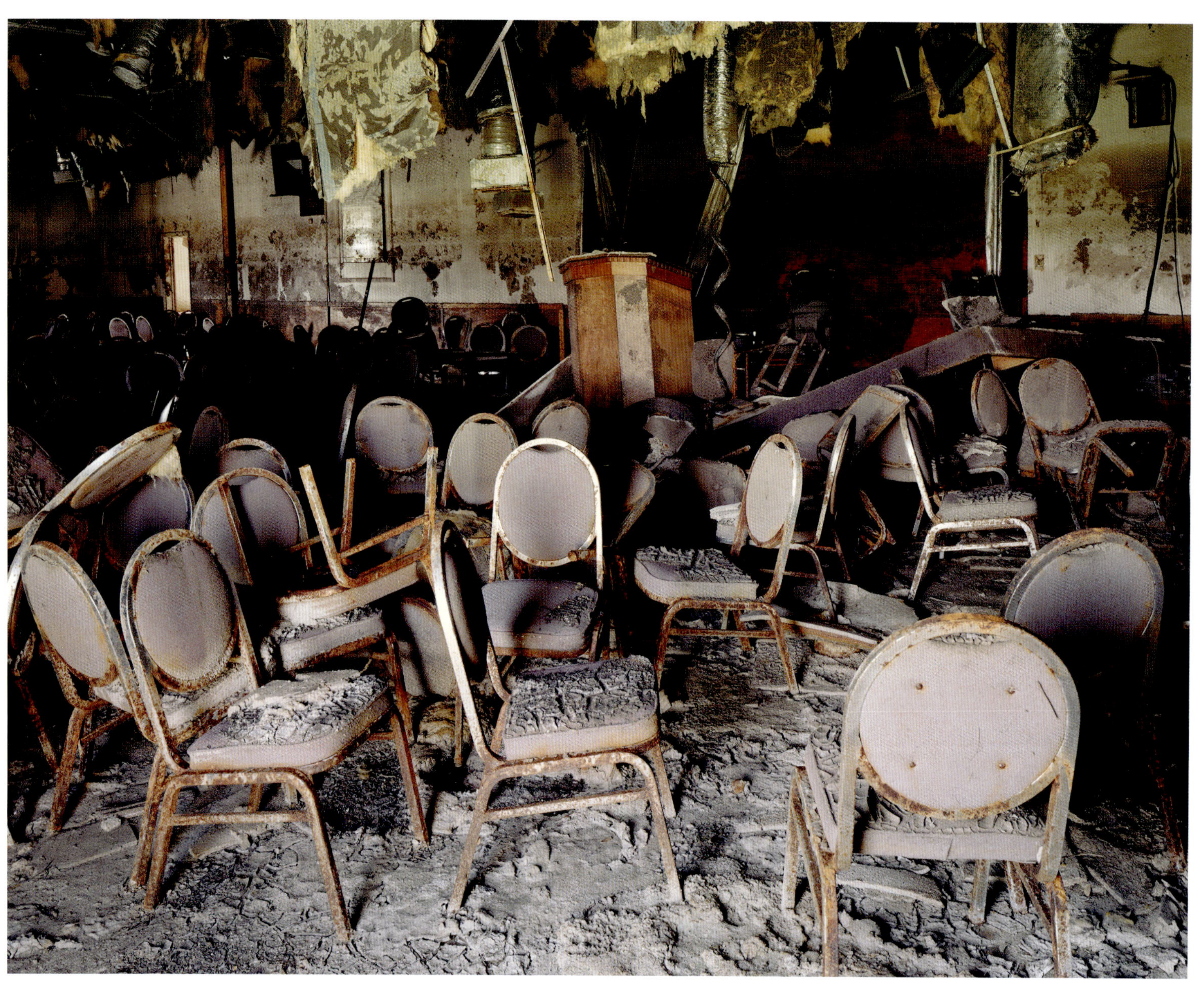

Katrina, Presbyterian Chairs, 2006

FS: The Choctaw from Mississippi are my ancestors. My intentions are to draw attention to the fact that it is getting hotter, land is sinking, sea levels are rising, and if not abated, pollution and our [carbon] footprint are dooming the planet.

RF: How are your interactions with communities impacted by these problems important to your working process?

FS: By the time I get to a place, the calamity has already befallen the community, and with the fires, there were not many people left in the areas. I did meet a few people, and it was like being in the aftermath of a war. Hundreds of thousands of acres of woods were just burned up on the West Coast.

On the island, I met the fifty-five people who are left from the three hundred people who were there originally. They were hiding out on the island as refugees from the Trail of Tears. This was when five tribes from the Cherokee were driven off their land east of the Mississippi. Most moved west. Others were the original inhabitants of that island. Talking to them, I told them who my people were, and they welcomed me into the tribe, so to speak, and they let me take pictures of them and their homes. Everyone on the island is related in some kind of way. The landscapes I shot talk about subsidence [which occurs because of pumping the oil from beneath the island] and that the sea is rising, so the island is getting devastated in two different ways. The salt water came into the marshlands and killed off the cypress trees.

As for New Orleans, it is one of my favorite cities, and it has long been a place that I've gone for its unique African American culture and as the seat of jazz music. New Orleans has had its share of devastation by hurricanes before Katrina. But Katrina's wrath hit the densest section of the Black community, so that was what I saw when I went to the Lower Ninth Ward after Katrina. Concentrating on the Black churches where the culture begins—before Katrina there were more than a hundred Black churches, and after Katrina there were eleven. Half of the ones that had flood insurance didn't have a constituency anymore, as the people left and never came back. The pictures I took in 2005, '06, and '07, I could take today and they'd be the same. Nothing has changed; there's nobody to come back to change it.

RF: These are devastating stories, and I'm sure there is much more to tell.

But let's shift subjects again. We started talking about people in your life, so let's close with a similar topic. Let's talk about your children and grandchildren. You are clearly a very loving part of their family, two daughters, Sing and Bining, and six grandchildren.

FS: Sing is a film producer, and I get to work with her sometimes. We've done projects together. Bining is the head of an alternative school in Austin, Texas, and I've visited her. Her office is in a yurt. I have four grandchildren living with me, and that fact is very interesting. They are all different, have different temperaments and emotions: two boys, William and Lukie, and two girls, Malaya and Lyra. I'm watching them go through life and grow up, go to school, being a part of their lives every day—what they gotta do, what they're not going to do. I like the fact that I am a part of their world, and I'm sorry I am not more a part of the lives of my other two grandchildren in Austin—a girl named Kay Ling, and a boy named Boaz.

RF: One of the nonfamily members important to your life is Romare Bearden. My main interest there is how you think his inclusive approach to art and life impacted your own inclusivity. For example, one of his important collaborators was journalist Harry Henderson, who was White. And Bearden had a keen interdisciplinary relationship with writer Albert Murray. You, too, seem to have many diverse and interdisciplinary connections throughout your life.

FS: Me and Romie were both from the South and being from the South you learn how to—what they say—take a bone and carry a bone. He would have these stories that he would embellish, that he would hear from somebody and he would make it like it was his own. And they were always interesting. He would like put yeast in them, yeast them up. He was very superstitious, too. Like I would be driving him down the street and a black cat would cross the road, so we would have to back out of that street.

He was a great teacher as well, and he loved children. He didn't run across them too much, but when he did, he took a lot of time out, introducing them to art. He was a voracious reader. He read all the time, so he was up on everything, especially sports.

There was never a time he asked me to take pictures of him. I just started because we were hanging out. I'm a photographer; he looked like a willing subject.

As to his collaborations, the fact that Harry was White wasn't particularly important. Romie was also very close to photographer Sam Shaw, who also was White. Bearden was inclusive with anyone he found interesting. Although sometimes he would suffer fools, because they made him laugh, so he found them interesting. And if you are inclusive, you are always inclusive. Sam Shaw was like a movie star—he knew Marilyn Monroe and other movie stars. So being a friend of Romie's and through Romie of Sam Shaw, I was automatically taken in by his movie star friends, too.

RF: And what about your work helping Bearden?

FS: I did all sorts of things—driving him to lectures, like a series he did at Yale, went with him once or twice a year when he went to Saint Martin, to help with whatever he needed. We bought a car together so I could drive him around. For his lectures, say, I would take pictures of his work, or copy other works out of books, and then prepare the slides. He would tell people about what a work of art was, and who made it, and what the story was behind it, and how he came to make the piece if it was his own work. And what memory it jogged for him, and what it was like when he was young, and living through all this. It's all personal. Sometimes it would be memories and sometimes it would be events, like the goddess of the forest, or the ritual of bathing. But when it was a memory, he would talk about growing up. Nanette [Bearden's wife] always went out of town with him; he went with her whenever she would go with her dancers.

They shared a passport. It's the first time and the last time I've ever seen that. They had to be handcuffed, I guess. They never went too far from each other, ever. Mostly our conversations were about art. He would talk about Picasso, Matisse, Raphael, Michelangelo, Van Gogh, people like that. He was a roving history lesson on art. He wasn't interested in things; he was interested in philosophy, history, the Civil War, his time in the army in Europe. He talked about race all the time; that was ever-present. We talked about culture a lot; yeah, he called himself a race man, as they say. I think that connotation meant something else to him than it means now. A race man back in the day, before integration, all Black people lived together in the community, so you were part of that race that was in that community. Today, that term is mostly applied to older Black men, and people don't all live in the same community, so the term doesn't have the same weight to it. Bearden loved African American culture, African American art, artists. He loved the whole history of it, thought Aaron Douglas and Henry Ossawa Tanner were the great masters.

RF: Another artist, David Driskell, was important to you in many ways. It would be fascinating to hear about some of the projects you worked on with him, including the book you were developing with David at the time of his death.

FS: I told you earlier about meeting David at Fisk. After a month, David came over to me and asked me to come talk with him after class. And he said, "Young man, you're not enrolled in this class, are you?" And I said, "Adrienne Jenkins is my cousin and I'm auditing your class." Because I was Adrienne's cousin, he let me stay. I worked with him at the start, in the archives at the Los Angeles County Museum of Art for the *Two Centuries [of Black American Art]* film, but mostly I worked with Carlton Moss and Johnny Simmons on the film, out in the field. And that's how I met Romie, and Alma Thomas and Loïs [Mailou] Jones, those last two in DC, and Selma Burke, who had a home in New Hope, Pennsylvania, and sculptor John Rhoden, who lived in

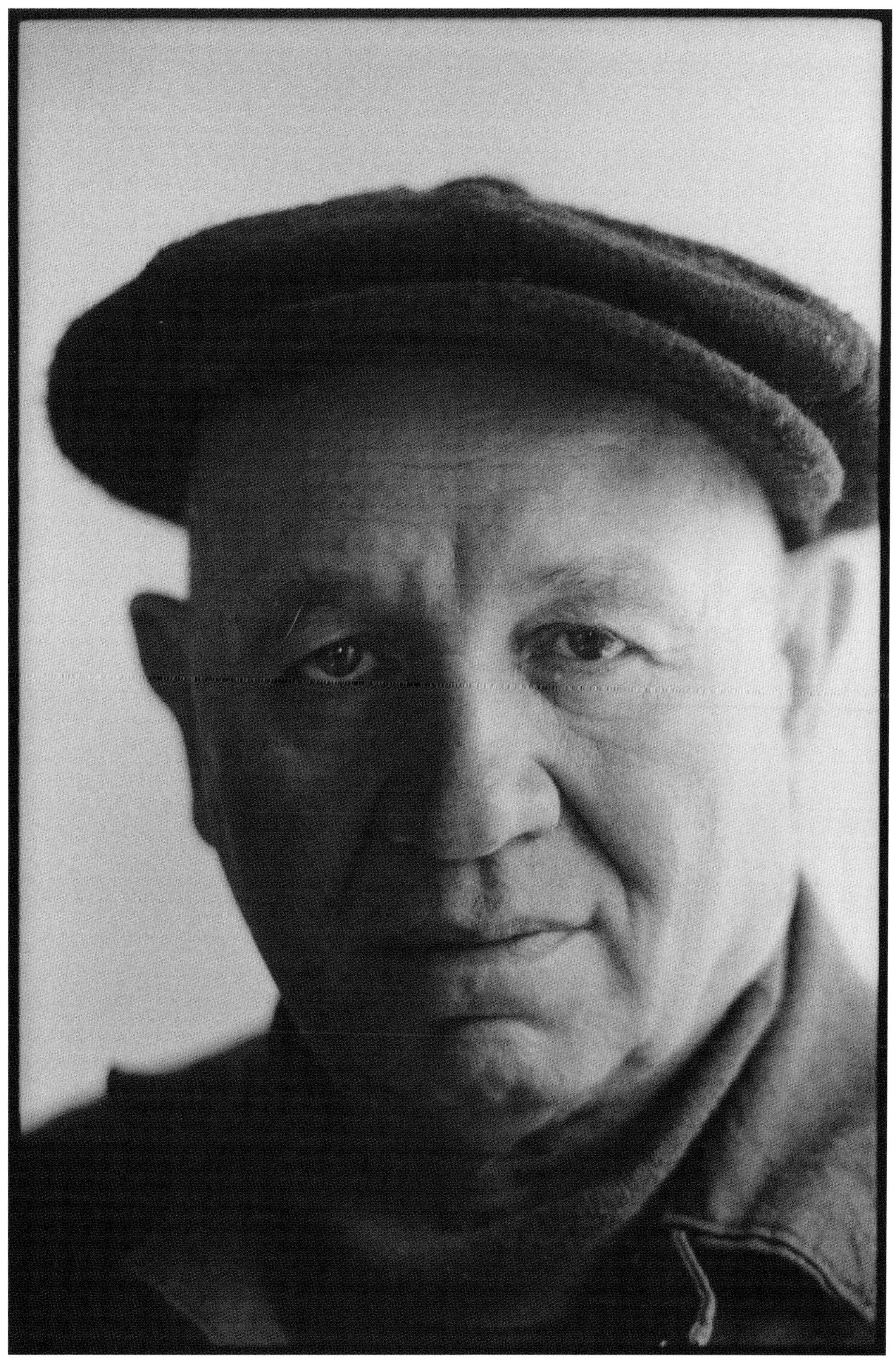

Romare Bearden, 1979

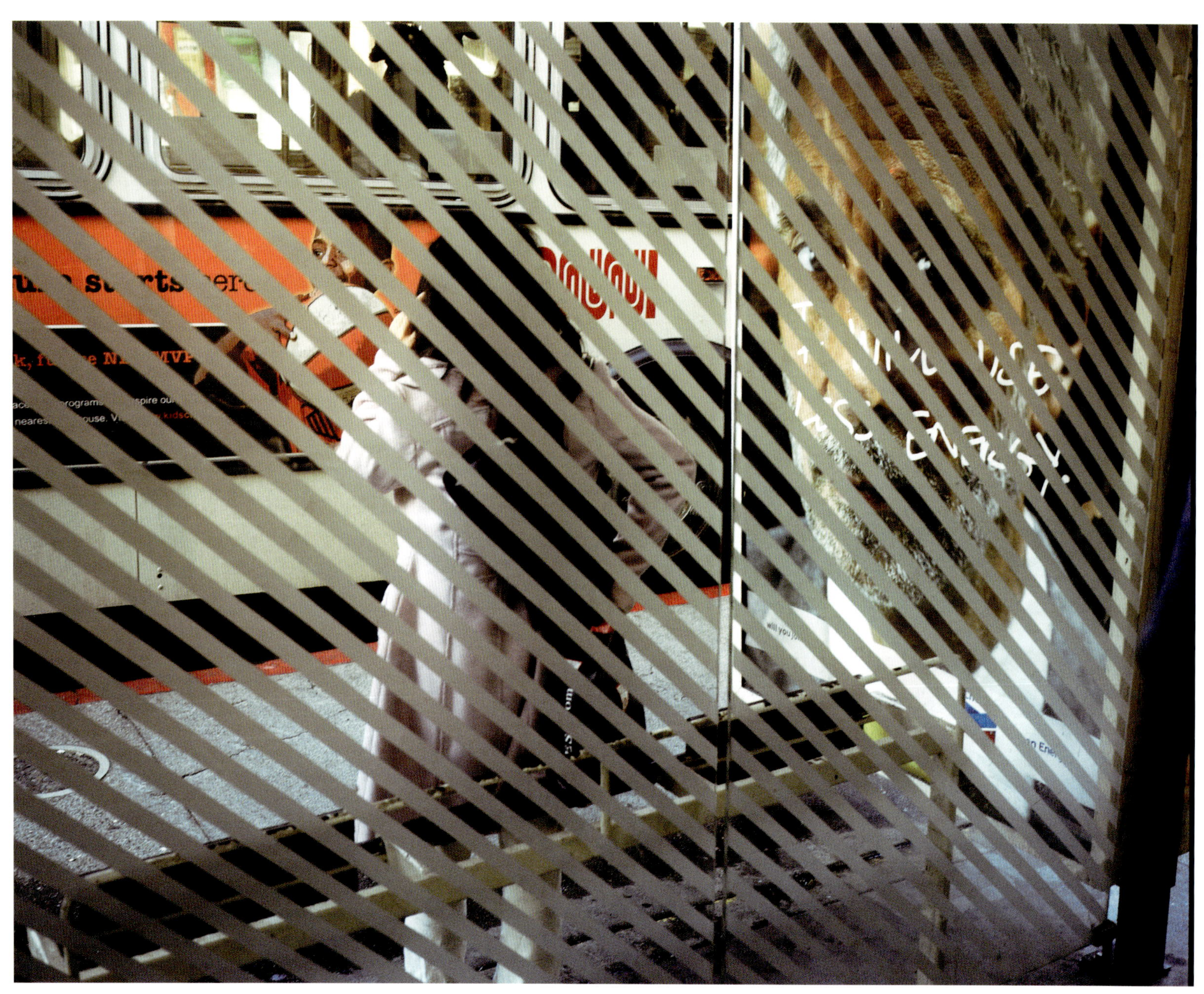

Stripes, San Francisco, 2009

Brooklyn, and Aaron Douglas. I shot photographs of all of them and others, and of their art.

Later I worked with David along with Camille Cosby on the book *The Other Side of Color,* shooting the Cosby collection. My older daughter, Sing, lived with David and Thelma and the Driskell family when she did her semester out of NYU to go to a historically Black college, to Howard [University]. David also wrote the foreword for the book you and I did of my photographs of Bearden.

My last project with David was intended to be with the frontline civil rights worker Dr. Rudy Lombard, who lived in Chicago, but was from New Orleans and died there. It was going to be a book on the education of a sharecropper. David was the subject, having grown up with his father, who was an itinerant preacher early on, but was also a sharecropper. David grew up with this vast knowledge of wild plants, herbs, from his grandmother, mother, and father. The book we were doing was about these plants, and the stories attached to them, and how he learned about them. David was doing the watercolors of the various plants and herbs and telling us their names, sometimes a slave name, sometimes a Native American name, sometimes a scientific name. He was telling us about the medicinal properties and how the plants were used in his family, but David got sick and it got stalled. And then Rudy got sick and died. Before he died, he researched and wrote about David's life, the time when he was a sharecropper and went with his father to these various churches. David did some preaching as well. That probably set him on his course to being a lecturer, the roots of his learning how to lecture, which he did all around the world. I was traveling with David—went with him to the first house that his father built in Eatonton, Georgia, and also to North Carolina, where he had family and where there also were some of the plants and herbs. He was drawing and painting these forms in nature and I was photographing the environment. Unfortunately, he passed before we could finish the book.

RF: You have had so many relationships with great artists. Talk about your own collection of art. What are your most precious possessions?

FS: The first things came from my colleagues at Cooper: George Mingo, Juan Cash, Jeanne Moutoussamy-Ashe. Then Bearden gave me a few things; at first, I asked him, "Why don't you pay me with art instead of cash?" So, he gave me a few things. The first one was a small watercolor that I gave to a friend who lent me a camera to use for copying art when I first met Bearden. Then he would give me prints from time to time. And one time he gave me one of his first collages that was in the National Gallery exhibition. He did it in 1956, but signed it the 1980s, so the difference in his signature at different times shows. It was one of only two that were from 1956 like it.

RF: What about your Norman Lewis?

FS: I gave a group of photographs to Bill Hodges in trade for my Norman Lewis drawing, an abstraction that I picked out from a group he had at the time. When I had Onyx Gallery, prints would come across the desk, and two [Elizabeth] Catlett showed up one day, and the one I have is one of them. Two Charles Whites came across also, including a proof from *Sound of Silence* [1978], which I kept. It doesn't have color in it. Bill Hutson was the second Onyx show, and the two pieces I have are from that show. I guess we bought them. The print I have from Al Loving, he gave me just before he died; I was in upstate New York around Nyack, and he was there, too, so he took me to his house, and as I was leaving, he gave me that print. I made a nice portrait of him, 8 by 10. I bought a few pieces from Terry Adkins when we had Onyx. David Driskell bought pieces from him at the same time I was buying them. He bought more than I did.

RF: What about your African art pieces?

FS: In 1971, I had the African art class with George Preston, and he basically gave me the rudiments of the classic works, and then I went to Africa in 1974 and brought some pieces back. And I was friends with Merton [Simpson] and a childhood friend named Marvin Jones, he's a chef now, who went to Africa and met a runner, who brought works back from the villages, and we used to sell African art together in New York.

I would do photography for Eric Robertson, at Grove Street Gallery, an African art gallery, and he would pay me with small pieces, like a Senufo pulley for a loom. I am still interested, look for it when I go to Africa, am on the board of the Museum of Art and Origins, so I spend a lot of time with George's historical collection, museum pieces. All of them have been ceremonialized before coming to the States, sold to runners by the villagers.

RF: Let's finish by you talking about what has been keeping you busy during these last few years, during Covid.

FS: What's been keeping me busy has been going through thirty years of Jazz at Lincoln Center negatives and printing images for a book I want to be called *The Absence of Sound Called Jazz*. I'm finally having the time to go through and edit all of these thousands of negatives that I never got the time to edit before. To cull images that I've never seen before. I have over four hundred images right now and another hundred to print before I start putting the book together.

RF: Can you describe some that stand out for you?

FS: The ones that stand out are the ones that I took for myself on the streets of various cities around the world. It's not only going to be jazz photographs; it's going to be how I view the world.

RF: Do you have a sense of the percentage of jazz and non-jazz images you want to use?

FS: I'm thinking it's going to be in chapters, and every transition to a new chapter will be one of these "drawings" from the streets of one of these cities around the world that we played in.[5]

RF: So, it is mainly jazz.

FS: Yeah, it will be mainly jazz. The newest man on the planet has come up with the newest art form on the planet, which is jazz, improvisation, and my photography comes out of that genre of thought. As I'm working on the streets, it's all improvisation. It's all made up on the spot, just like a jazz musician improvises on a riff. That's what I'm doing. I'm improvising on a riff.

1 This conversation is a compilation of many conversations and emails over several years.

2 Janet and Harold are Dotty's younger siblings, closest to FS in age.

3 Lee (from Lehman) was Stewart's nickname as a child, and longtime friends still call him by this name.

4 Painters, photographers, and other artists Stewart studied with are mentioned throughout the chronology in this book.

5 Stewart's "drawings" are fast thoughts that come to him as he confronts them on the streets. See a selection in this catalogue, pages 149–53.

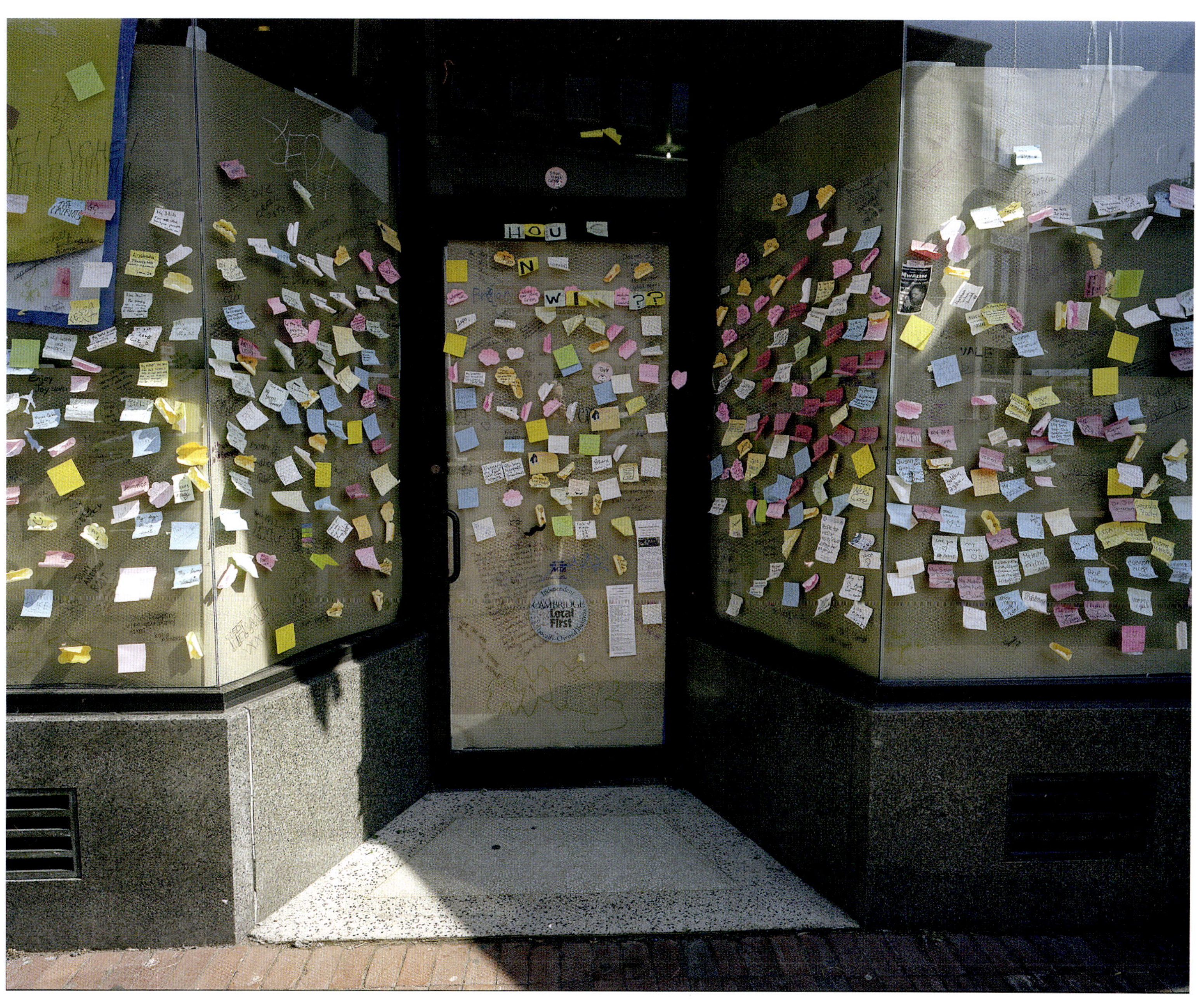

Cambridge Window, 2011

Ancestors: Africa, the Caribbean, New Orleans

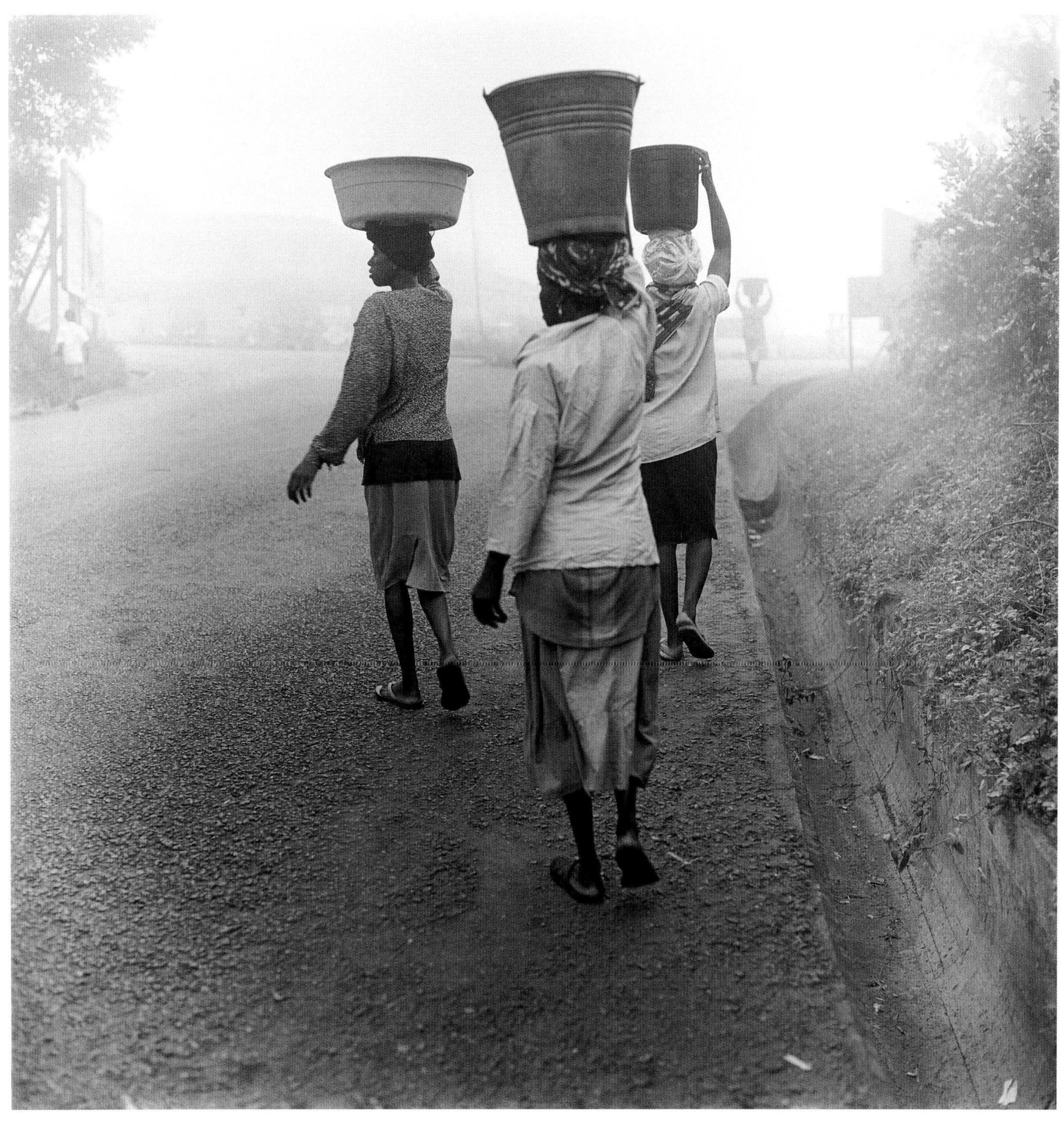

Clock of the Earth, Mamfe, Ghana, 1998

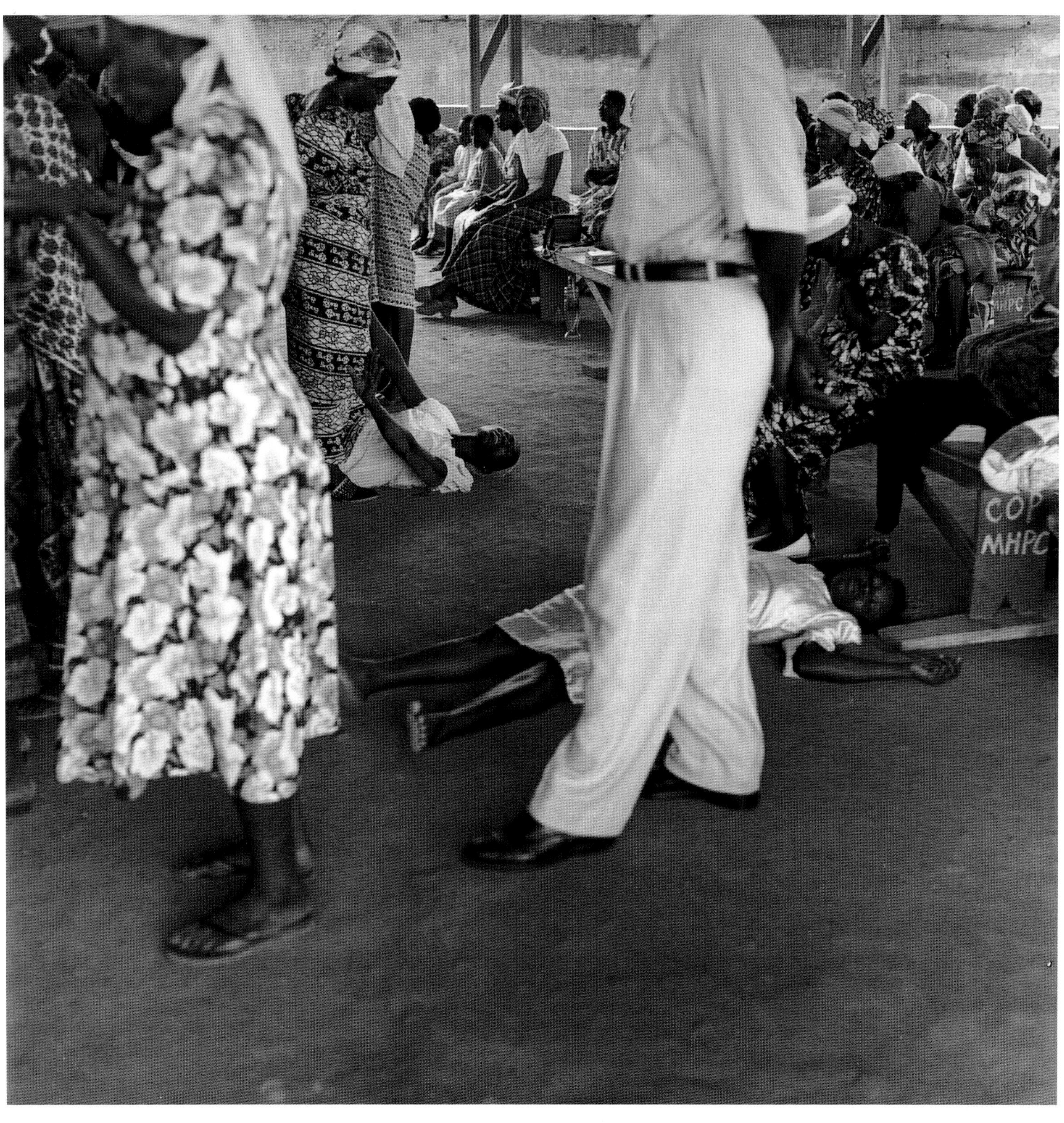

Getting the Spirit II, Mamfe, Ghana, 1998

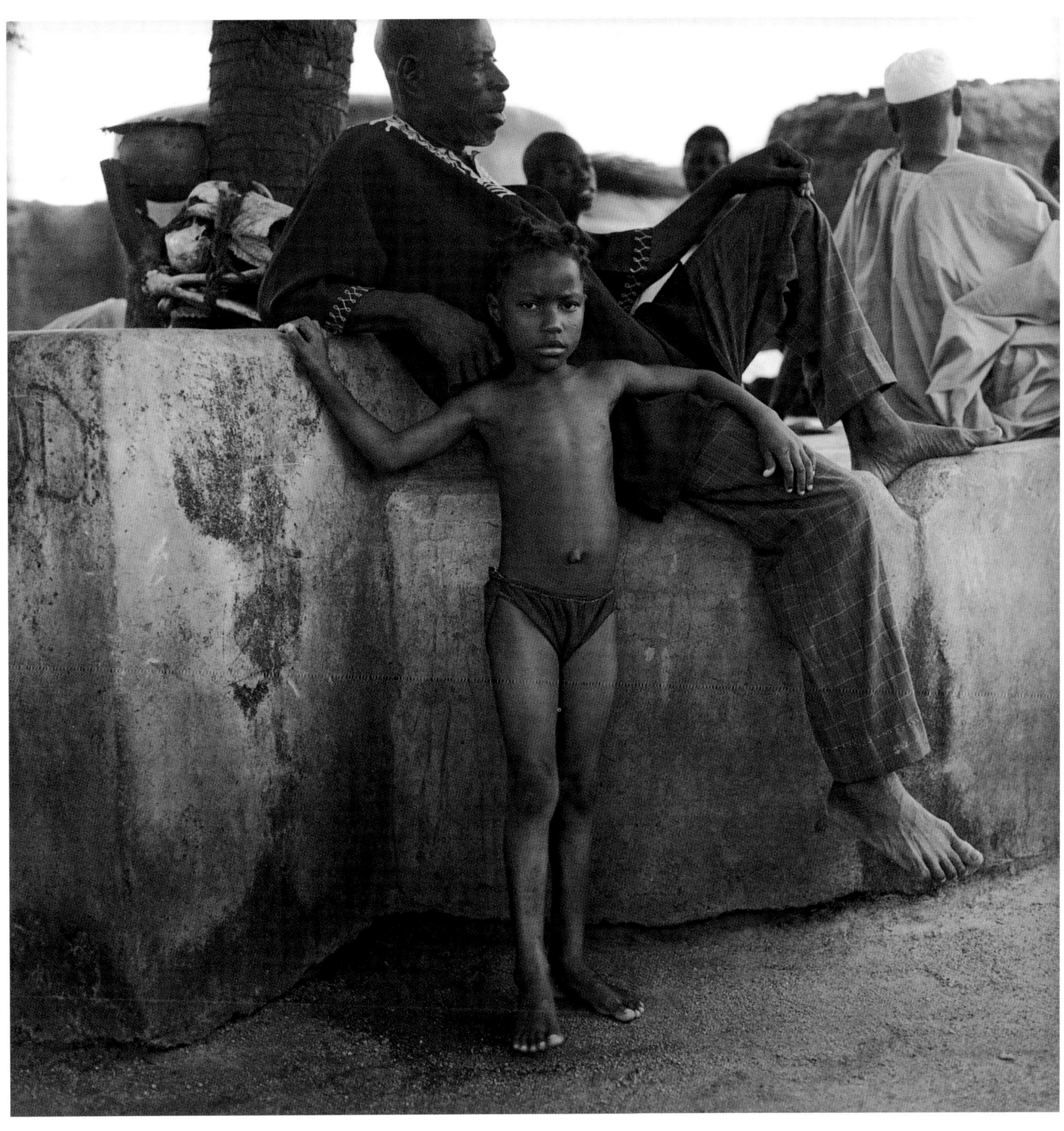

Chief's Granddaughter, 1999

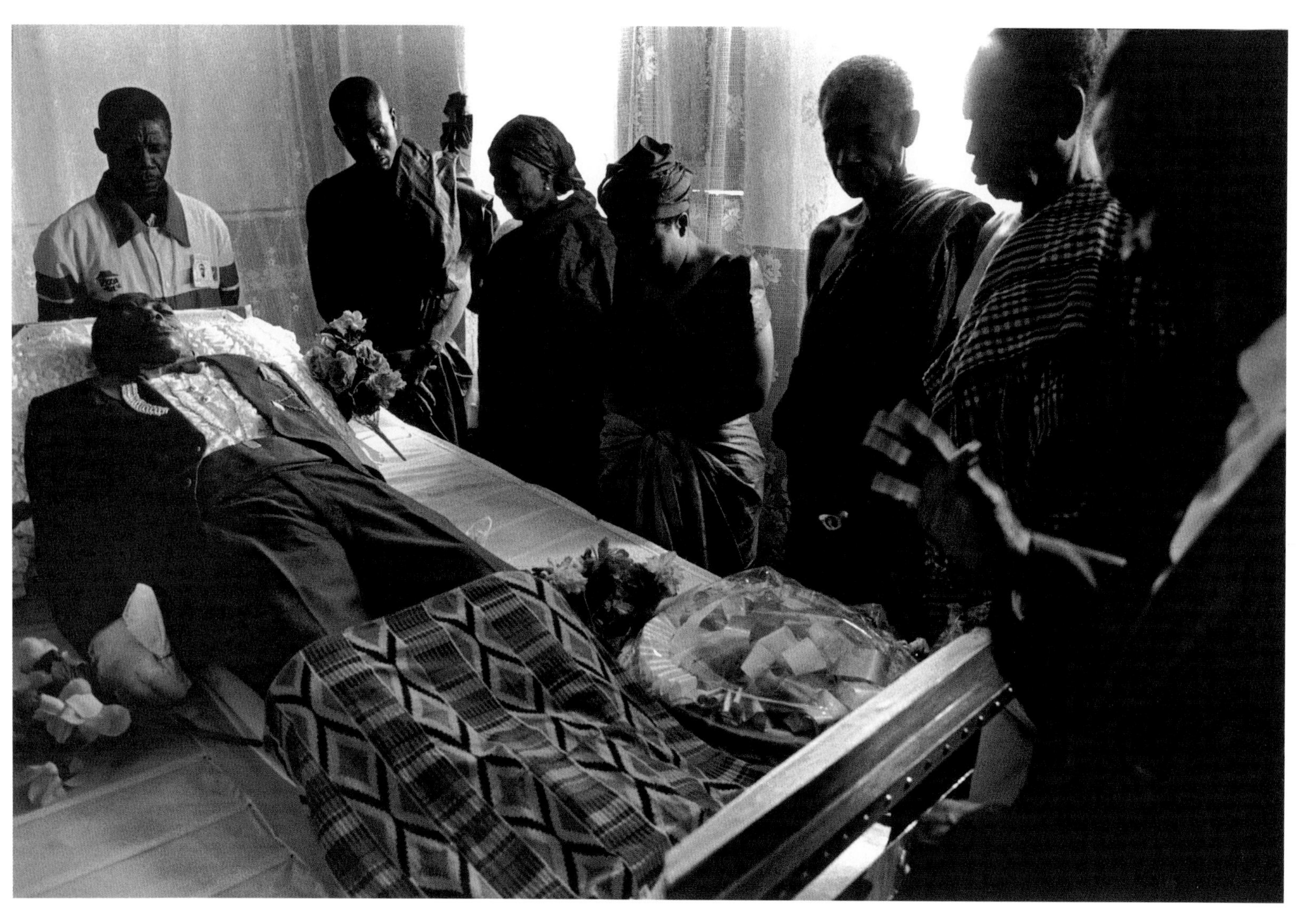

The Dead Man, Amanokrom, Ghana, 2004

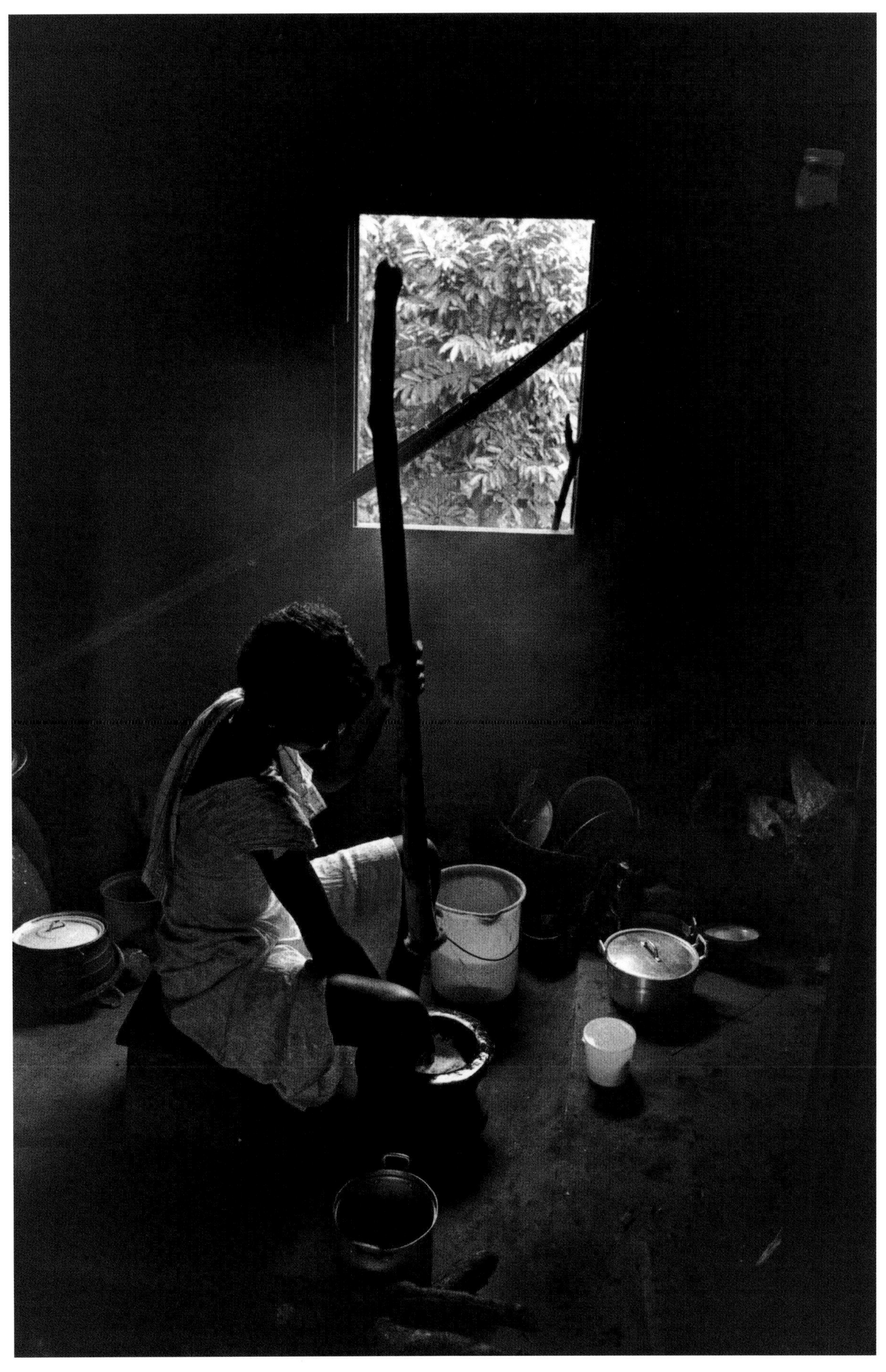

Abena Pounding Fufu, Mamfe, Ghana, 2000

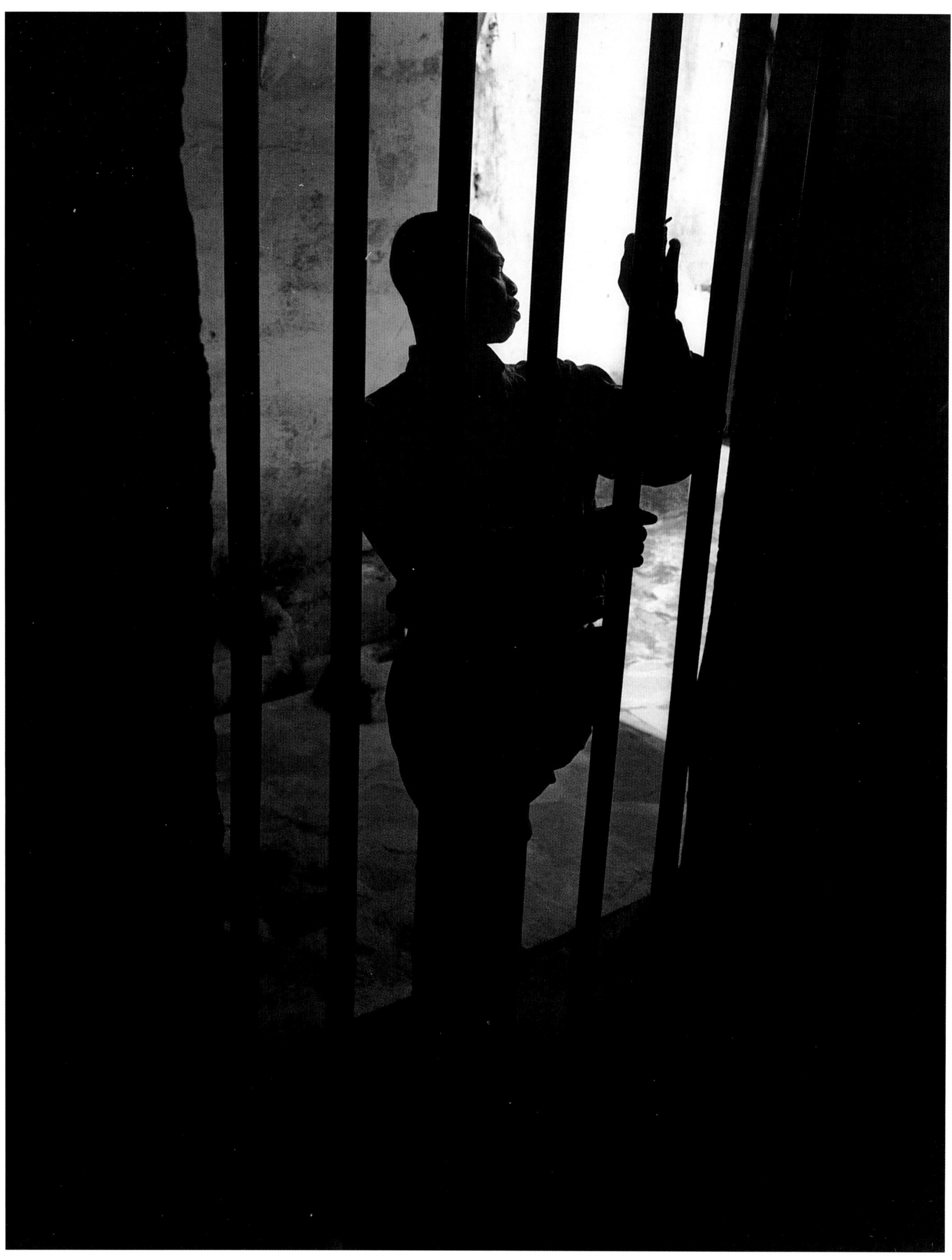

Slave Castle, Cape Coast, Ghana, 2004

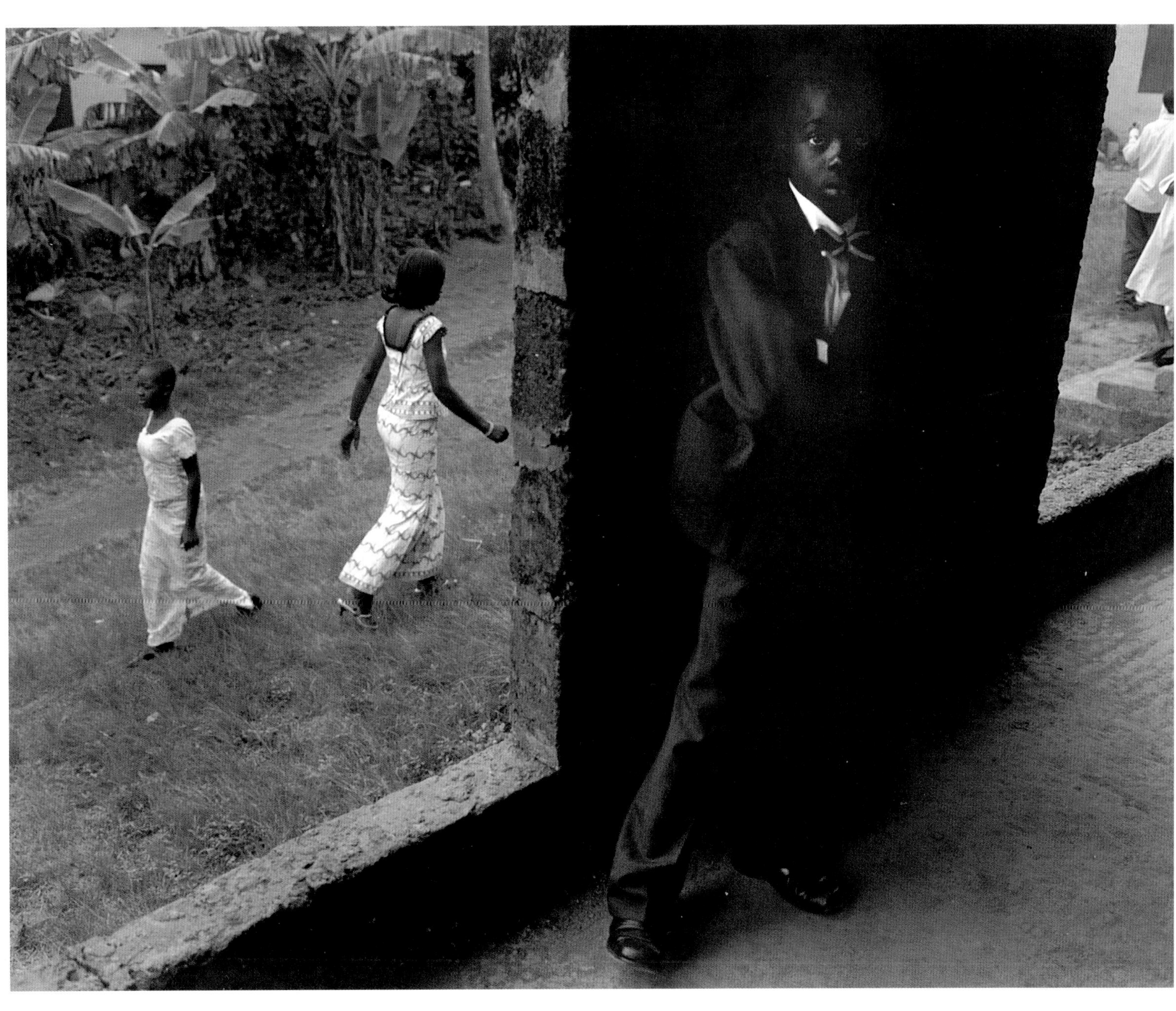

Boy and Two Girls, Mamfe, Ghana, 2004

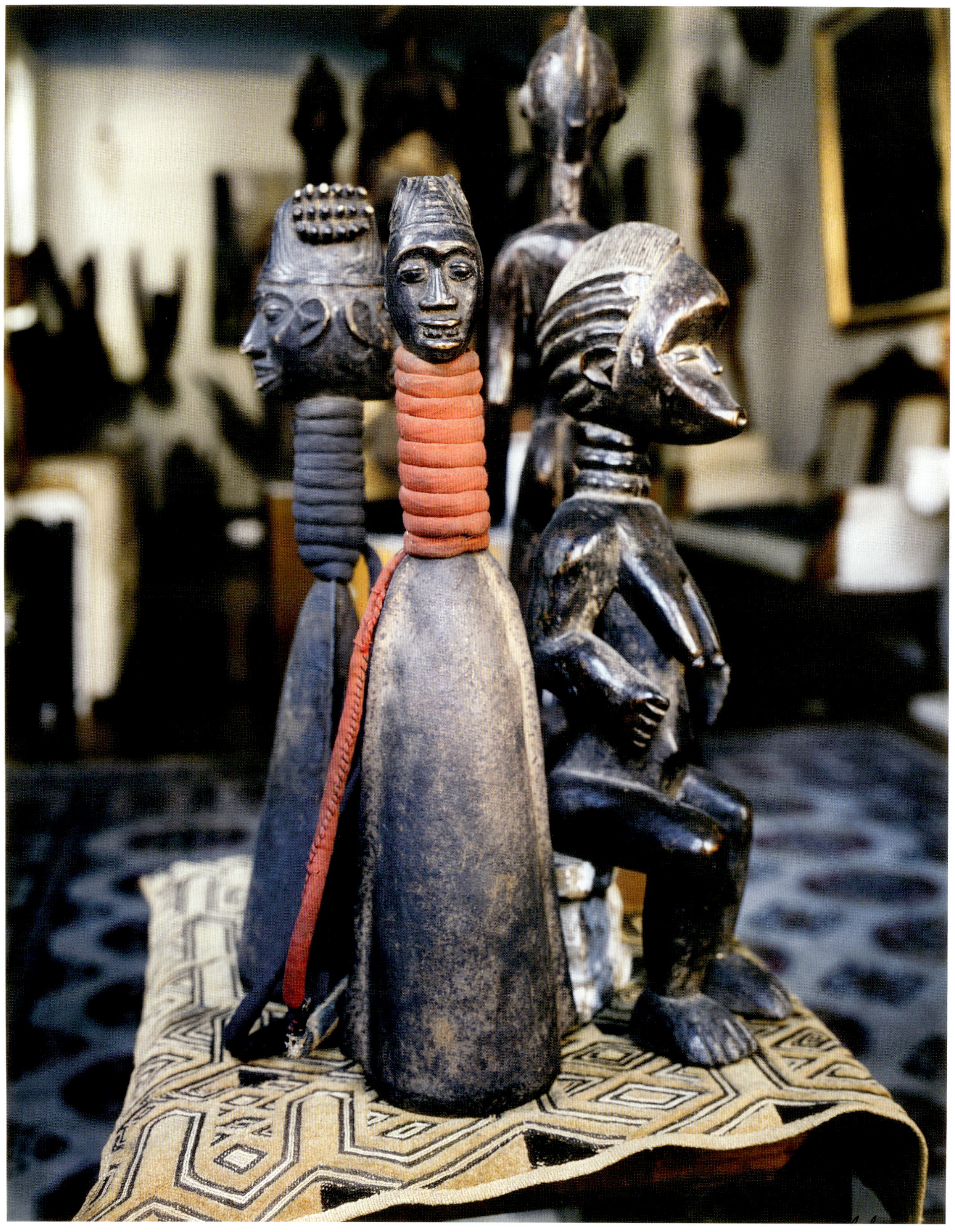

George's Parlor, 2004

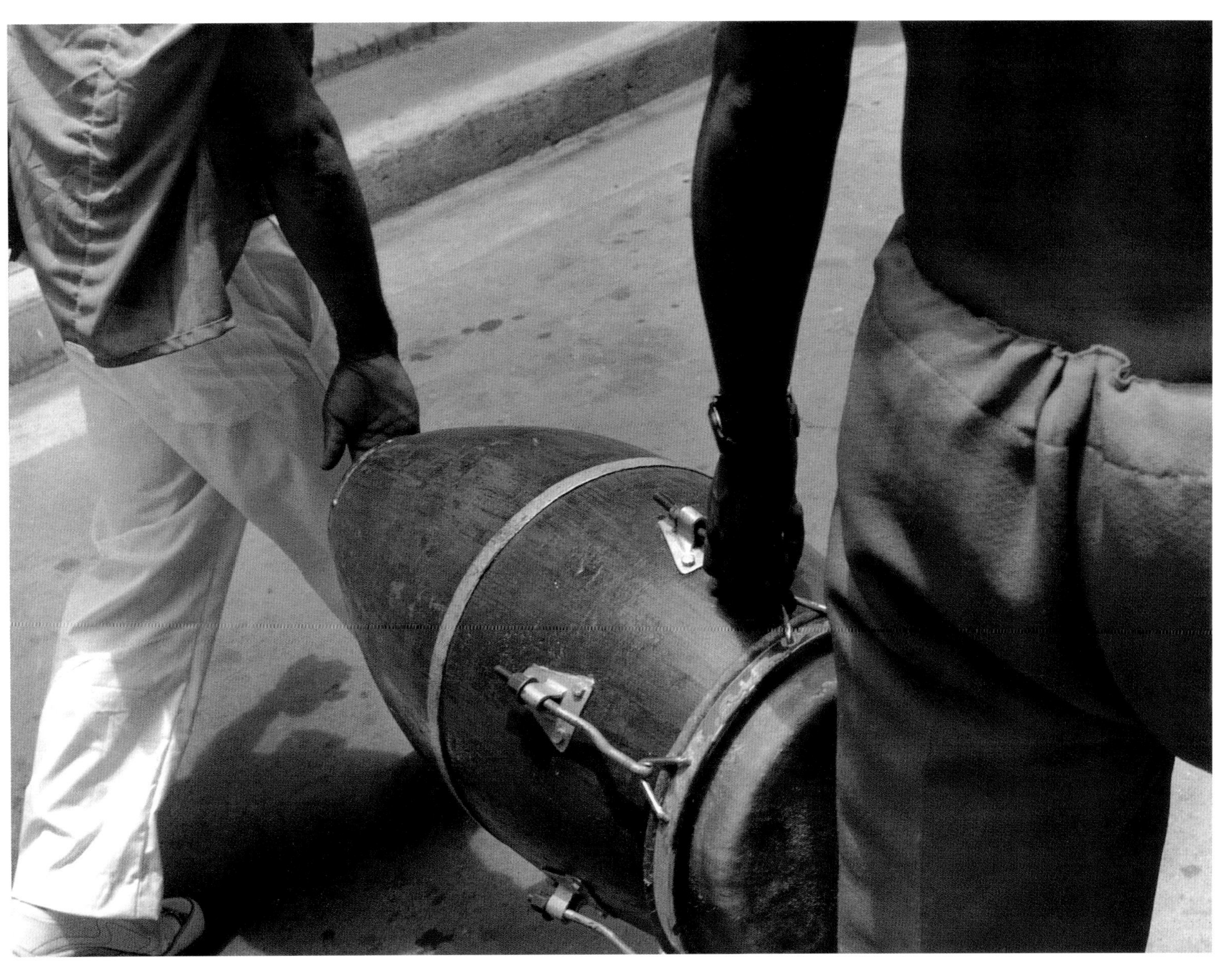

Going for Salsa, Santiago de Cuba, 2003

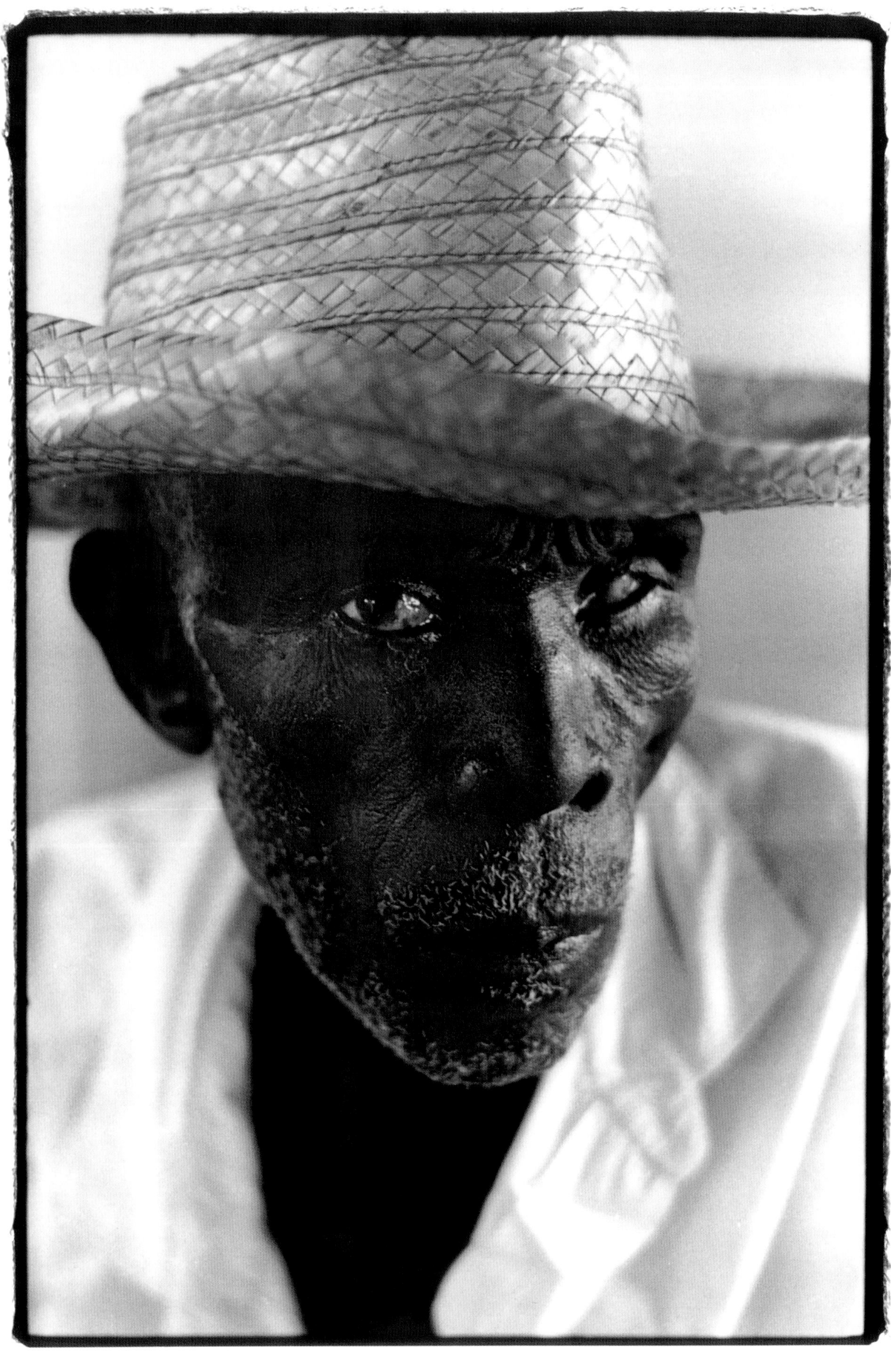

One-Eyed Man, Santiago de Cuba, 1977

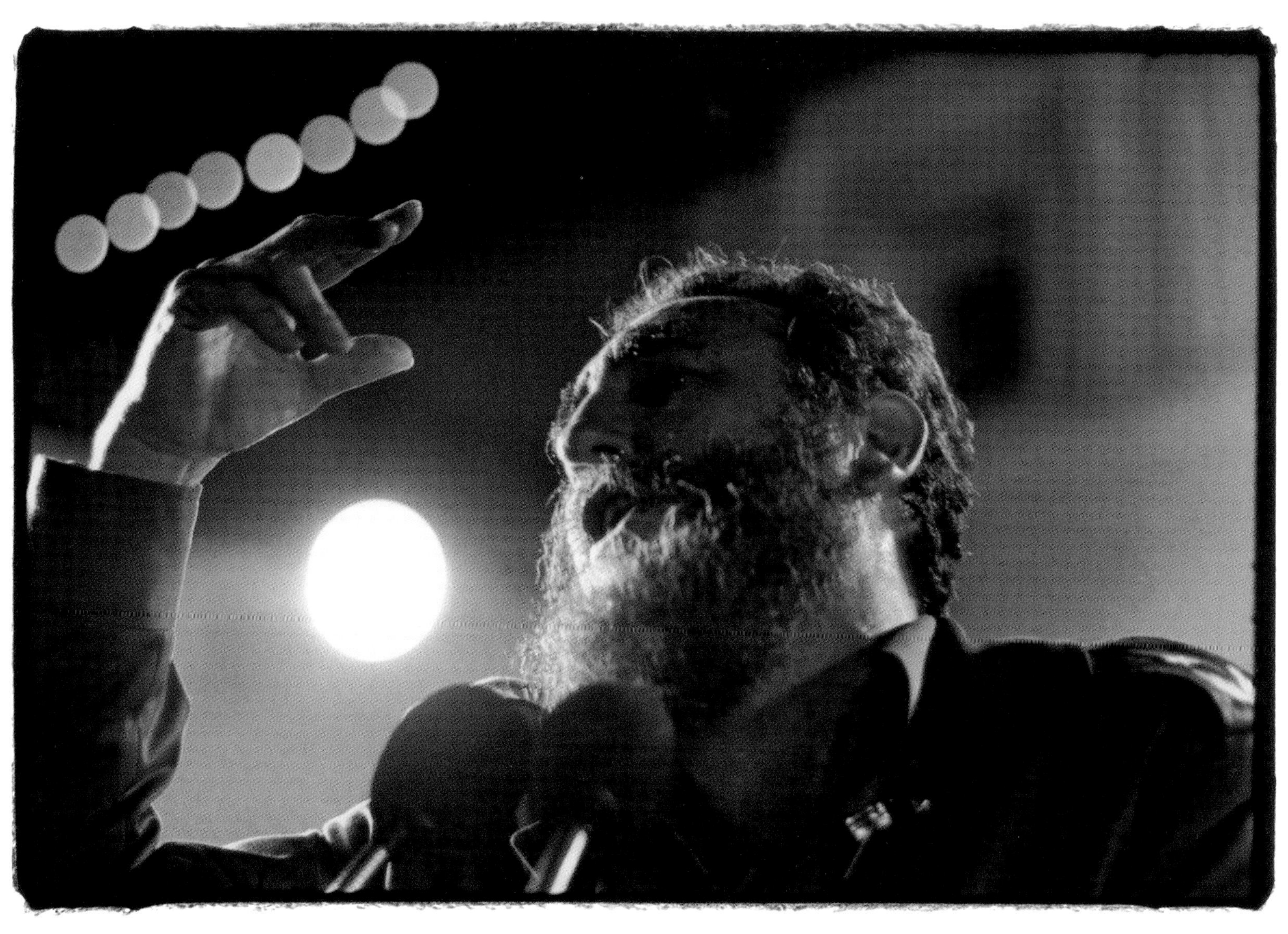

Number 1, 1978

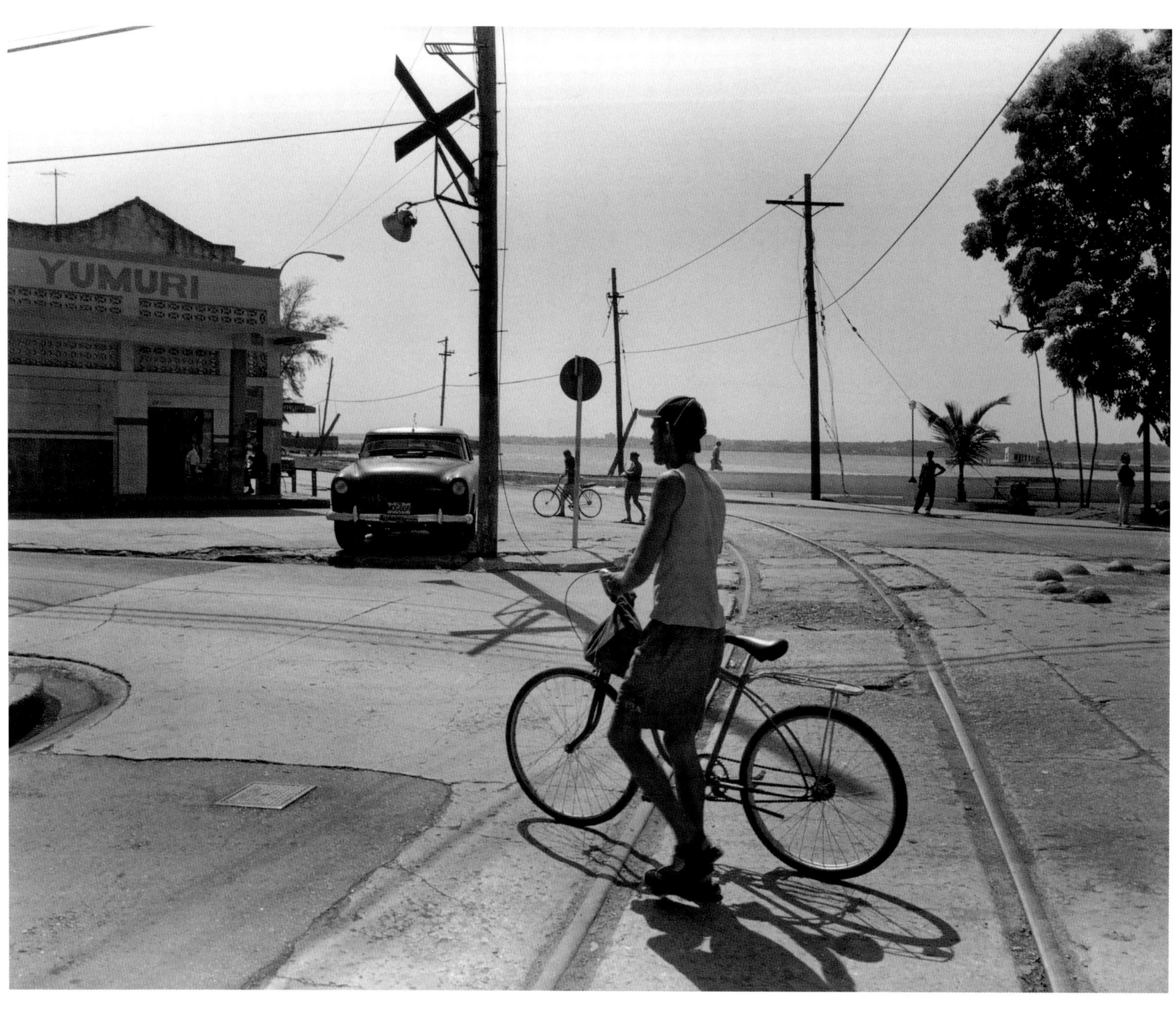

Bicycle II, Cienfuegos, c. 2004

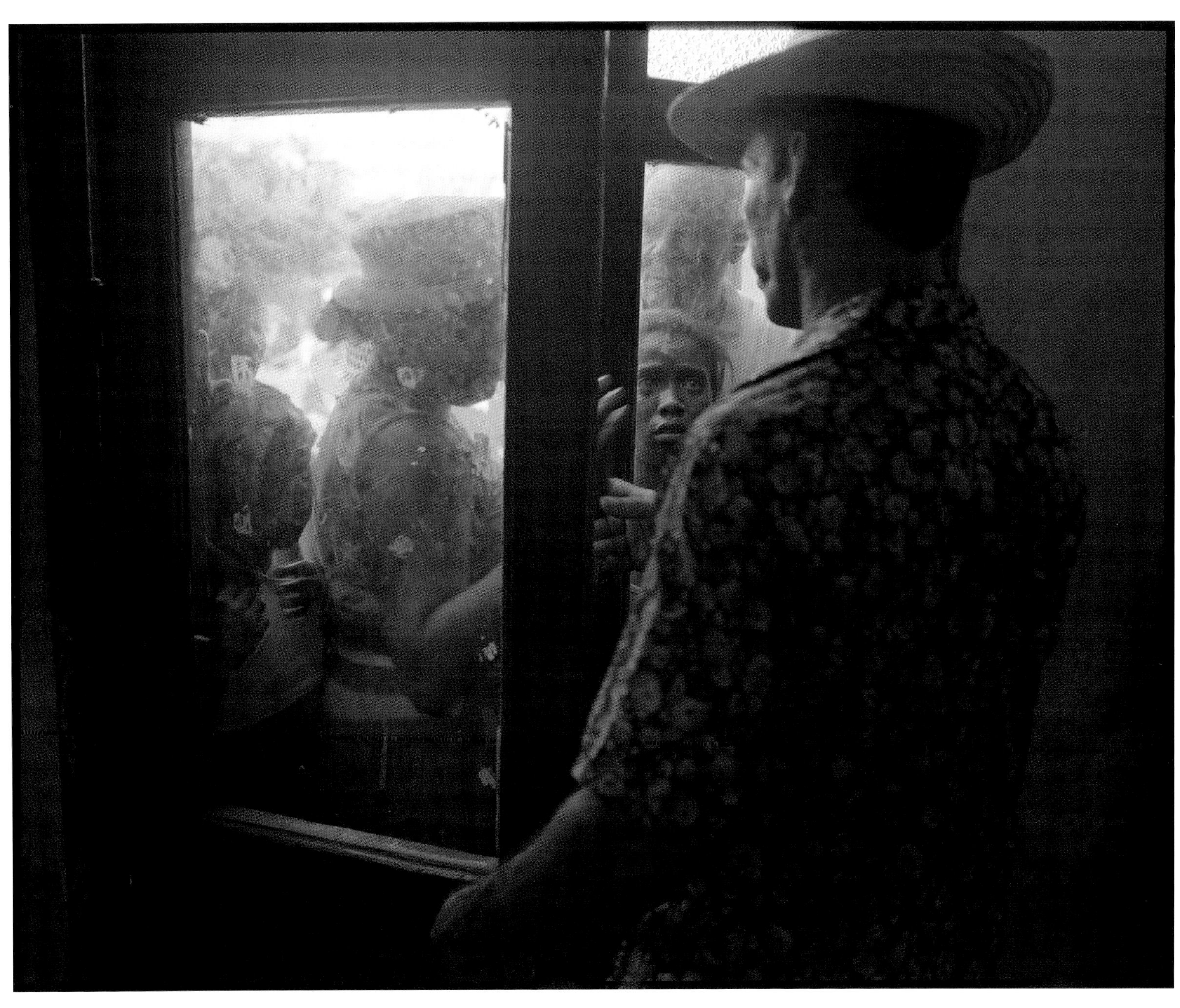

Inside Out at La Conga,
Santiago de Cuba, 2003

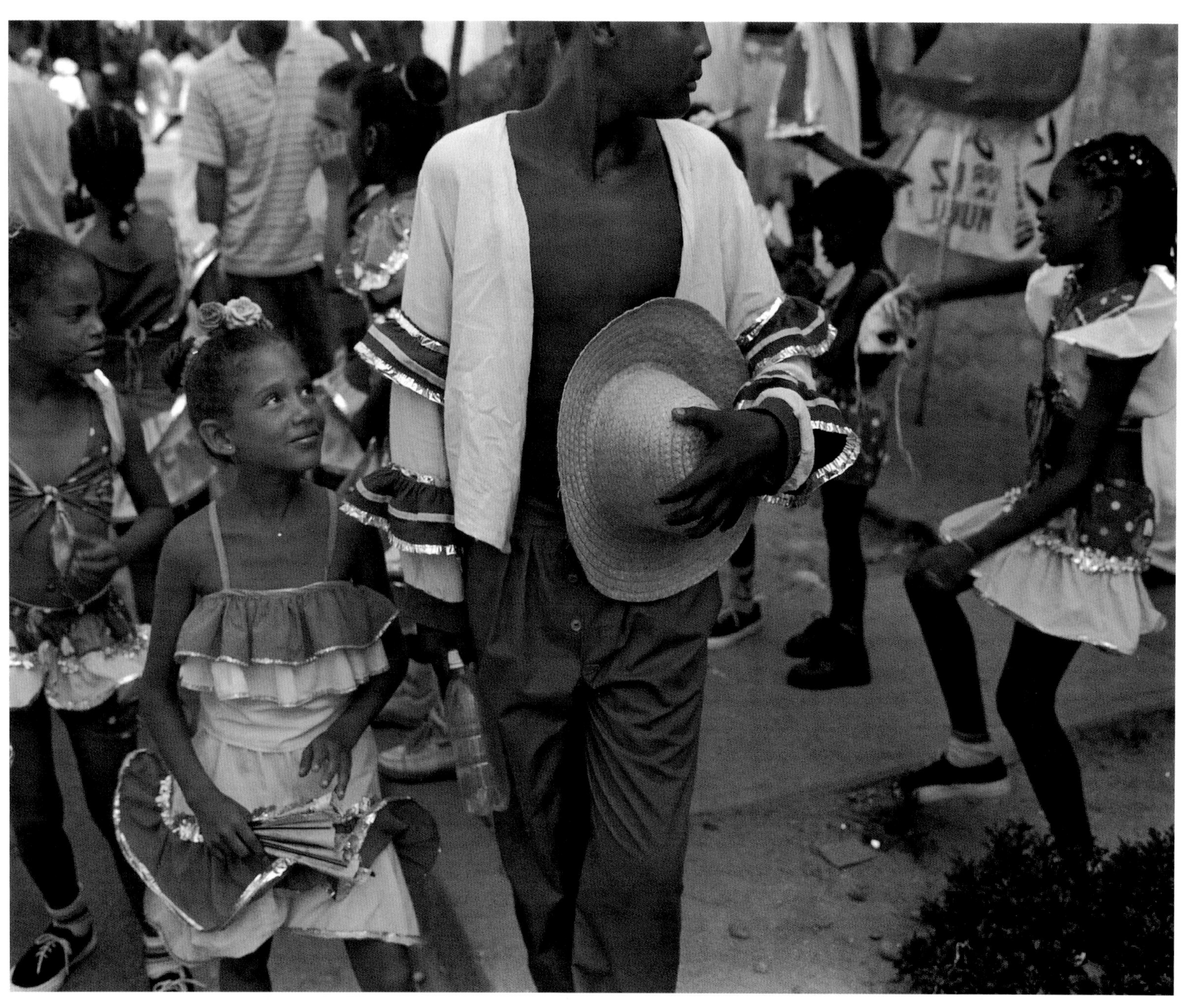

Santiago Carnival, 2003

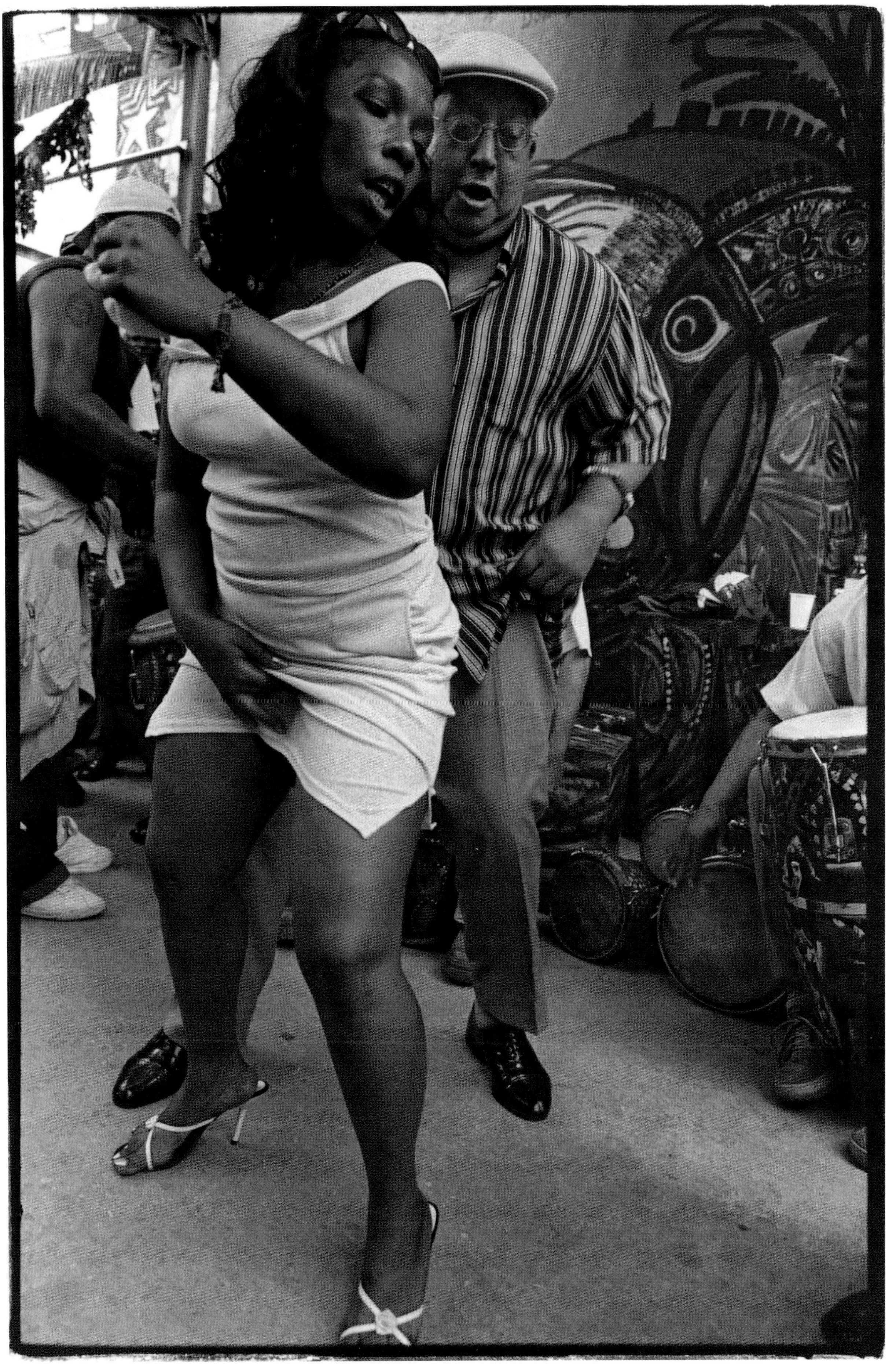

Callejón de Hamel, Havana, 2002

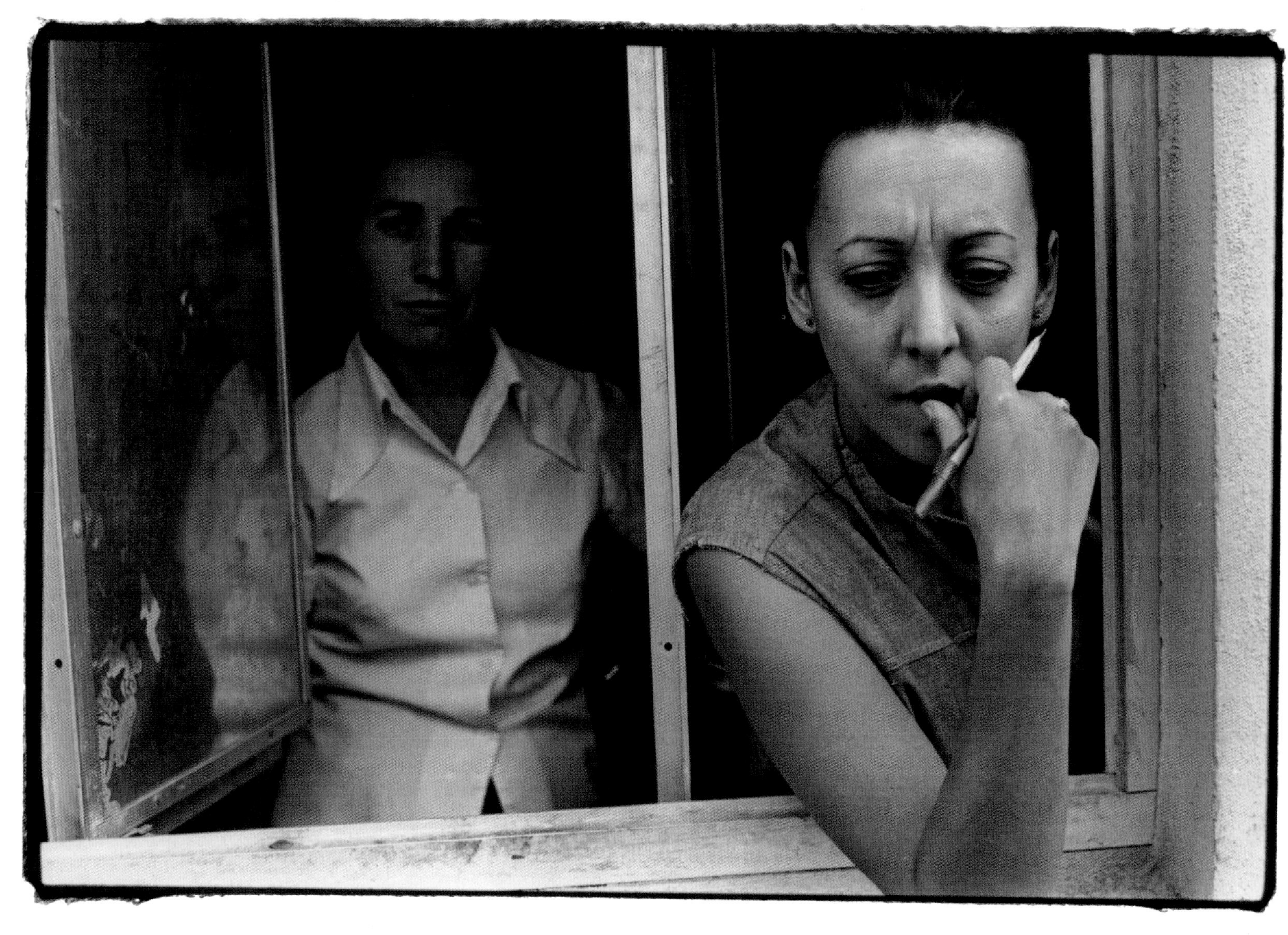

Homage to Cartier-Bresson,
Camagüey, 1977

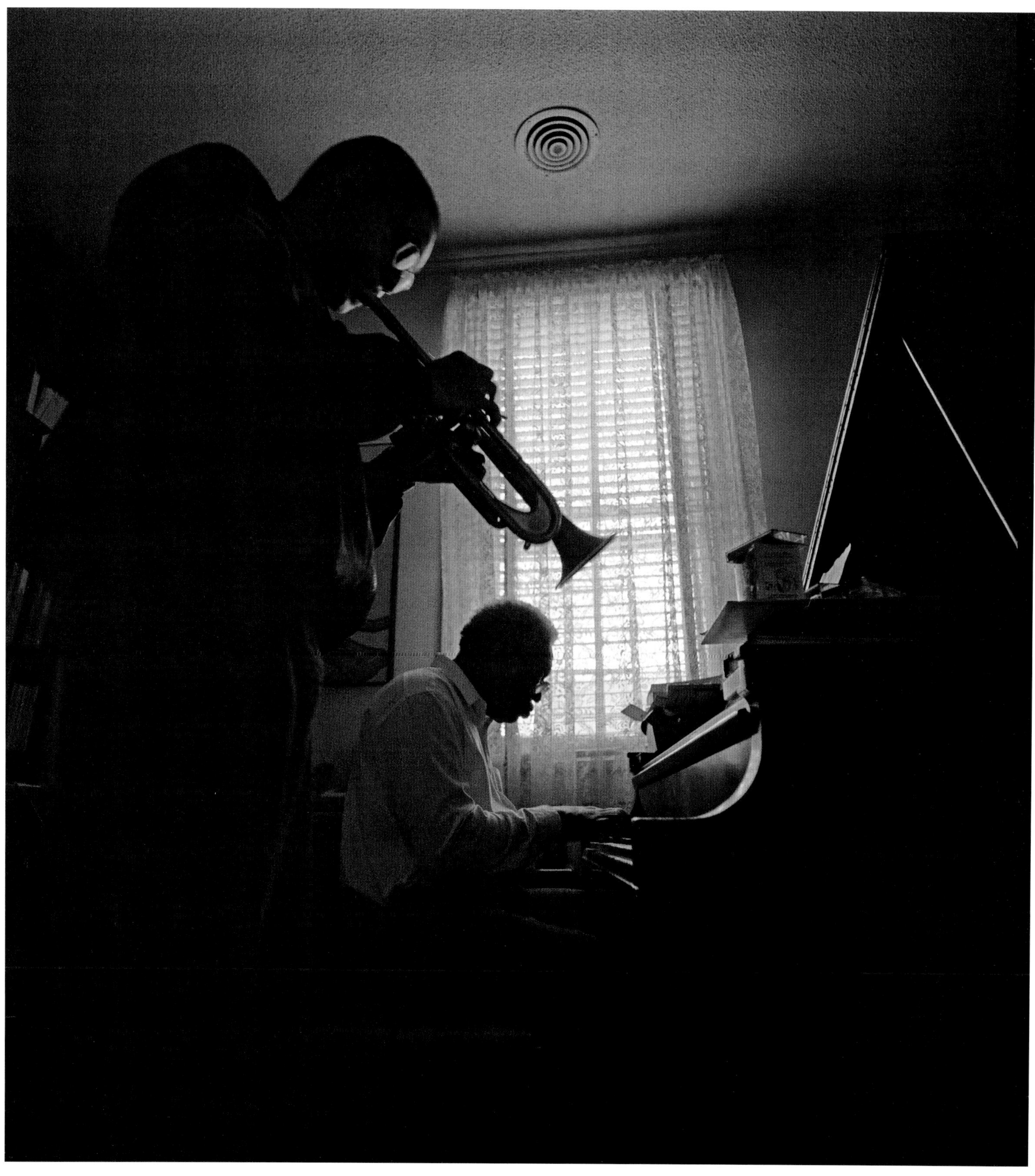

Ellis and Wynton Marsalis, 1991

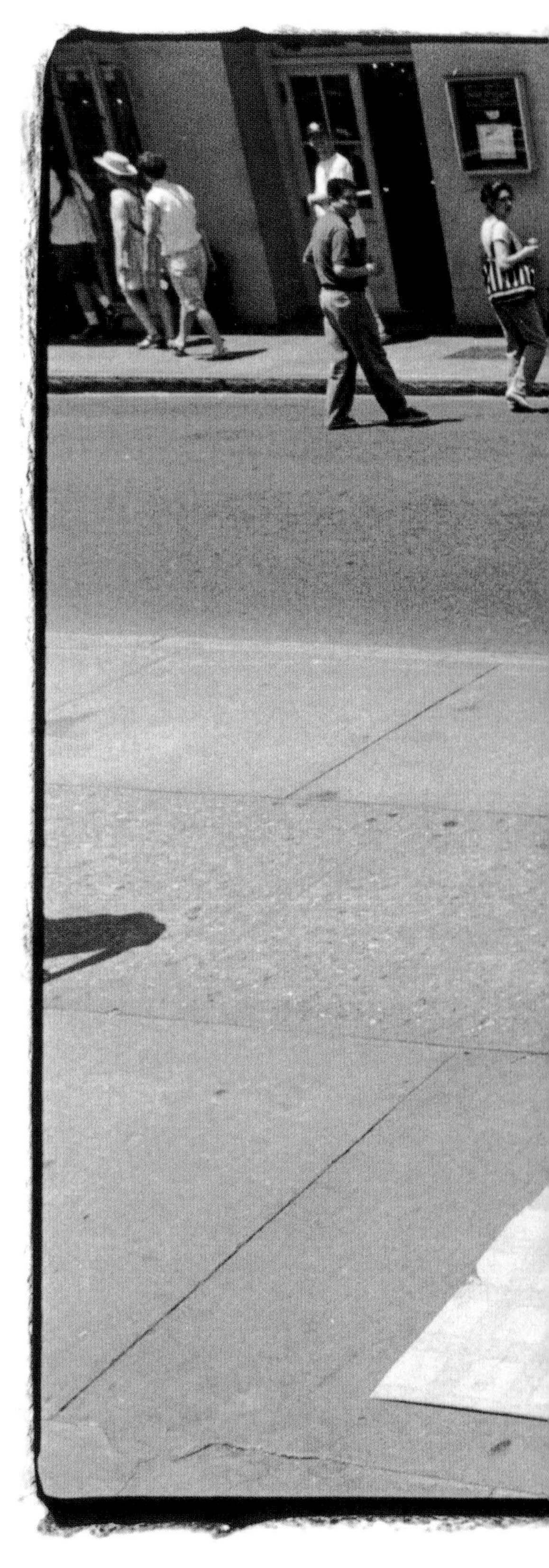

I'm Still Here, New Orleans, 1991

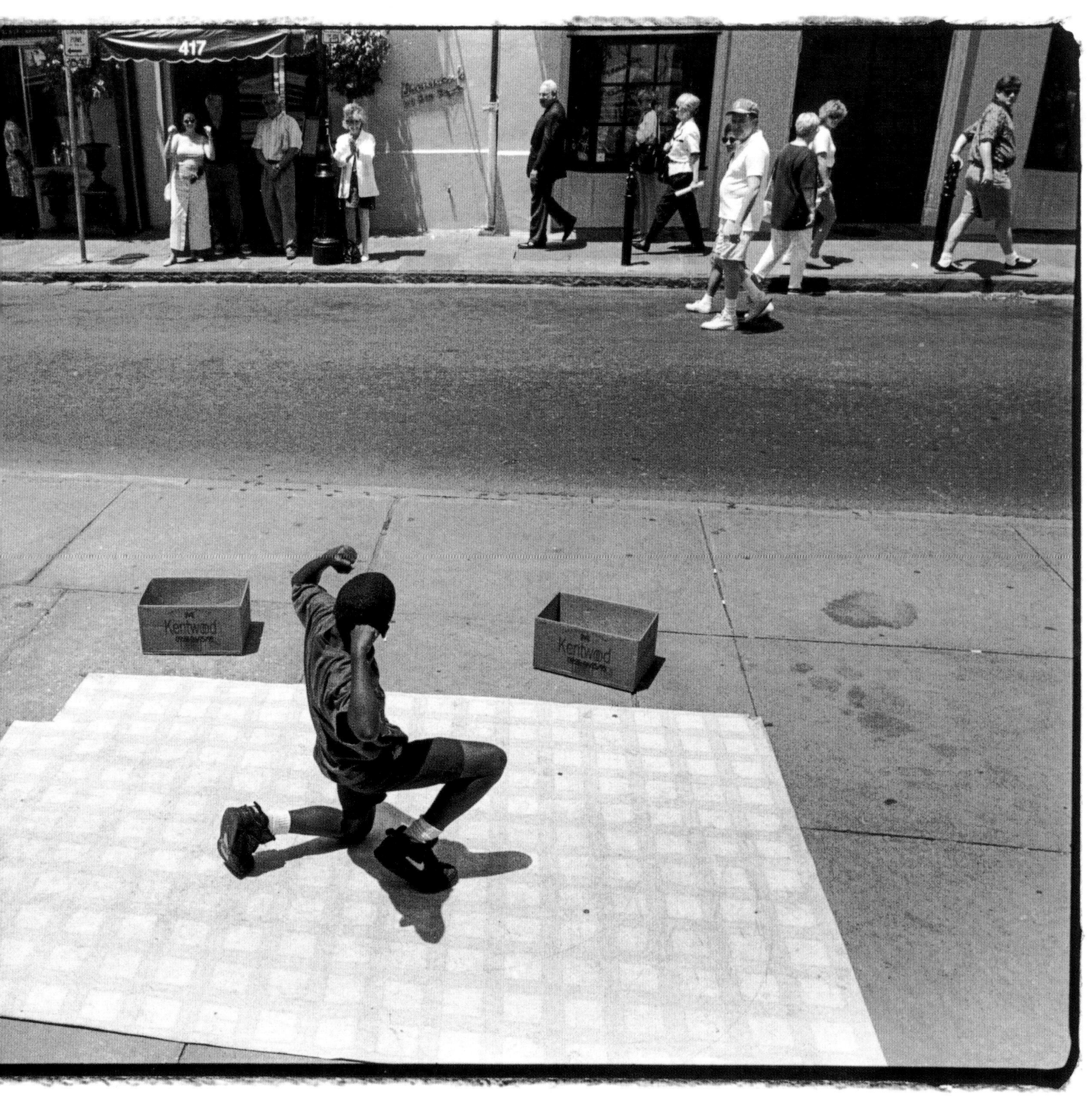
417
Kentwood
Kentwood

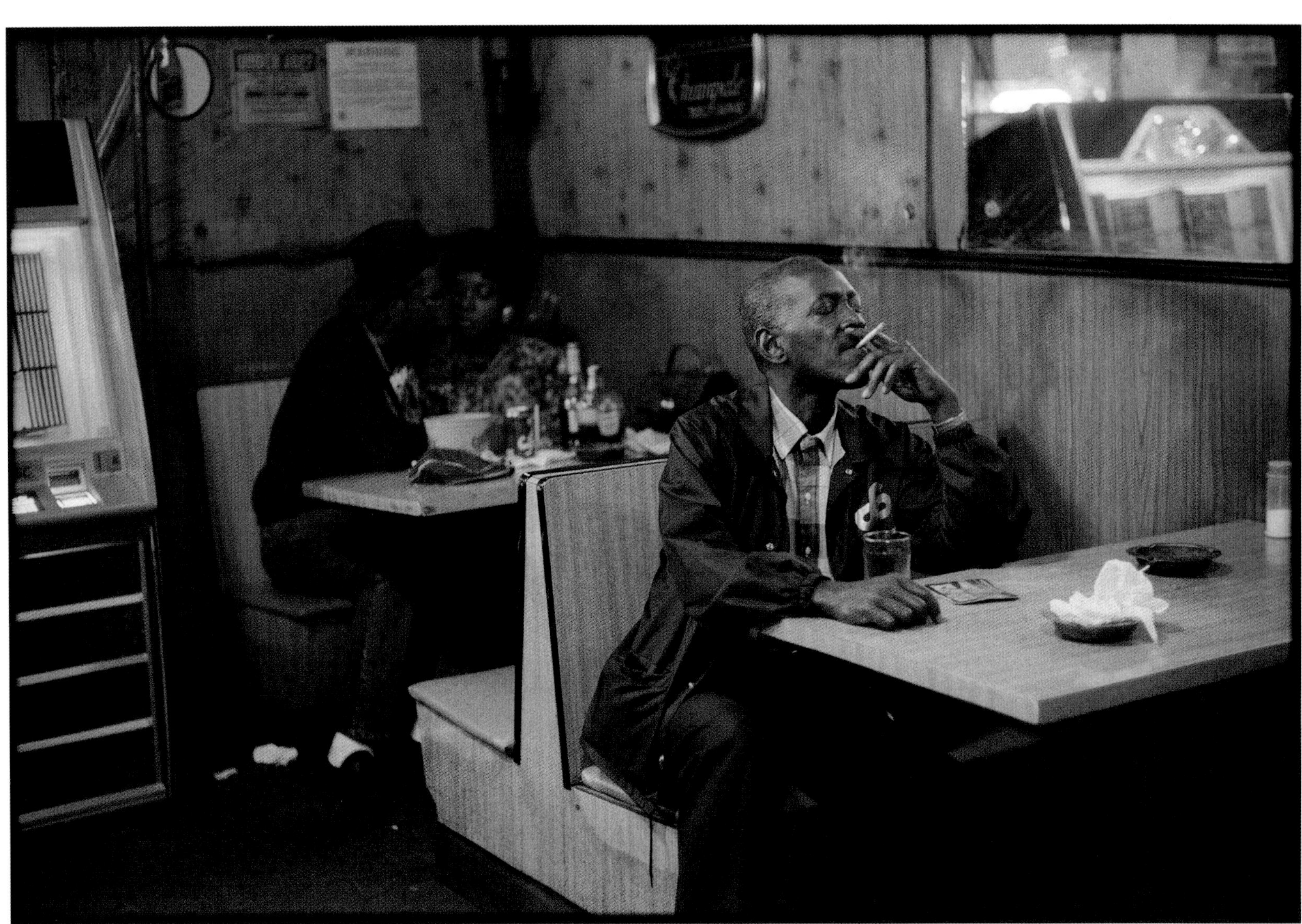

FEAST FOR THE SENSES

Fred Moten

I would do a painting and it would take a couple of days to find out that it's a disaster. But with photography, I had thirty-six images to find out that they were all disasters, quickly. . . .

Something I'm curious about is how reality changes through the medium . . . Well, you know, the thing that's happening through the medium is your capturing light on surface, right? . . . That's part of the intelligence of the medium. It's that this is the best tool to capture light on surface. I mean, that's what it's all about for me. . . .

I'm working not only with the subject matter, but I'm working with the medium and trying to stretch the medium out. I'm using a flash like a brush, the light of a flash like a brush, and I am bouncing it off the floor, so you get a different perspective of where the light comes from. There's motion and I am stopping the motion with the light. And she fits into that space. She's bending over backwards and she's filling up that space. . . .

At this point I'm experimenting with the medium anyway. I don't know what's going to happen. You don't know how it's going to change through the medium. This is negative black and white. It's not digital, so you can't see it right away. I don't know what I'm going to get until I get into the dark room. That's a whole other gestation there.

—Frank Stewart interviewed by Victoria L. Valentine, *Culture Type,* June 18, 2020

Smoke and the Lovers, 1992

Nexus and journey go together because they don't. Focus, center, crossroads, hub, a bunch of ways gone through, a pointless point of collection and release, gathering and dispersal, both beginning and end and neither, where one and one make three and none in constant proof of one stillborn in motion, of one and one's impossible afterlife in solid air. The natal occasion is tragicomically avoided one mo'gin in the bad, expectant faith we keep with fate and time. Meanwhile, Frank Stewart regularly celebrates a feast of the senses, playing on the Feast of Ascension, which marks the day when Christ's body went into heaven, and all is in the wake and on the edge of disaster. Stewart is interested in that kind of interplay of the material and the immaterial in their differential inseparability, not just when sensual experience becomes nonsensual and meaning is made, but also when a certain madness of brushed light and bent or tangled form pervades the image and evades the imaged, and when sensual experiences move over or across the boundaries that are supposed to separate sensual registers. In these ways, index turns on itself as meaning unravels, while content and form collude in brokenness. This is to say that surface is broken open. The image and the imaged are affected, vulnerable. They are foregiven in and as the next disaster, where Stewart makes findings in the art of loss. What's sacramental in Stewart's work is that it makes conditions in which the viewer can all but walk or rise or, deeper, fall into the photographic space. We are required and allowed to be made aware of having joined him in grave somersault and low-ridden tumble. What light we are, or have, is transferred, too, and shared, in barely airborne surfacing. This pandimensionality is as miraculously close as heathens get to divine experience, but it is, as when Jesus rises, an experience of the flesh and of the senses. Not resurrection so much as an insurrection, this feast is given also, and all but primarily, as aroma. Now, how does somebody who's not trying to make a picture of scent make such great pictures of what it is to have been sent by scent, and to it? There's some kind of alchemical and pansensual sorcery going on. It's a matter of spirit, and Stewart preaches the gospel of barbecue, using a flash like a brush to share light from one surface to another. And light is the surface in question, and the implement that makes surface instrument. All this arranging and deepening where surface, medium, and instrument are inseparable is surfacing. The interplay of foreground and background is not the point. What matters is the pointlessness, the intra-active nonlocality, which is given when the very idea of foreground and background are no longer backdrop and foregone conclusion. We're not lost in the photograph, but we find that they can't quite find us. For the moment, in the moment, they're not there. It's that there is gone, too, and so is here. Even now is given over to presencing, where reality changes and emplotment fails. Having been taken to the club by Phineas Newborn, and on the road by Ahmad Jamal, Stewart has been long engaged in mobile, anthemic, anathematic, anamathematical monasticism. Jazz pianists' extended tilling of the trio field, in the ancient neoplasticism of Smalls or Lola's or some other cup of trembling, where one and three are subject to under-trinitarian confusion, forms a school for surfacing, where number gives way to recess and felt curve. It's like when somebody singing a song about a creek to the creek that accompanies her becomes the sound shining in a photograph of light applied to light with light in shade. In and through Frank Stewart's immersed, immersive, echomusicological photography, we see the glorious rise and even more glorious fall of the Black creative intellectual.[1]

This essay is just some questions laid out on top of one another, augmenting and obscuring one another, addi(c)tive and redactive and diffractive in all this compulsive pointing, and invasive seeing, and violent, loving regard. Maybe this essay *are* some questions. There might be no (such thing as an) essay, at all, all this incompleteness all for naught in constant asking. The questions are laid out, not posed. This laying out and layering gets deep when matter and medium lay down with one another and get (us) involved. It's like what happens when you close this book and the compact of surfacing goes mad, light on light in light all heavy with and through one another. Light, which is said to reveal, covers over some other layer of itself, as if in recovery of certain shades of the blues and the abstract truth, wherein a mystery is shown but not divulged. After hours, there's no telling what goes on in a book like this. And after unfolding, when the light goes on, stillness can't quite hide the sound of rearrangement, shit getting itself correct in secret resistance to every point of view; mantic, pan-African approach divining all the way to China. The rub is this rubbing of the photographs and the various flavors it induces. Smoke, as in *Smoke and the Lovers* (page 102), reveals some drawn out sharing of attention. Light turns the surface, seasons it, lightning lightening the heavy paper; but the paper, the surface, having been held in light's (ab)solution, its foregivenness, is not to be seen beneath the appearances that tell of it and tell on it, thereby disclosing its inexistence like an aura, all but aural, in études of elemental fade.[2] Isn't that how overtone bears fundament out into nothingness? Out into was it ever there? Out into was there ever any surface underneath this practicing of surfacing that light takes up in and with and through its medium? Out into "I'm curious about . . . how reality changes through the medium"? Light's medium is photography. Photography's medium is Frank Stewart. Frank Stewart's medium is the open secret.

Surfacing is the diffusion, dispersion, disruption, and deepening of surface. In the digitalization of photography, what is the fate and practice of surfacing's ongoing intensification of the refusal, in rehearsal, of surface? Can brushing light survive cybernetics' arrest of development? A certain motion of light in water, or

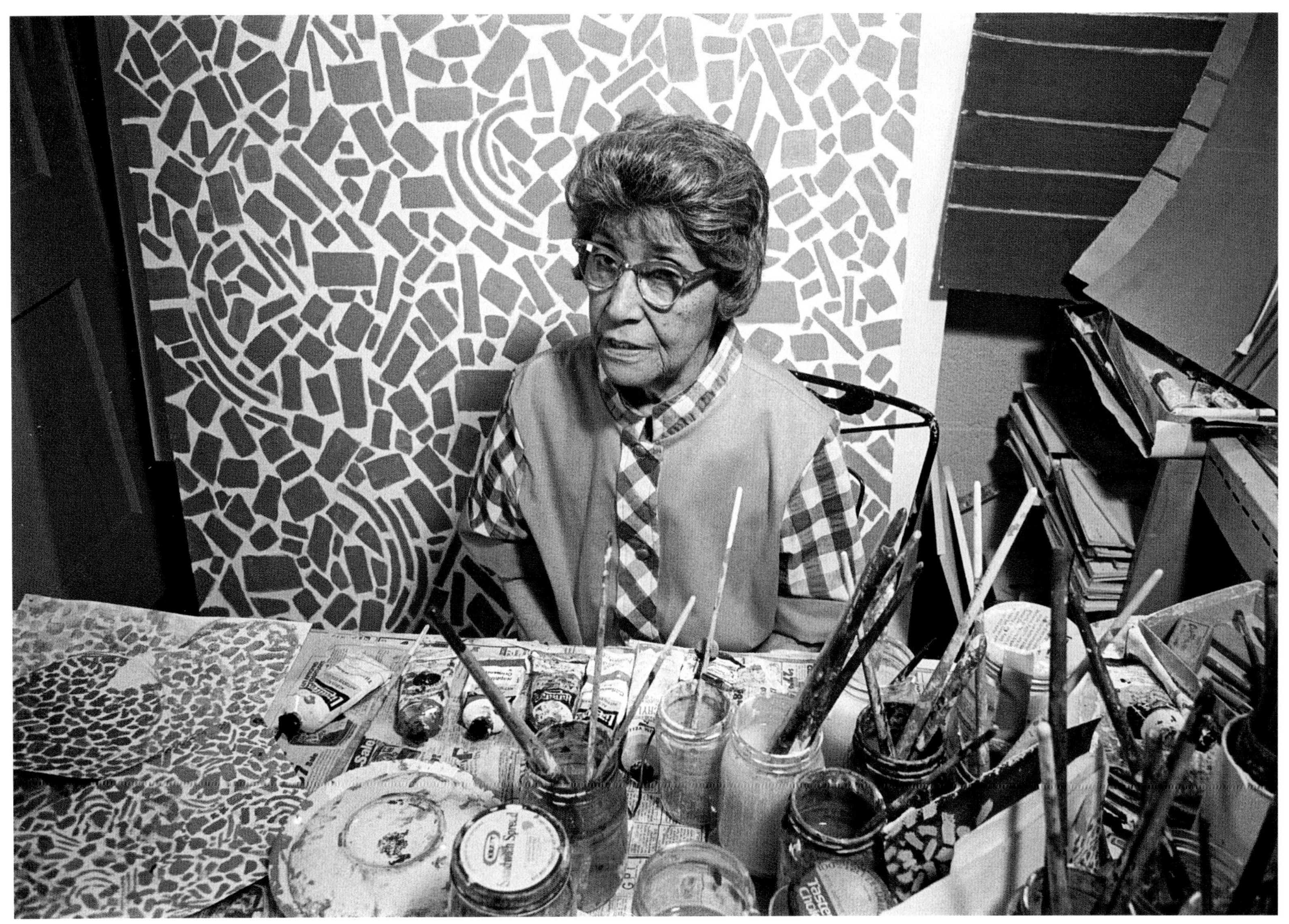

Alma W. Thomas, 1976

movement of light through fluid, seems necessary.[3] More questions concerning the alignment visage and portraiture emerge with others concerning the entanglement of medium and pigment. These are questions Glenn Ligon has asked of and by way of Chris Ofili and David Hammons.[4] These are Sam Gilliam's questions for drapery, and Jack Whitten's questions of fabric(ation). These are questions for laundresses and seamstresses and quilters and schoolteachers, questions Stewart asks, in light, of Alma Thomas. These are kitchen table questions for cooks and collagists and painters and photographers. These are tense questions. These are Hortense Spillers questions. Such questions of wave and vapor are concerned with not only the specific problem of the non-particular but the general problem of the pre-particulate, where the convergence of light, pigment, instrument, medium, and surface is fabulous and fabulant. When Stewart's description of his practice as brushing light with light is endowed with absolute clarity, then the very nature of reality, and not just its representation or reproduction, comes into the play of changes. Who gets to ask these questions? Who has to ask these questions? Because they are unsettling it should come as no surprise that the unsettled ask them best and with the most terrible precision. These questions of framing are sacraments of the enframed. Abstract truth is blue's (people's) special concern. It is played out in black (and white). There, it's read, and understood, by students of the frame. They abstract persons from the frame, suspending personality in the frame in favor of shook arms and moved forms. They know what it means that, for the sake of

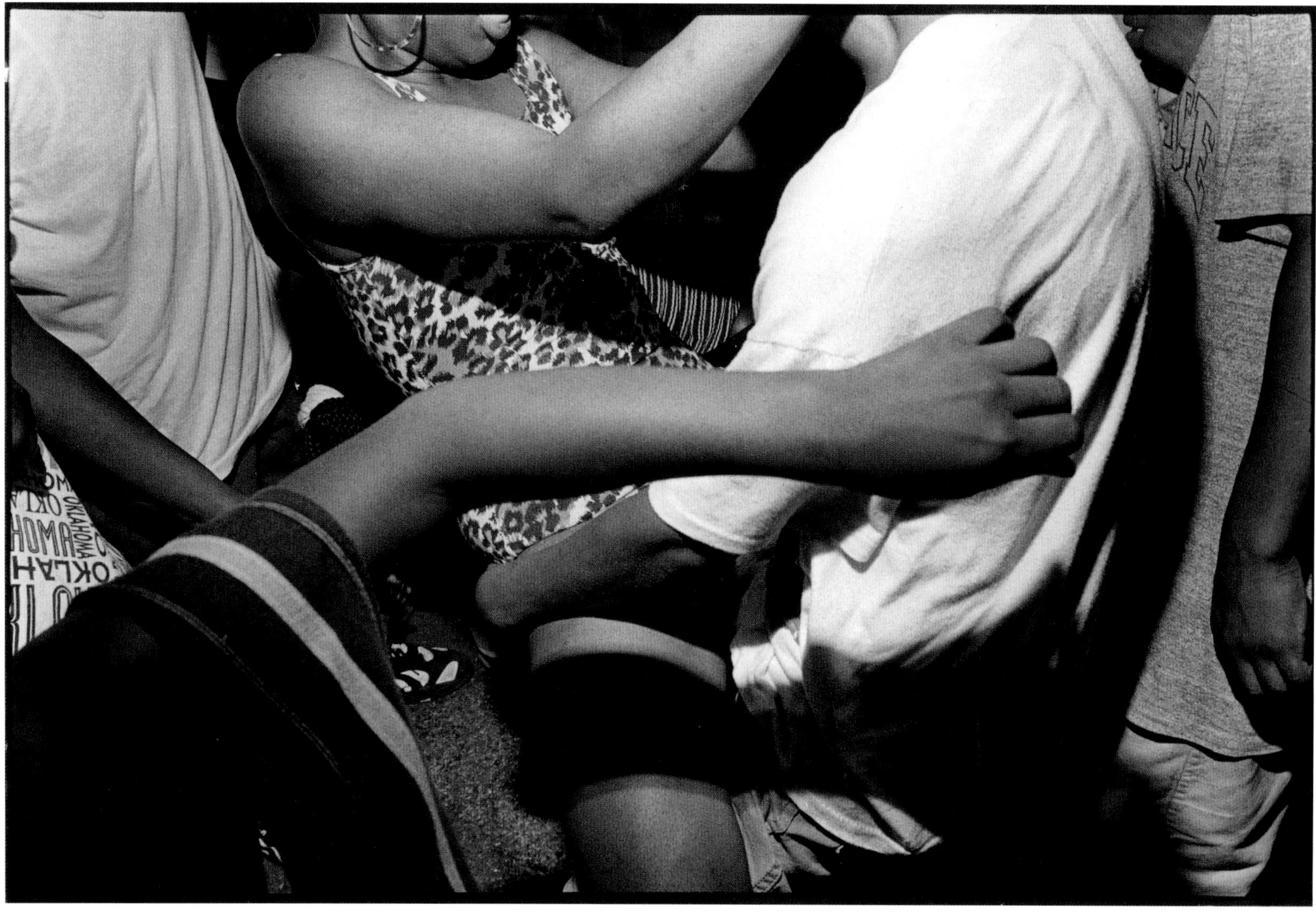

movement, motion is stopped with light. They stay on the scene, they stay with the seen, where there's some work going on, people working shit out, working their way out of something.

It looks like the unowned, the un-self-possessed, are working their way out of work, and of the work, and we're all up in there with them, and Stewart's all up in there, too. Light's been rubbed around up in there—you can taste it. They're studying, but they ain't studying you, or any human calculation. The passionate attachment of the people is impersonal. If you want to know what disaster is, here it is. There is no concept of the human that will have been able to withstand the distinction between the owned, ownable, but incapable of owning and the owner. And it's in this regard, by way of this distinction, that the human fully comes into his own, as enacted self-possession, to which he submits in and as the image, the framed picture. This, in its turn, both requires and allows us to consider the relation between the owned, ownable, but incapable of owning and those who improve and are improved, and who conceive and are conceived. The problem is given already in the concept, and in conceptualization, and in their relation to the interplay of separation and grasp by which self-picturing and self-regard are held. And the problem this problem bears and hides is a wound at the heart of the human insofar as all ownership begins with the separative self-possession of the one who owns. The extent to which the owner must be self-owned is the extent to which the owner is always already revealed as incapable of owning. His picture of himself is incomplete, though the frame is absolute for him and absolutely brutal for those he sees as owned and owns.

Juneteenth '93, 19th of June Celebration, Mexia, Texas, 1993

For the one who will have owned all this is, as it were, inconceivable. Self-consciousness looks outward for itself. You can't look out for yourself like that. You can't understand yourself that way. It is the inconceivable, generalized as a generative non-conceptuality, that we share in/as practice.[5] But you can't stand where we ground together. Man, we be grounding without ground. I wish this essay were a brush, or a sheaf of sheaves of light, on photography as a kind of grounding, a kind of surfacing. I wish it could reveal and then abjure the relays between institution and personality, taking and having.

The question concerning the taking of the photograph is one of attitude. Consider by way of the undergeometrical in Spillers, who refuses the norms of verticality in and as grounding rather than in and as the having, which is to say the standing, of ground or the occupation of a point of view. The point of flew, or flown, in grounding, in touching, in approaching is that the medium is intimate. Spillers and Stewart are homelessly homegrown confidants of the zero-degree of social (non)conceptualization.[6] He whispers, "Look where this light is coming from," and her reply is "The empathic luminosity we share." But here's a paradox: the way to get (the) people out of being-framed is to get down in it and irrupt. It is to prefer the horizon(t)al in approaching, surfacing, in relation to a sociological hesitation, a solicitation, a rhythm-n-ing that is before the concept, as its depth charge. At the same time, there's a de-objectification of the real that's intimated in the thought that it must change, that it's already otherwise, and that this is what photography reveals. If the concept of the object is a remedy for the simplifications and ossifications of the real object it is not, finally, a de-objectification but is, rather, a re-objectification whose power of abstraction and extraction is too awesome. This is why the re-materialization of work is crucial, why Spillers reads the way Althusser reads Marx so closely and tells them all about themselves. She's working with the people who be working something out. Stewart all but puts it this way: "At this point [we're] experimenting with the medium anyway. [We] don't know what's going to happen. You don't know how it's going to change through the medium. This is negative black and white. It's not digital, so you can't see it right away. [We] don't know what [we're] going to get until [we] get into the dark room. That's a whole other gestation there."[7] They're experimenting in the darkroom, in the basement at the house party on Juneteenth, in the corner booth by the jukebox at Hawkins Grill. That abstraction and extraction from the bodies of the workers, which is crucial to the operation and the critique of capital, demands another intellectual and affective (dis) comportment that bears sufficient attunement to the terrible utility of the concept is a matter of concern for photography. A re-materialization, a surrealization of work, in the flesh, in and as our monstrous claim upon the monstrous, which is manifest as sharing, in open and empathic handing, is at hand in Stewart. The echology is maternal. The passage is eternal. The middle lasts forever. The medium is massage. Spillers and Stewart share expectations in Memphis, which opens on the delta, where things change. They see with what they see, not so much catching people in the act but rather studying with them their releasement, their preformative practice, before the act, and their critical practice in the aftermath of what never, finally, passes for the act. There's a culinary and intoxicant sociality in flavor's entire sensual range. This is all essence, but it's estuarial, too, something flown and flowing through, where the idea of the natal community is all but always already dispersive, a cosmopolitan slide, some kind of phono-photographic gliss that animates (the) work. Call it unrest, or restlessness, or nervous muscularity; something ante-kinetic; some new, and off, an ante-genetic rebirth of the newly neverborn.

Scene set, sound seen, light table overturned. Turn—is that the set you see? Descend. Let's try approaching surfacing again. Is photography contingent on its printing? Is photography the print, the thing in hand? Now, after the digital, where is photography? When does it happen? Does the photograph give photography or is the photograph what photography withholds? Or, what if the thing photographed, as if it were some idea of the thing itself, is what photography withdraws? It seems that the essence, or maybe the condition, or maybe the instance of the photograph is never there before us. What you hold in your hands, or what you behold

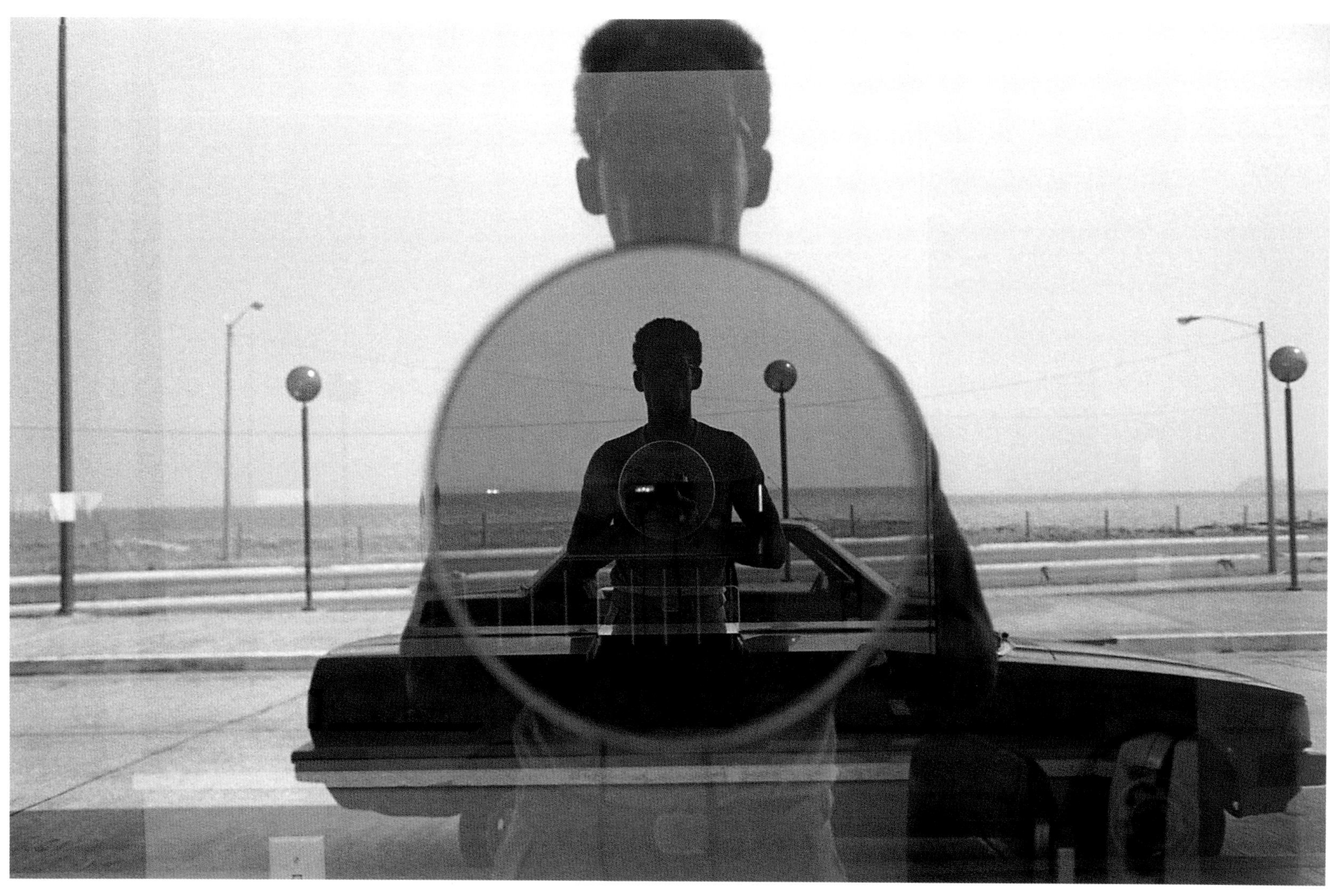

on the wall, is not quite there. What if the central fact of the photograph is not that it captures but, rather, that it withholds? When it seems like it's all right there in front of us, showing or representing itself or its making or its maker, it's hiding, sliding, moving on in plain sight as if it were plainsong.

Photography removes in drawing with and drawing on. Photography is given in the withdrawal of and in the photograph; not only of what's photographed, but also of the photograph's own fade, when it loses all it has, or all that has been taken. With the chemistry of the Polaroid, which emerges before our eyes and fades in our hands, a scene is set, and seen, and then recedes, in a kind of fluidity, as when a river shines and sways. This recess, or recession, is a double session, words written out in chalk and palimpsestically, in the residue of all that had been written, the never fully erasive noise from which the figure, or the shape, or the form, or the word emerges, and back into which it falls or lays. Is drawing also always the withdrawn? This intraplay of leaving and accompaniment is given again and again in folded service (I mean surface).

To describe rather than depict, rather than explain; to view with rather than provide a theoretical overview; to see with the seen when they are seeing: all these are to do much more than merely see them. Moreover, such withness is so much more than witnessing. Photo-phenomenological description shares experience for whom no person, and never the merely personal, comes first. There's no question of or questing for personality. At stake, instead, is something of prefor-mance. Is the *per* in person(ality) the same as the *per* in perform(ance)? There's something of complete-ness, of finishing, of being-through that demands and

Self-portrait, Dominican Republic, 1986

justifies refusal. What would it mean to pass, or go past, through? What is it to sound this passing through, never getting through it, or over it, never being-through with it? This sojourn on the road, this big road blues, this constant delta, is the holding and releasement of intelligence. It's the simultaneous sharing and keeping of a secret, where the sharing of the secret keeps it safe. There's something withdrawn in the telling, this doubleness of holding out, this cutting seriality of perseverance, dis continuity, dis place/meant. Perhaps in some continual withdrawal of telling, even of the telling of a story, something is said. What's the difference between the saying, or the sharing, and the telling of a secret? Is there an opening of the secret into which the secret withdraws? We go there with it, into that sousveillant recess to find that the rendezvous of victory is involvement. This is a C. L. R. James/Aimé Césaire/Martin Carter imperative, a pan Caribbean affordance when Memphis is rightly seen as the sea's upper partial.[8] T/here, in study, the figure of the intellectual gets up to get down.

> So it is that the "homegrown" intellectual is addressing her hermeneutic demand not only to the cultural dominant but to her natal community as well. Furthermore, it is by sectors of both that she is, in effect, interpellated, or summoned, as a responsible subject and subjectivity. And how could it be otherwise? How could it not be double trouble that her very vocation is itself a space not yet entirely cleared out, as it were, by a culture that maintains no obligation at all to believe her, especially; to treat her, to imagine her, as a credible discursive subject, working on an intellectually identifiable object, at the same time that she encounters it as contradictory, if not adversarial, that she moves on in a "negative capability"? The other tale, then, that the black creative intellectual confronts marks the weave of contradiction as a fruitful one, but only if . . . It is, perhaps, too soon here to speak of bravery, but I suspect that that must be our destination through the reversals of assumption that now make it difficult, if not impossible, to (1) reconstitute a "talented tenth," which is itself the culminative position of the myth of representation (as both DuBois and Cruse embraced it from their common historic past); (2) sustain the idea of the intellectual as a leading and heroic personality rather than a local point of oscillation among contending conceptual claims; and (3) continue to pursue a theory and practice of intellectual or cultural work that is performative rather than, for lack of a better word, unfortunately, "scientific," or responsible to a "cognitive apparatus," or a "thought-idea."[9]

What if the primary way to "sustain the idea of the intellectual as . . . a local point of oscillation" is photography? What if photography is such oscillation's field, its radical nonlocality? The leading and heroic personality of the Black intellectual fades in the impersonality of working through the work. If personhood persists in performance rather than posture, then *preformance* is dis-place/meant of the person.

> Furthermore, if Steiner and Foucault were right, man is not only no longer the linchpin of historical movement but history itself demonstrates a minimal resiliency of meaning as a self-reflective tool in the current inventory of media-inspired, constructed punctualities. Certain idols of narrative have lost their explanatory power for American culture in general and for African American culture, in particular, if its contemporary music tells us anything, so that the key question for the black creative intellectual now is: How does one grasp her membership in, or relatedness to, a culture that defines itself by the very logics of the historical? Or, as I queried earlier, What is the work of the black creative intellectual, *for all we know now?*
>
> The short answer is that the Black creative intellectual must get busy *where he/she is.*[10]

Get busy. Get down. Fall through. Where s/he is is all up in there; and man, above, is mere "media-inspired, constructed punctualities." That's all. The human will have been the generalization of that point, that particle, but still. No way that where we are is here, says Nathaniel Mackey; like he was really nowhere, says Amiri Baraka.[11] And Stewart shows dis-place/meant, here and now, is nowhere in presencing, which is approaching, surfacing. If the contemporary is generally understood as now/here, this spatio-temporal coordination, this posture, this emplotment, which will have then been placed on the move, in history, the timeline spread brutally out in smooth-curved plane all over the globe, then Afro-diasporic work, its spirit-physics, its crowds of common wind, bespeak the strange anacontemporaneity of no/where, its anarrhythmia.[12] What if the incessant photography of Black artists, in the recesses of Black social life, in the wake and on the edge of catastrophe, asks us to ask again? What if play, in/as dis place/meant, is the condition in which "the black creative intellectual" becomes instrument or God's trombone? If, as Spillers says, "the intellectual has imagined flight only in its negative instance as a supposed rejection, when his very status, or standing, *as an intellectual requires* that he take on a language and disposition that are 'foreign,'"[13] then photography, for Stewart, is where a preference for fallenness is exercised. If, as again, Spillers lays it out and lays it down,

> In other words, the work of the academy [or of the museum, or of the gallery], or more specifically, the "cognitive apparatus," is defined, symbolically speaking, as "not-mother," a "not-my own" . . . [then] I am referring less to the maternal and paternal objects here as gendered actants of precisely defined sexual role than the *ground of intimacy* that the subject assumes: the more or less harmonious ensemble of impressions that bound me not only to my body, but my body as it is reflected back to me in the eyes of others that I recognize *as like myself*.[14]

Then the "ground of intimacy," as reflection fades in our Black share, all over the world till earth is seen before world's end, is photography, which is surfacing, which is the medium of its medium, Frank Stewart—the Black creative intellectual to end them all.

1 See Steven Feld, "From Ethnomusicology to Echo-Muse-Ecology: Reading R. Murray Schafer in the Papua New Guinea Rainforest," *The Soundscape Newsletter*, June 1994, https://static1.squarespace.com/static/545aad98e4b0f1f9150ad5c3/t/5465b2bee4b0c4e0caea1605/1415951038575/1993+From+Ethnomusicology+to.pdf.

2 See Wallace Stevens, "The River of Rivers in Connecticut," The Collected Poems of Wallace Stevens: The Corrected Edition (New York: Vintage, 2015), 564.

3 See Samuel R. Delany, *The Motion of Light in Water: Sex and Science Fiction Writing in the East Village* (Minneapolis: University of Minnesota Press, 2004).

4 See Glenn Ligon, "Blue Black," in *Chris Ofili: Night and Day*, ed. Massimiliano Gioni (New York: Rizzoli, 2014); and Glenn Ligon, *Blue Black* (St. Louis: Pulitzer Arts Foundation, 2017).

5 See Hans Blumenberg, *Begriffe in Geschichten* (Frankfurt: Bibliothek Suhrkamp, 2016); and Hans Blumenberg, *Theorie der Unbegrifflichkeit* (Frankfurt: Bibliothek Suhrkamp, 2019).

6 See Hortense Spillers, "Mama's Baby, Papa's Maybe: An American Grammar Book," in *Black, White, and in Color: Essays on American Literature and Culture* (Chicago: University of Chicago Press, 2003), 203–29.

7 Victoria L. Valentine, "Culture Talk: Frank Stewart on His Jazz Photographs, Approach to Image Making, and Forthcoming Museum Retrospective," *Culture Type*, June 18, 2020, https://www.culturetype.com/2020/06/18/culture-talk-frank-stewart-on-his-jazz-photographs-approach-to-image-making-and-forthcoming-museum-retrospective/.

8 See Martin Carter, *Selected Poems/Poesías Escogidas*, trans. Salvador Ortiz-Carboneres (Leeds: Peepal Tree Press, 1999); Aimé Césaire, *The Collected Poetry*, trans. Clayton Eshleman and Annette Smith (Berkeley: University of California Press, 1983); and C. L. R. James, *At the Rendezvous of Victory: Selected Writings* (London: Allison and Busby, 1984).

9 Hortense Spillers, "*The Crisis of the Negro Intellectual*: A Post-date," in *Black, White, and in Color: Essays on American Literature and Culture* (Chicago: University of Chicago Press, 2003), 445.

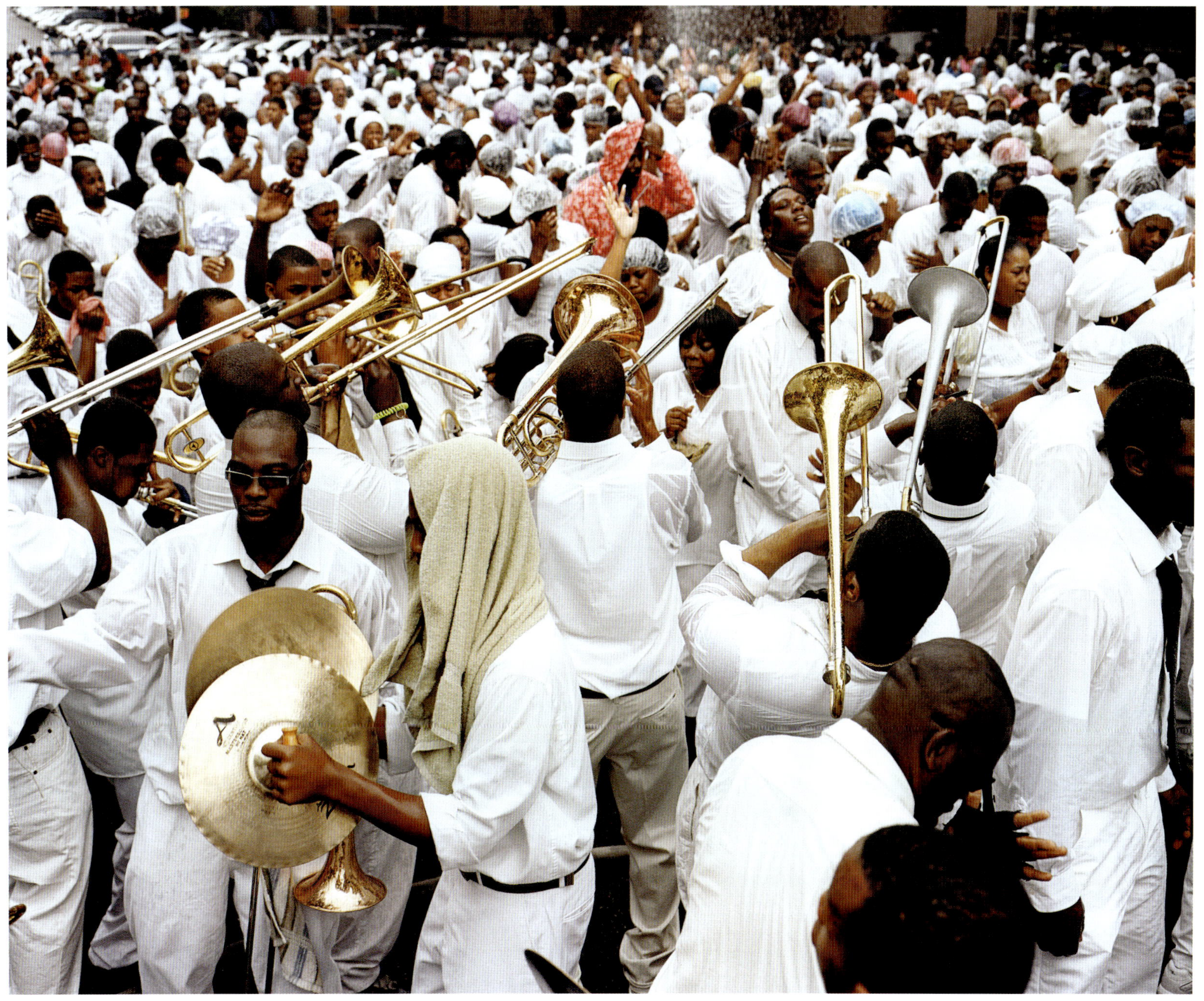

God's Trombones, Harlem, New York, 2009

10 Spillers, "*The Crisis of the Negro Intellectual*: A Post-date," 450.

11 See Amiri Baraka, *S O S: Poems 1961–2013* (New York: Grove Press, 2016); Nathaniel Mackey, *Splay Anthem* (New York: New Directions, 2006); and M. NourbeSe Philip, *A Genealogy of Resistance and Other Essays* (Toronto: Mercury Press, 1997).

12 See Julius S. Scott, *The Common Wind: Afro-American Currents in the Age of the Haitian Revolution* (London: Verso, 2020).

13 Spillers, "*The Crisis of the Negro Intellectual*: A Post-date," 460.

14 Spillers, "*The Crisis of the Negro Intellectual*: A Post-date," 460.

Around the World: Windows

Three Partitions, 1971

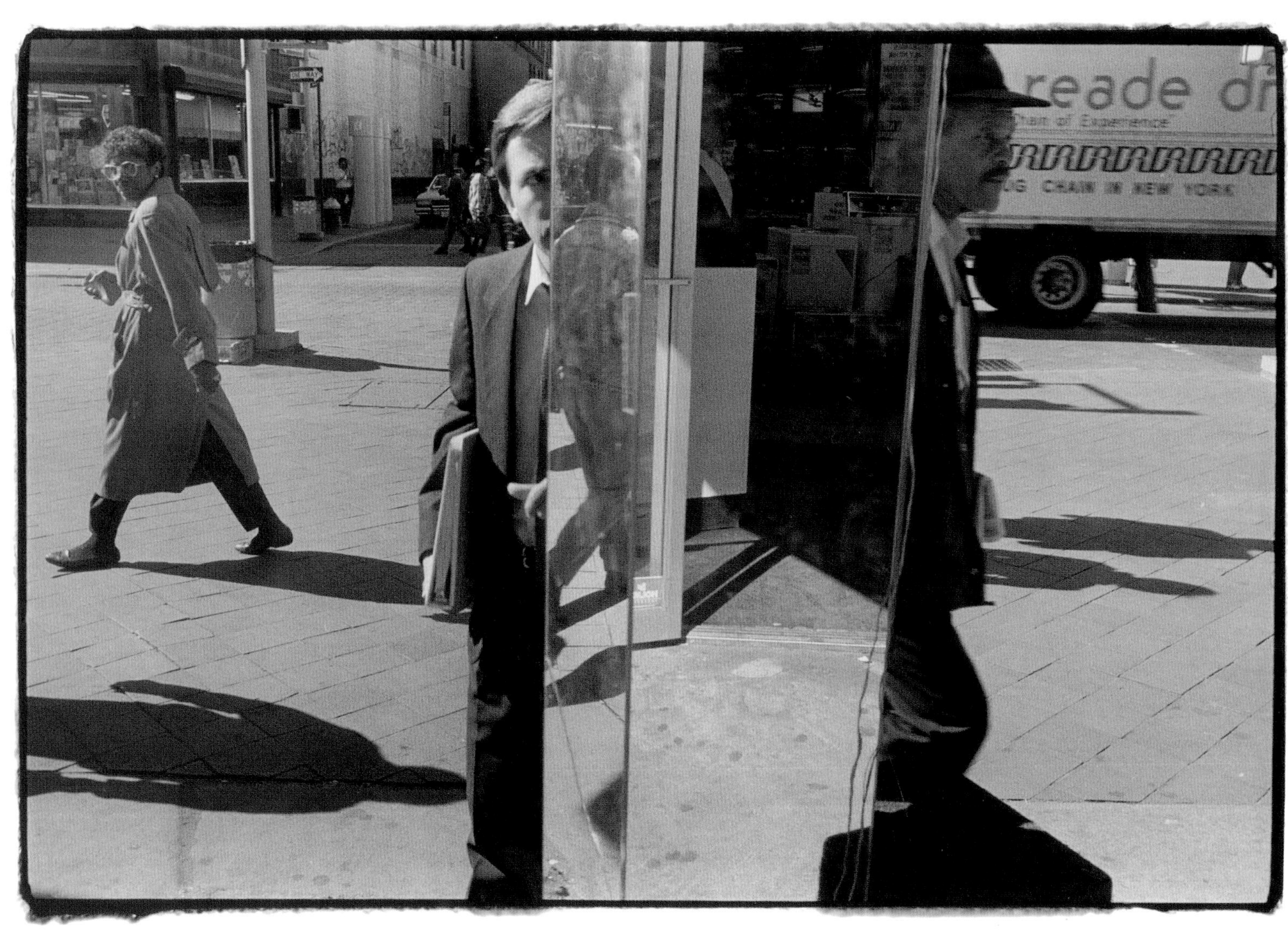

Fulton Street, 1990

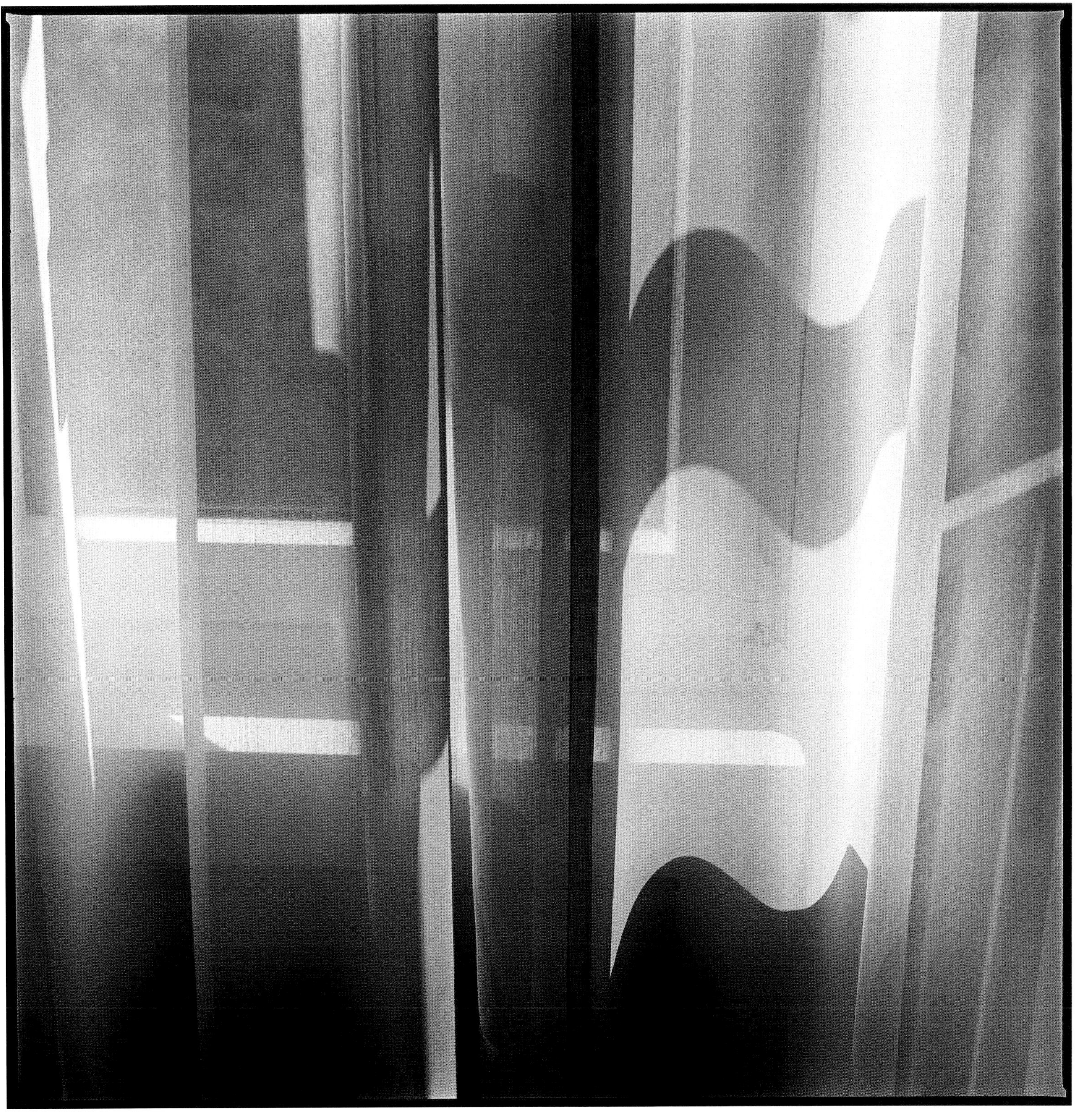

Perugia, 1996

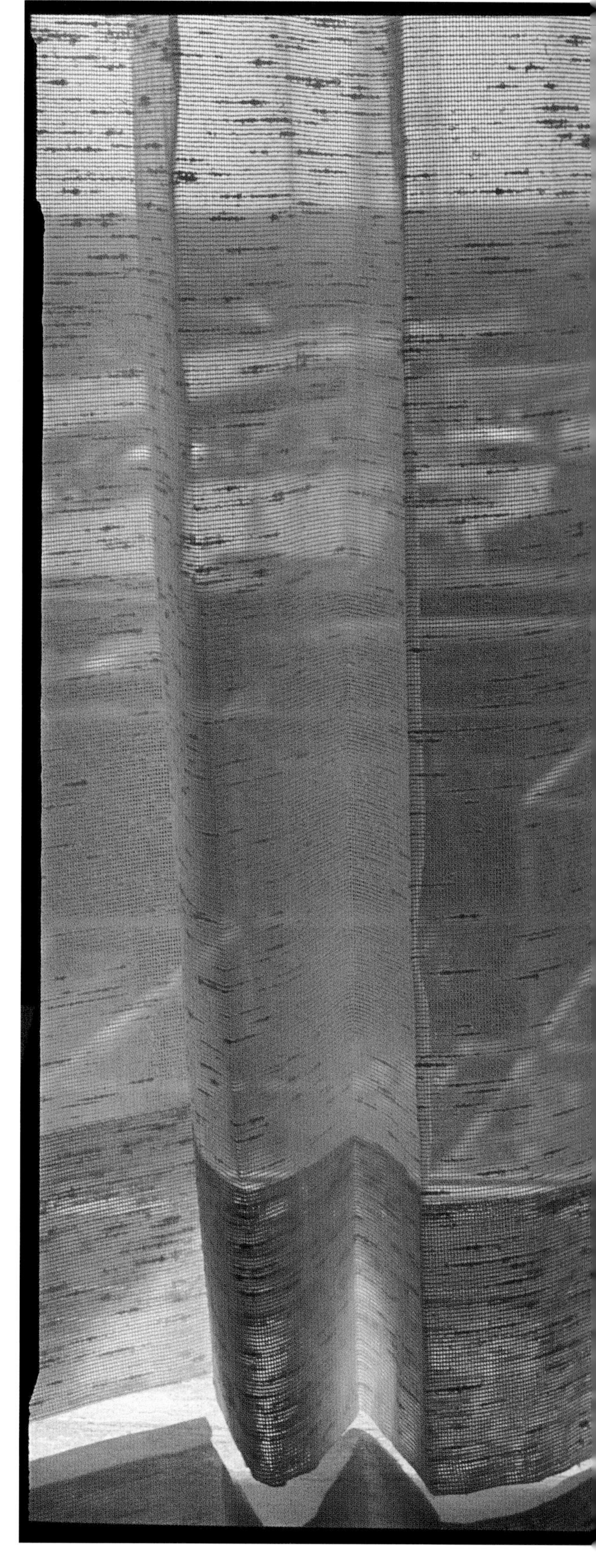

Louisville, 1998

Following spread: *Communist Windows* (detail), see page 147

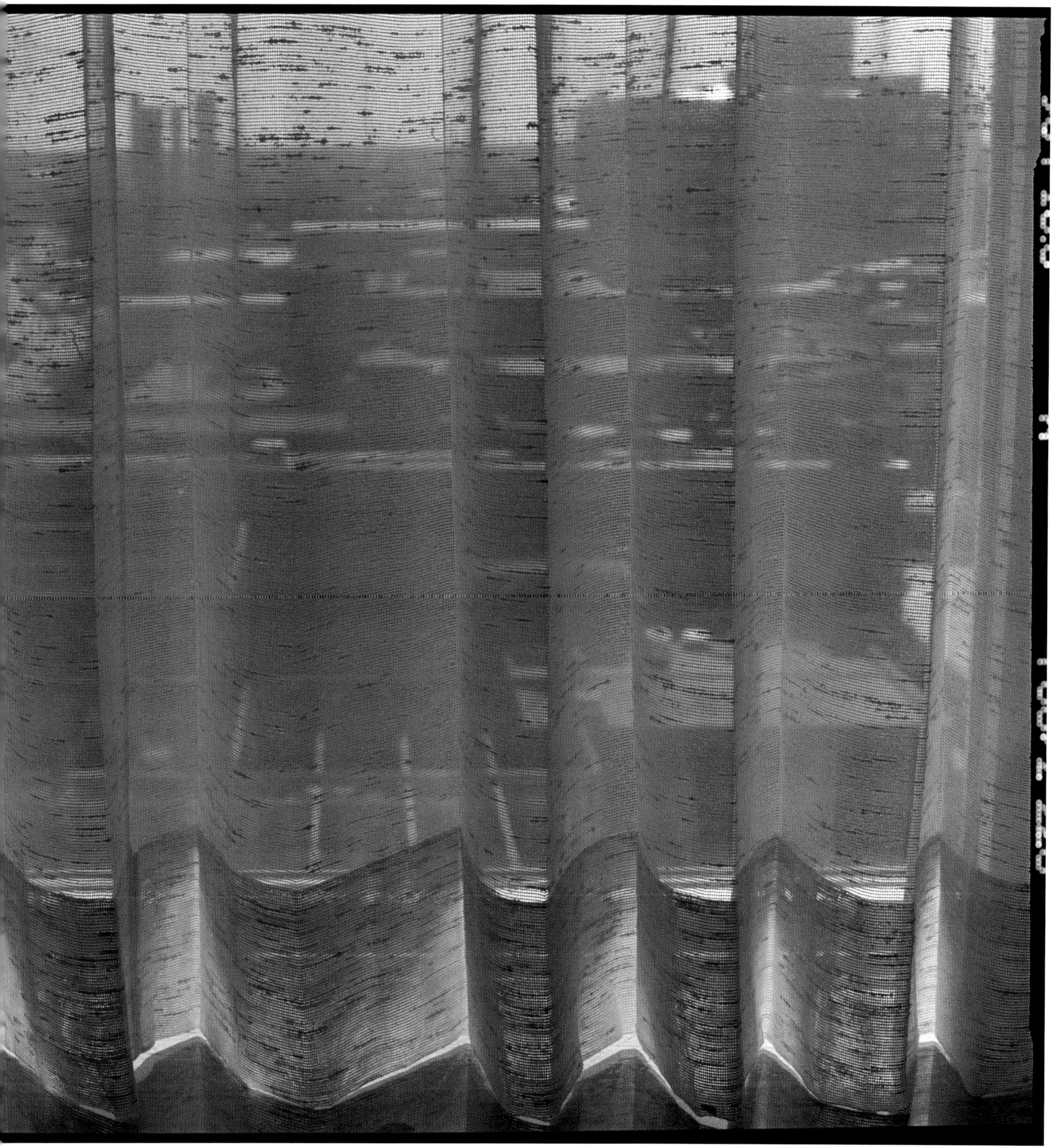

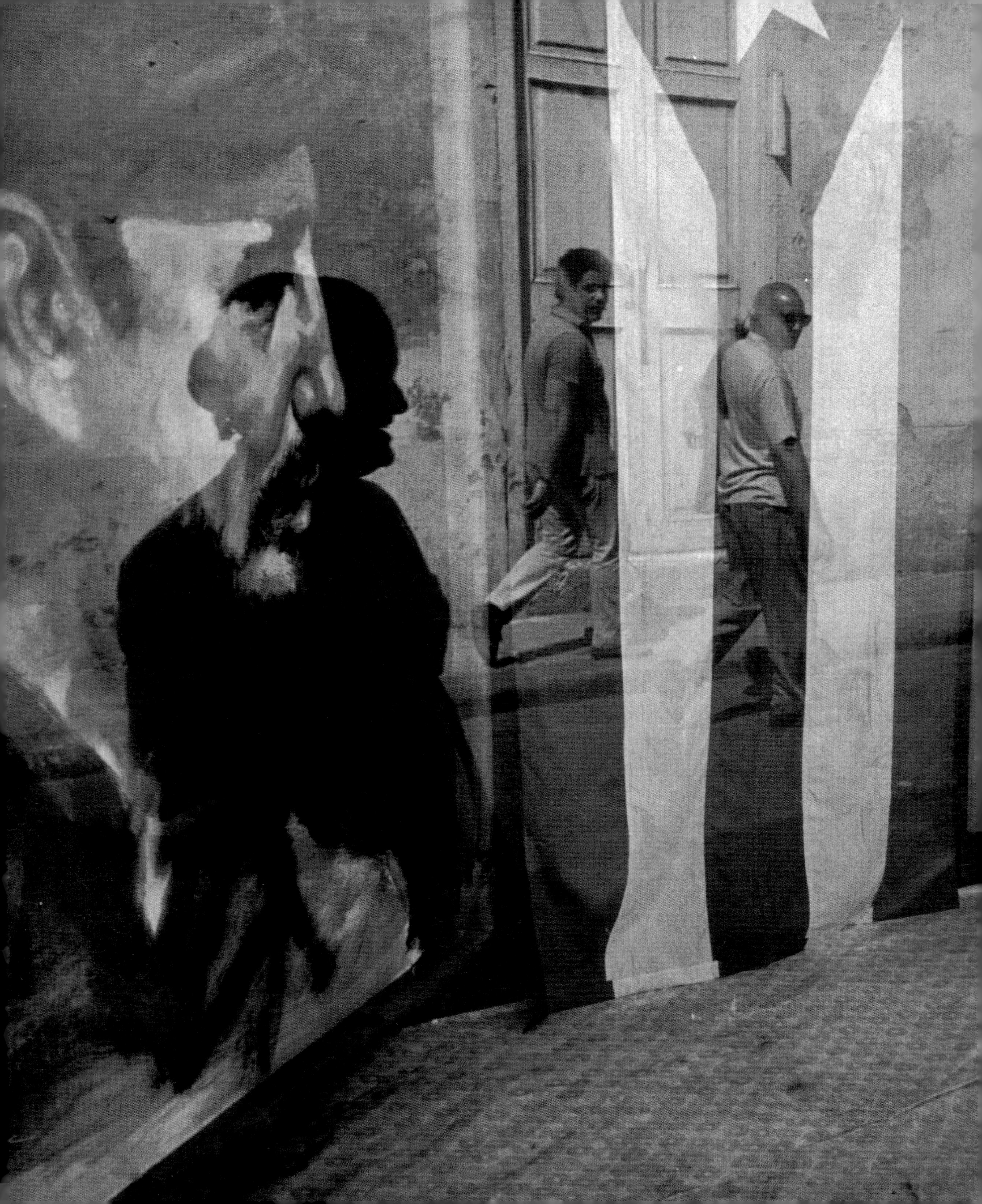

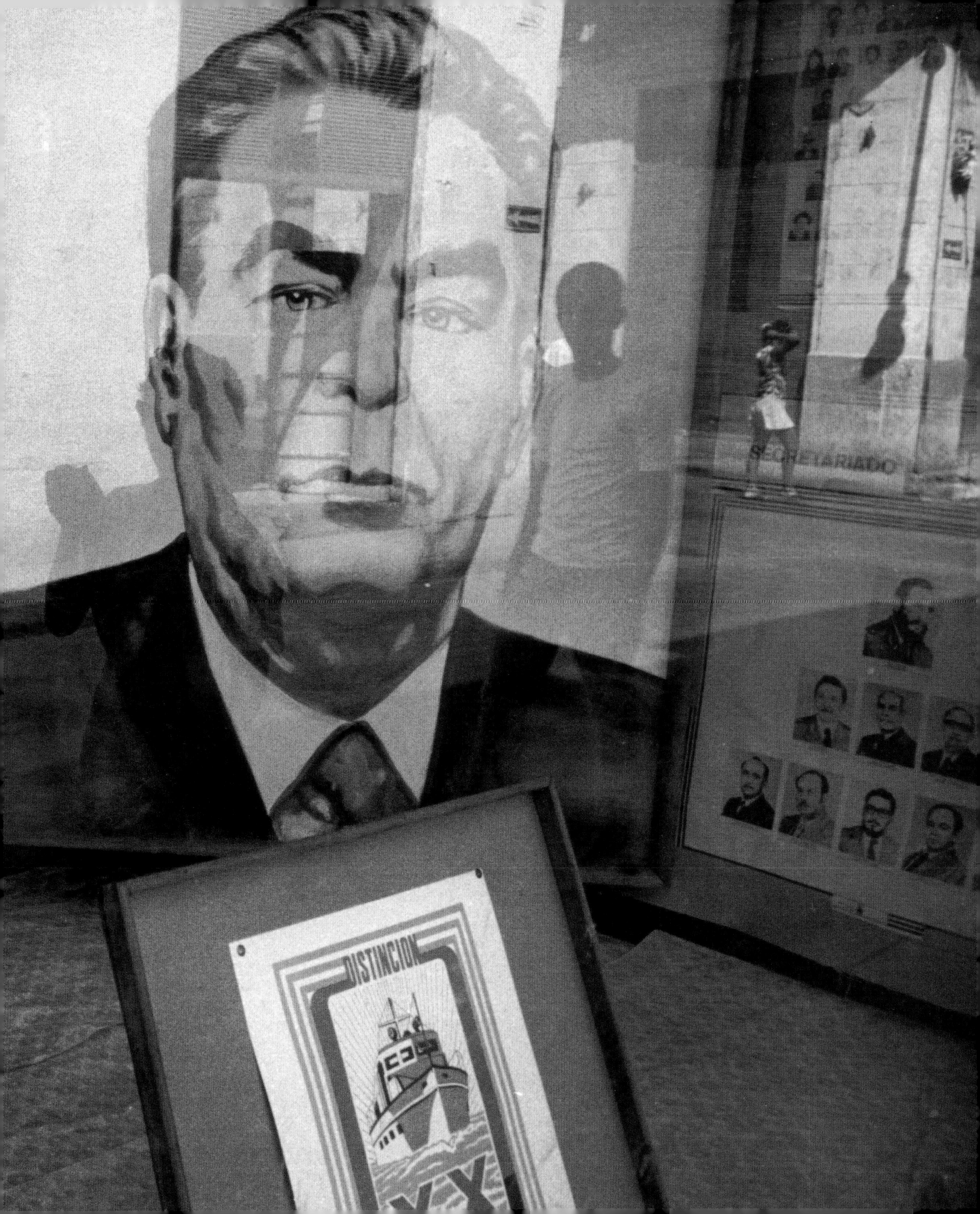
DISTINCION

Around the World: Chromatic Music

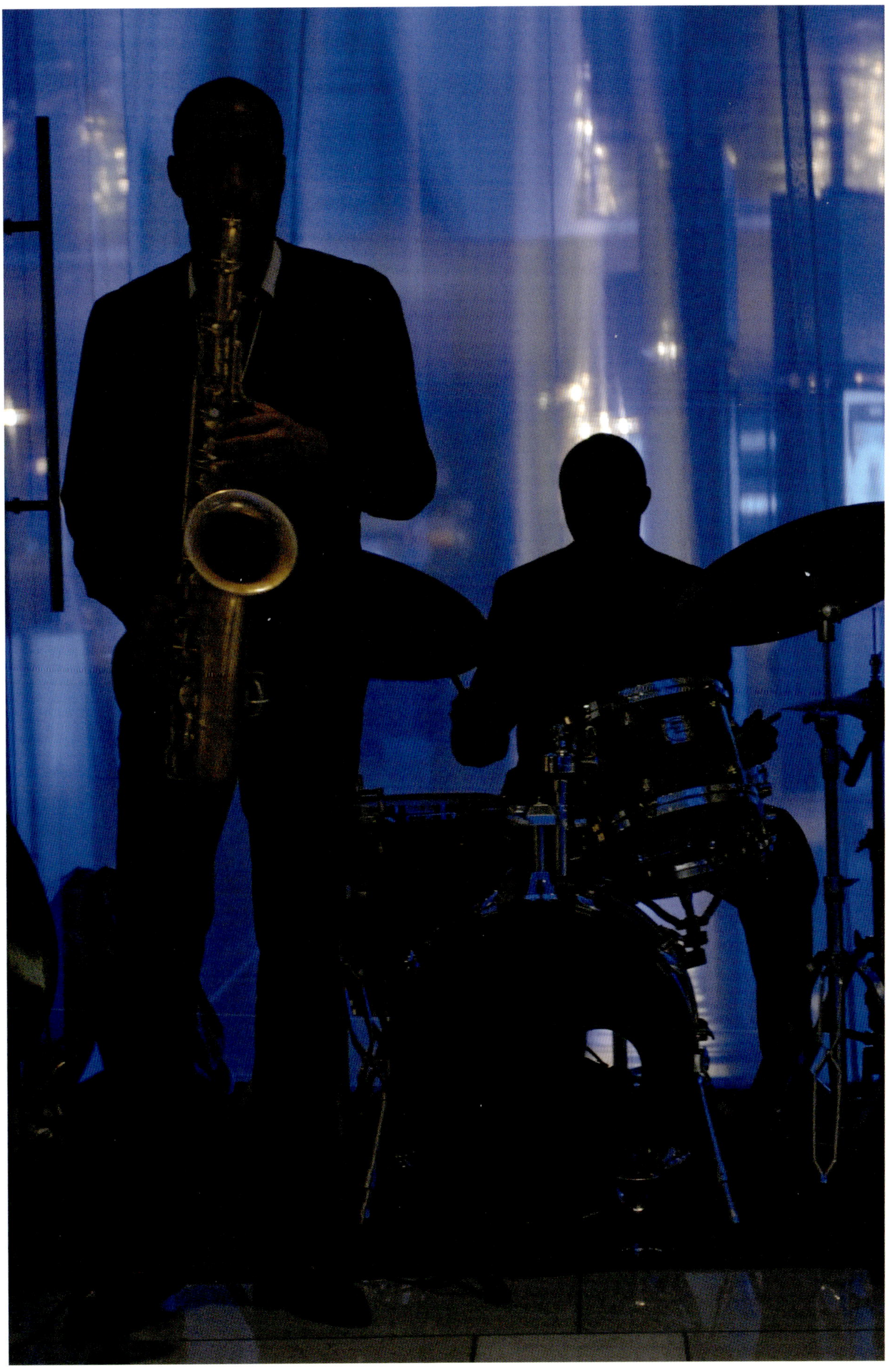

Walter and Willie, 2004

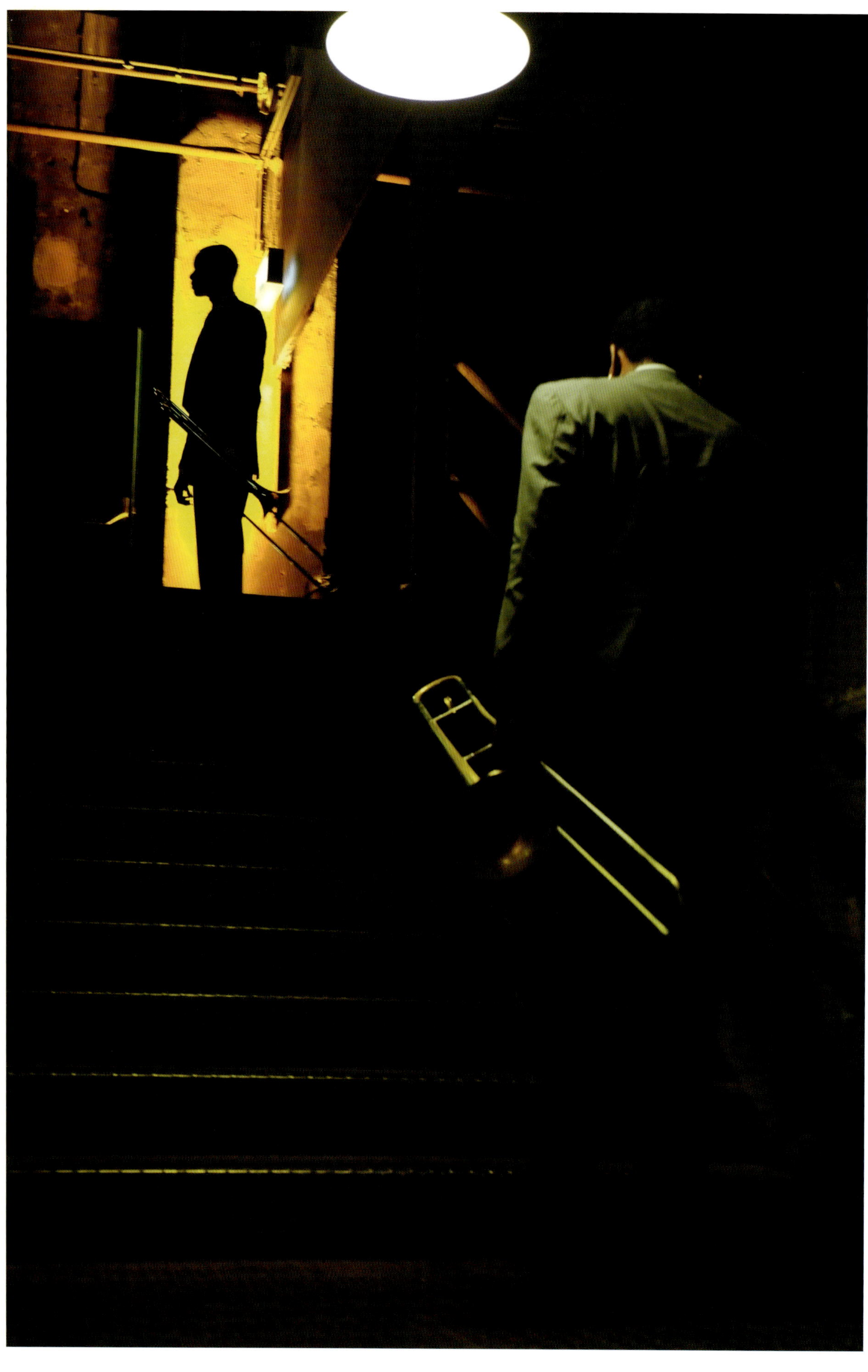

Bone and Silhouette, 2009

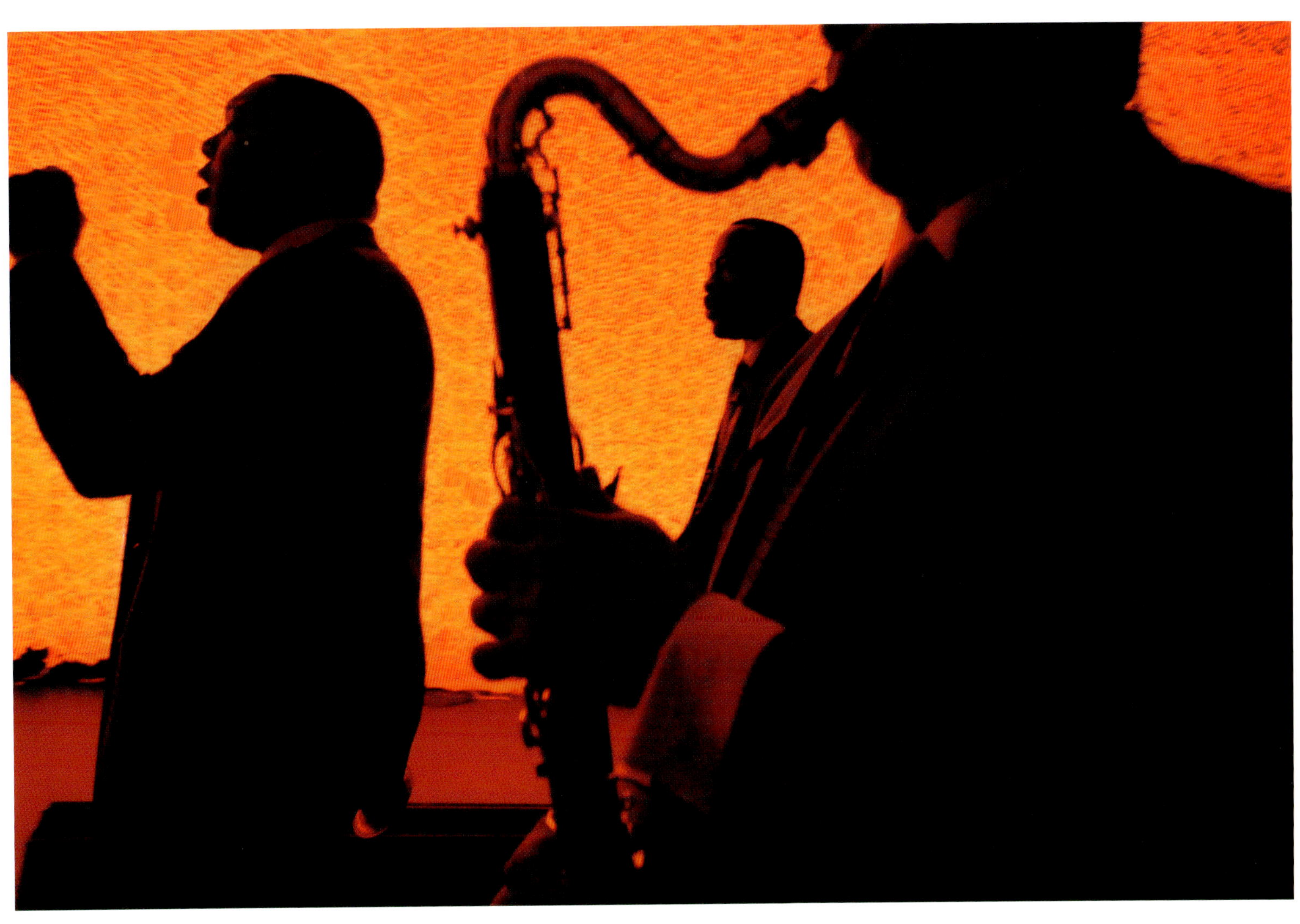

This page and following spread:
Blood on the Fields, 2014

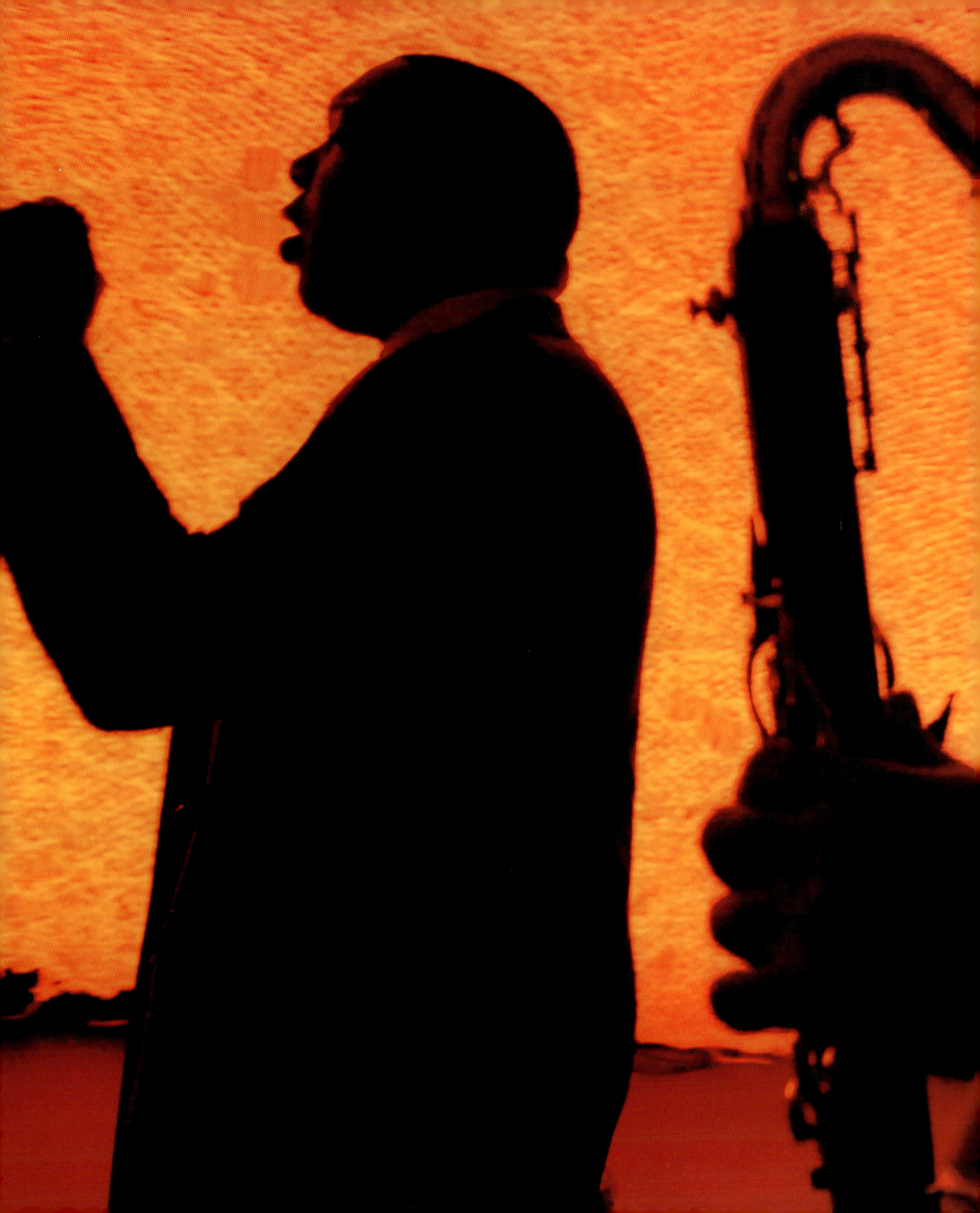

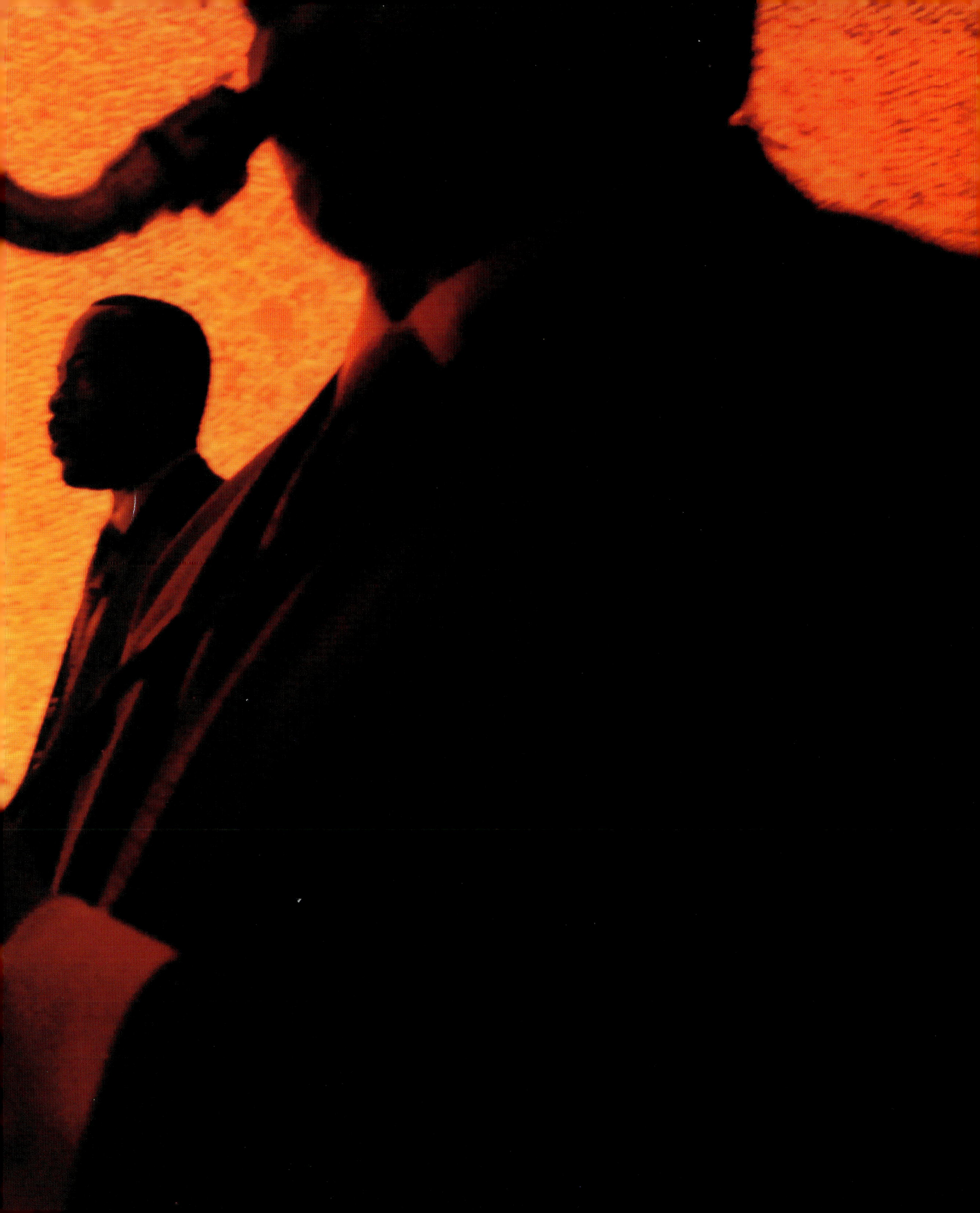

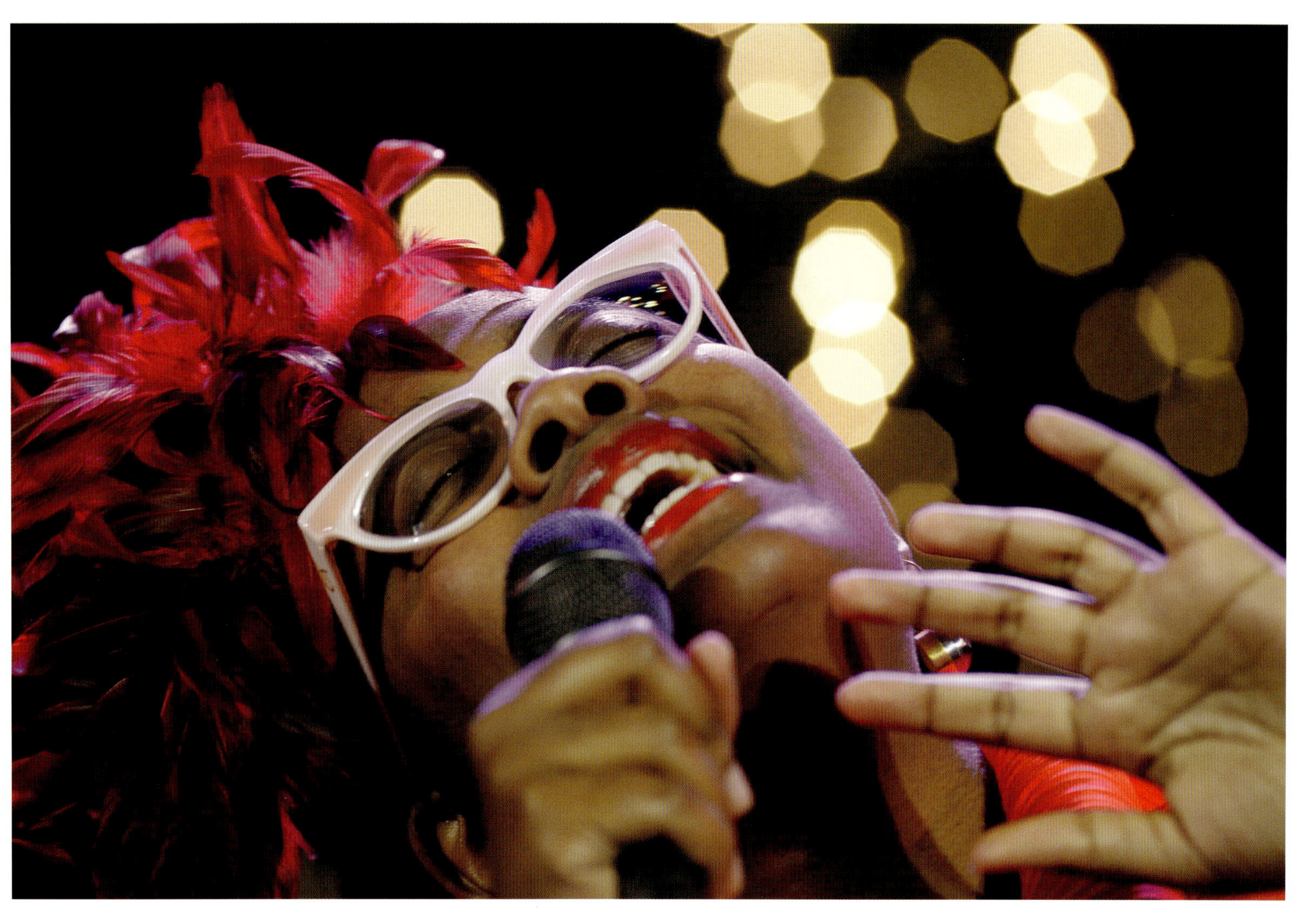

Cécile, New Year's Eve, 2016

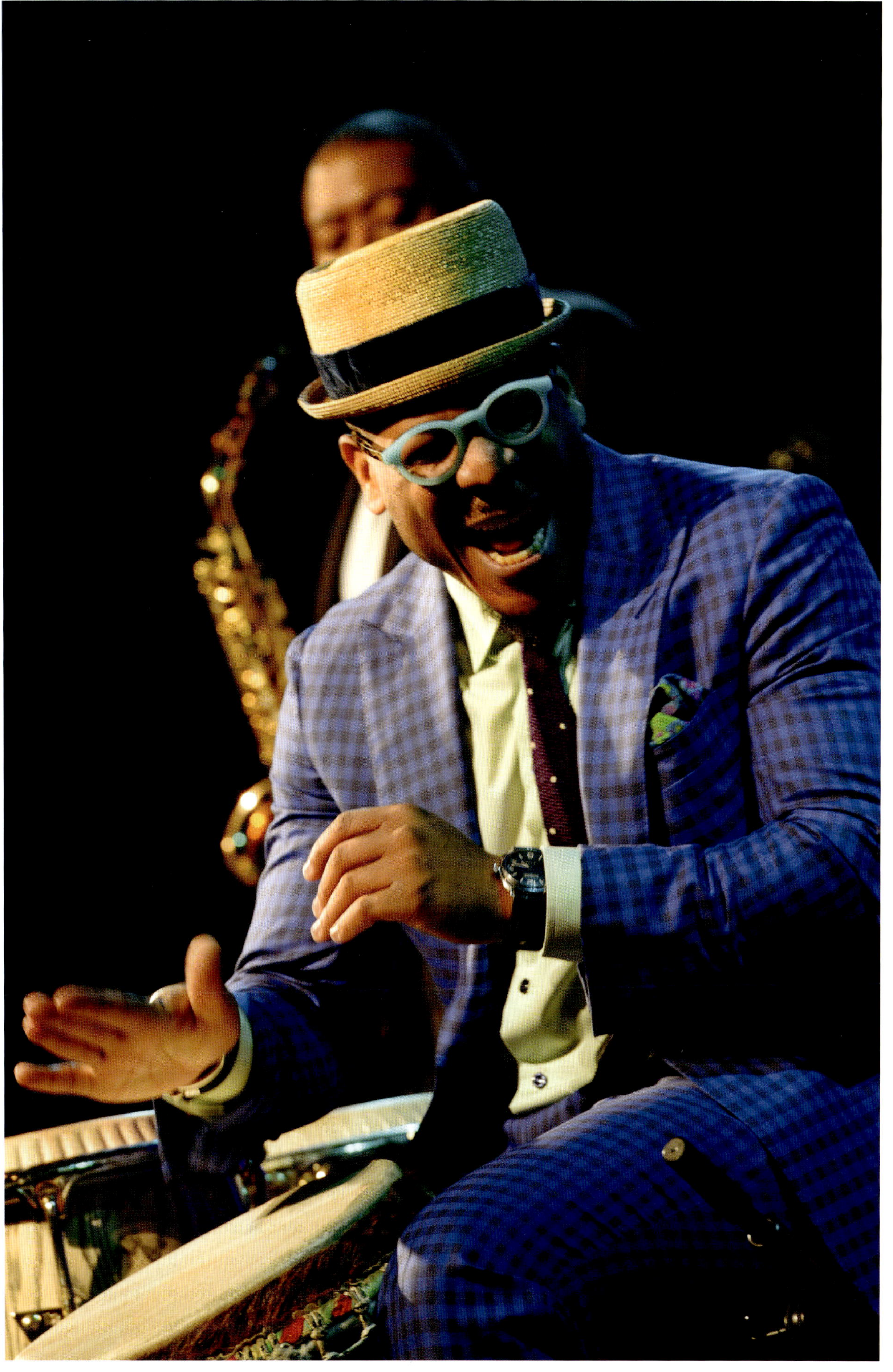

Etienne, 2017

Around the World: Cultures in Color

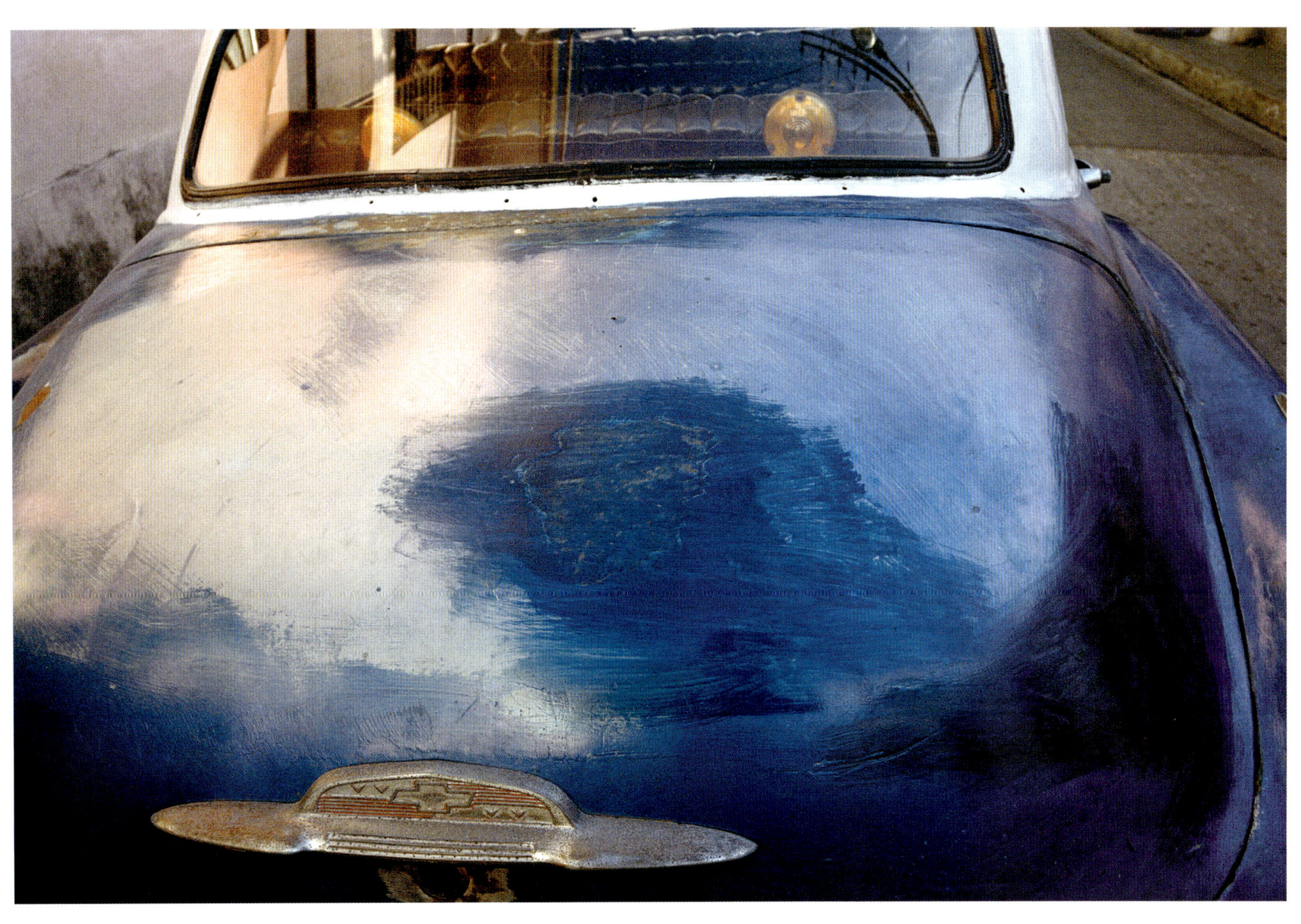

Blue Car, Havana, 2002

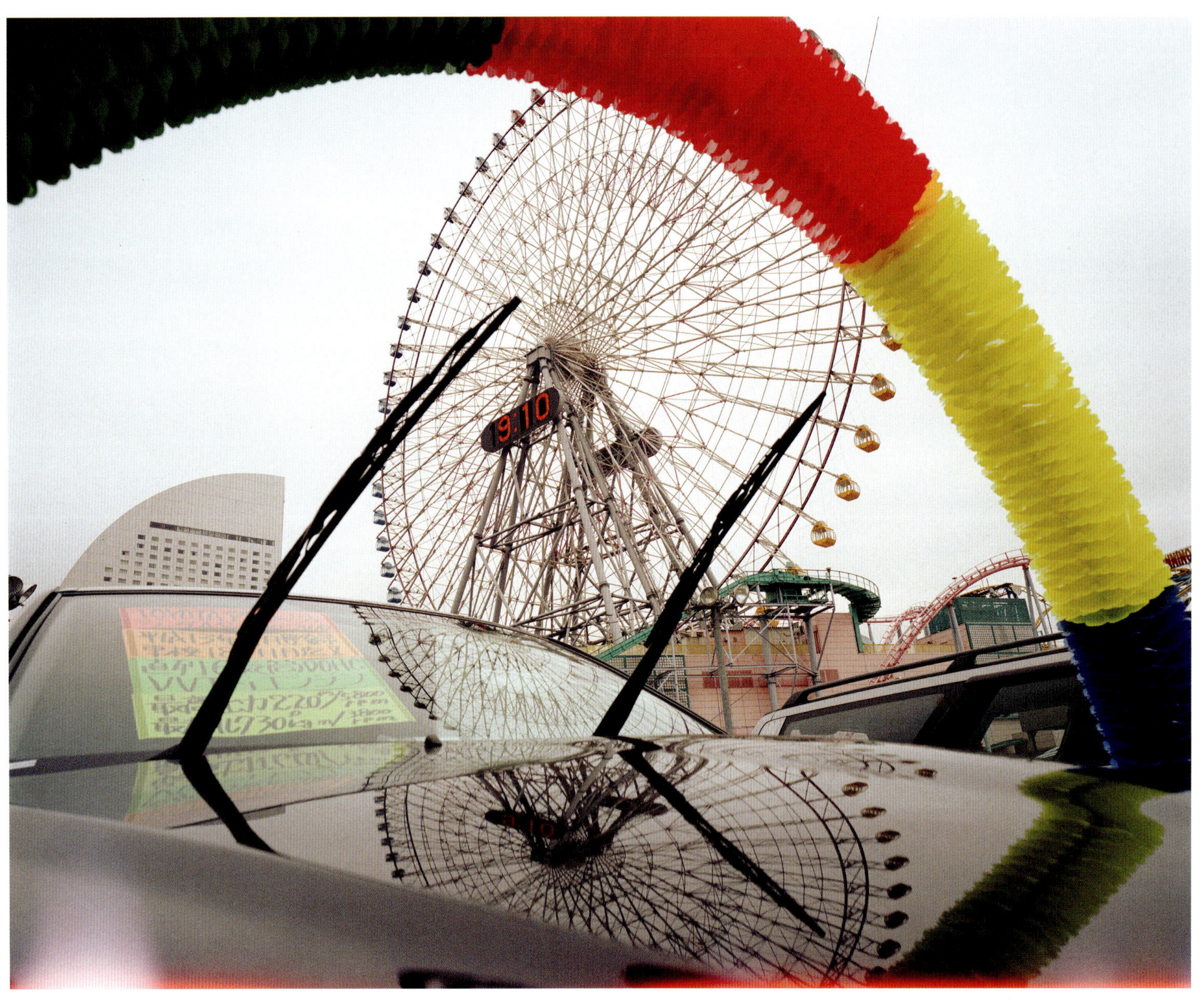

Yokohama, 2004

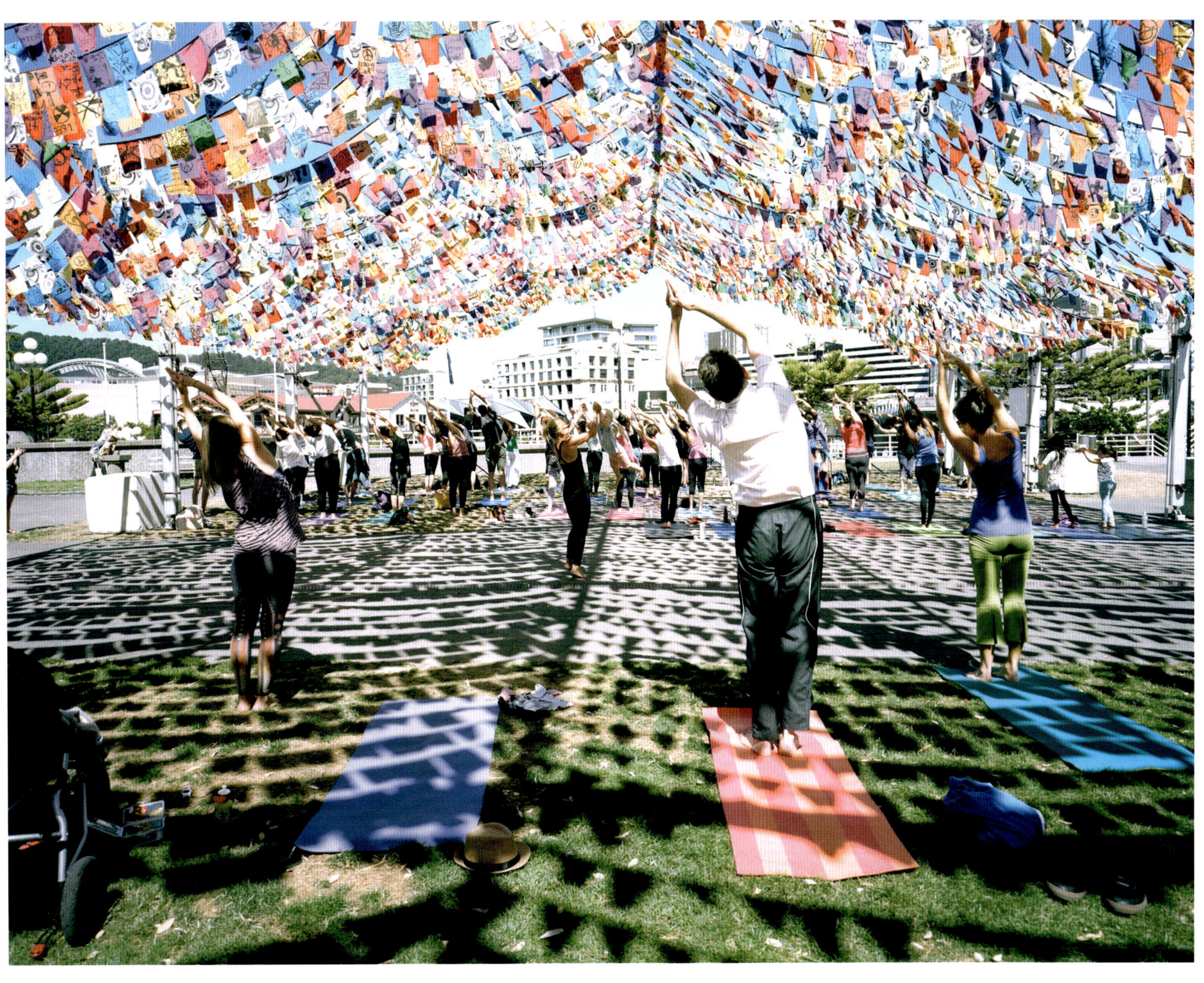

Auckland, 2016

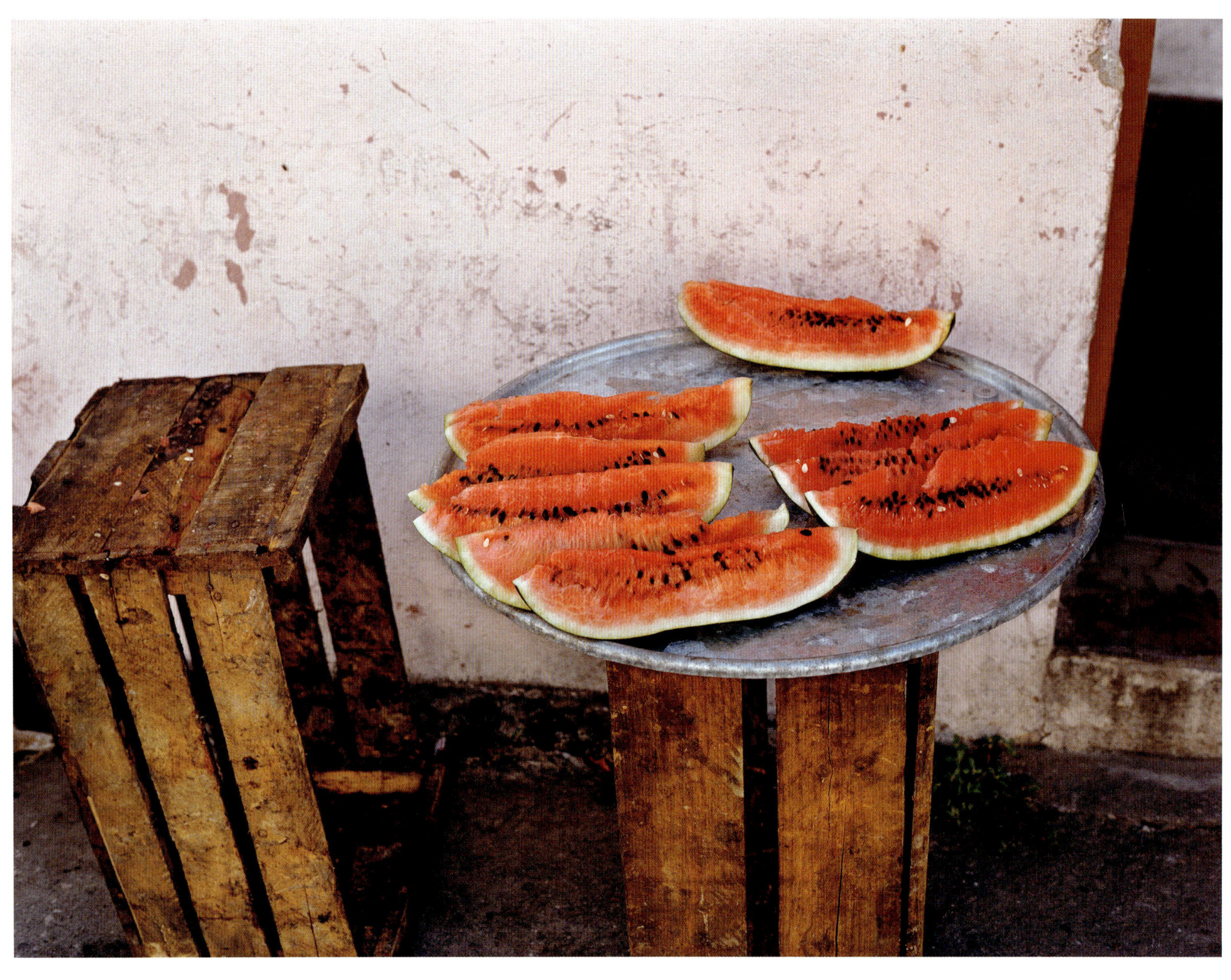

Watermelons, 2003

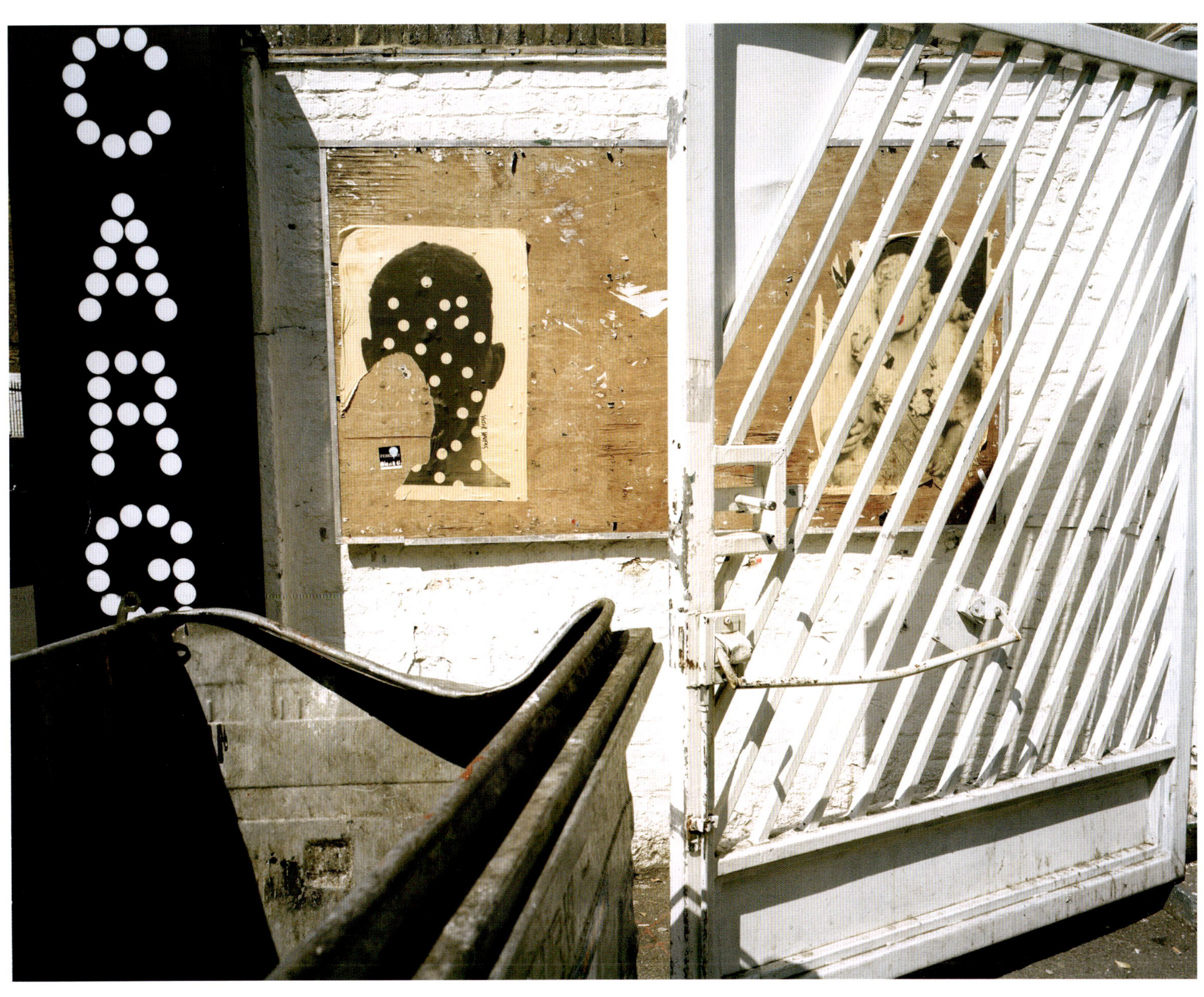

Cargo, England, 2020

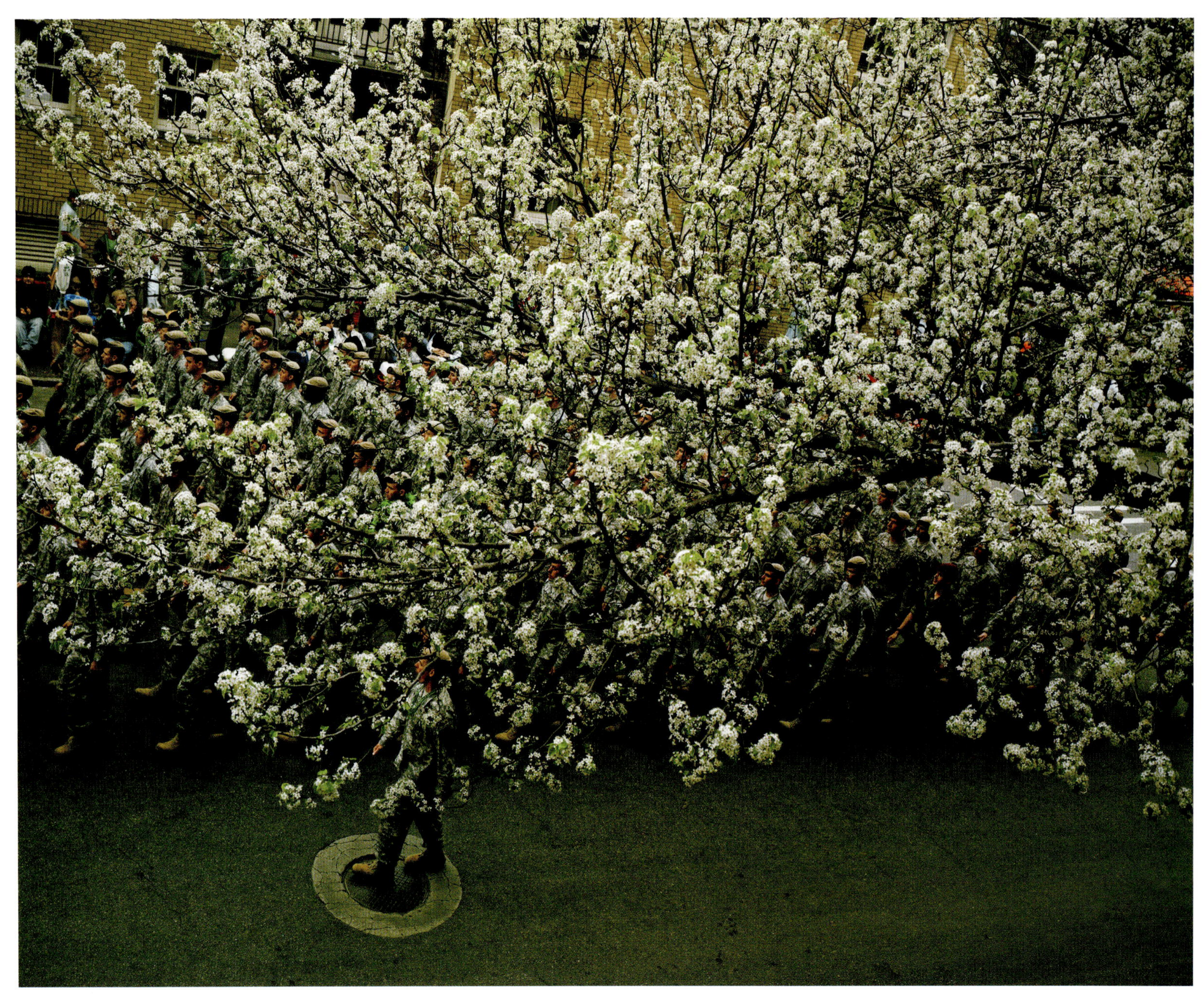

St. Patrick's Day, Savannah, Ga., 2012

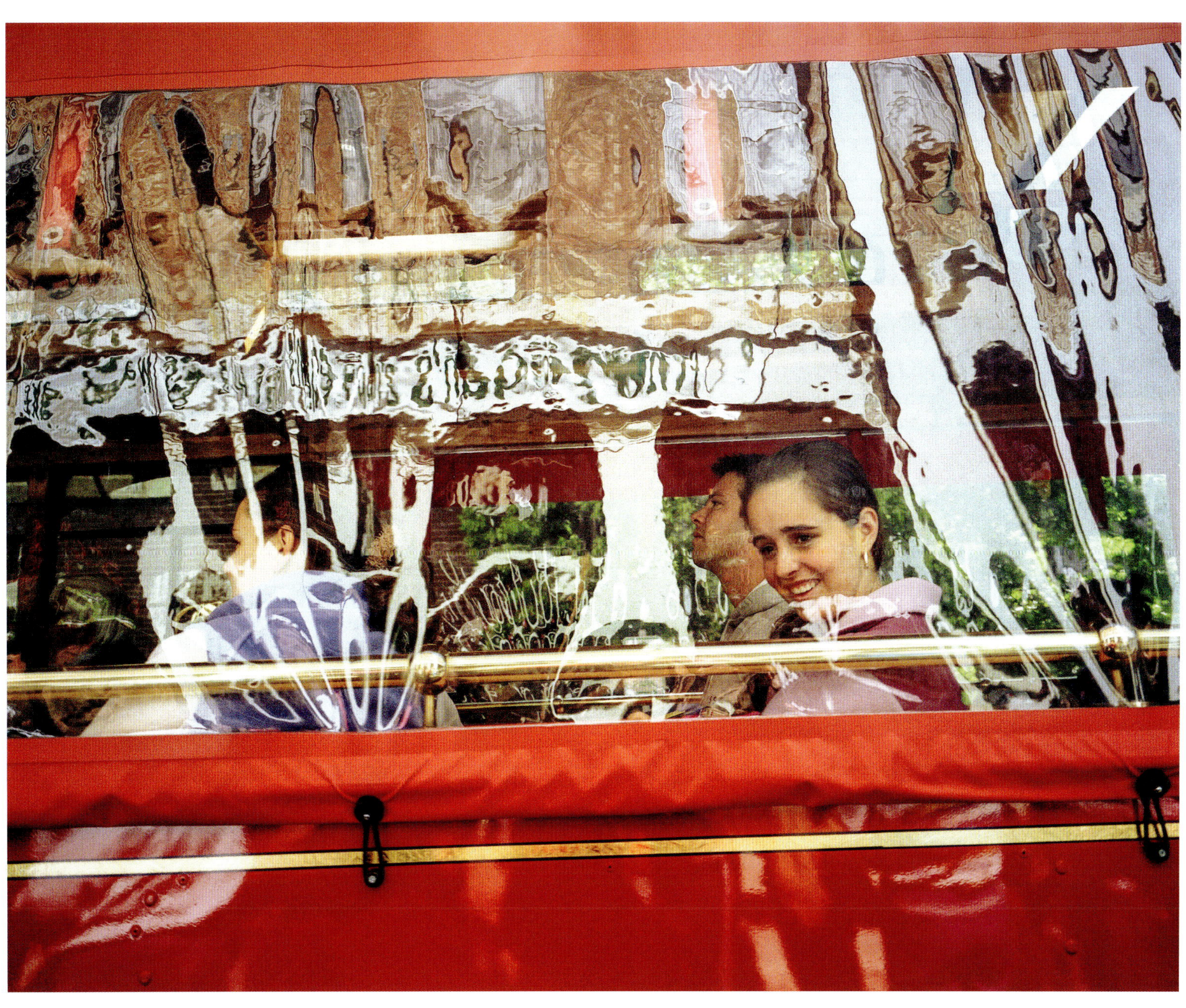

Savannah Tour Bus, 2006

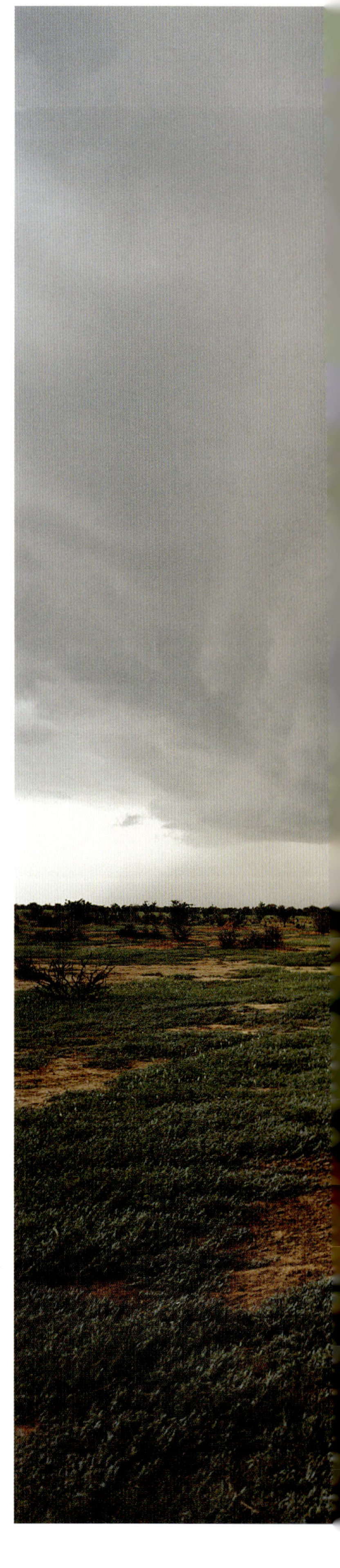

Three Young Camels, Mali, 2006

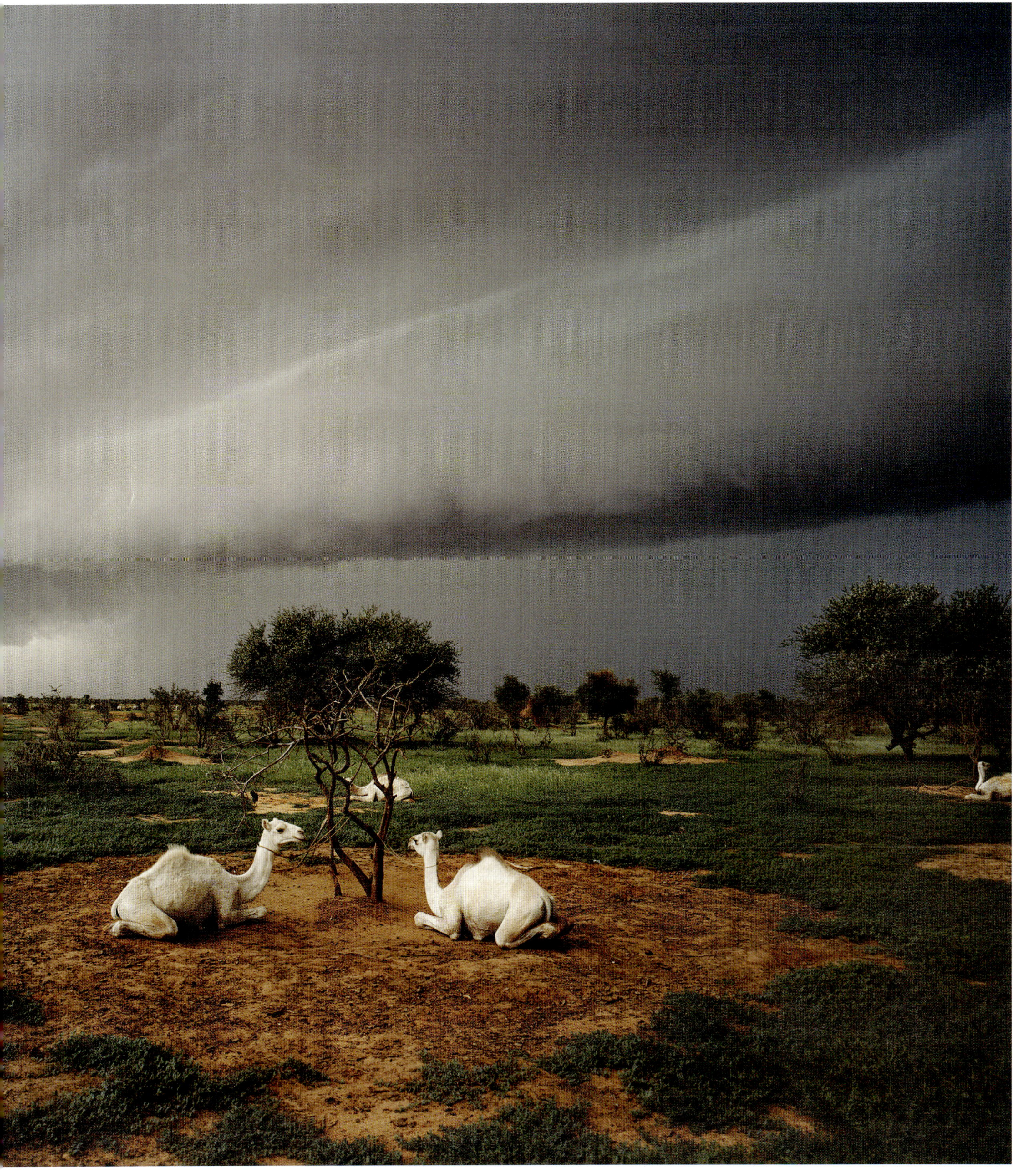

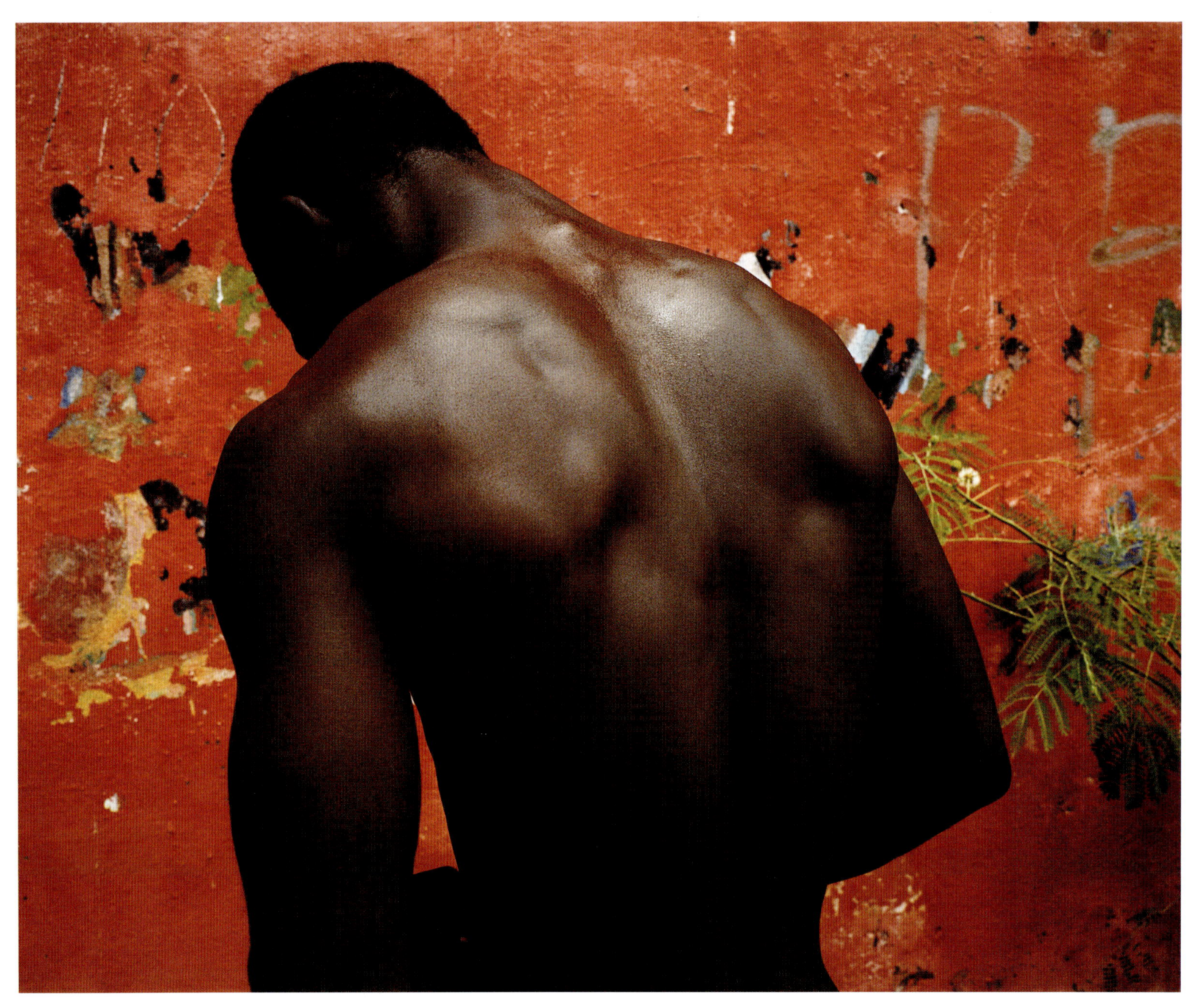

Gorée Island Painter, 2006

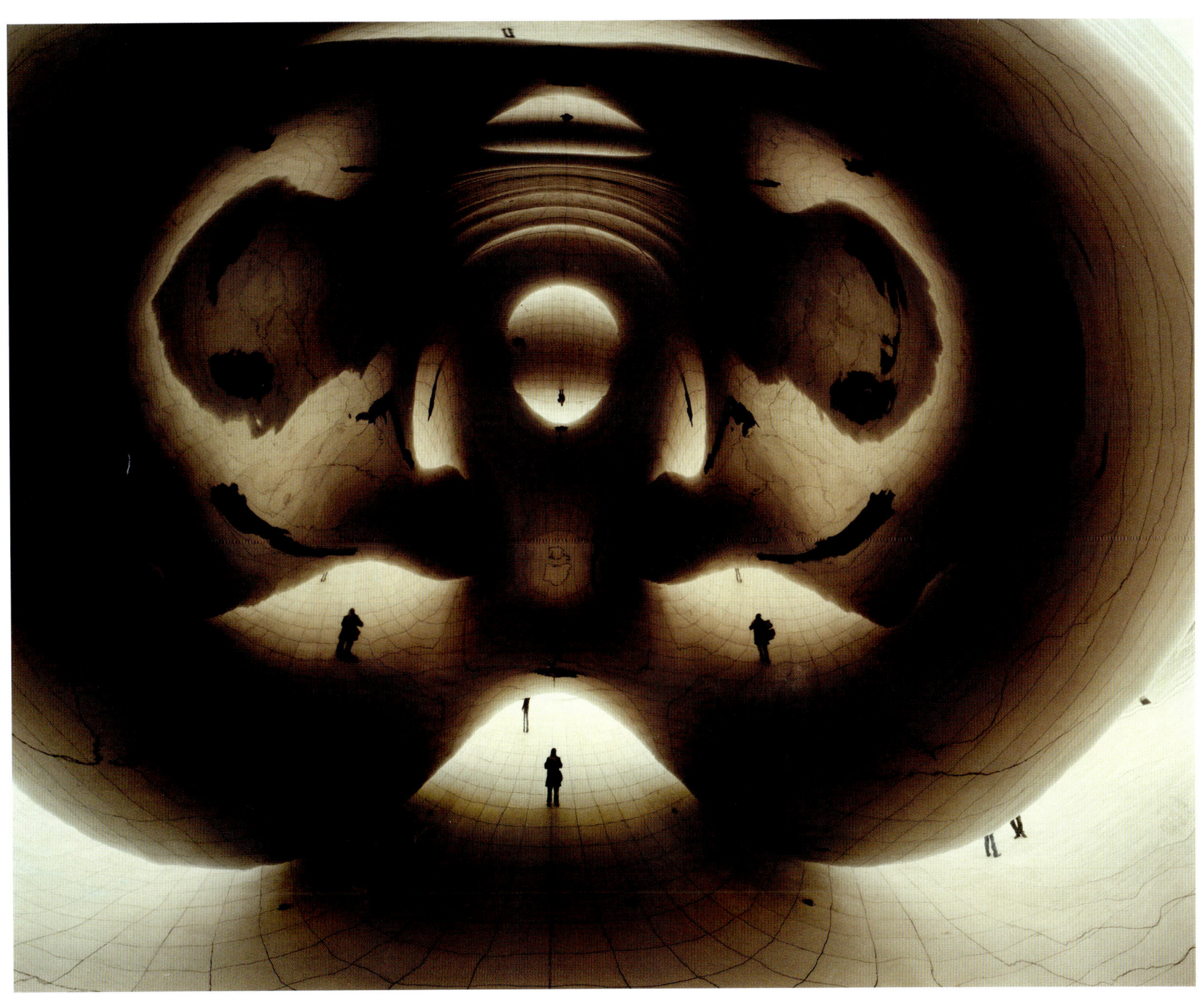

Bean, Chicago, 2018

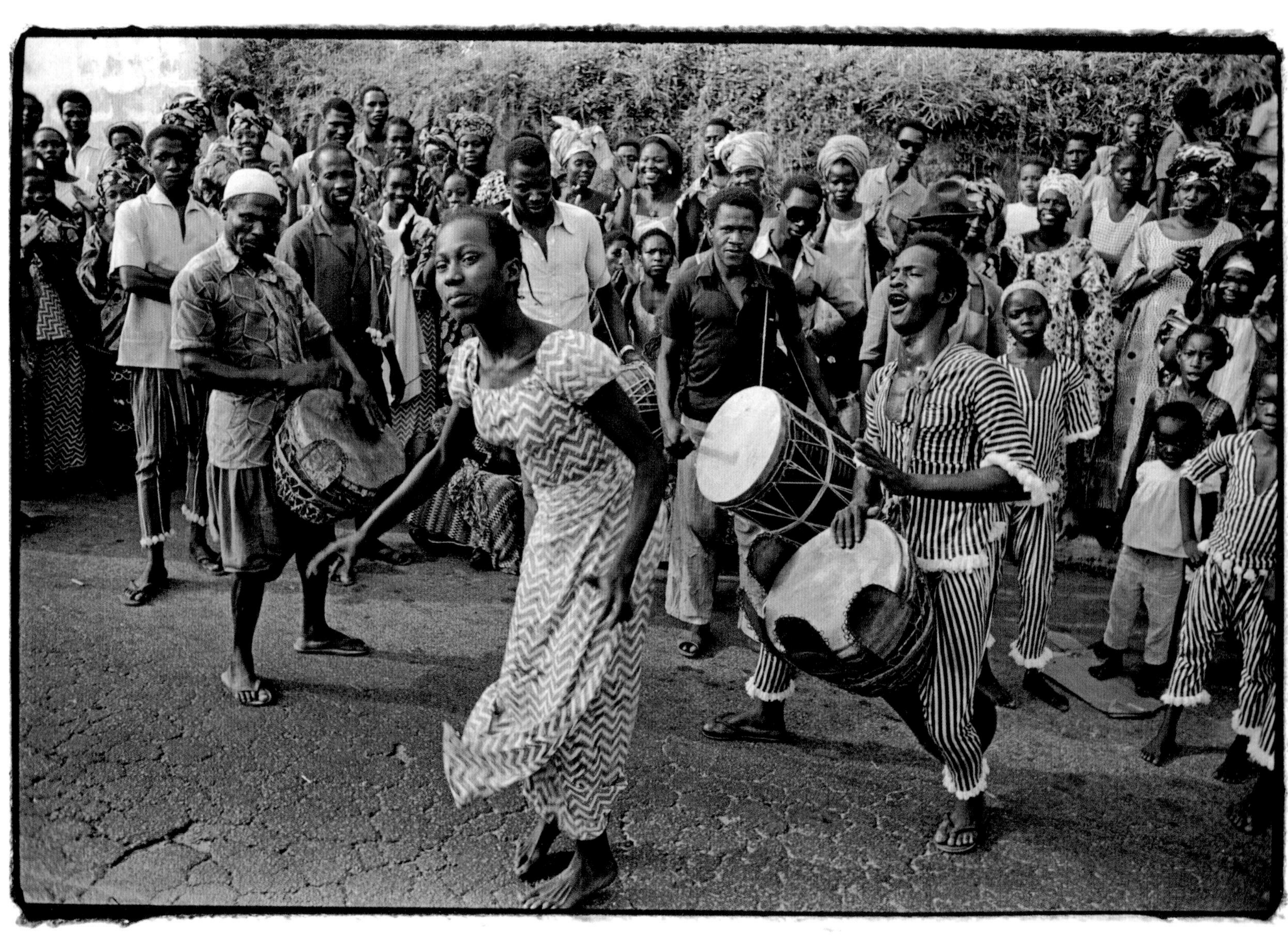

FRANK STEWART'S INTERNATIONAL LENS

Cheryl Finley

I think Frank wants to convey what his world is.

—Ruth Fine in "The Soul of a Jazz Man" by Colleen Walsh, *Harvard Gazette*, October 1, 2019

Frank Stewart's career in photography has spanned more than fifty years and encompassed a dedicated and exploratory practice on just about every continent, including international travel to capture indelible images of the human spirit: life, music, art, culture, and joy! Stewart began his career just as photography as a contemporary art medium was taking off in the art market and students began vying for spaces in BFA and MFA programs at some of the most coveted art schools in the nation. Stewart attended the School of the Art Institute of Chicago, where he was a student of the photographer Garry Winogrand, known for his rigorous, gritty, wide-angle street photography of everyday Americans. At the Cooper Union for the Advancement of Science and Art in New York City, where Stewart earned a BFA in 1975, he was exposed to some of the most exciting artists of the era, notably two seeming aesthetic opposites, Roy DeCarava and Joel Meyerowitz. DeCarava's exceptional control of black-and-white photography produced memorable street scenes in Harlem and photographs of jazz greats with deep intensity and high contrast, while Meyerowitz's masterful treatment of color in street photography, landscape, and other genres pioneered anew the possibilities for color photography in the 1970s. Stewart was particularly drawn to DeCarava's photography through his classic photo book, *The Sweet Flypaper of Life* (1955), depicting the story of a Harlem family with a narrative written by Langston Hughes. Of DeCarava's work, Stewart recalled, "I had never seen the black form depicted in such a manner—with dignity, pride, and humanity."[1] Cooper Union was known for experimentation and innovation, and these essential qualities have shaped Stewart's choice of subject matter and way of seeing. As a result, his oeuvre is characterized by an insistence on making connections between the global, through an international practice, and the local, through a conscious study of the capaciousness of the African diaspora around the Atlantic rim.

Stewart's first international field study took place in 1974, while he was a student in the Cooper Union Independent Study Program. He traveled to nearly ten nations in West Africa, including Liberia, Nigeria, Upper Volta, Mali, Togo, Dahomey, Côte d'Ivoire, and Ghana, where some of his first classic studies were made. His choice of sites coincided with a resurgent interest in sub-Saharan Africa on the part of African Americans as the impact of African liberation movements of the 1960s intersected with the Civil Rights, Black Arts, and Black Power movements of the same period in the United States. His exploration of Black art, culture, and music helped to deliver powerful images in Africa such as *Call and Response, Abidjan, Côte d'Ivoire* (1974, page 140). In that aptly titled work, Stewart captured a local performance with drummers and a dancer responding to their call. The title, referring to a foundational tenet

Call and Response, Abidjan, Côte d'Ivoire, 1974

of African and African American oral tradition, draws attention to the dancer's rhythmic body as she moves to the beat of the talking drums. Onlookers heed the call as well in this classic street photograph that would become a signature of the artist's practice in the years to come. For Stewart, street photography was a way to engage with and record people and their distinctive cultures, while the thought-provoking practice also served as fodder for other compositions, whether jazz photographs, abstract images, or pictures from the road.

Another photograph from Stewart's first trip to Côte d'Ivoire, *Tailor Shop, Abidjan, Côte d'Ivoire* (1974, page 143) cleverly demonstrates his range while also referring to some of the history of photography's pioneers, including Eugène Atget, known for his photo-essays of turn-of-the-twentieth-century Paris, including storefronts. In that minimal work, Stewart simply photographs a pair of trousers and a shirt, suspended like cardboard cutouts behind the plate-glass shopwindow. This work signals Stewart's penchant for abstraction early on, while also hinting at what would become his lifelong study of windows and abstract forms. This could be seen as early as 1971 in *Three Partitions* (page 113), an early window study with muted figures behind a dimly lit translucent window.

Stewart would return to Africa on many occasions, notably to Ghana in the late 1990s and early 2000s. He photographed most often in Mamfe, where culinary practices, daily routines, and cultural events were his subjects. In *Girl Reading, Mamfe, Ghana* (1997, page 20), Stewart focuses on a young blind girl intently reading braille written on a single piece of paper, her determination shown by the expression on her face and caringly delivered by the artist's framing of her silhouette against a light background. *Clock of the Earth, Mamfe, Ghana,* (1998, page 83) shows three women carrying head burdens as they walk down a dirt road, a daily routine of transporting foodstuffs and water, and a classic profile of female domestic labor in West Africa. In *Abena Pounding Fufu, Mamfe, Ghana* (2000, page 87), the artist records the traditional way cassava or yam is pounded into *fufu*, a starchy staple of West African cuisine. In Ghana, Stewart was drawn to cultural practices, as shown in *Getting the Spirit II, Mamfe, Ghana* (1998, page 84) and the simple beauty of everyday life. *Boy and Two Girls, Mamfe, Ghana* (2004, page 89), riffs on the work of Stewart's mentor, DeCarava, in its contrast of black and white and attention to youthful delights.

Ghana and Senegal were magnets for Stewart due to their rich historic sites of memory related to the transatlantic slave trade. In Ghana, there were more than sixty fortified structures used to operate slaving ventures controlled by Europeans, including outfitting slave ships and holding enslaved Africans captive until ships were full and ready to sail across the Atlantic. The most notorious of these include Cape Coast and Elmina, structures often called "castles" due to their enormous size and multiple functions. *Slave Castle, Cape Coast, Ghana* (2004, page 88) shows the brutality and inhumanity of the slave trade with remnants of metal bars demonstrating how millions of people were held and stolen away against their will. Stewart photographed Cape Coast and Elmina on many occasions, almost as a rite of passage, delivering necessary and indelible images of African, African American, and African diasporic history. Designated as UNESCO World Heritage monuments in the 1970s, Cape Coast and Elmina in Ghana and Gorée Island in Senegal are magnets for diasporic Africans, drawing many "back" to Africa for pilgrimages to these powerful sites of memory.

In Senegal, Stewart's vibrant photograph *Gorée Island Painter* (2006, page 138) depicts a man's glistening back against a visibly worn and graffitied crimson facade at the site of another key entrepôt for the slave trade just three kilometers off the coast of Dakar in Senegal. The symbolism of the man's bare back was not lost on Stewart and is seen through the history of slavery and the unforgettable image of torture captured by the famous Civil War–era photograph of Sargent Peter's (formerly identified as "Gordon") whipped back.[2] Widely circulated as a carte de visite, it was used to enlist supporters in the abolitionist cause. Once again, in *Gorée Island Painter*, Stewart positions a figure against a relatively monochrome background,

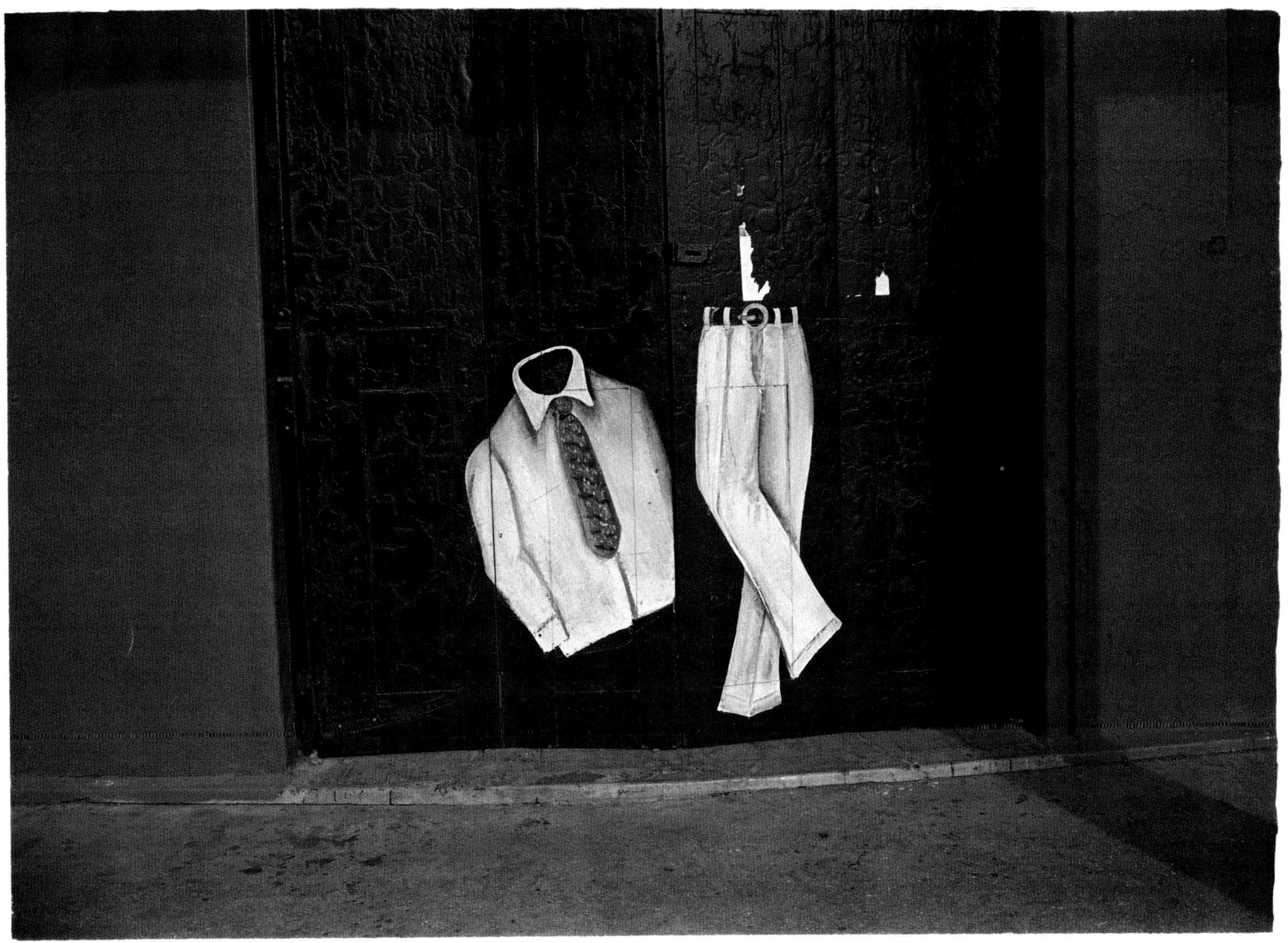

Tailor Shop, Abidjan, Côte d'Ivoire, 1974

creating a silhouette and proposing a suture of layered forms, recalling the work of two other important artist mentors, painter Jack Whitten, who was one of his teachers at Cooper Union, and painter/collagist Romare Bearden, for whom Stewart worked from 1975 until his passing in 1988.

Stewart graduated from the Cooper Union in 1975 as the influential Black Arts Movement began to fade.[3] The following year, he showed his work alongside that of Jeanne Moutoussamy-Ashe and Dawoud Bey in *Sun People*, a critically acclaimed exhibition at the Weusi Gallery on Strivers' Row in Harlem. *Weusi*, the Swahili word meaning "black," was a Harlem-based artists' collective formed in 1965 dedicated to making work inspired by African themes. It was one of a handful of artists' collectives that were formed during the Black Arts Movement; another was the Kamoinge Workshop, established in 1963 by two groups of photographers in New York, who sought to take control of and reverse the largely negative portrayals of social issues within Black communities through artistic innovation. They chose the Kenyan Kikuyu name Kamoinge, meaning working together, to inspire artistic empowerment and promoted mentorship from seasoned photographers, including Henri Cartier-Bresson, Gordon Parks, and Roy DeCarava. In weekly meetings, often centered around jazz, improvisation, or social issues, the members of Kamoinge set aesthetic goals based on shooting, timing, framing, assignments, and darkroom

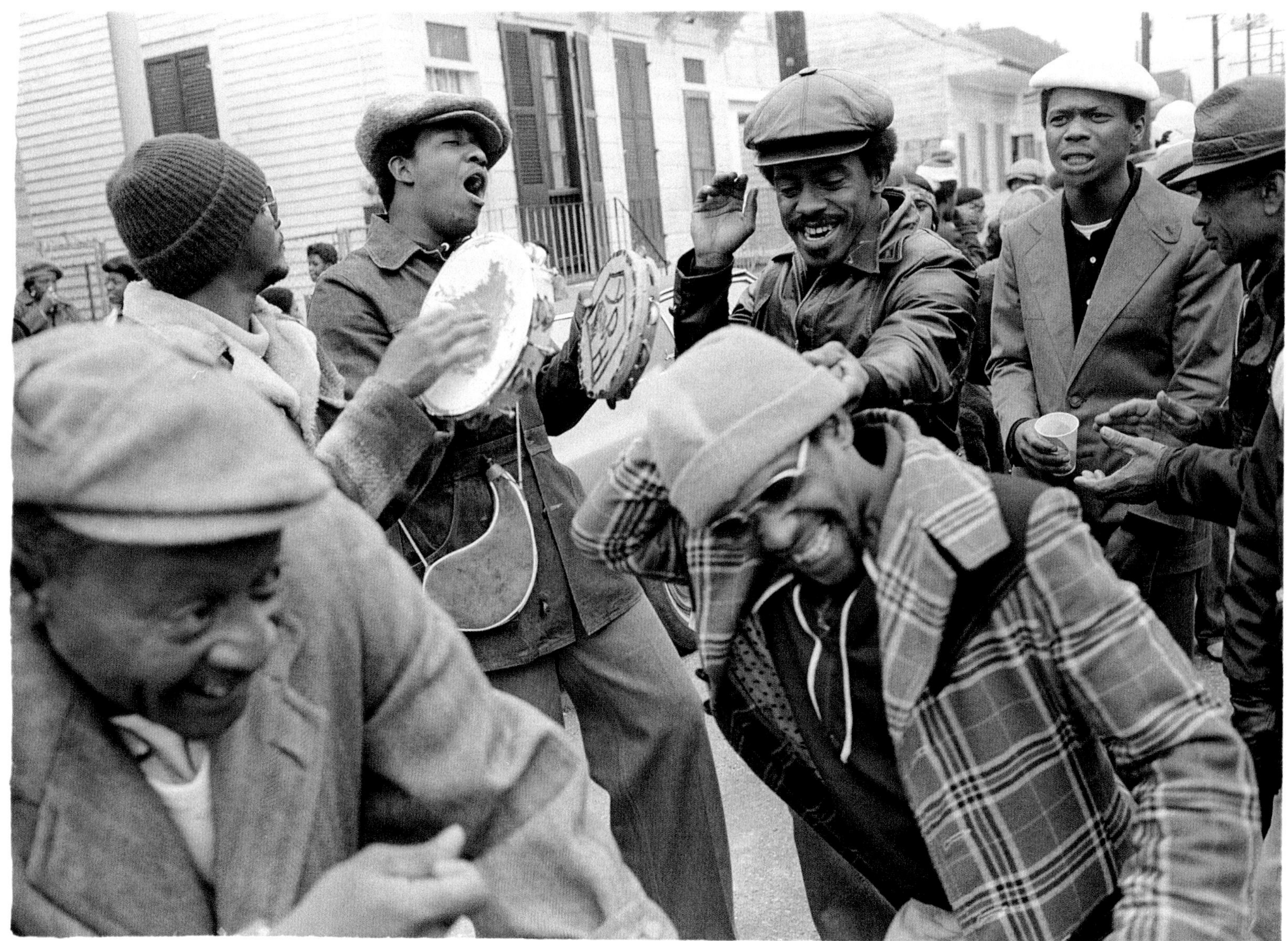

techniques. Stewart was invited to join Kamoinge in 1982, and his choice to frame his works within the viewfinder is but one way Kamoinge has affirmed his practice. Other significant ways Kamoinge has paralleled Stewart's work over the years include its focus on African diaspora themes, as well as a call for global (diasporic) travel.

Upon graduation from Cooper Union, Stewart accepted a life-changing job shooting stills for a documentary based on the landmark exhibition *Two Centuries of Black American Art*, a 1976 bicentennial show at the Los Angeles County Museum of Art curated by David C. Driskell. Stewart met many of the most important African American artists of the day in this role, including Bearden, Jacob Lawrence, and Alma W. Thomas, whom he photographed. This job was a springboard to future opportunities, presenting a wide network of African American artists who would mentor Stewart in the years to come.

New Orleans has been a recurring site of photographic interest for Stewart, a fertile ground of African American and African diaspora history and culture with a direct link to the ancestors. The city's connection to Africa long has appealed to the artist, who has recorded its celebrations, burial rites, and musical traditions, notably jazz. He first photographed there in 1976 for a project on the Mardi Gras Indians, a secretive organization drawn from African American communities in

Calling the Indians Out, 1978

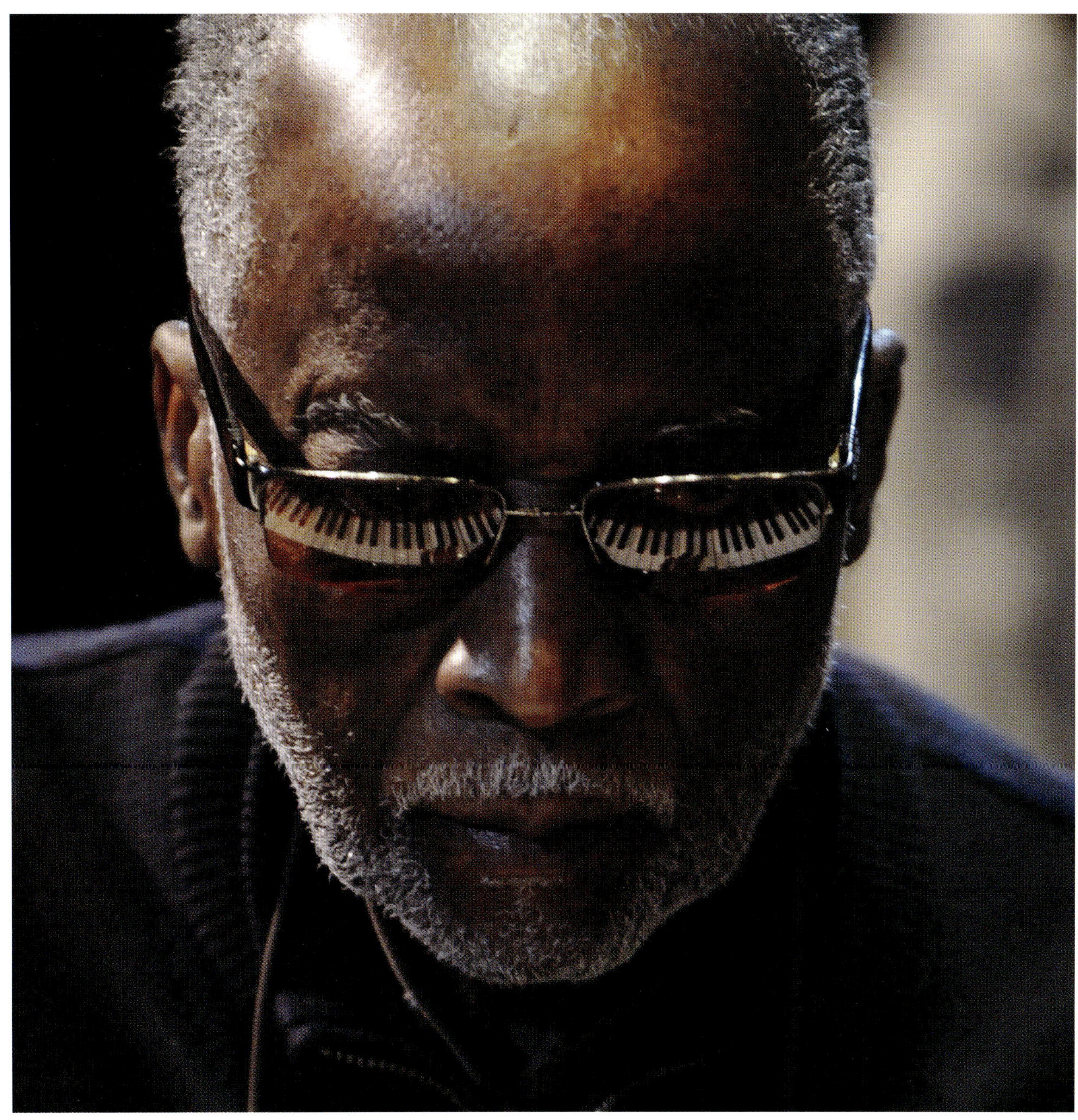

Ahmad Jamal, 2013

New Orleans who were prevented from participating in mainstream Mardi Gras parades due to racism and Jim Crow segregation. They named themselves in honor of the Native Americans who frequently took in and aided African Americans escaping from slavery in the seventeenth, eighteenth, and nineteenth centuries. Over the years, the Mardi Gras Indians developed their own style of costuming, dancing, and naming, using neighborhood street names or the names of Native American groups to identify their "krewes," or Mardi Gras organizations. Stewart returned to New Orleans to photograph the Mardi Gras Indians again in 1978 for *Calling the Indians Out* (1978, page 144), a lively portrayal of their distinctive costumed street procession. *Untitled* (from the *Second Line* series) (1976, page 48) shows a woman dancing with a decorated parasol and the vitality of the city's celebrated brand of funerary rites. She is part of a famed second line of revelers led by a grand marshal and accompanied by a jazz band. New Orleans' second line jazz funerals and celebrations also originated in Black communities, and they share with the Mardi Gras Indian tradition a history related to offering social aid to freed slaves. Nearly thirty years later, Stewart returned to shoot the devastation of many historically Black neighborhoods and homes in the aftermath of Hurricane Katrina. Starting in 2005, he produced heart-wrenching images of loss with attention to abstract detail, such as *Katrina: Hammond B-3, 9th Ward, New Orleans* (2007, page 159). Stewart, like many other artists, often favors the mode of abstraction to portray difficult events and painful histories, offering the viewer (and the artist) space for introspection, understanding, and compassion that figuration and realism often do not allow.

Stewart first traveled to Cuba in 1977 at the invitation of the Cuban government through the New York City–based Center for Cuban Studies. He traveled throughout the island for a period of one month along with seven North American photographers. *Communist Windows, Havana* (1977, page 147) is a time capsule of the era, an abstract, layered work showing the Cuban flag with superimposed images of communist leaders. Part of Stewart's ongoing *Windows* series, this work stands apart from the artist's later photographic explorations of Cuba. He returned to Santiago de Cuba and Havana to document different forms of African-derived music and dance, including salsa and conga. In these instances, Stewart's camera was trained on the details. In *Going for Salsa, Santiago de Cuba* (2003, page 91), he shares a glimpse of two men carrying a drum, a detail of a bigger picture. *Callejón de Hamel, Havana* (2002, page 97), on the other hand, shows the response to the beat of the drum as a couple dances to the groove! Making a connection between Santiago and New Orleans, Stewart also photographed the *Santiago Carnival* (2003, page 96), showing how the legacy of slavery, through the dispersion and retention of music, religion, art, and culture, connects Africa to Cuba to New Orleans.

Stewart has toured the world with jazz artists since as far back as 1975 with Ahmad Jamal, whose image he captured in 2013 with the reflection of piano keys in his glasses. Stewart met Wynton Marsalis in 1989 and has traveled with him regularly. From 1993 through 2019, as senior staff photographer for Jazz at Lincoln Center, Stewart traveled globally with the world's leading jazz musicians creating memorable abstract, documentary, and portrait photographs of the musicians and their performances. While on tour, Stewart frequently picks up on recurring series—as he did with the series *Windows* in the elusively undulating *Perugia* (1996, page 115)—or discovers new themes. In addition to frequent trips to Europe and the Americas, Stewart has traveled to Korea, China, Japan, and New Zealand, where he has continued to photograph unique and unrivaled subjects. Many of these more recent works are in color, and often they portray abstract geometric forms highlighted by vibrant colors or patterns, such as *Yokohama* (2004, page 130), *Auckland* (2016, page 131), and *Cargo, England* (2020, page 133).

Stewart's prolific career has shone a spotlight on the importance of international contemporary photography, highlighting global connections across the African diaspora through jazz music, abstract work, self-portraiture, and street photography. His 1986 self-portrait taken in the Dominican Republic (page 108) commands symmetries and layers meaning. His dedication to exploration and to pushing the limits of the medium of photography has produced an oeuvre worthy of further study by future generations. To see the world through Stewart's lens is to understand the world in a nuanced light reflecting compassion, knowledge, and purpose.

1 "Behind the Lens: An Interview with Frank Stewart," *Jazz Blog*, November 18, 2015. https://www.jazz.org/blog/behind-the-lens-an-interview-with-frank-stewart/

2 https://npg.si.edu/learn/classroom-resource/gordon-lifedates-unknown

3 The Black Arts Movement was a key arts and advocacy movement of the late twentieth century, spurred by the activism of the March on Washington for Jobs and Freedom in August 1963 and later solidified by the assassinations of Malcolm X in 1965 and Martin Luther King, Jr., in 1968. Artists, writers, and performers created collectives, such as Kamoinge and Spiral (both established in 1963) to advocate for Black artistic representation in mainstream museums and galleries, while frequently creating figurative works aligned with African and African diasporic themes.

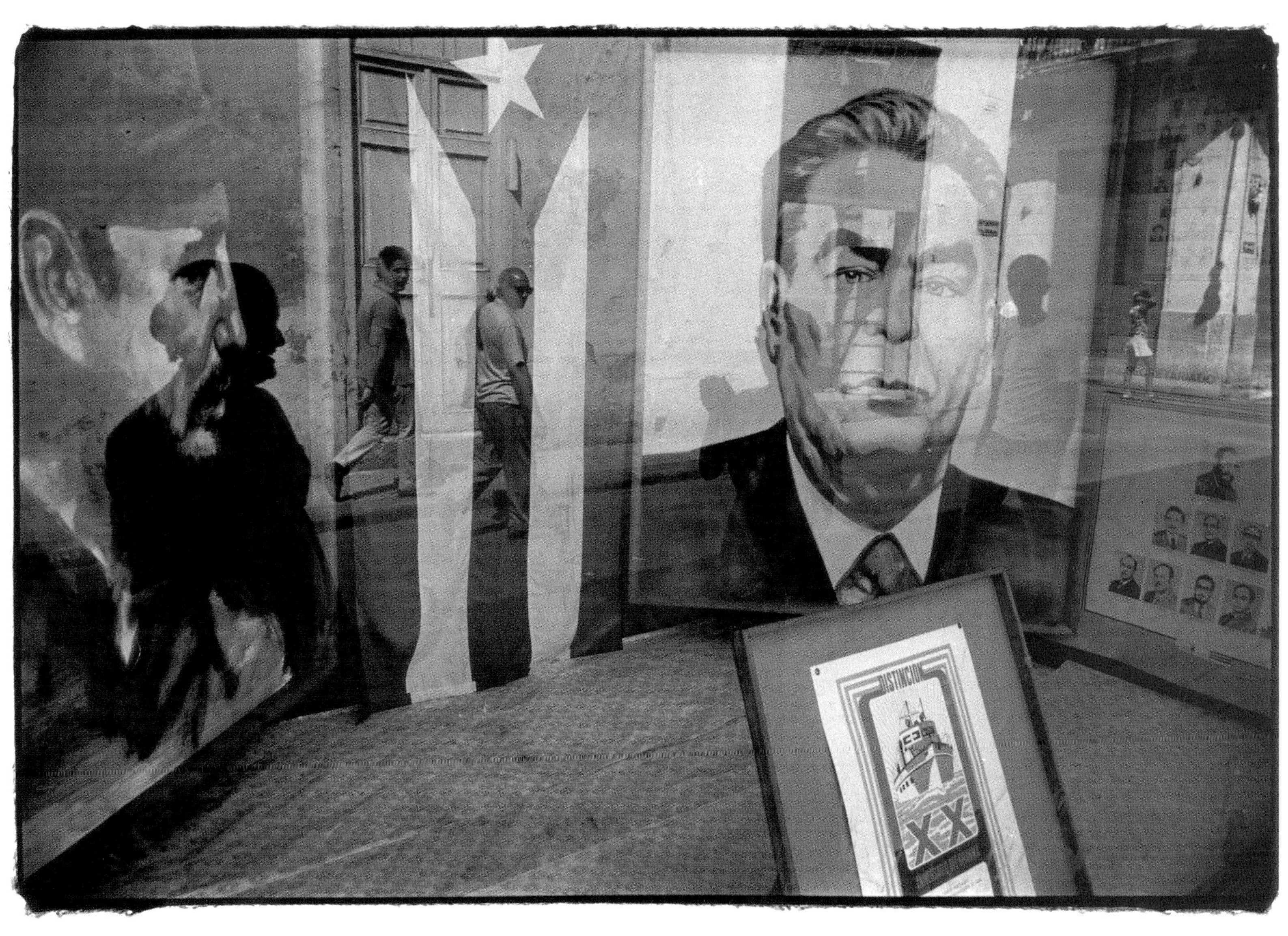

Communist Windows,
Havana, 1977

Drawings: The Photographer's Sketchbook

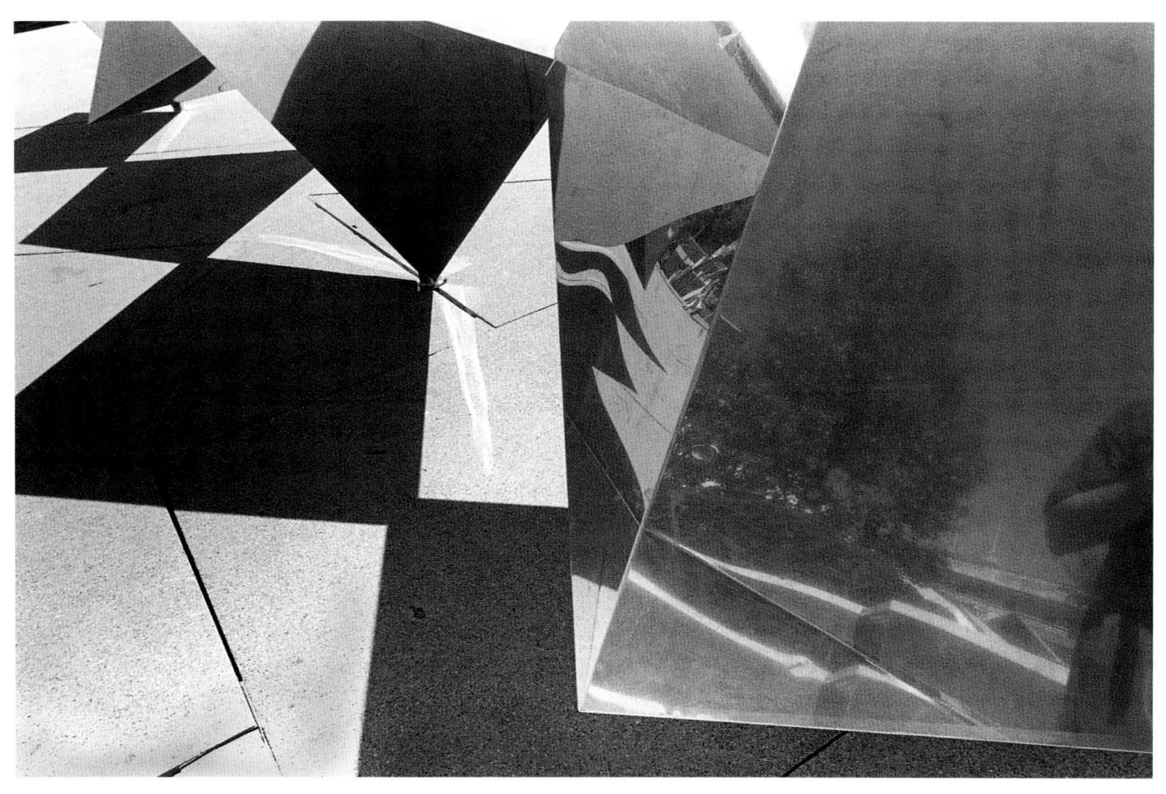

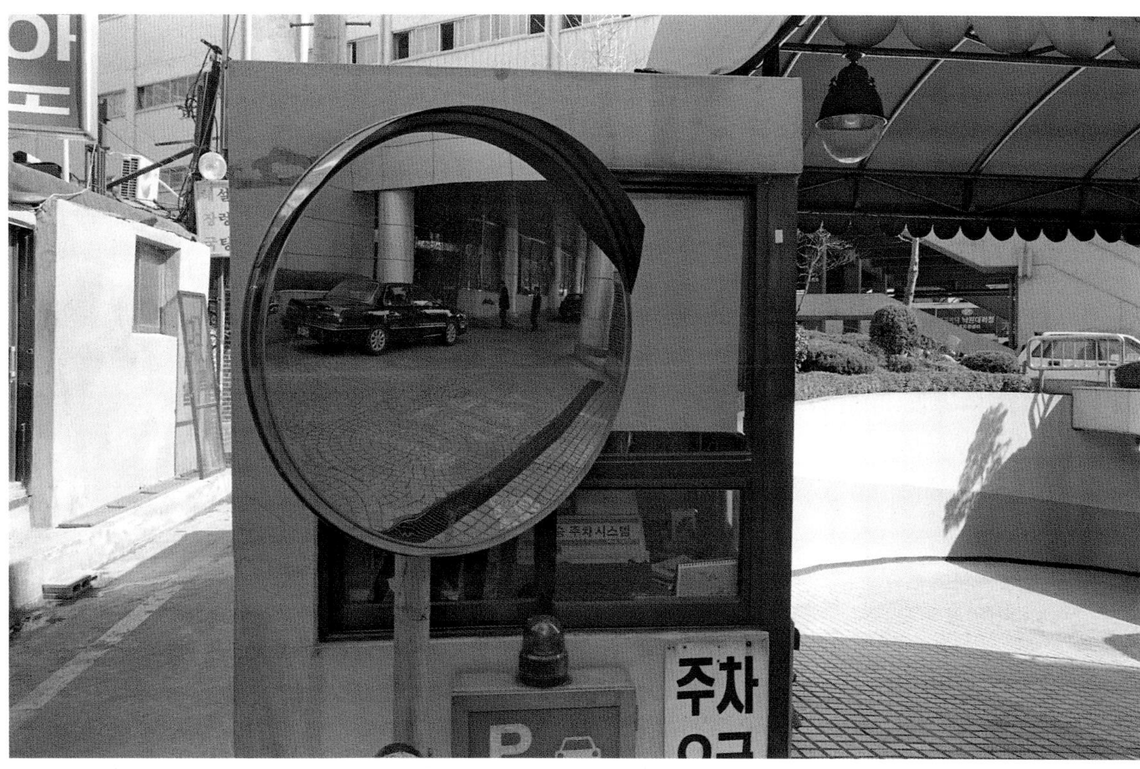

Lisbon, 1998

Seoul, 1998

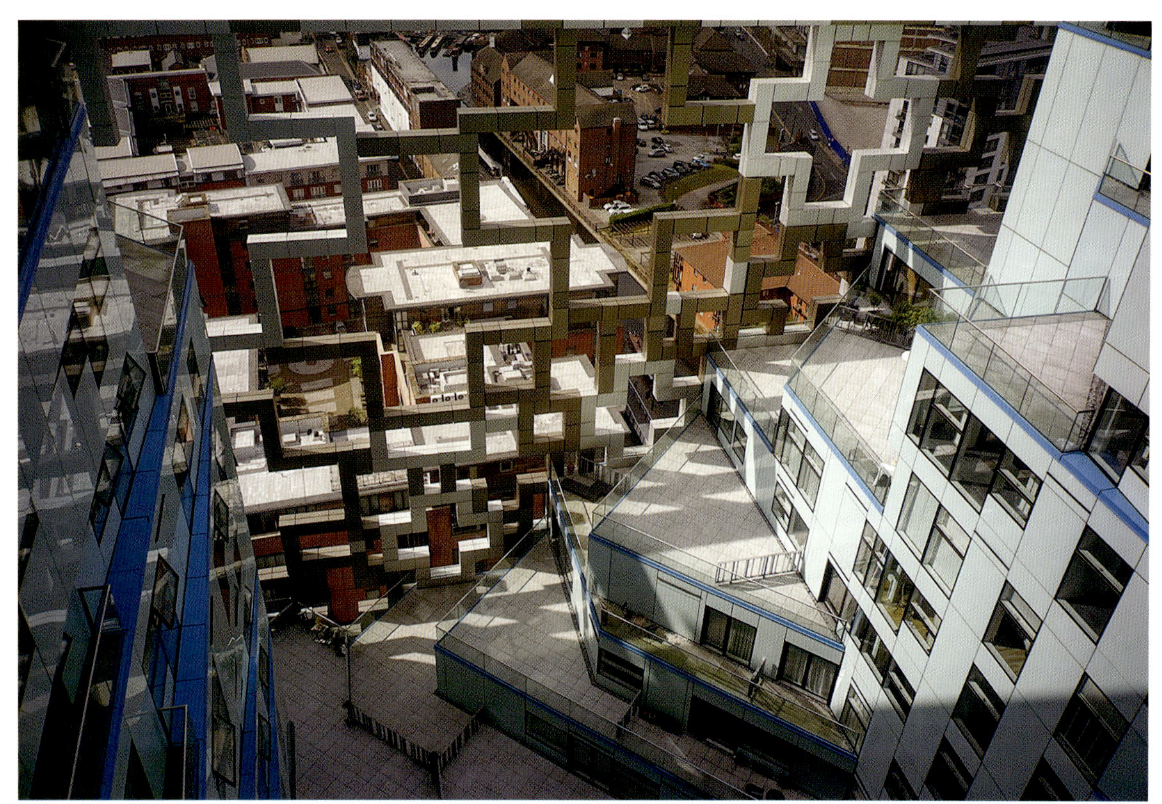

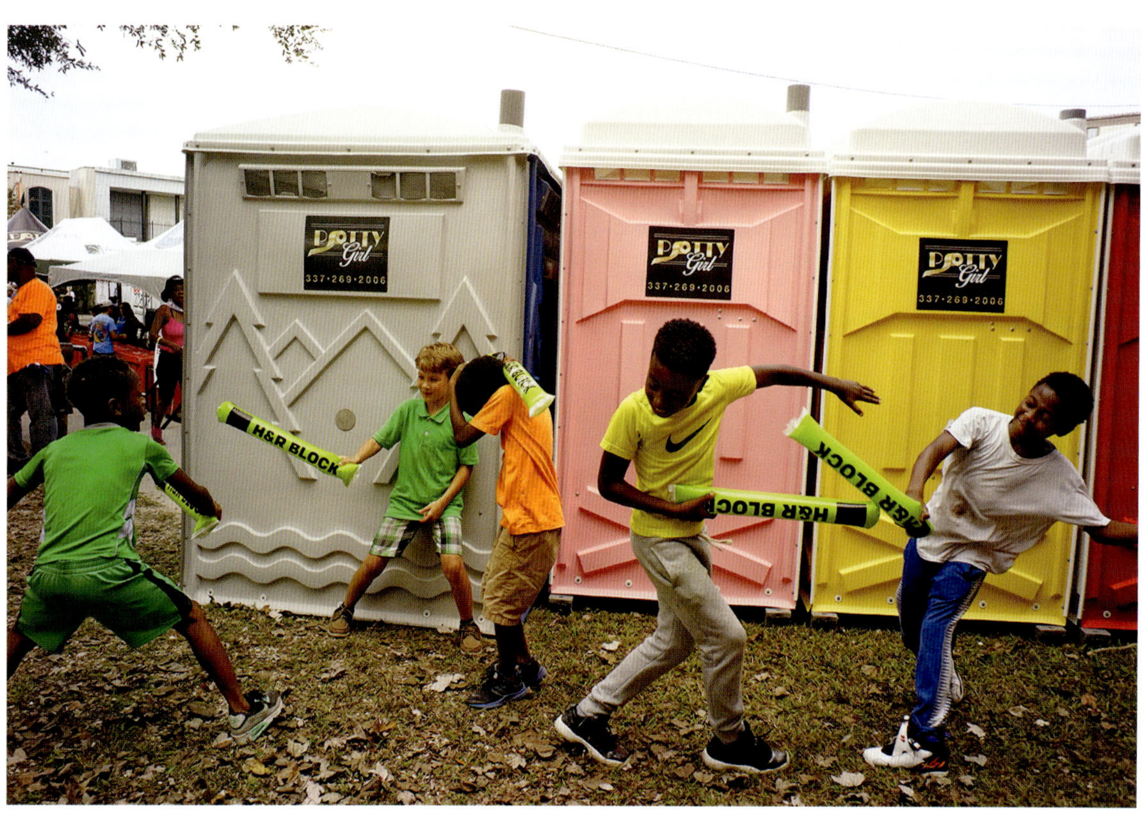

Manchester, England, 2014

Swordsmen, New Iberia, LA, 2015

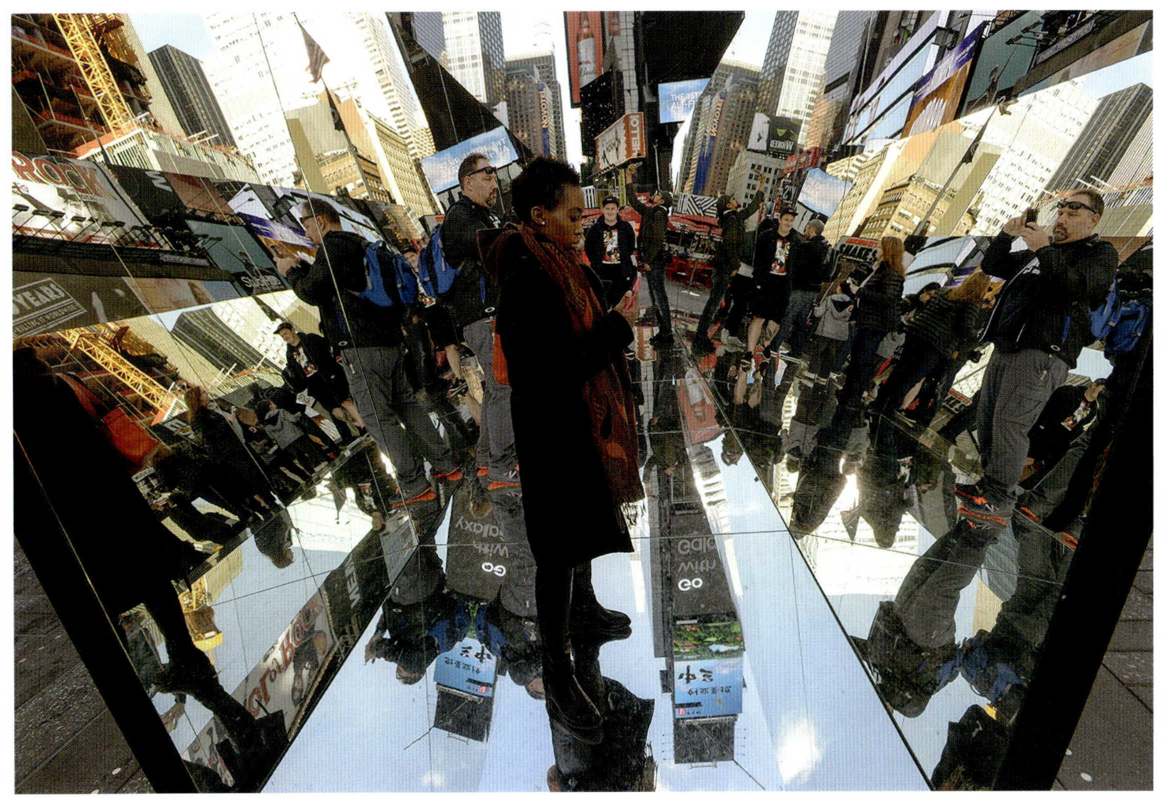

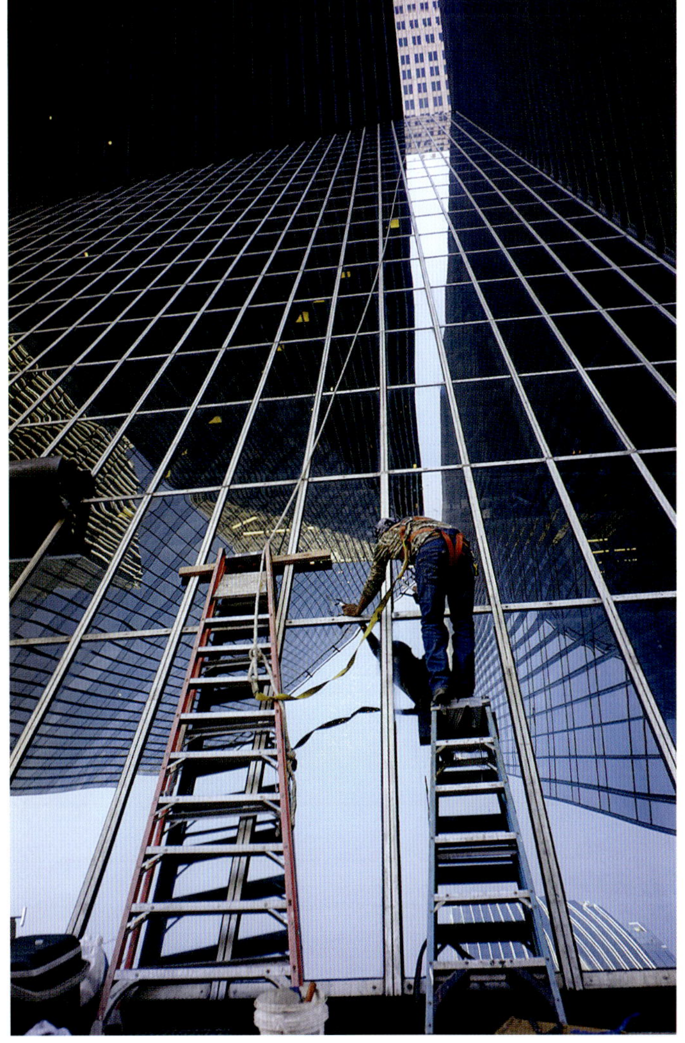

Cubism, Times Square, 2016

Cityscape, 2018

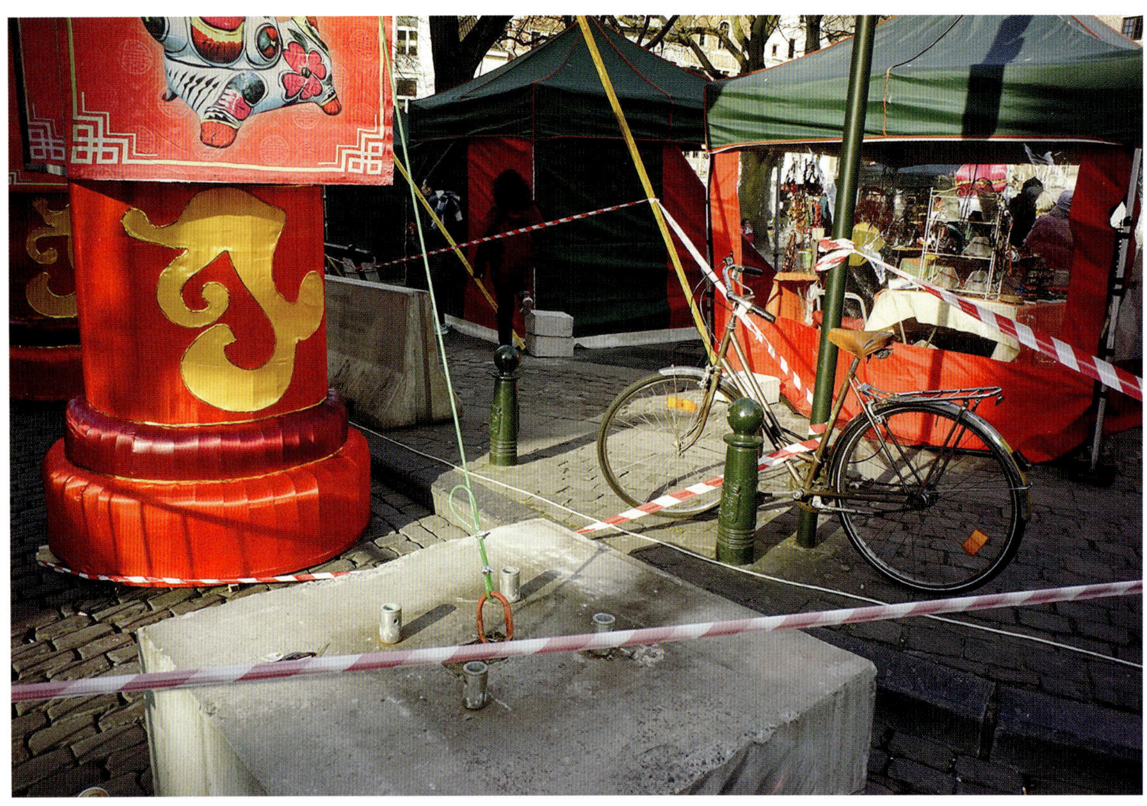

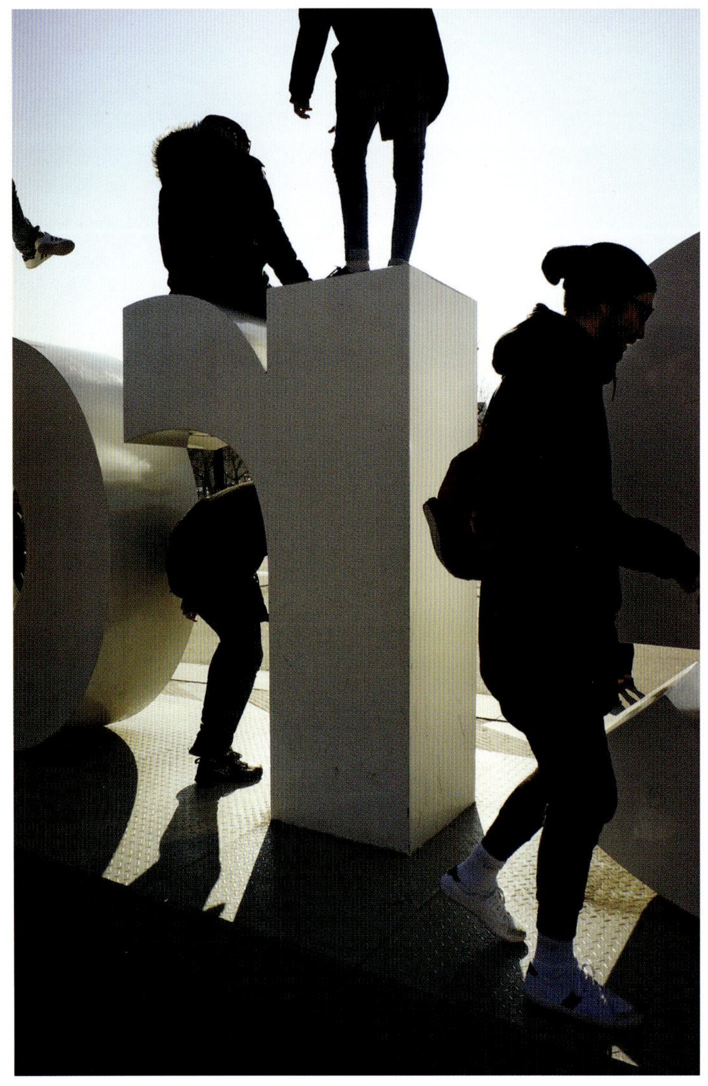

China, 2019

Amsterdam, 2019

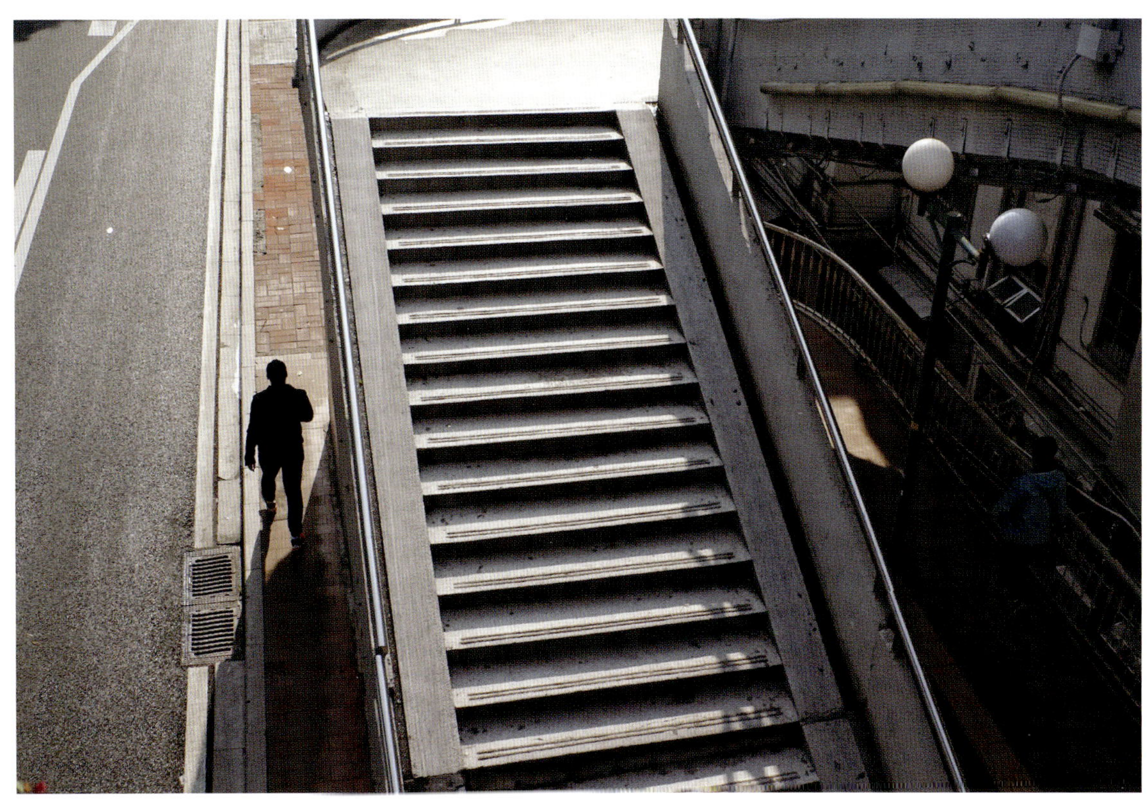

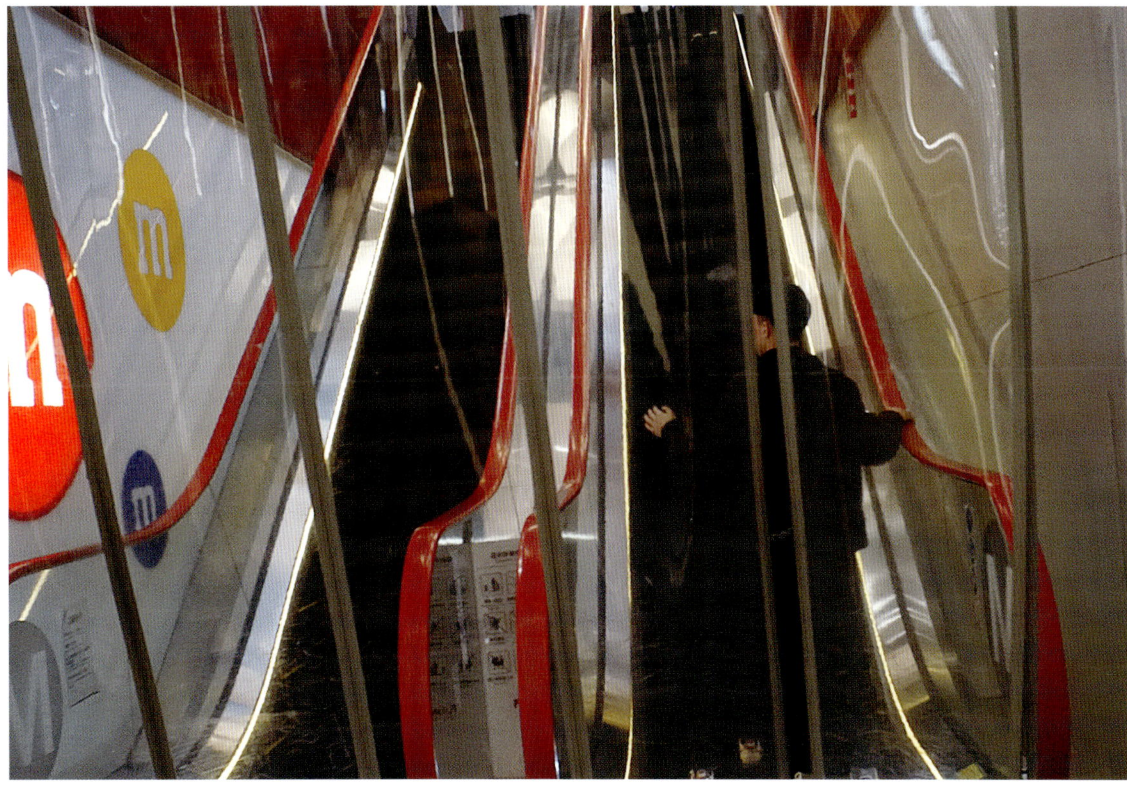

Wu Han, 2019

Shanghai, 2019

Environmental Catastrophe

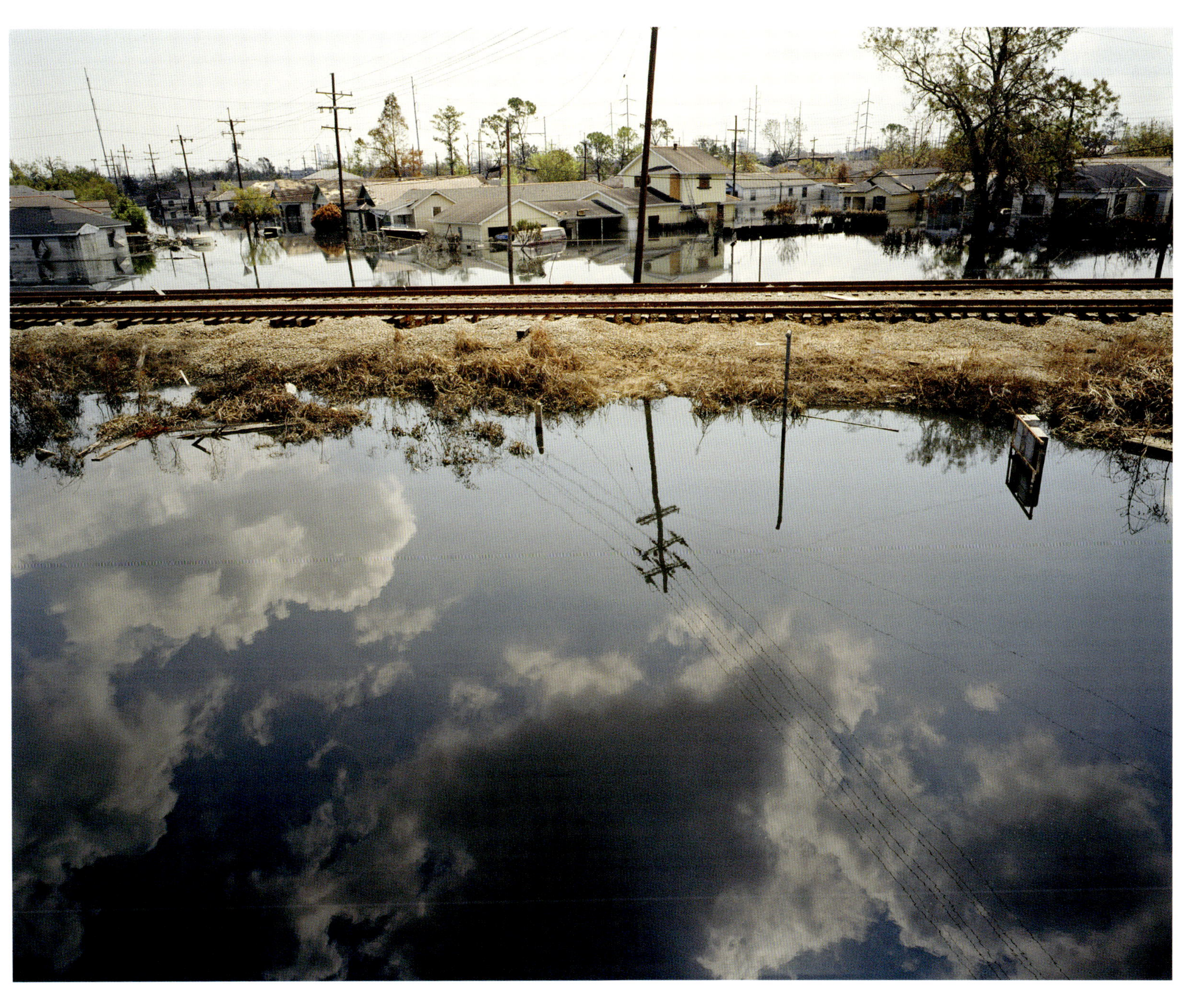

Katrina: Clouds and Railroad Tracks, 2005

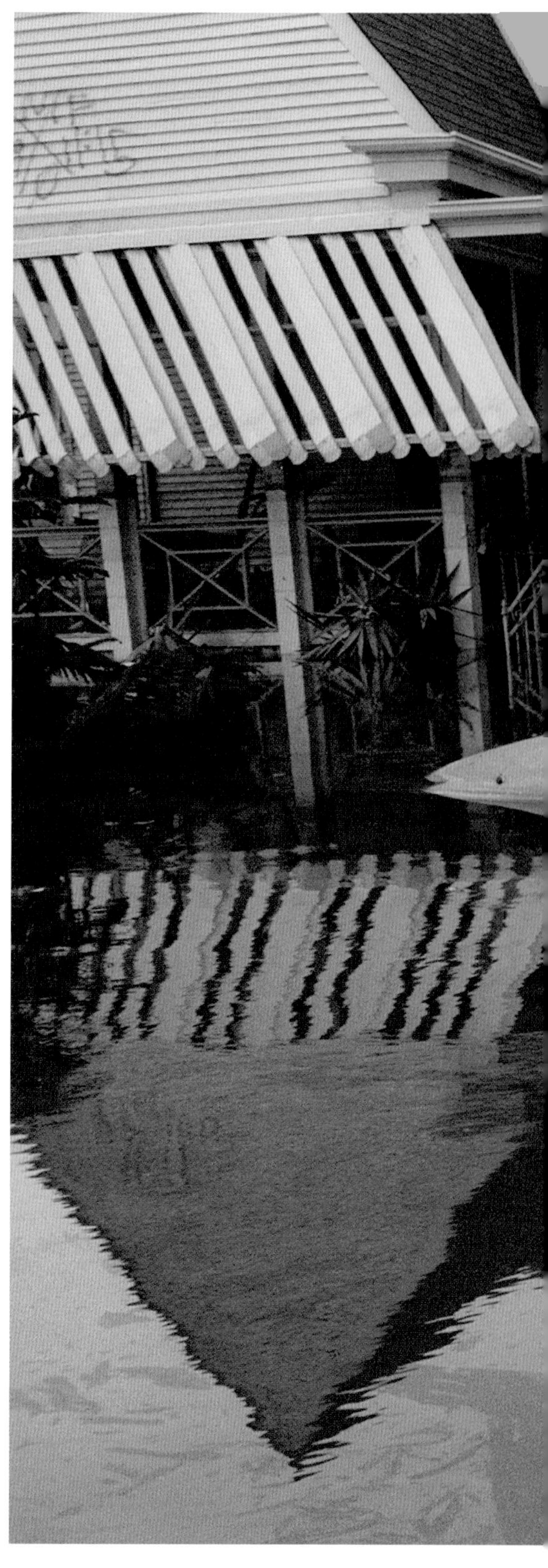

Katrina's Houses I, 2005

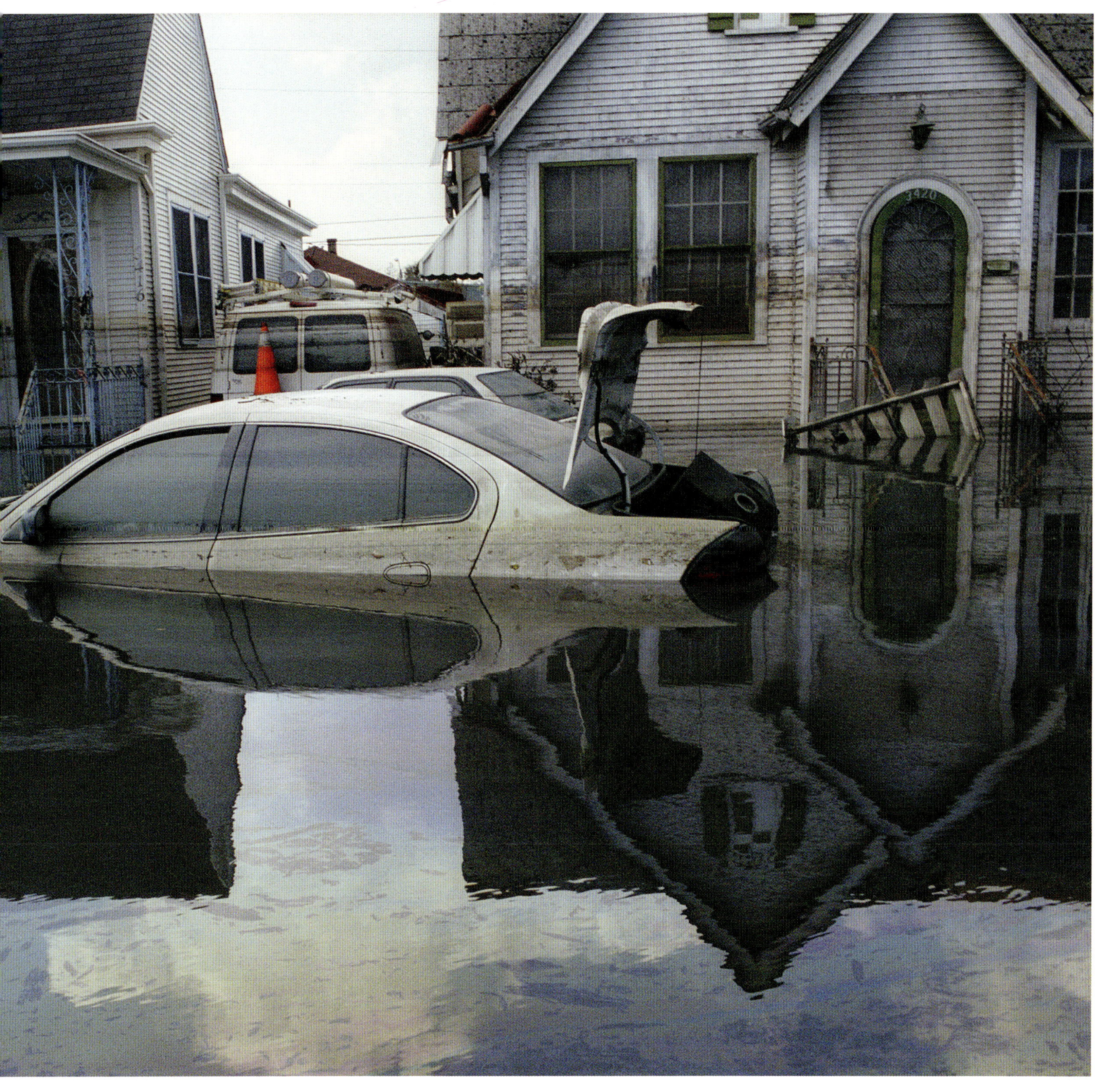

Opposite and following spread:
Katrina: Hammond B-3, 9th Ward, New Orleans, 2007

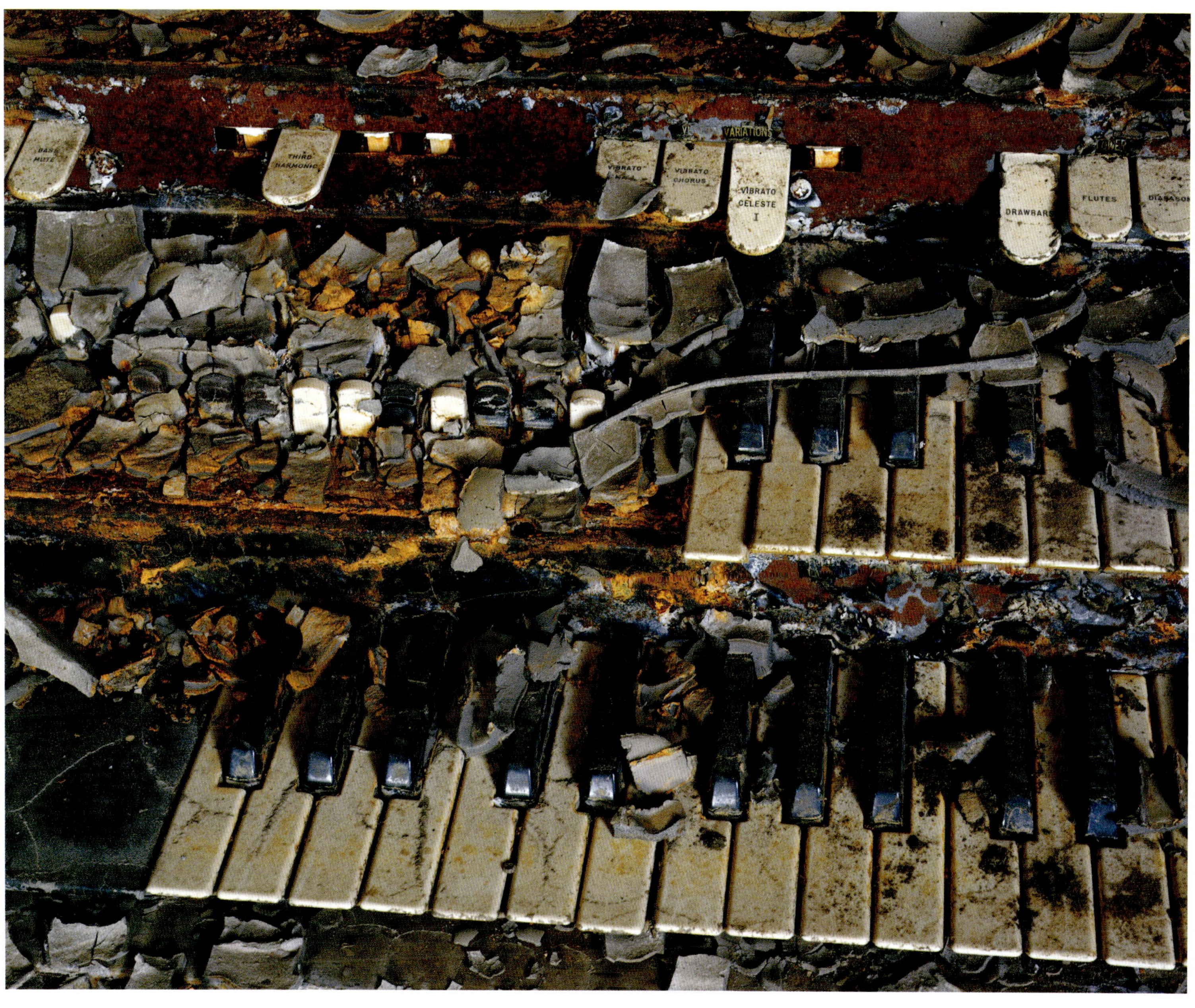
BASS MUTE
THIRD HARMONIC
VARIATIONS
VIBRATO
VIBRATO CHORUS
VIBRATO CELESTE I
DRAWBARS
FLUTES

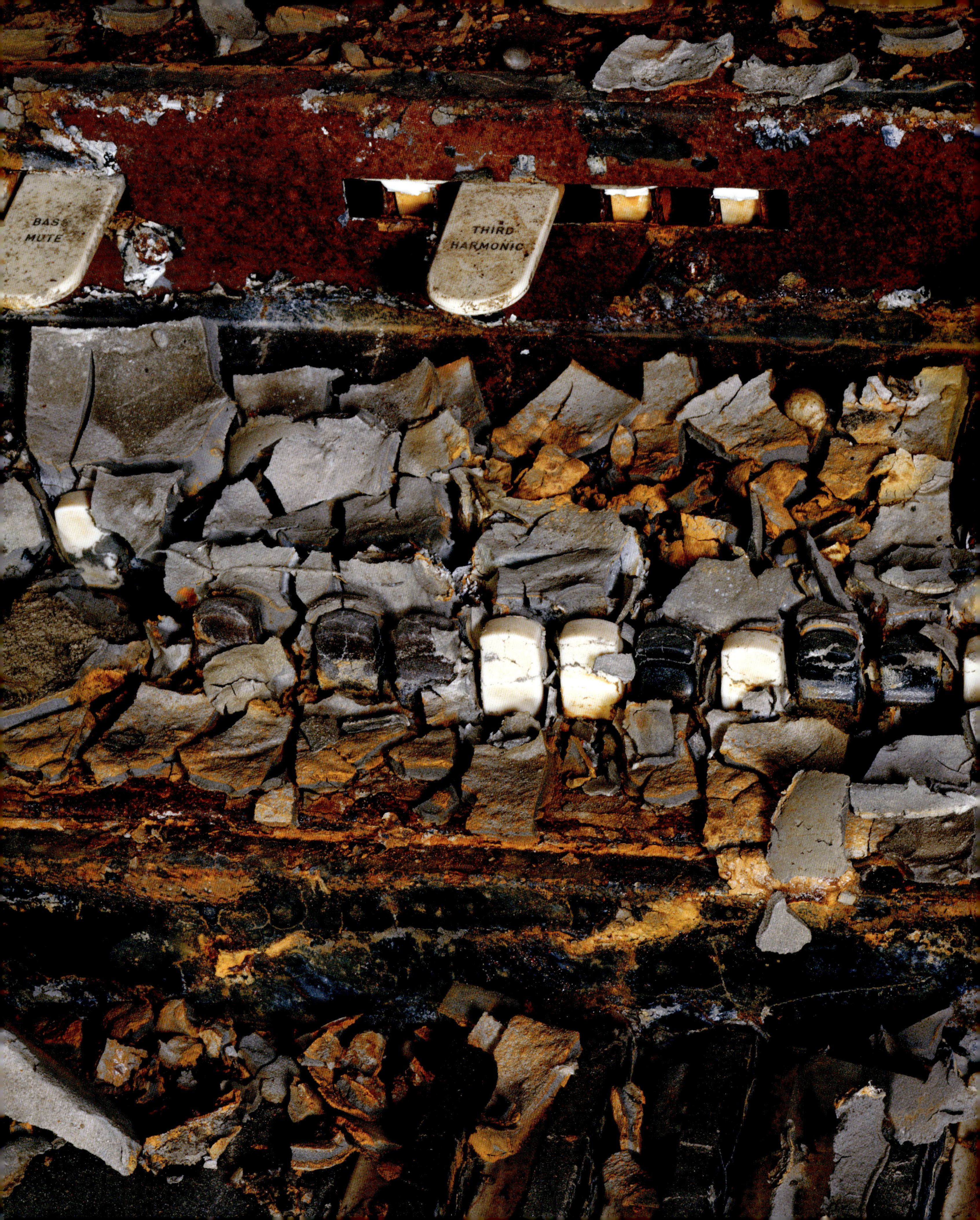
BASS
MUTE
THIRD
HARMONIC

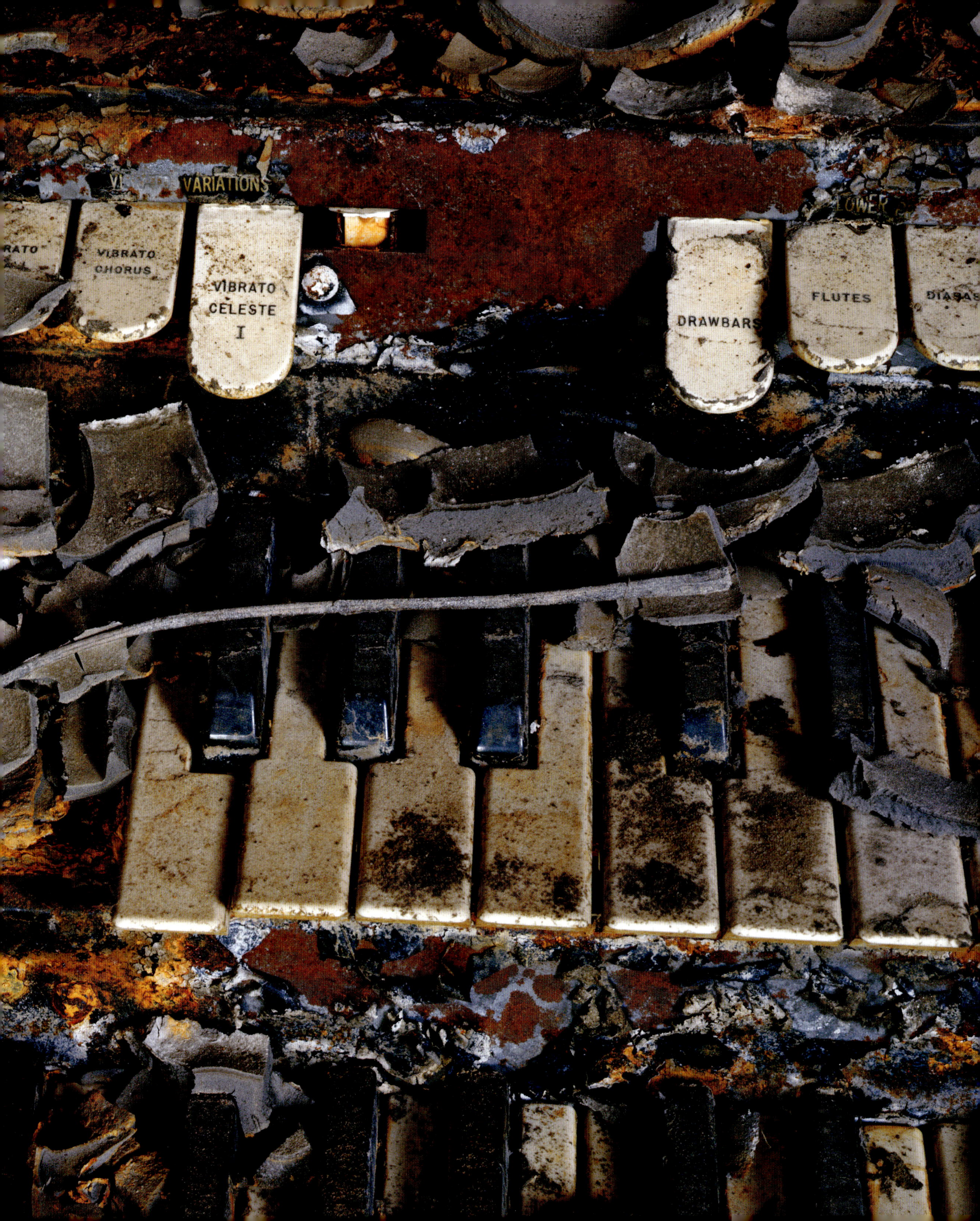
VARIATIONS
VIBRATO CHORUS
VIBRATO CELESTE I
LOWER
DRAWBARS
FLUTES

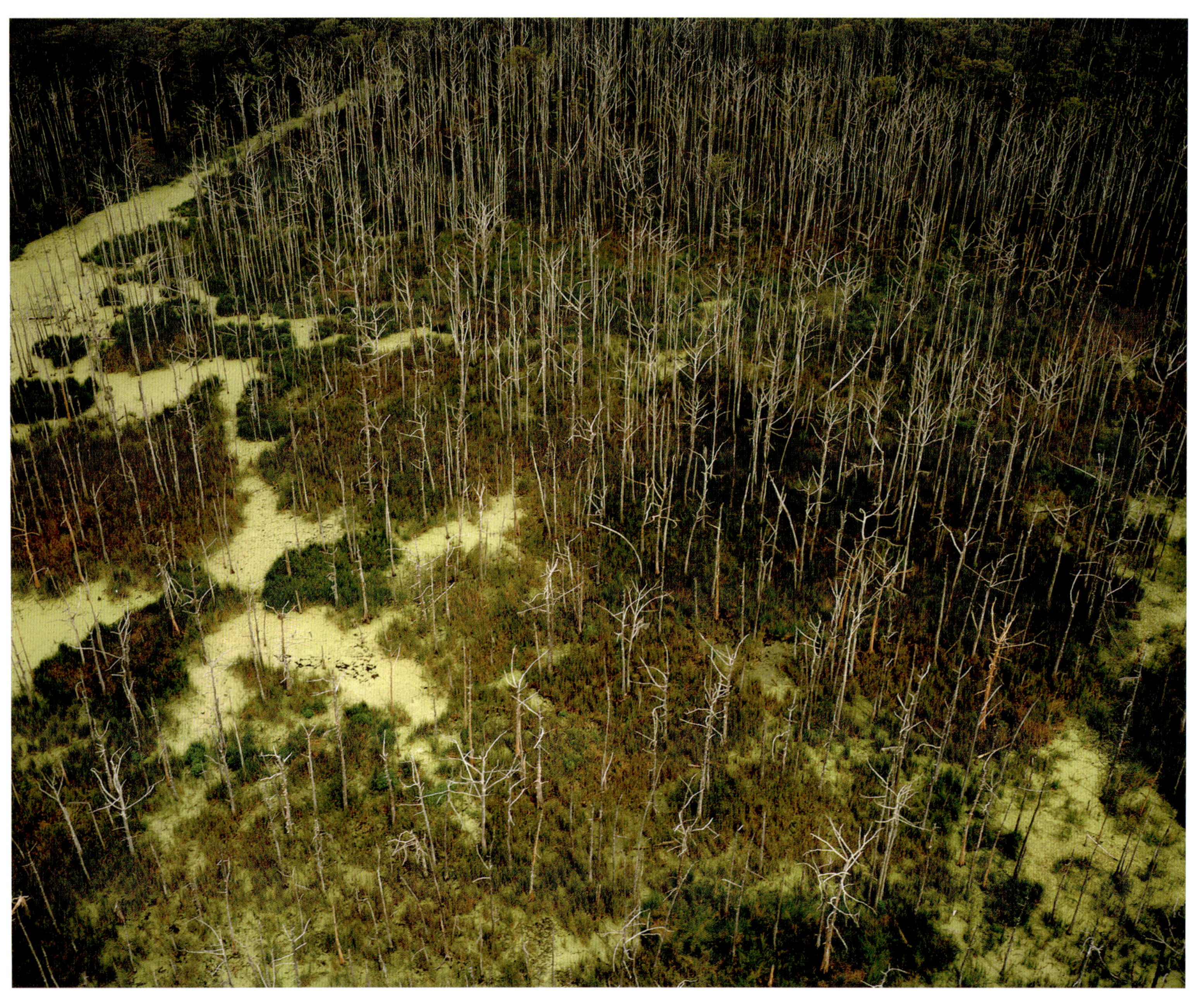

L'Isle Jean Charles, 2017

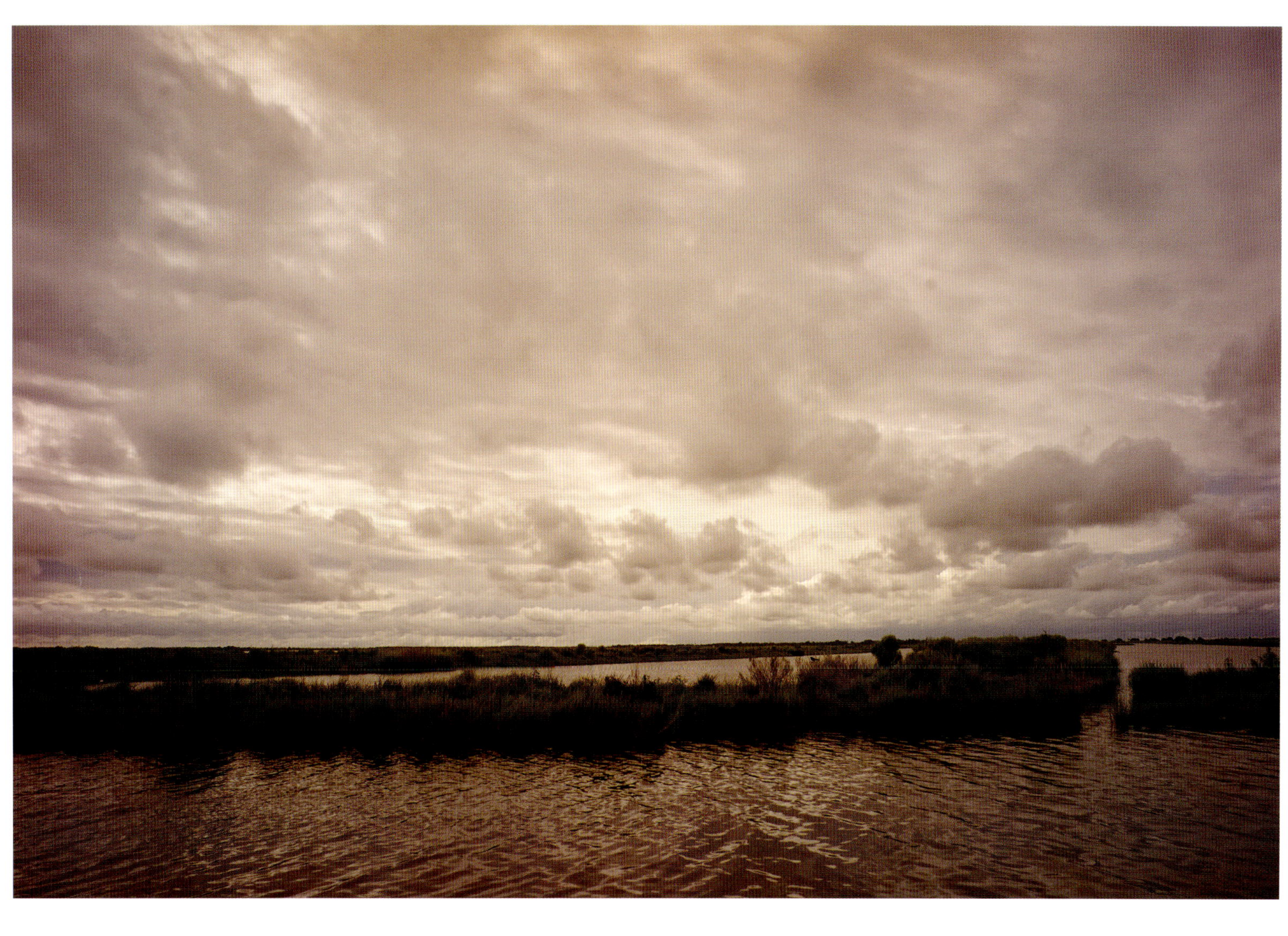

L'Isle Jean Charles: Man-made Reefs, 2017

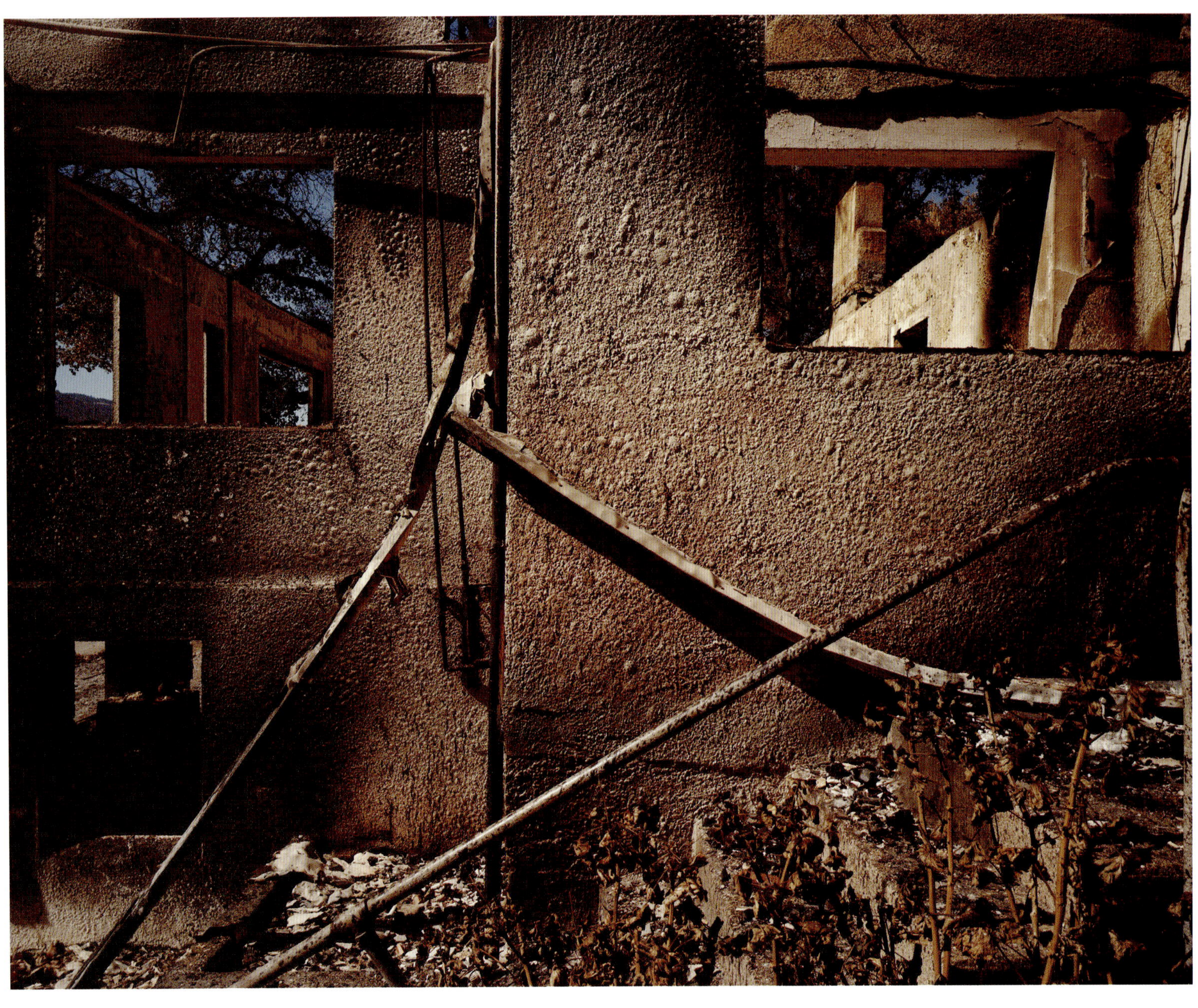

California Fires Series,
St. Helena, 2020

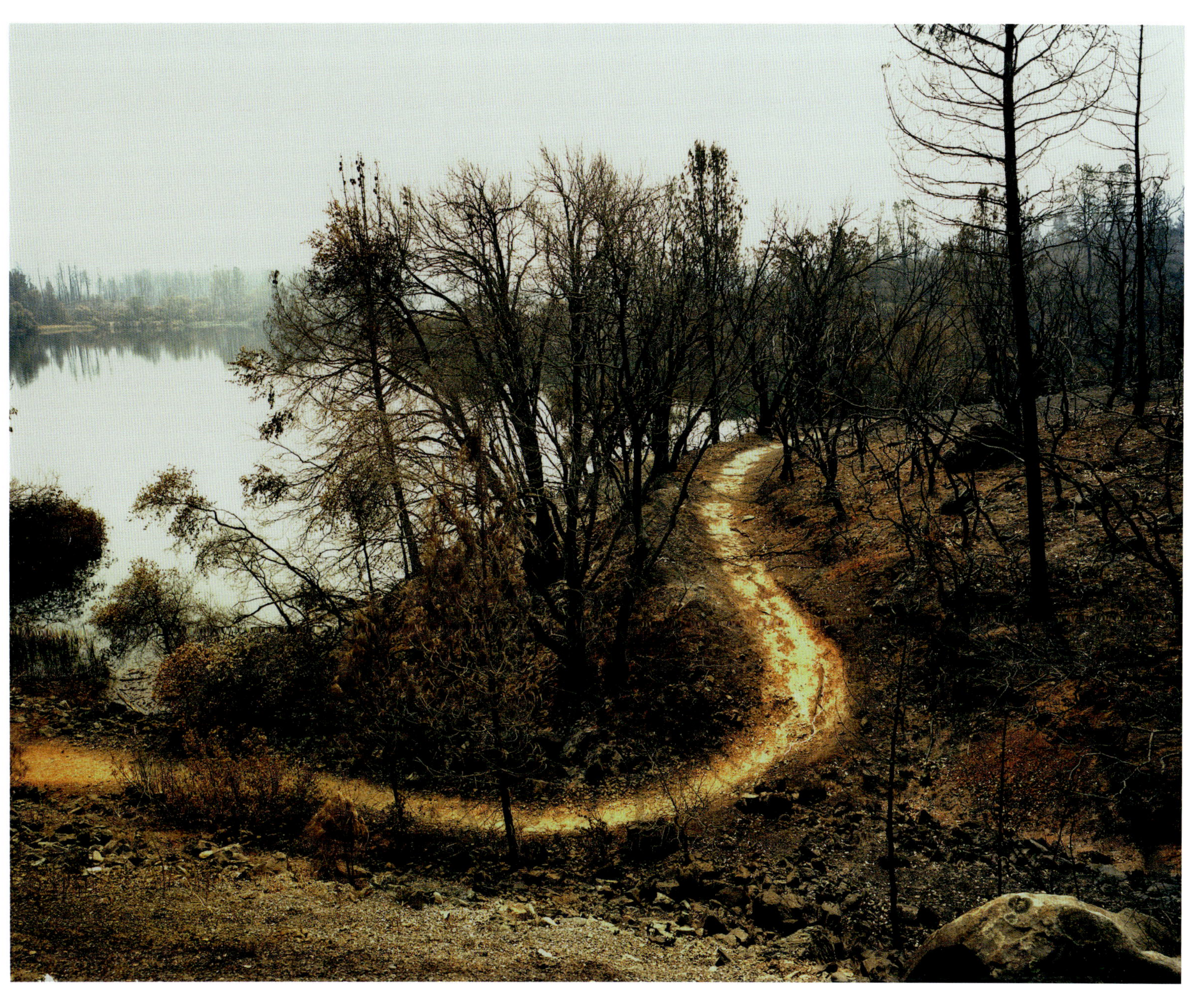

California Fires Series, Camp Fire, 2018

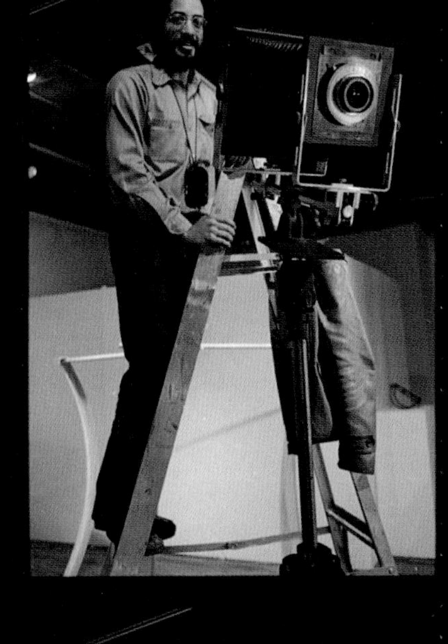
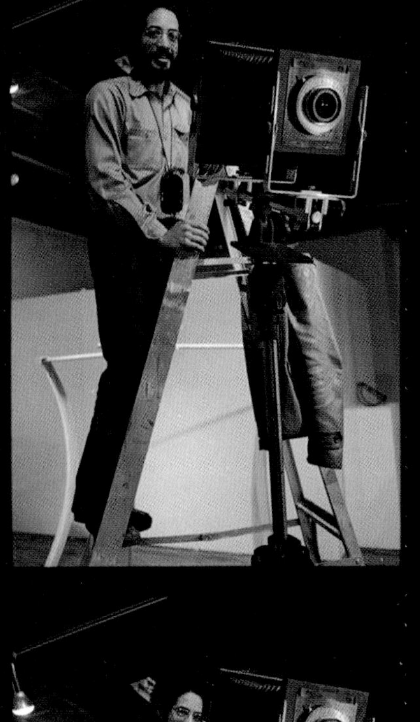
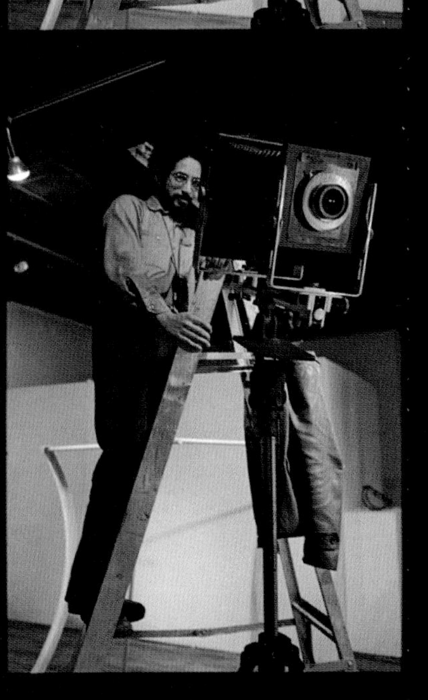
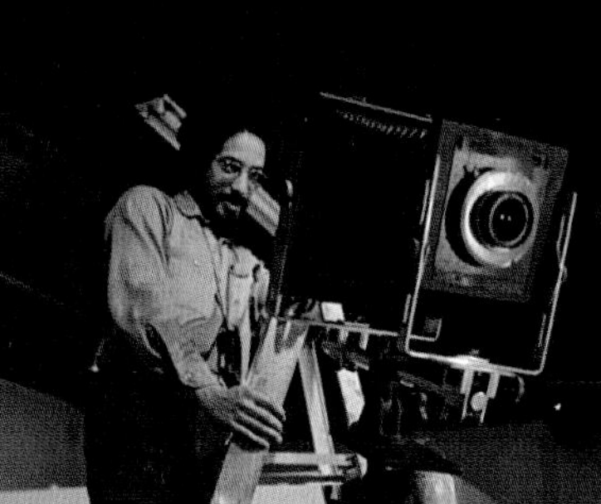
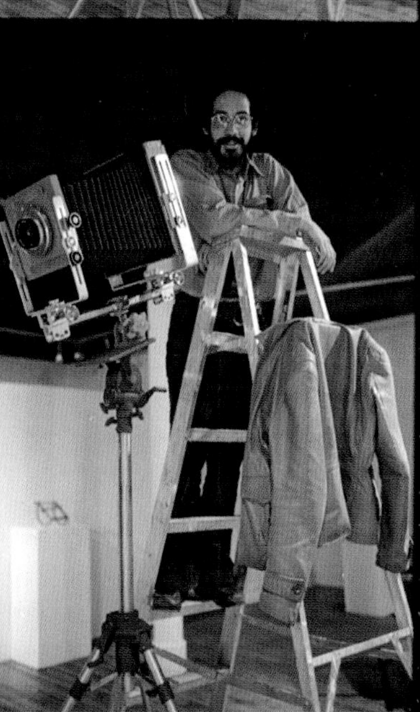
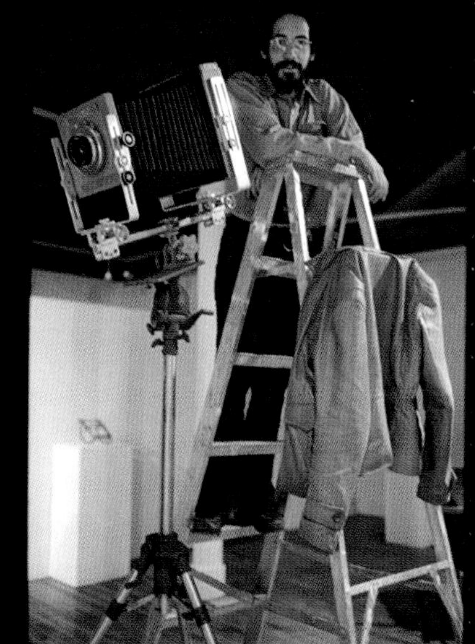
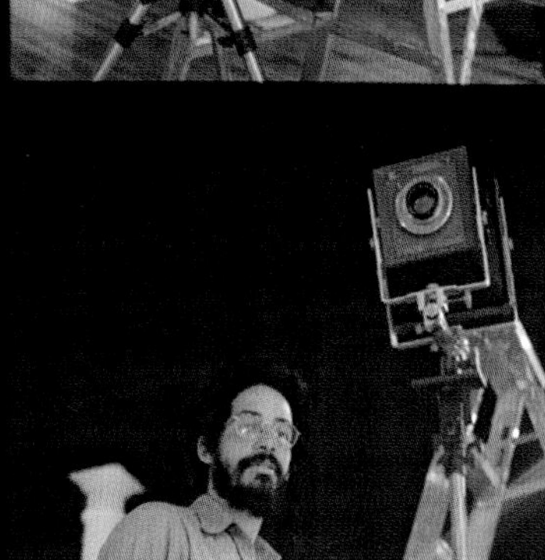
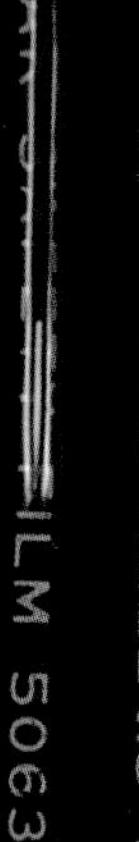
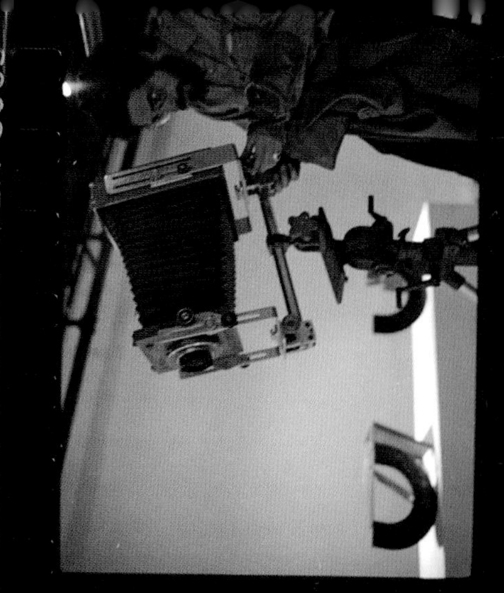
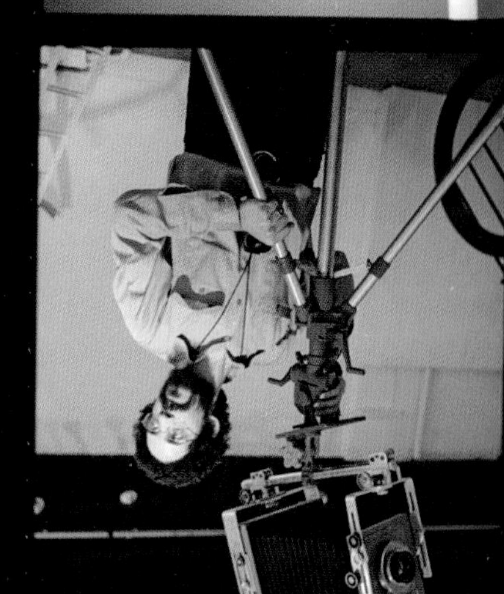
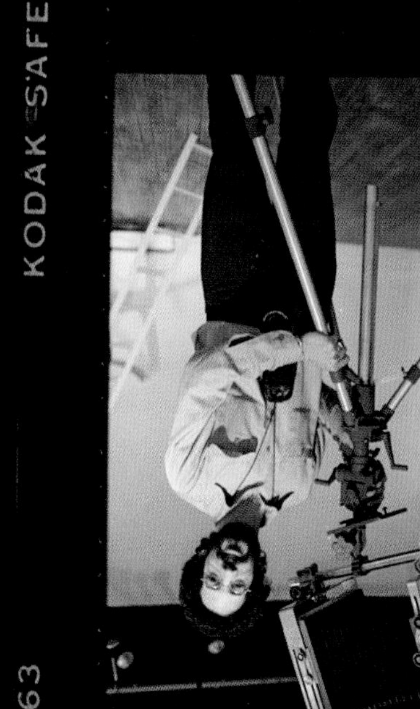
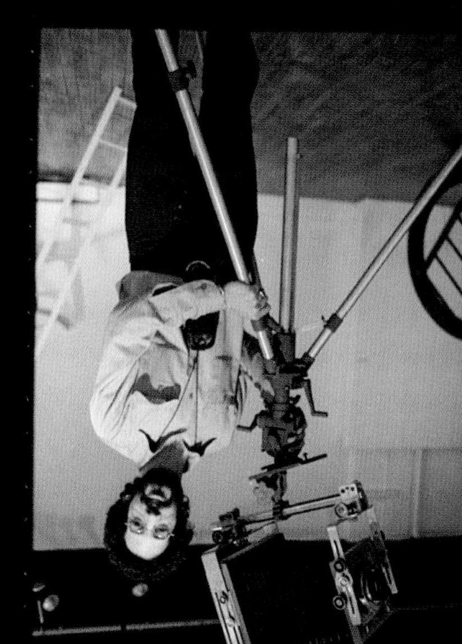
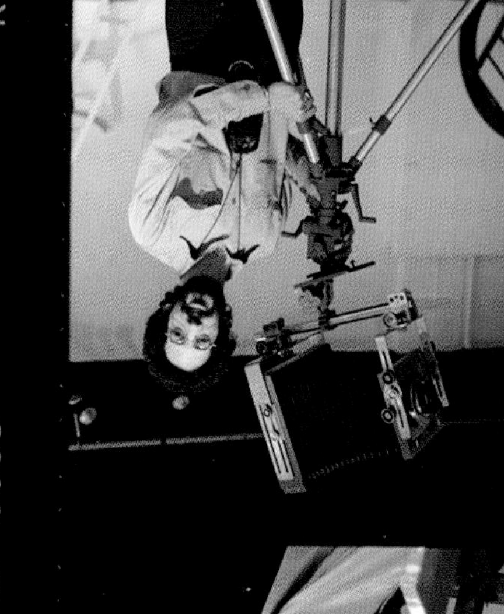
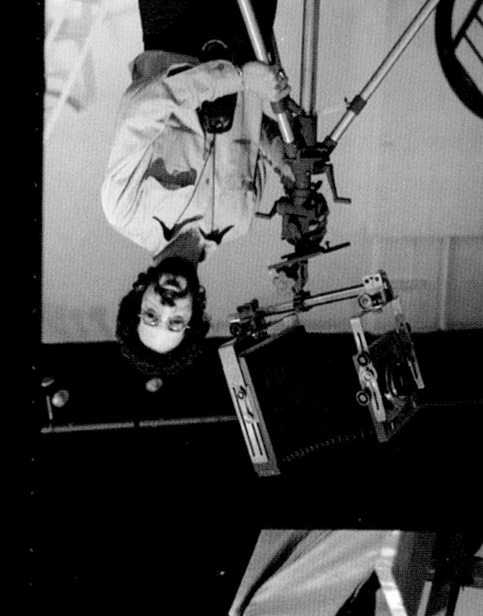
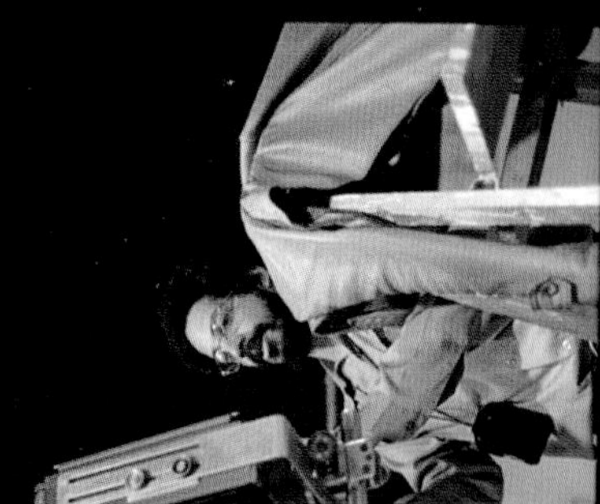

CHRONOLOGY

The Covid pandemic limited library access while this chronology was being compiled. Data is provided as known, with hopes that future researchers will contribute additional information. Institutional names change or vary from project to project: they are cited as we understand them to have been called at that specific time. Frank Lehman Stewart Jr. is referred to as FS throughout. He was and continues to be called Lee by family and friends.

1949–55

FS is born on July 27, 1949, in Nashville, Tennessee, to Dorothy "Dotty" Jean Lewis Stewart (1929–2010) and Frank Lehman Stewart Sr. (1925–1992). Parents met at what was then known as Tennessee Agricultural and Industrial State Normal School for Negroes, now known as Tennessee State. Father was on a swimming scholarship; mother was on a scholarship earned in a beauty pageant, the Memphis Spirit of the Cotton Carnival, the African American version of the Cotton Carnival celebrated by the White population. Parents' marriage dissolves when FS is approximately one year old. He and Dotty remain in Nashville.

1955–57

Dotty moves to Manhattan to pursue a career as a model and dancer; FS moves to Memphis to live with maternal great-grandmother, Ruby Gillis (called Mama), and grandmother, Mildred Lewis (called Mudear), at 924 Mississippi Boulevard, now destroyed. Household at the time includes Dotty's younger siblings, Andrew, Janet, and Harold, who are children themselves when FS moves in. He attends St. Augustine Catholic Elementary School grades one through three. Starts playing football, grows up listening to the radio—rhythm and blues in the daytime, blues at night, gospel on Sunday.

Coreen Simpson, *Frank Stewart at The Studio Museum in Harlem*, 1978

In the summer, FS briefly visits Dotty and partner, later to be husband, jazz pianist Phineas Newborn Jr., living on Thirty-Fourth Street in Manhattan. Also visits Richmond, Virginia, to see his father and then-wife Peggy.

1958–60

FS lives with Dotty and Newborn at 62 West Ninety-First Street in New York. He is held back one year in school, on the assumption that a Memphis education is not as advanced as one in New York. FS joins the school track team. Spends many nights with his stepfather at jazz clubs, including Birdland, the Five Spot, the Village Gate, and the Village Vanguard, meeting such legends as Count Basie, Paul Chambers, Miles Davis, and Roy Haynes.

CIRCA 1960

Newborn seeks independence from standard music business control factors and leaves for Europe. During his time with Dotty, they have two daughters, Rochella and Pamela. Dotty's career outside the home means FS and his half-sisters spend the year in a Jamaican family's foster home in Brooklyn, where FS attends several different schools in one year. Dotty and the children then return to Memphis for several months, after which they return briefly to Manhattan, then move to 501 Seneca Avenue, Mount Vernon, New York, where

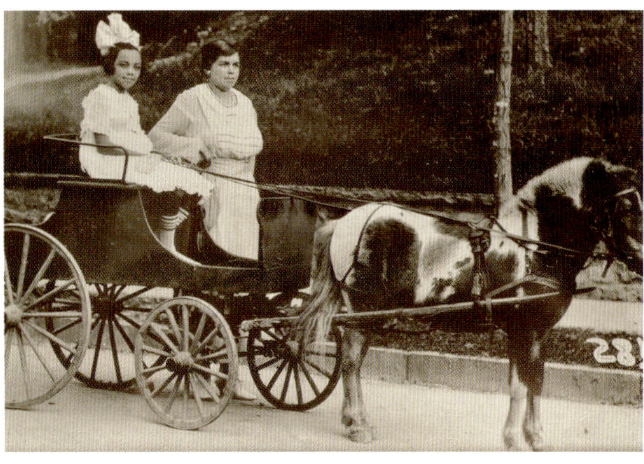
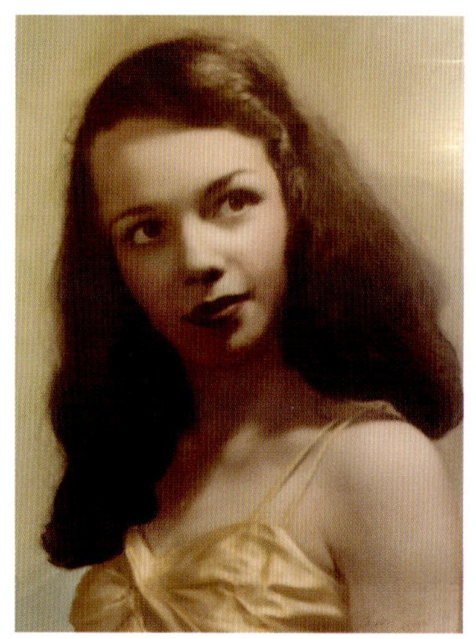
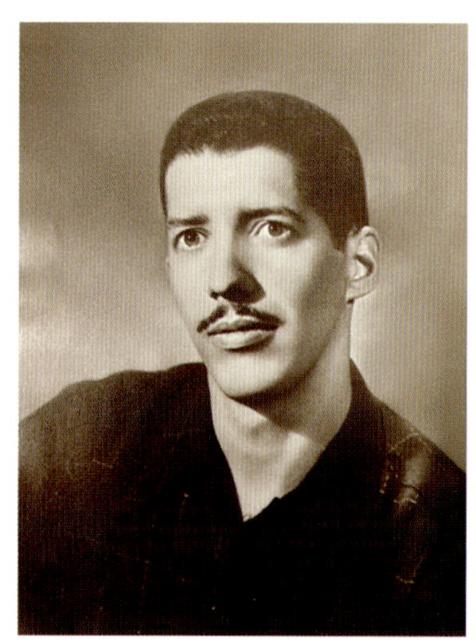

(from left) Unknown photographer, Frank Stewart's grandmother and great grandmother, c. 1905

Unknown photographer, Dorothy "Dotty" Jean Lewis Stewart, c. 1945

Unknown photographer, Frank Lehman Stewart Sr., c. 1955

FS lives for about a year before moving to Chicago to live with his father.

1961–68

FS enters fourth grade in Chicago; lives on Chicago's South Side, first at Eighty-Sixth Place with father and his father's third wife, Mary, next to Miles Davis's elder and only sister, Dorothy Milburn, and her husband, Vince Milburn, with whom Davis stays when in Chicago. Vince sets FS on the path to make barbecue; FS later becomes an expert. FS moves next to Eighty-Fifth Street and Maryland Avenue with his father and paternal grandmother, Cora; then to the Lake Meadows housing complex, first at 3420 with father, then with Cora at 601 Lake Meadows, where the Sengstacke family also lives. FS becomes friendly with Lewis, the youngest brother of photojournalist Robert "Bobby" Sengstacke. The Sengstacke family owns the *Chicago Defender*, the *Tri-State Defender* (Arkansas, Mississippi, Tennessee), and other important African American newspapers; Lewis introduces FS to budding photographer John Simmons, who becomes a lifelong friend. FS then lives at 401 Lake Meadows with father and his fourth wife, Irene. Owing to family conflict, during his last two years of high school FS lives with two different friends' families in Lake Meadows; he also lives with the Moonies, with whom he will live again later, and at the Hyde Park YMCA. Attends several Chicago elementary and middle schools and De La Salle Institute high school, where he excels in basketball, football, and track. His coaches become father figures.

1962

FS attends drawing and painting classes at the School of the Art Institute of Chicago on Saturdays during the summer.

1963

In August, FS goes to the March on Washington for Jobs and Freedom with Dotty, borrowing her Kodak Brownie camera to take his first photographs; they reveal visual interests that remain important today, including African American culture, the inner personalities of his subjects, spatially complex compositions, and shooting from unusual vantage points.

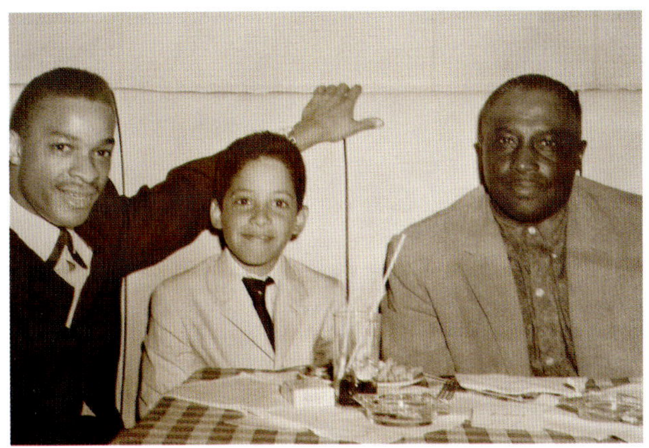

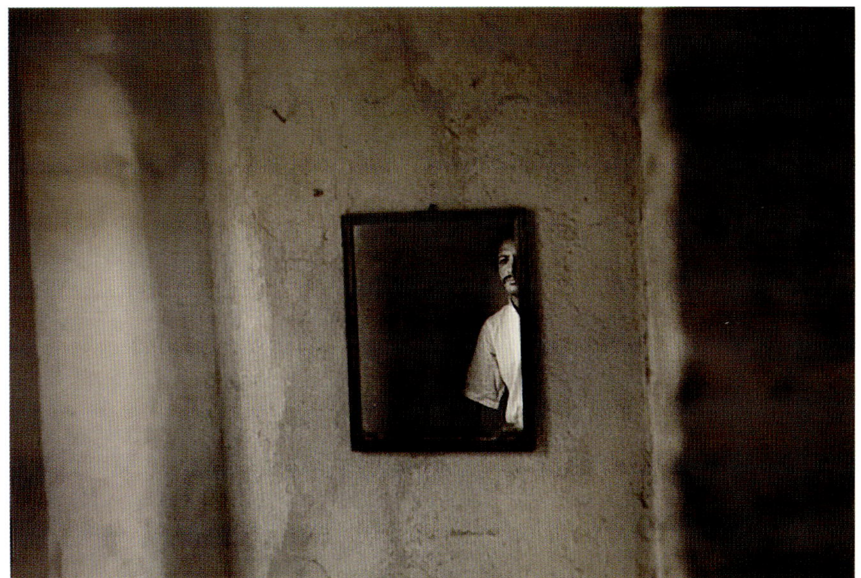

Unknown photographer, a young Frank Stewart with Phineas Newborn Sr. and Jr. at the original Birdland, 1957

Self-portrait, Mexico, 1975

Shortly thereafter, through John Simmons, FS meets Bobby Sengstacke, who shows him the collaboration between Roy DeCarava and Langston Hughes, *The Sweet Flypaper of Life* (1955).

1967–68

Takes photographs with a Canon AEl camera borrowed from a friend's father.

1968–69

Receives a track scholarship and attends one semester (fall 1968 to winter 1969) at the previously all-White Middle Tennessee State College, Murfreesboro, about twenty-five miles from Nashville. Frequently travels to Fisk University to visit his cousin Adrienne Jenkins (later Patel). Sengstacke is teaching photography at Fisk with Simmons as assistant. From Carlton Moss FS learns about the production of films. Audits artist and art historian David C. Driskell's classes about African American art. Driskell, like Sengstacke and Simmons, remains a lifelong friend and collaborator. After one semester, FS returns to Chicago, where he lives with the Moonies, before moving to New Rochelle in Westchester County, New York, where Dotty is living. Buys a motorcycle and shoots photographs "in the hood."

CIRCA 1969–70

FS's father moves to Jocotepec, Jalisco, Mexico, on the shores of Lake Chapala, where Stewart visits him and Irene approximately every two years until his father dies in 1992.

1969–71

FS meets Roy DeCarava through an introduction from photographer and music producer Esmond Edwards. DeCarava is on the faculty of the Cooper Union for the Advancement of Science and Art (known as Cooper Union) and supports FS's application to attend.

Lives in New Rochelle. He is threatened by draft for the Vietnam War, which he opposes. FS drops discussion regarding athletic scholarship to Harvard University in favor of attending Cooperative College (known as Co-op College) in Mount Vernon through 1971 to study political science. He continues taking photographs, primarily in his New Rochelle neighborhood. Teaches photography at New Rochelle Community Action Agency. Briefly belongs to the Mount Vernon chapter of the Black Panther Party and sells newspapers and administers food for the breakfast program.

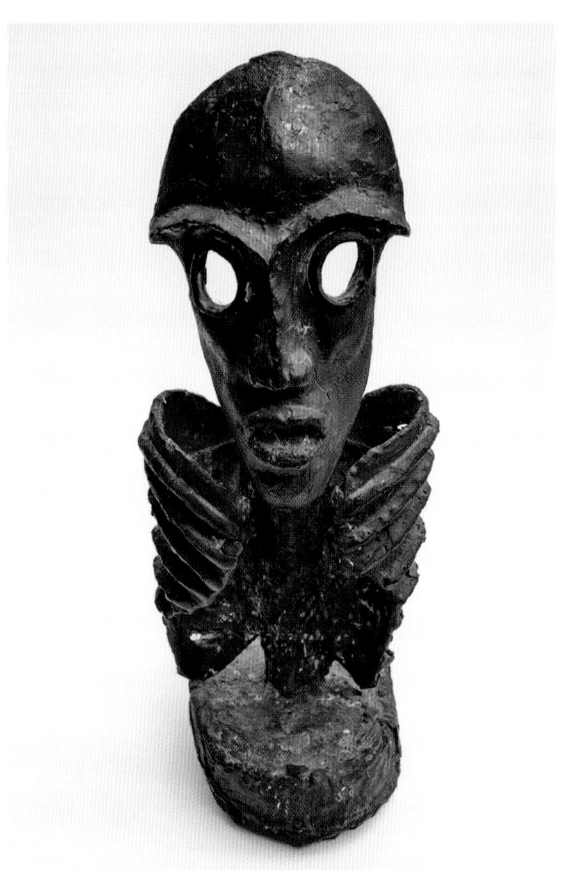

Frank Stewart, *Untitled,* early 1970s, bronze

Sells motorcycle to buy Honeywell Pentax camera and acquires first Leica camera.

SOLO EXHIBITIONS

1969

Tarrent's Grocery Market, New Rochelle. Features primarily photographs of community residents and is turned into a permanent installation until the store is sold many years later.

1970

New Rochelle City Hall. *Photographs by Frank Stewart.* The exhibition is such a hit that some of the photos are stolen.

1971

Fisk University Student Union, Nashville. *Frank Stewart.* The exhibition is organized by John Simmons.

1971–76

Attends Cooper Union, majoring in photography, but also studies a broad swath of the humanities, including the Irish poets and philosophy. Photography teachers include DeCarava; Gene Tulchin, head of photography department; Charles Harbutt, Jay Maisel, and Joel Meyerowitz for color photography; Arnold Newman; Stephen Shore; and Tod Papageorge. Other important faculty for FS's development include Jack Whitten for painting; Reuben Kadish for sculpture; Stephen Anderson for printmaking; John A. Williams for African American literature; George Nelson Preston for African and pre-Columbian art. FS sustains himself by driving taxicabs, working in restaurants as cook and dishwasher, and delivering food for a restaurant called Dial and Dine.

1971–72

Lives in loft on Great Jones Street, Manhattan.

Starts working on *Windows* series, which continues to the present time.

1972

On the advice of Tulchin, FS studies at the School of the Art Institute of Chicago in the summer with Garry Winogrand, who later teaches at Cooper Union.

1972–73

Lives on West Eighty-Fifth Street between West End Avenue and Riverside Drive.

1973

Portfolio of FS's work is published in *Black Photographers Annual*, volume 1.

Jamaica Wedding Reception, 1972, wins first prize in contest sponsored by *Black Creation: A Quarterly Review of Black Arts and Letters* (volume 4, number 3).

1973–85

Lives at 54 West Seventy-Fourth Street.

1974

Almost exclusively prints on 11 by 14–inch paper at this time.

Takes first trip to West Africa on Cooper Union Independent Study Program and visits Liberia, Nigeria,

Friday Evening, 1970

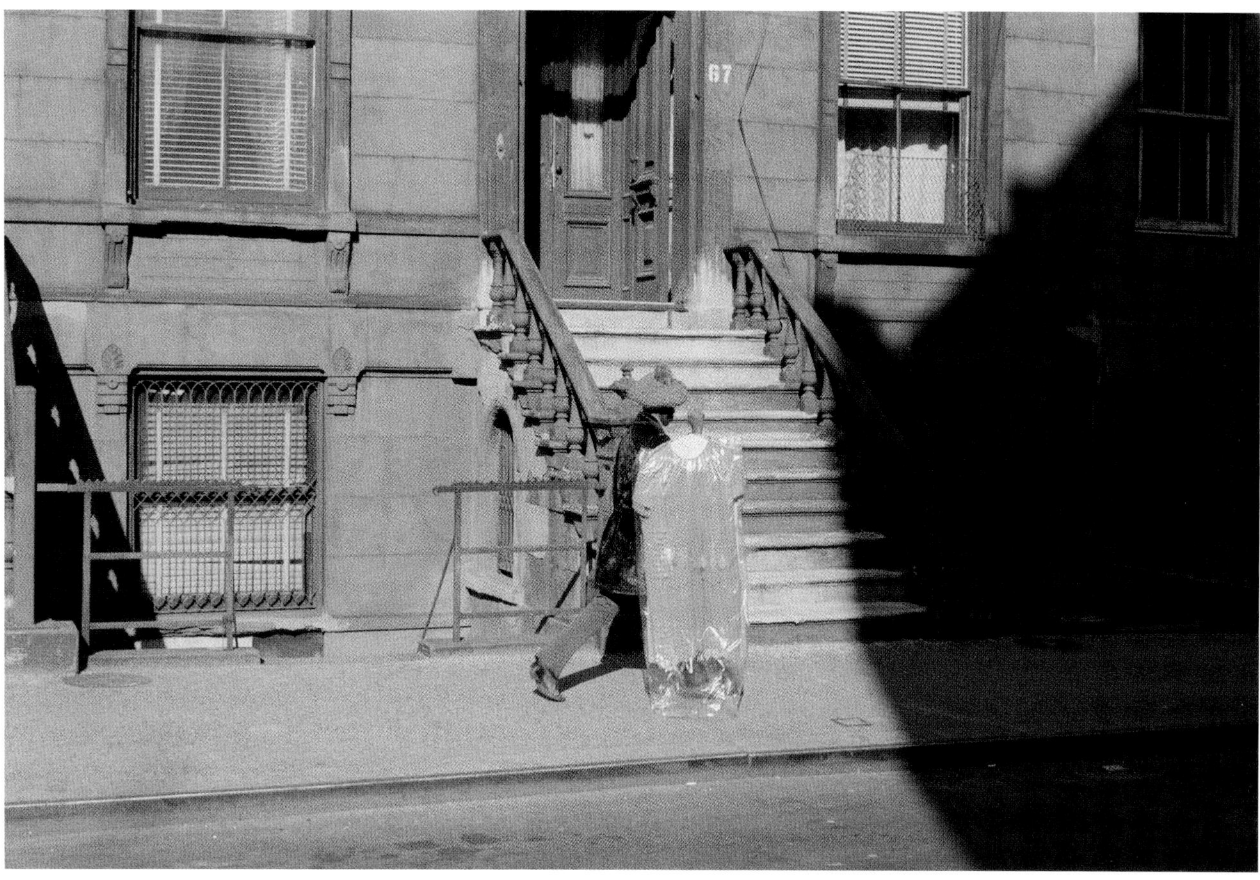

Upper Volta, Togo, Dahomey, Ivory Coast, Ghana; FS makes subsequent trips to Africa starting in 1996.

CIRCA 1975

Teaches photography at Co-op College and continues the course at SUNY Purchase when the photography program moves there.

1975

Graduates from Cooper Union in June with a BFA degree in photography.

Photographs stills for film related to *Two Centuries of Black American Art*, the bicentennial exhibition organized by David C. Driskell for the Los Angeles County Museum of Art that traveled to additional venues. Prior to working with Moss and Simmons on the *Two Centuries* film, FS worked informally with them on other documentaries about African American culture, including *The Life of Frederick Douglass: The Slave Contribution to the Plantation.*

Meets Romare Bearden on the *Two Centuries* project and is closely associated with him through 1988, the year of Bearden's passing. Through Bearden, FS meets many artists and becomes connected to many institutions central to the African American arts community, including The Studio Museum in Harlem (SMH), Kenkeleba House, and Cinque Gallery, where he photographs openings, the artists, and sometimes the art.

1975–76

Through Dotty, FS meets Ahmad Jamal, the first jazz musician with whom he travels, driving the equipment van and shooting photographs while on the road. Bass player Jamil Nasser (formerly known as George Joyner) came from Memphis with Newborn, FS's stepfather, and is like an uncle to FS, watching over him while they are on the road; trip includes FS's first trip to California with a visit to his uncle Clarence "Zoog" in Monterey.

1975–85

Becomes SMH staff photographer (a position he will hold through 1977, when he then begins freelancing for the museum through 1985), at original 125th Street and Fifth Avenue location and continues after 1979 when the museum moves to 144 West 125th Street, working with directors Edward Spriggs, Courtney Callender, and Mary Schmidt Campbell. Photographs the SMH art collection and art in private collections for exhibition catalogues; documents symposia and other programs, including, exhibition openings and meetings of the curatorial council. Teaches photography at SMH through 1977.

1976

During Mardi Gras in the spring, FS takes the first of many trips to New Orleans. He is following interest in Bearden's depictions of Storyville, which is long gone, and jazz's second line. However, the primary purpose is to research the Black Indians—Blacks who paraded on Fat Tuesday (in secret) as Indigenous people in an homage to their ancestors, who took enslaved people into their homes during the winter and helped them survive. FS discovers it is necessary to go out at five a.m. to encounter them in full dress. Connects with photographer Jules Allen in Memphis, and they take the train to New Orleans. Meets sculptor Clifton Webb and his wife, Jo, through Yancy Dent, Nexus Gallery owner; the Webbs host FS and Allen in their home and introduce them to the culture and explain how it metastasized from Africa to New Orleans.

During a second trip to New Orleans, on an SMH fact-finding mission about folk art, FS meets Wynton Marsalis, who is playing with his father, Ellis, and brother Branford at the Jazz and Heritage Festival.

Shoots Democratic convention in New York for *Chicago Defender*, with Sengstacke, from July 12 to 15.

First artist-in-residence in photography at SMH.

Prints on different papers, trying out whatever sheets he can afford, and learns how the paper impacts the image.

Primarily uses Leica camera.

GROUP EXHIBITION

June 12–19. Weusi Gallery, New York (owned by photographer Edward Sherman). *Sun People*. Three-person show with Jeanne Moutoussamy-Ashe and Dawoud Bey.

1976–77

Partners with writer Ntozake Shange.

1977

FS takes his first of many trips to Cuba, this one by invitation from the Cuban government to the Center for Cuban Studies, New York, with a team of North American photographers who travel throughout the island for a month.

GROUP EXHIBITIONS

July 21–August 31. Parsons School of Design, New York. *Impressions of Cuba*. Brochure.

Corcoran Gallery of Art, Washington, DC. *Black Photographers Annual*.

1978–80

Works as photographer for United Negro College Fund and Urban League annual reports.

From this period forward are listed primarily photography commissions and projects related to fellowships and grants. Also during this time, FS independently photographs the subjects and motifs he personally finds compelling.

1978–85

Photographs art and artists' portraits for exhibition catalogues for Gallery 62, at the National Urban League.

LATE 1970S

Documents art collection as the photographer for the New York Public Library's Schomburg Center for Research in Black Culture, working with Jean Blackwell Hutson, director, and Ruth Ann Stewart, curator of collections.

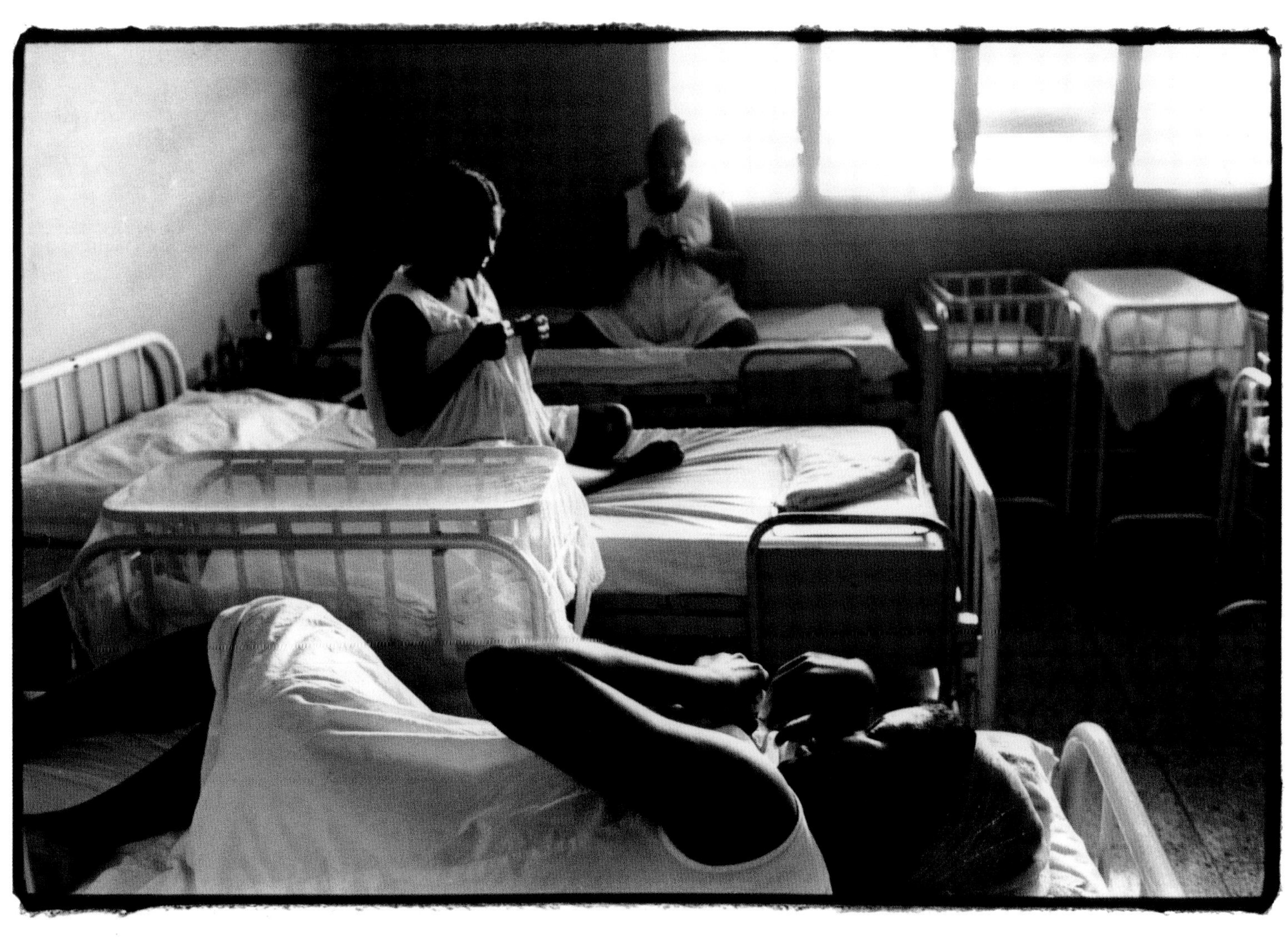

Maternity Hospital, Santiago de Cuba, 1977

1978

Through the Center for Cuban Studies, FS, Allen, and Simmons become the official photographers for the eleventh World Festival of Youth and Students in Havana, shooting still photographs and film.

1979–85

Partners with artist Mei Tei-Sing. Has two daughters: Sing Lee (Lathan) born 1980, Bining Lee (Taylor) born 1982.

Works as New York–based photographer for *Ebony* magazine when Monetta Sleet is on vacation.

Photographs collection of Reginald C. Lewis, working with his curator, Larry Randall.

1979–88

Acts as assistant cameraman and production crew-member on award-winning documentaries with producers/directors Nelson E. Breen, Julius Potocsny, and Dan Weissmann. Three productions broadcast nationally on PBS: *Bearden Plays Bearden* (about the late artist Romare Bearden), *Grand Central* (about the landmark New York City railroad terminal), and *The Precious Legacy* (a history of Czech Jews). His work also includes many corporate films sponsored by Philip Morris, the 7UP company, and Tilcon.

1977

GROUP EXHIBITION

Haitian-American Institute, Port-au-Prince, Haiti. *Diaspora II*.

1978

GROUP EXHIBITION

February 26–March 15. Peg Alston Fine Arts, New York. *Art in Photography: Anthony Barboza, John Pinderhughes, and Frank Stewart*.

1979

GROUP EXHIBITIONS

March 22–April 22. International Center of Photography, New York. *Harlem on My Mind, 1968–78.*

The Studio Museum in Harlem, New York. *Black Eyes/ Light* (with Allen). Travels to Augusta Savage Gallery, University of Massachusetts, Amherst.

1980–90

FS works for numerous organizations and institutions, among them Bronx Community College, the Institute for Urban Family Health, and Albert Einstein College of Medicine.

1980

Photographs Democratic Convention, New York, for *Chicago Defender*, with Sengstacke, from August 11 to 14.

Receives New York State Creative Artists Public Service (CAPS) award, which he uses to photograph in the South, including shooting in New Orleans and photographing the Ku Klux Klan in Jackson, Mississippi.

Uses the first of two National Endowment for the Arts fellowship awards to photograph primarily New Orleans, Memphis, and Civil War battlefields in the areas of Jackson, Meridian, and Natchez, Mississippi. FS's Indigenous ancestry is rooted in Clarksdale and Tunica, Mississippi.

GROUP EXHIBITIONS

January 21–February 22. Gallery 62, National Urban League, New York. *Jules Allen, Beuford Smith, Frank Stewart: Photographs*. Catalogue with foreword by Roy DeCarava. The exhibition features ten works by each artist.

April 12–May 18. Chicago Cultural Center. *Still Photographs: Recent Photographs by Frank Stewart and Jeanne Moutoussamy-Ashe*. Catalogue with introduction by Gordon Parks.

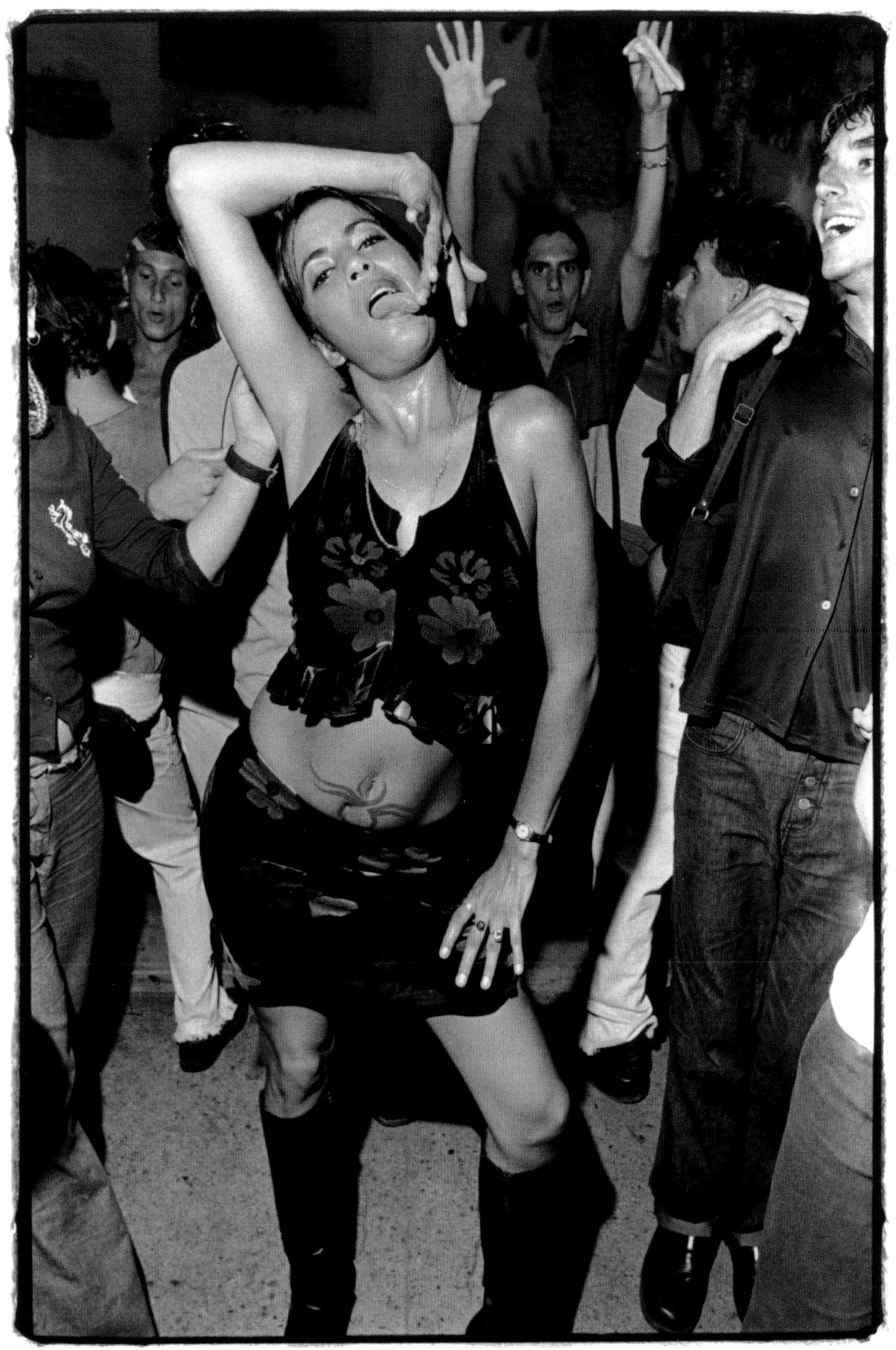

Friday Night Party, Cuba,
c. 2016

1982
Invited to join the Kamoinge Workshop, a New York–based collective of African American photographers. John Pinderhughes is also invited at this time.

GROUP EXHIBITION
New York Public Library, Schomburg Center for Research in Black Culture. *New Acquisitions*.

1983–90
Shoots art and gallery events as photographer for Kenkeleba House, New York.

1983
GROUP EXHIBITION
October 6–November 27. Allen Memorial Art Museum, Oberlin College, Oberlin, Ohio. *Contemporary Afro-American Photographers.* In conjunction with Equality: The Education of Black Americans conference. Catalogue.

1984
Accepts invitation to be one of ten photographers to photograph Los Angeles Summer Olympics after proposing to shoot the crowds and their interaction with the athletes.

1984–85
Receives $15,000 National Endowment for the Arts Young Master fellowship in photography.

1984–86
Cofounds Onyx Art Gallery, 54 Irving Place, New York, with Swiss backer who wants to promote African American art. FS serves as art director with art historian and curator Halima Taha as assistant director. First exhibition is the work of Jack Whitten, followed by exhibitions of Bill Hutson, Al Loving, Joe Overstreet, Ed Clark, and Sam Gilliam. Terry Adkins does telemarketing for the gallery in the evenings. Onyx closes in 1986.

1985
GROUP EXHIBITION
November 18–January 6, 1986. Museum of Contemporary Art, Los Angeles. *10 Photographers: Olympic Images*. Catalogue. Other participants include Louis Carlos Bernal, Robert Buitron, Jo Ann Callis, Jack Cornell, Robert Cumming, Jim Dow, Peter Reiss, Charles Traub, and Bonnie Donohue.

1986–92
Resides in Clinton Hill, Brooklyn, with partner, then wife, Halima Taha.

1986
FS serves as associate director, Dotty as CEO and director for Contemporary American Artists Series, a nonprofit documentary film company that produces one film, on the artist Benny Andrews.

GROUP EXHIBITION
April 20–May 18. Kenkeleba House, New York. *Two Schools: New York/Chicago, Contemporary African American Photography of the 60s and 70s.* Catalogue. FS curates the exhibition.

1987
Spends approximately three weeks touring Italy, including Sicily, for the Harlem Cultural Council, photographing for an exchange program that sends jazz musicians and dancers, including Cab Calloway and the Commodores, to work in Italy.

Travels to Port-au-Prince with Nanette Bearden Contemporary Dance Theatre under the auspices of the Haitian-American Institute, accompanied by Romare Bearden and African American dance and social historian Richard Long.

1987–88
Is the artist-in-residence at Kenkeleba House, New York.

1988–89
Works primarily with 4 by 5–format camera.

1989–94
Travels with the Wynton Marsalis Septet shooting photographs that will eventually form a book titled *Sweet Swing Blues on the Road.* FS generally becomes

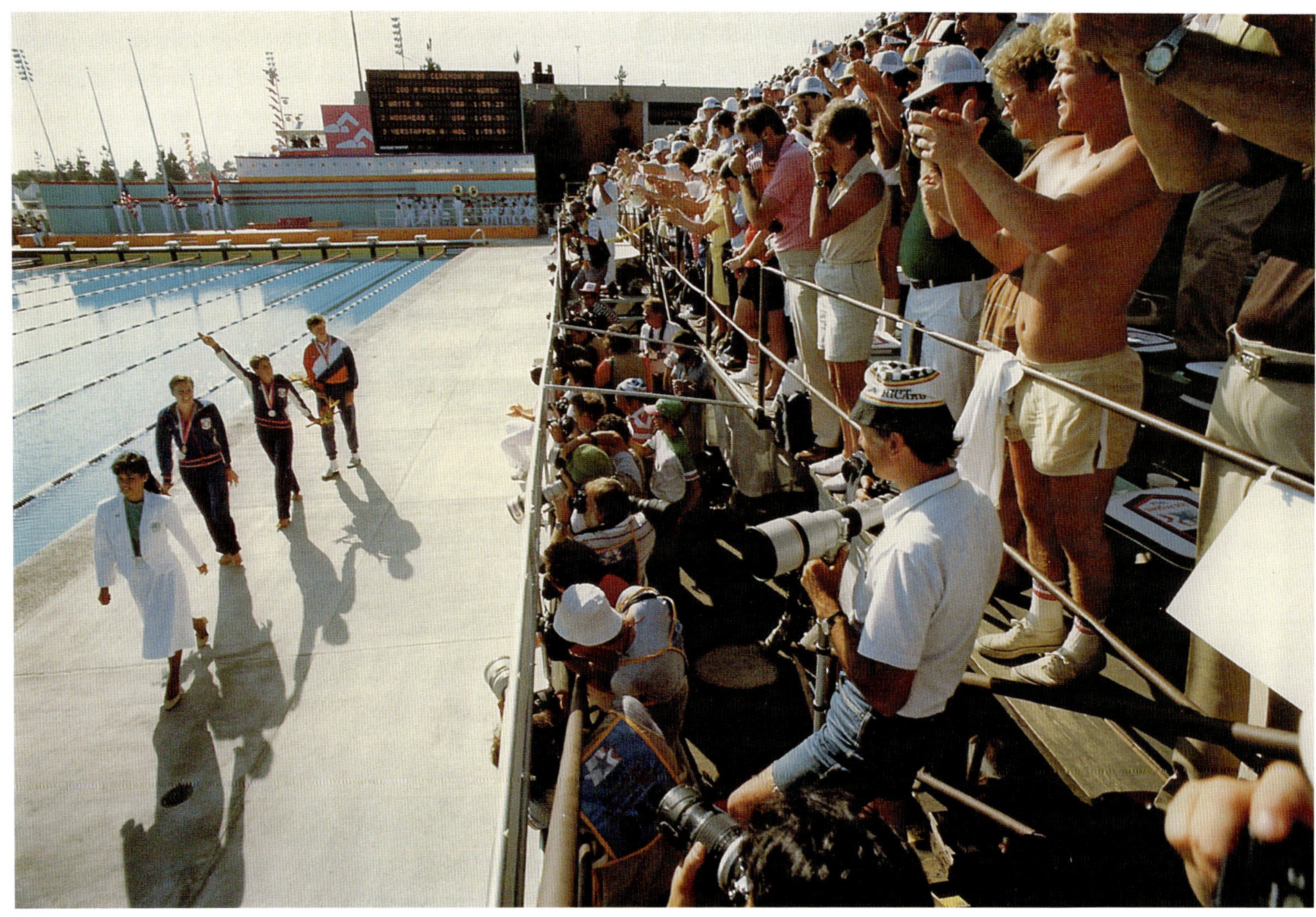

American Gold and Silver, University of Southern California, 1984

indispensable by also driving, helping set up and take down equipment, moving baggage, and so on.

1988

GROUP EXHIBITION

February. Mounted at State Office Building, New York. *Black Women in the Arts: A Tradition of Distinction and Accomplishment.* The exhibition is initiated by Kenkeleba House and sponsored by the New York State Division for Women. Donald Vogel acts as curator with FS as photographic specialist.

1989

GROUP EXHIBITION

September 14–December 9. Washington Project for the Arts, Washington, DC. *The Blues Aesthetic: Black Culture and Modernism.* Catalogue. Travels through December 1990 to California African American Museum, Los Angeles; Nasher Museum of Art at Duke University, Durham, North Carolina; Blaffer Art Museum, University of Houston; The Studio Museum in Harlem.

1990

Is the artist-in-residence at the Light Work gallery at Syracuse University.

1992

Submits a chapter, including image of *Smoke and the Lovers* for what will become *Smokestack Lightning: Adventures in the Heart of Barbecue Country* with writer and food historian Lolis Eric Elie.

SOLO EXHIBITION

November 15–December 17. Kenkeleba House, New York. *Frank Stewart: Blues & Abstract Reality*.

1993
Travels for six months with Elie to complete *Smokestack Lightning*.

1993–2019
Works as road manager and senior staff photographer for Jazz at Lincoln Center, working with music directors Marcus Roberts, Jon Faddis, and Wynton Marsalis.

1994
Celebrates publication of *Sweet Swing Blues on the Road* with text by Wynton Marsalis.

SOLO EXHIBITION
December. Bill Hodges Gallery, New York. *Sweet Swing Blues on the Road*, featuring images from the recent publication.

1995–96
GROUP EXHIBITION
March 26, 1996 (closing date). Art in the Atrium, Morristown, Pennsylvania. *Kamoinge Photographers Group Show*.

1996
Photographs Wynton Marsalis's Pulitzer-prize winning oratorio *Blood on the Fields* with Jazz at Lincoln Center Orchestra American and European Tours.

Smokestack Lightning: Adventures in the Heart of Barbecue Country is published.

GROUP EXHIBITION
Crawford and Sloan Gallery, New York. FS and David Ellis collaborative project using FS's photographs as the basis for Ellis's collages.

1997–99
Serves as vice president of Kamoinge.

1997
SOLO EXHIBITION
Leica Gallery (Broadway location), New York. *Frank Stewart: Riffs, Rectangles, and Responses: 25 Years of Photography*.

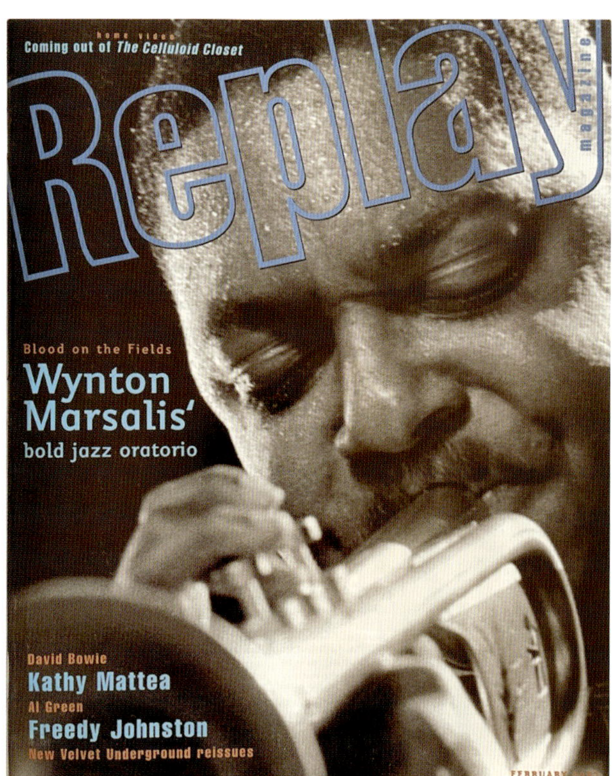

Cover photograph by Frank Stewart, *Replay Magazine*, February 1997

1998
GROUP EXHIBITION
September 4–30. The 4th Street Photo Gallery, New York. *Sight Sound in the Subway* (with Petra Richterová).

1999
SOLO EXHIBITION
June 15 (closing date). A+ Resources Fine Art Gallery, Miami. *Frank Stewart: In the House of Swing*. Curated by gallery owner Denise Andrews.

GROUP EXHIBITION
New York Public Library, Schomburg Center for Research in Black Culture. *Black New York Photographers of the 20th Century: Selections from the Schomburg Center Collections*.

2000
Curates discussion of jazz photography for Jazz at Lincoln Center, which opens on October 31 and features Bill Gottlieb and Herman Leonard.

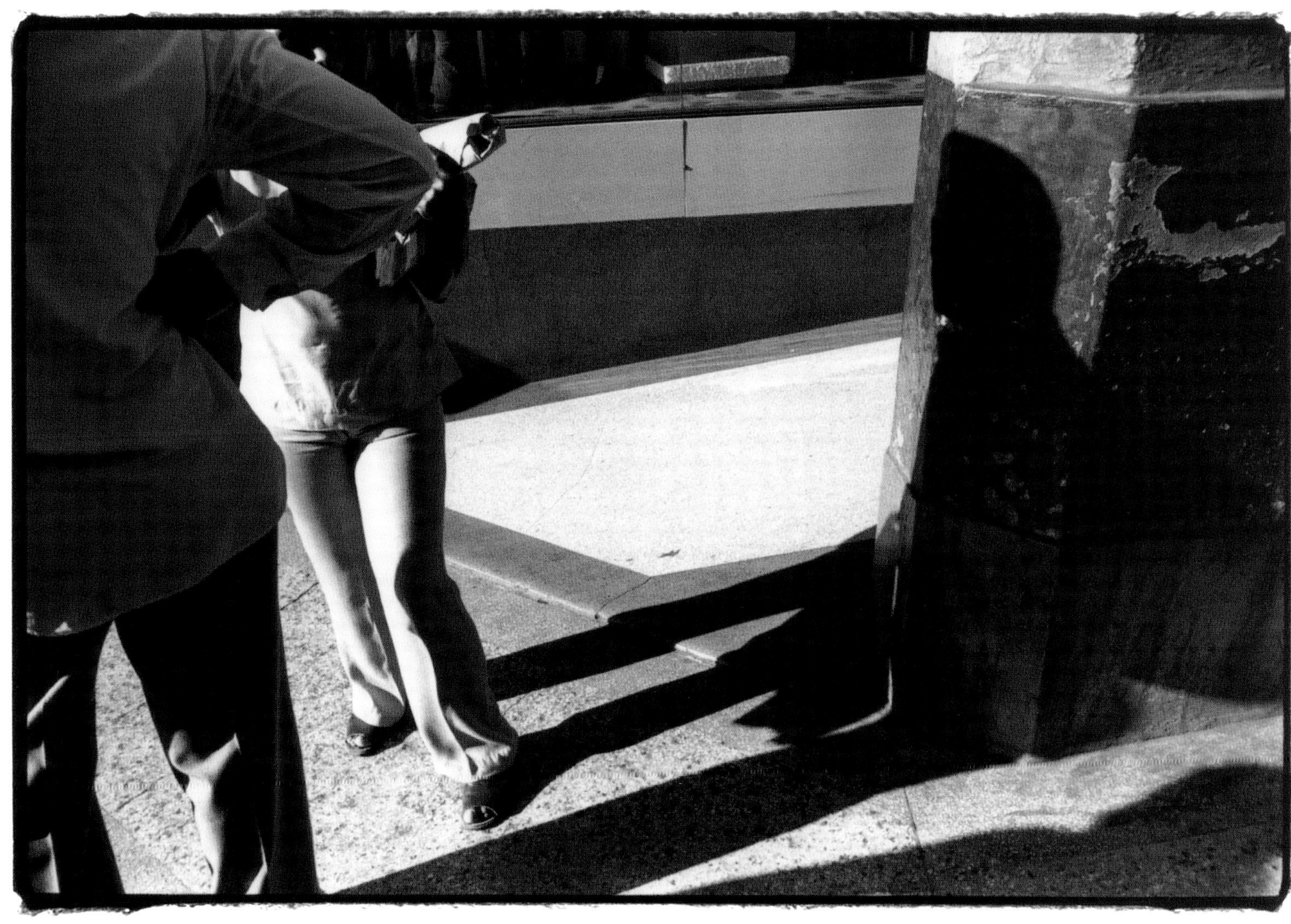

Two People and an Emotion, Santiago de Cuba, 1977

2001

FS photographs Harry Belafonte for a fundraiser at Avery Fisher Hall (now David Geffen Hall) at Lincoln Center that Susan Sillins produces for the Center for Cuban Studies. FS and Sillins form Black Light Productions, which lasts through 2011.

Travels to Cuba with Sillins and FS's daughter Sing, which leads to *Slice of Light* exhibition at Cuban Art Space, New York, the following year.

2001

GROUP EXHIBITIONS

February 16–April 29. Brooklyn Museum. *Committed to the Image: Contemporary Black Photographers*. Catalogue.

Leica Gallery (Broadway location), New York. *Harlem: A Group Exhibition*.

2002

SOLO EXHIBITIONS

July 5–August 31. Julie Baker Fine Art, Grass Valley, California. *Frank Stewart: Photographs*, featuring jazz-related photographs, coincides with Jazz at Lincoln Center performance in Grass Valley.

Cuban Art Space, Center for Cuban Studies, New York. *Frank Stewart: A Slice of Light*.

2002–3

As a New York Foundation for the Arts fellow, FS uses the funding to photograph in New Orleans.

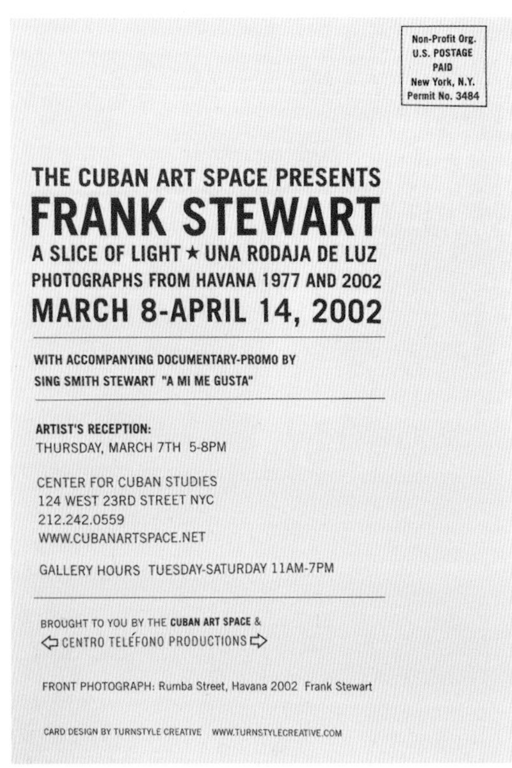

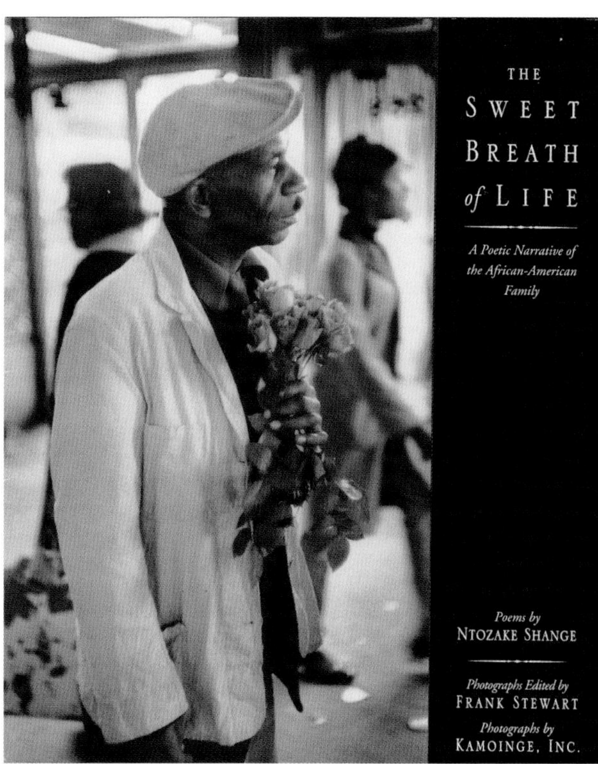

Announcement card for the exhibition *Frank Stewart: A Slice of Light*, 2002

Cover of *The Sweet Breath of Life: A Poetic Narrative of the African-American Family*, 2004. Cover image by Beuford Smith

2003

SOLO EXHIBITIONS

September 14–October 18. Kenkeleba House, New York. *Frank Stewart: Windows.*

September 14–January 4, 2004. Martin Luther King, Jr. Memorial Library, Washington, DC. *Frank Stewart: Romare Bearden* (in association with the National Gallery of Art exhibition *The Art of Romare Bearden*).

GROUP EXHIBITION

Leica Gallery (on West Broadway), New York. *Saturday Night Sunday Morning.* Curated by Deborah Willis.

2003–2018

Works as photographer for Savannah Music Festival each year in spring and privately shoots the legendary Savannah Saint Patrick's Day parade.

2004

Wynton Marsalis is appointed music director for Jazz at Lincoln Center.

Publishes *The Sweet Breath of Life: A Poetic Narrative of the African-American Family*, which features text by Ntozake Shange. FS serves as editor of photographs by Kamoinge members.

December 11. Conversation at National Gallery of Art among FS, David C. Driskell, and Ruth Fine followed by book signing to celebrate the publication of *Romare Bearden: Photographs by Frank Stewart*.

SOLO EXHIBITIONS

September. Time Warner Center atrium installation for opening of Jazz at Lincoln Center, New York. *Frank Stewart.*

September 18–November 18. Basta Pasta, New York. *Frank Stewart: Windows.*

October 8–November 9. June Kelly Gallery, New York. *Frank Stewart: Romare Bearden, The Last Years.*

Peg Alston Fine Arts, New York. *Romare Bearden by Frank Stewart.*

Galerias del Instituto Cubana del Arte e Industria Cinematográficos (ICAIC), Havana, Cuba. *Frank Stewart: Dos Momentos en La Vida/Two Moments in a*

Shanghai Mirror, 2004

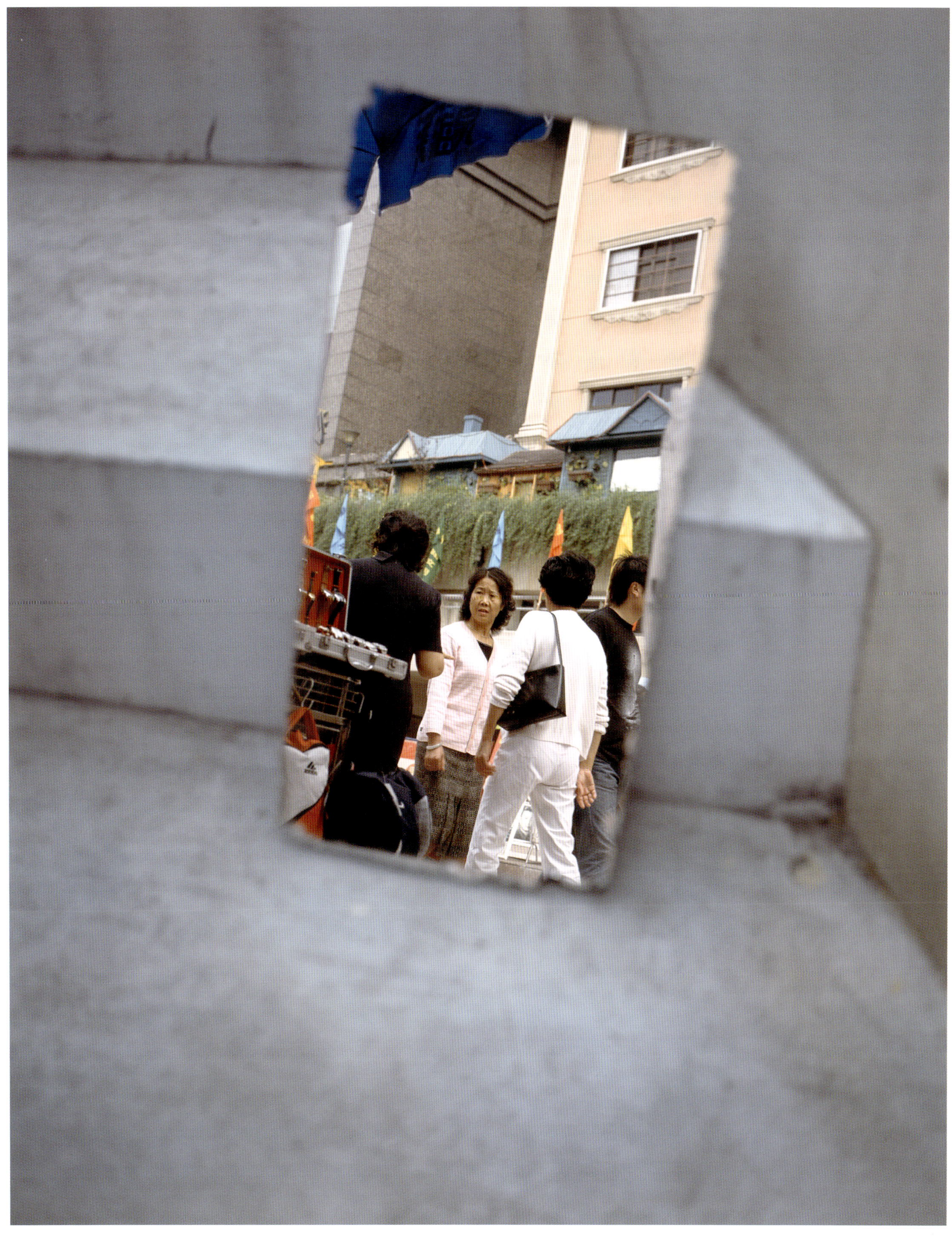

Life. The Charles Chaplin Theater hosts an installation of approximately ten 30 by 40–inch color prints, and the nearby cultural and community center features approximately thirty black-and-white prints of jazz subjects.

GROUP EXHIBITIONS

October 9–November 6. Peg Alston Fine Arts, New York. *Images of Romare Bearden by Frank Stewart and Anthony Barboza.*

New York Public Library, Schomburg Center for Research in Black Culture, New York. *Romare Bearden.*

G.R. N'namdi Gallery, New York. Exhibition based on *The Sweet Breath of Life*. Curated by Herb Robinson and Beuford Smith.

2005

Travels to New Orleans to observe the damage caused by Hurricane Katrina in September.

Drives cross-country in autumn to shoot images over more than 10,000 miles, with Carolyn Appel assisting. She later writes unpublished essay about the experience titled "Under the Black Cloth."

SOLO EXHIBITIONS

February 5–May 2. High Museum of Art, Atlanta. *Frank Stewart: Romare Bearden, The Last Years.*

April 20–May 23. Laumont Editions, New York. *Frank Stewart: Recent Color*, featuring photographs from cross-country trip.

October 15–December 17. Basta Pasta, New York. *Frank Stewart: Recent Color Photography.*

Installed in spring and on view for several years: 514 West, Savannah. *Frank Stewart: Jazz and Cuba.* Works on loan from the Walter O. Evans Collection.

Circa 2005. Little Black Pearl, Chicago. *Frank Stewart: Steppin'.* FS and Rudy Lombard, civil rights activist, professor of social sciences, and gourmet chef, set up a studio at the museum and FS photographs people from the community. After the negatives are processed, the photographs are installed in the same space where they were shot.

GROUP EXHIBITIONS

March 2–May 31. Museum of Art and Origins, New York (founded by George Nelson Preston). *Delta to Delta: From the Niger to the Mississippi.*

Nathan Cummings Foundation, New York. *Carnival.*

2006

Returns to New Orleans to observe long-term impact of Hurricane Katrina.

Blue Smoke Restaurant, Battery Park, New York. FS shows several large-scale photograph commissions.

SOLO EXHIBITIONS

Basin Street Station, New Orleans. *Frank Stewart.* Exhibition commissioned by Phoebe Jacobs, executive vice president and director of the Louis Armstrong Educational Foundation, featuring FS's photographs that highlight Wynton Marsalis's commitment to educating children around the world about jazz music and supporting the legacy of Louis Armstrong.

October 28. Adrian Ruehl Gallery, New York. *The Art of Frank Stewart* (single-day exhibition).

GROUP EXHIBITION

June 15–September 22. *Engulfed by Katrina: Photographs Before and After the Storm*. Nathan Cummings Foundation. Exhibition then moves to Tisch School of the Arts from October 19–November 18. Catalogue.

2007

Returns to New Orleans to further observe impact of Hurricane Katrina.

SOLO EXHIBITIONS

March 20–April 1. Jack Leigh Gallery, Savannah. *Frank Stewart: Jazz Improvisations.*

April 14–May 9. Essie Green Galleries, New York. *Frank Stewart: The False Face Mardi Gras.*

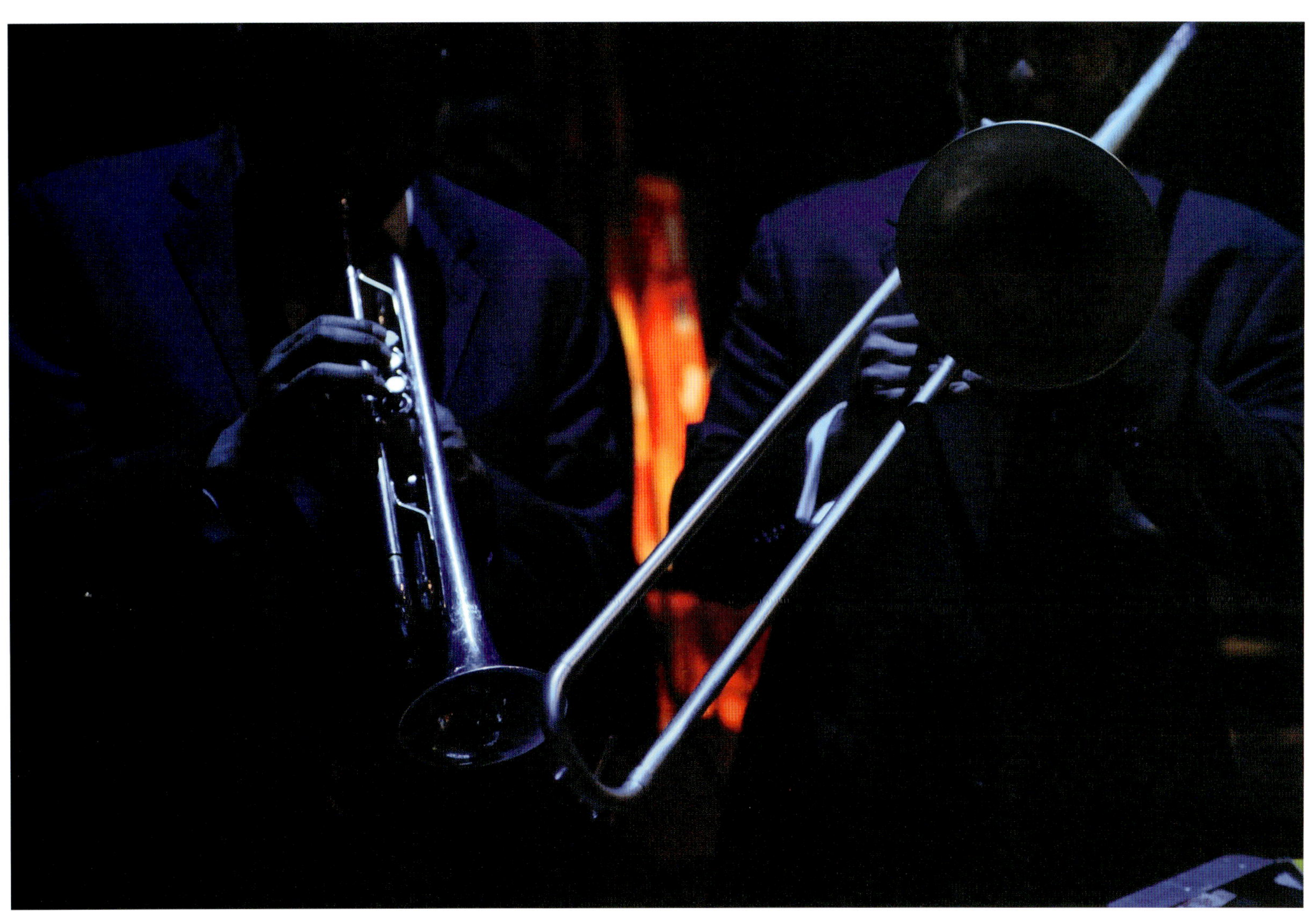

Trumpet and Bone, 2009

2009

SOLO EXHIBITION

October 15–November 5; and November 12–December 5. Essie Green Galleries, New York. A two-part exhibition titled *The Contemporary Frank Stewart: Painted Sounds* and *The Contemporary Frank Stewart: StreetScapes.*

GROUP EXHIBITIONS

September. Galerie Intemporel, directed by Laurence Choko, Paris. *Voyons Voir.*

September 2–December 6. University Museums, University of Delaware, Newark. *Sound: Print: Record—African American Legacies.* October 1–2: FS discusses his work during a symposium and conversation accompanying the show, partially sponsored by the Delaware Humanities Forum.

2010

July 8. Conversation between FS and jazz journalist Ted Panken at the National Jazz Museum in Harlem, intended to accompany portfolio of FS jazz photographs in *Aperture* magazine that was not published.

SOLO EXHIBITION

April 10–May 1. Bill Hodges Gallery, New York. *Frank Stewart: A Fulcrum of Time*, eighteen photographs spanning forty years

GROUP EXHIBITION

Panopticon Gallery, Boston.

2011

SOLO EXHIBITIONS

January 22–August 7. Time Warner Center, Jazz at Lincoln Center, New York. *Traveling Full Circle: Frank Stewart's Visual Music*. Brochure.

July 15–October 3. August Wilson African American Cultural Center, Pittsburgh. *Frank Stewart: Romare Bearden, The Last Years.*

September 2–January 22, 2012. Harvey B. Gantt Center for African-American Arts and Culture, Charlotte, North Carolina. *Frank Stewart: Romare Bearden, The Life.*

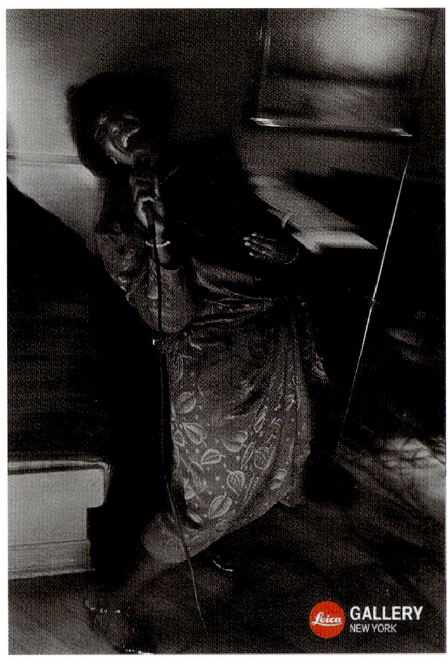

FRANK STEWART
BLUES PEOPLE

February 6 —
April 18, 2015

OPENING RECEPTION
Wednesday, February 25
6PM — 8PM

LEICA GALLERY
670 Broadway, New York, NY

Gallery Hours
Tuesday – Friday, 12PM – 6PM
Saturday, 12PM – 5PM

FRONT Frank Stewart, *Keisha at Lola's*, 1987

Two sides of exhibition announcement card for *Frank Stewart: Blues People*, 2015

2012

GROUP EXHIBITION

June. Design District during Art Basel, Galerie Intemporel, directed by Laurence Choko, Paris. *Ten Is One.*

2013

Jazz at Lincoln Center commissions a series of large Polaroid prints of the orchestra members. A video is made in association with this project.

GROUP EXHIBITION

Galerie Intemporel, directed by Laurence Choko, New York. *A Journey from Paris to New York.*

2014

SOLO EXHIBITION

November 8–January 4, 2015. Leica Gallery (West Broadway location), New York. *Frank Stewart: The Changing Face of Jazz.*

2015

SOLO EXHIBITION

February 6–April 18. Leica Gallery (Broadway location), New York. *Frank Stewart: Blues People*. Includes images from a span of twenty years.

Cover of exhibition catalogue *The Sound of My Soul: Frank Stewart's Life in Jazz*, 2019

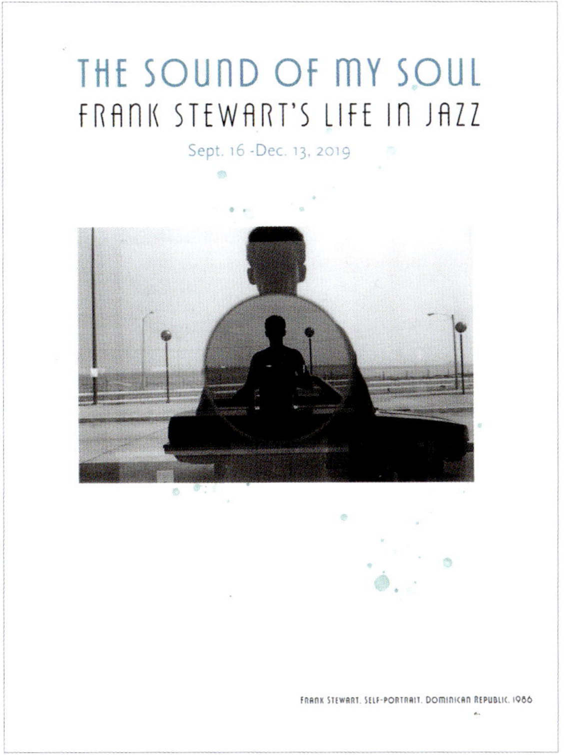

2016

Overview of FS photographs is acquired by newly opened National Museum of African American History and Culture, Washington, DC.

SOLO EXHIBITION

April 29–May 27. Essie Green Galleries, New York. *Frank Stewart.*

GROUP EXHIBITION

September 17–October 22. Essie Green Galleries, New York. *Artists and Style: Alexis Peskine, Charles Alston, Romare Bearden, Frank Stewart.*

2017

Receives the Lona Foote-Bob Parent Award for Career Excellence in Photography from the Jazz Journalists Association.

Travels to New Orleans in January to photograph pastors of Baptist churches in the Lower Ninth Ward.

Travels to Isle de Jean Charles in August to photograph effects of rapid climate change on Choctaw-owned land, stopping en route to photograph the funeral of Dolores Marsalis, wife of Ellis Marsalis.

SOLO EXHIBITION

April 29. Essie Green Galleries, New York.

GROUP EXHIBITION

June 4–July 29. Wilmer Jennings Gallery, Kenkeleba House, New York. *Time, Light, and Ritual: Photographs by John Simmons and Frank Stewart.*

2018

Travels to California in the fall to photograph the aftermath of the wildfires.

GROUP EXHIBITION

August 12–September 3. Featherstone Center for the Arts, Martha's Vineyard, Massachusetts. *The Beautiful Difference: African American Artists from Around the Country*. Curated by Sandra Grymes.

2019

SOLO EXHIBITIONS

February 12–April 30. New Rochelle City Hall, Rotunda Gallery. *The Photography of Frank Stewart*, presented by the New Rochelle Council on the Arts.

September 16–December 13. The Hutchins Center, Ethelbert Cooper Gallery of African and African American Art, Harvard University, Cambridge. *The Sound of My Soul: Frank Stewart's Life in Jazz*. Catalogue. Curated by Ruth Fine.

November 23–January 4, 2020. Gallery Neptune & Brown, Washington, DC. *Time Capsule: Photographs by Frank Stewart*. Curated by Ruth Fine.

2020

Travels to Washington, Oregon, and California in September to photograph the aftermath of the wildfires.

Becomes a teaching mentor at the Savannah College of Art and Design in Georgia and begins meeting with students to discuss their work.

During Covid lockdown period, begins reviewing negatives and doing work proofs of many images that had never been previously printed.

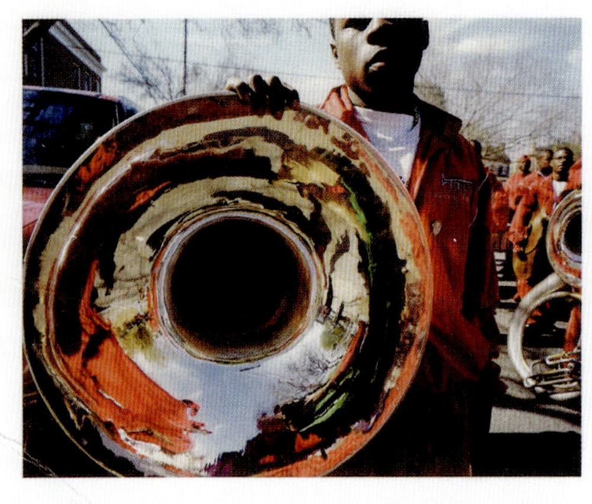

Exhibition announcement card for *Time Capsule: Photographs by Frank Stewart*, 2020

GROUP EXHIBITIONS

February 29–January 3, 2021. The Phillips Collection, Washington, DC. *Riffs and Relations: African American Artists and the European Modernist Tradition*. Five artist portraits included. Catalogue.

March 8–May 2. Wilmer Jennings Gallery, Kenkeleba House, New York. *Visions 1020*. Curated by Beuford Smith.

September 18–April 18, 2021. Telfair Museums, Savannah. *Youthful Adventures: Growing Up in Photography*. Includes *Circle in the Square, Savannah*.

2021

Travels to St. Helena Island, off the coast of South Carolina, to photograph the Penn Center community; also photographs St. Simons and St. Johns, islands sinking off the coast of Georgia.

SOLO EXHIBITION

October 23–November 27. Gallery Neptune & Brown, Washington, DC. *Frank Stewart: Diary of a Globetrotter*.

2022

Shoots the Savannah Music Festival in spring for the first time since 2018.

Travels to France to photograph in Normandy in June.

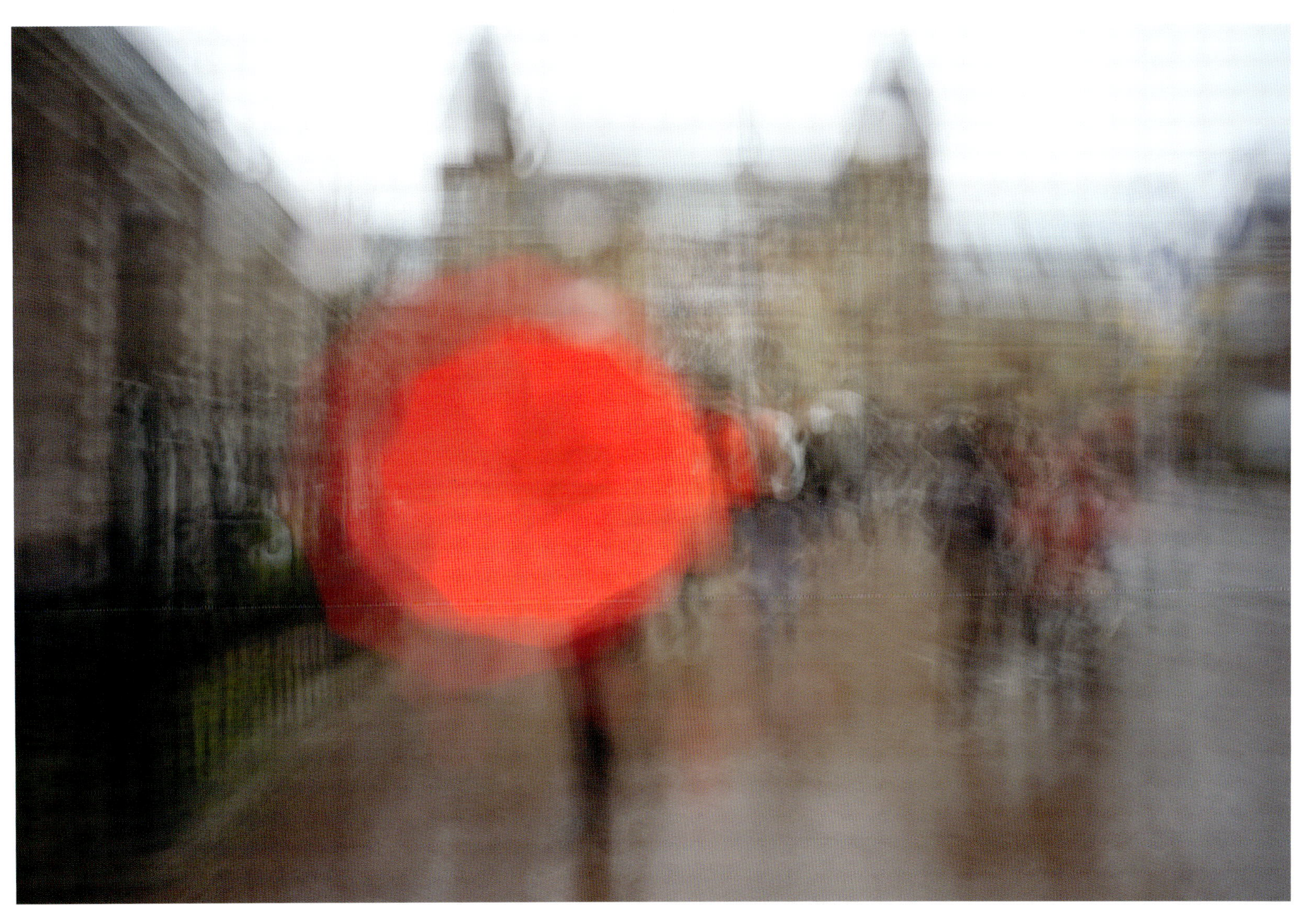

Red Umbrella, Amsterdam, 2020

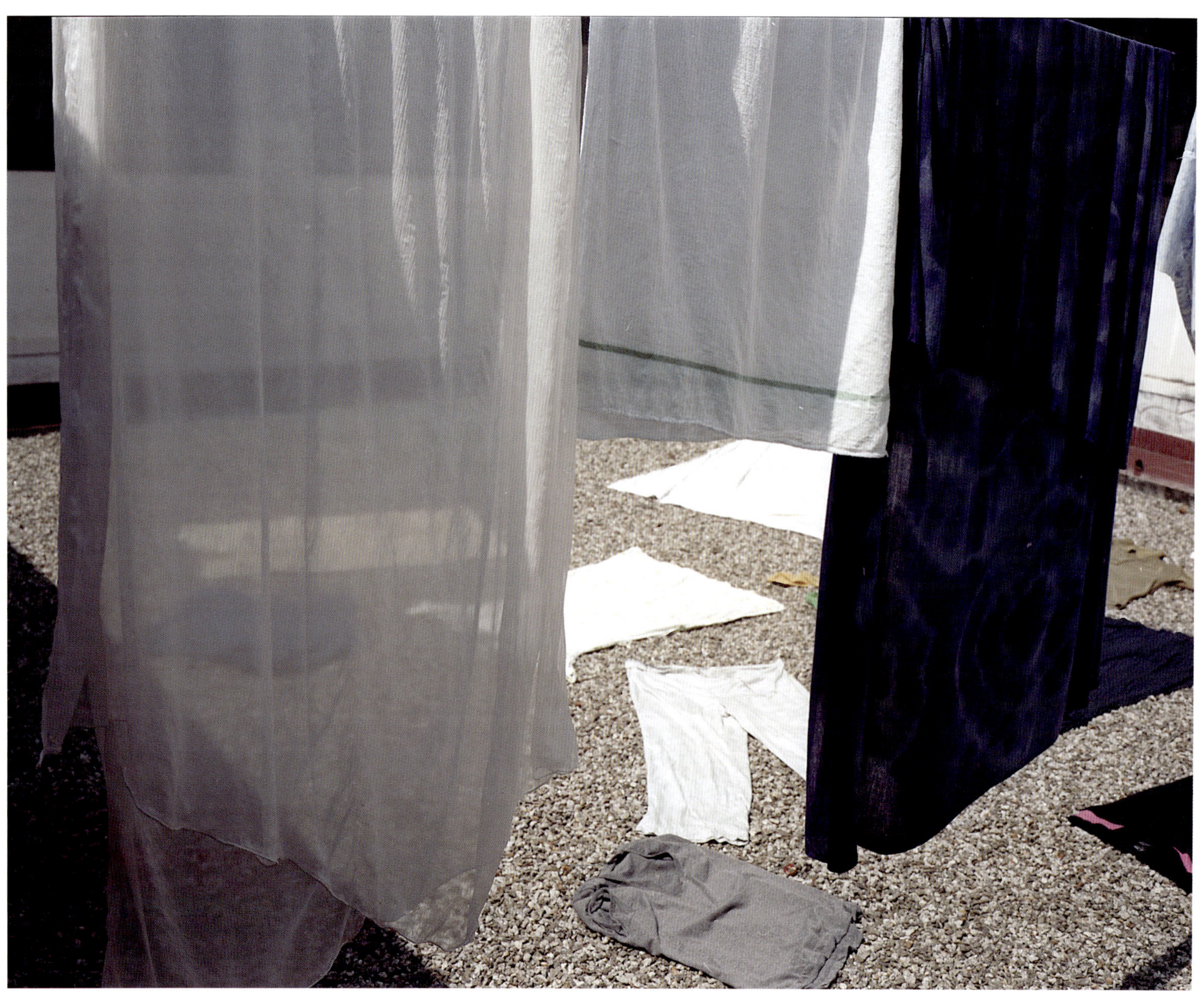

Towels and Gravel, India, 2011

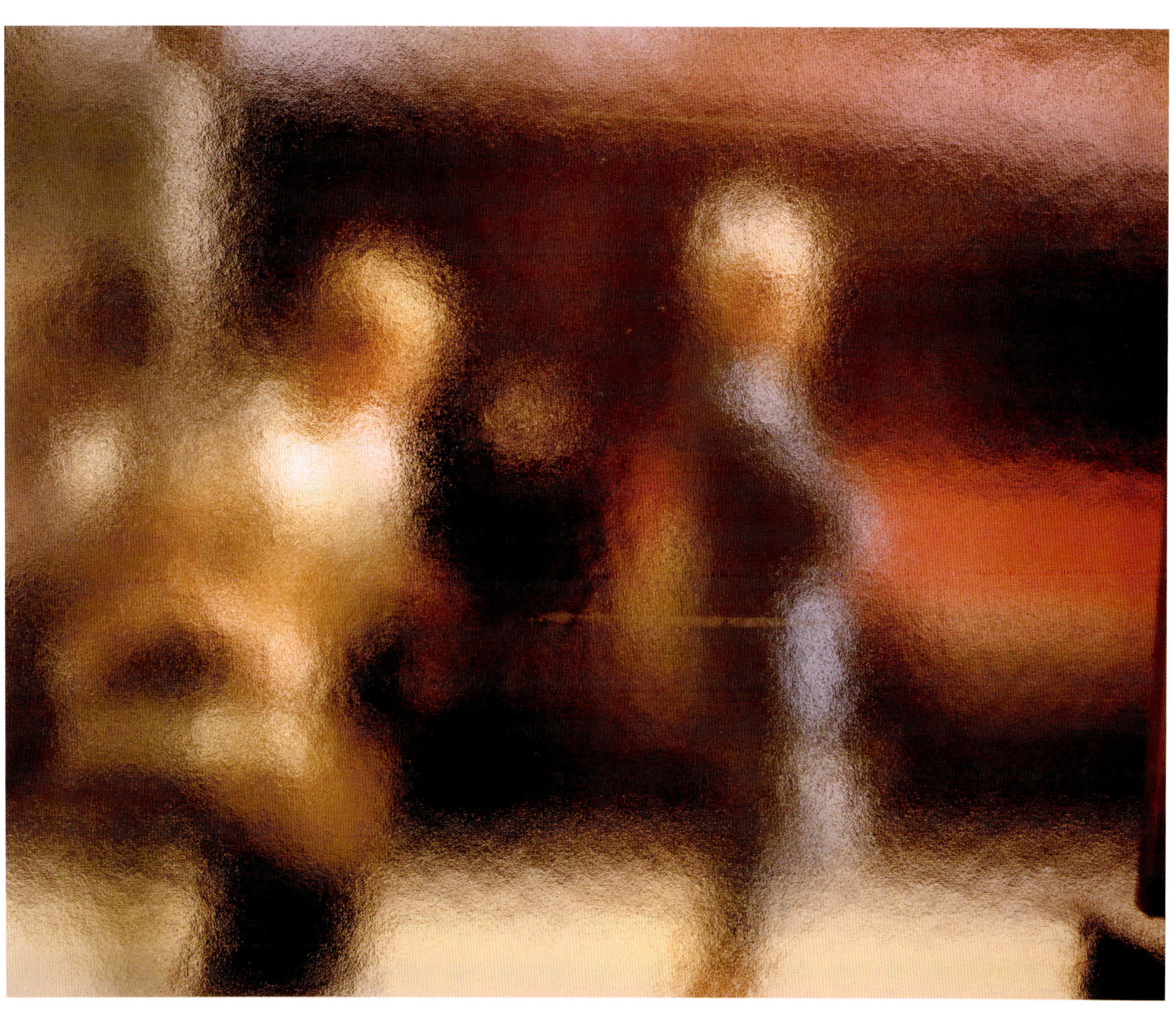

Bus Stop, Spain, 2009

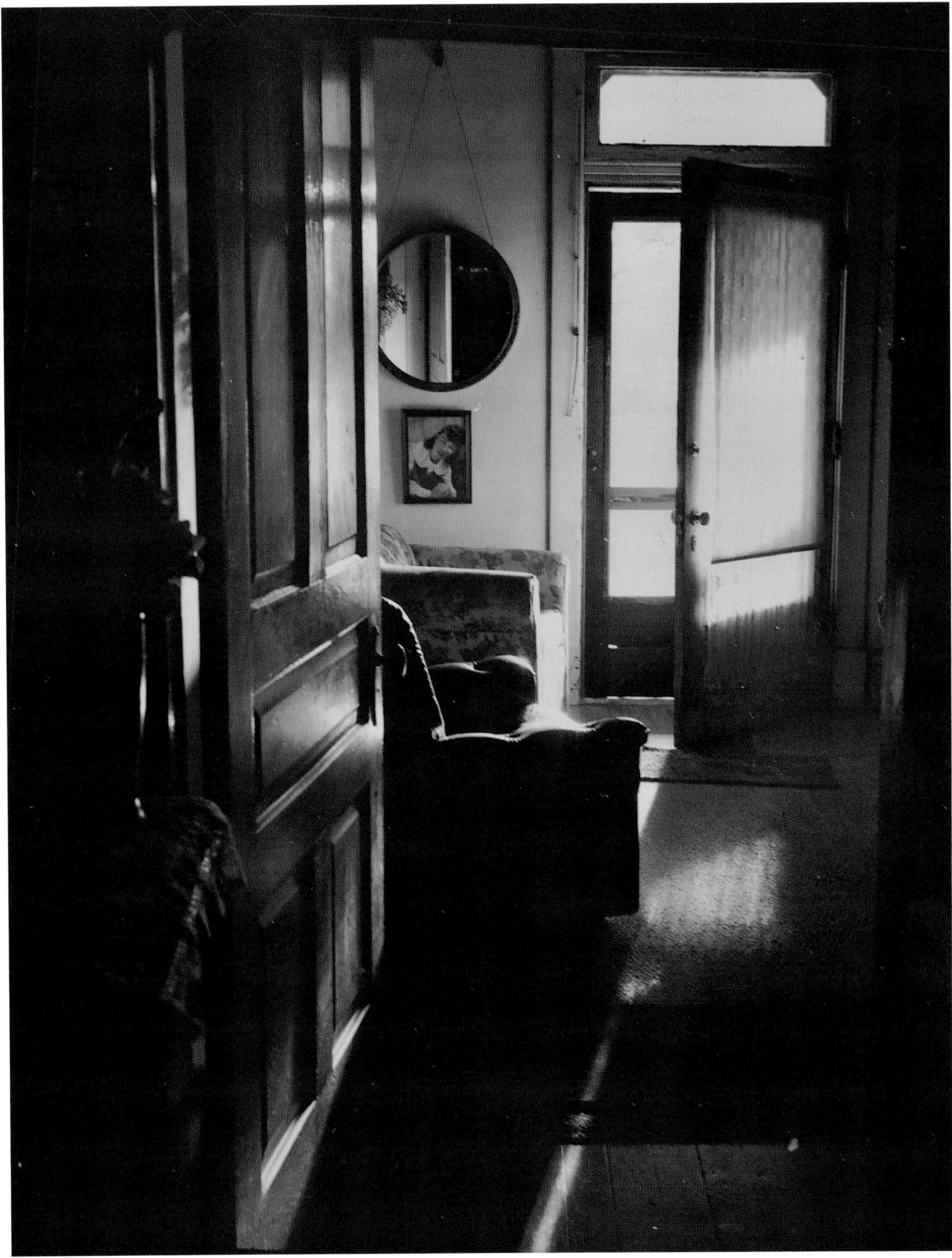

EXHIBITION CHECKLIST

Entries are chronological within each section and alphabetical within a given year. Unless otherwise noted, sizes refer to sheet sizes, or aluminum plate sizes, when relevant.

THE CULTURE: RITUALS

Nine Snapshots from March on Washington for Jobs and Freedom, 1963
Kodak drugstore processing
3 1/4 × 3 1/4 in. (each)
Collection of the artist
pages 23–25

George in the Doorway, 1969
Gelatin silver print
20 × 16 in.
Andre Kimo Stone Guess and Cheryl Peterson Guess Family Collection, Louisville, KY
page 4

George in the Doorway, 1969 (printed 1971)
Inkjet print
30 × 22 in.
Collection of Corrine Jennings, Kenkeleba House, New York

Chicago Wedding Reception (The Secret), 1972
Gelatin silver print
11 × 14 in.
Collection of Jeanne Moutoussamy-Ashe
page 26

Chicago Wedding Reception (The Secret), 1972
Gelatin silver print
16 × 20 in.
Collection of Corrine Jennings, Kenkeleba House, New York
page 27

Contrast in Black and White, 1972
Gelatin silver print
11 × 13 15/16 in.
Philadelphia Museum of Art, 2021-93-2
page 35

Alex in the Keyhole, 1975
Gelatin silver print
16 × 20 in.
Andre Kimo Stone Guess and Cheryl Peterson Guess Family Collection, Louisville, KY
page 30

Desnambuc, 1975
Gelatin silver print
16 × 20 in.
Collection of Corrine Jennings, Kenkeleba House, New York
page 16

Neon Pool Cue, Harlem, 1975
Inkjet print
16 × 20 in.
Collection of Sing Lathan and Bining Taylor
page 29

Boy and Motorcycles (or *Suffolk County Police*), 1976
Gelatin silver print
16 × 20 in.
The Studio Museum in Harlem, New York, Gift of the artist, 1979.3.1
page 34

Easter Sunday, Harlem, 1976 (printed 1978)
Gelatin silver print
16 × 20 in.
Collection of Eileen and Major E. Thomas, Jr.
page 17

Loop Auto Park, Chicago, 1976
Gelatin silver print
23 5/16 × 32 15/16 in.
Philadelphia Museum of Art, 2021.81.5
page 28

Radio Players Series (or *The Bus*), 1978
Gelatin silver print
14 x 11 in.
Collection of Sing Lathan and Bining Taylor
page 31

St. Louis Cemetery II, 1980
Gelatin silver print
16 × 20 in.
Andre Kimo Stone Guess and Cheryl Peterson Guess Family Collection, Louisville, KY
page 36

Klan Rally, Jackson, Mississippi (or *Ku Klux Klan*), 1981
Gelatin silver print
16 × 20 in.
Andre Kimo Stone Guess and Cheryl Peterson Guess Family Collection, Louisville, KY
page 37

Miles in the Green Room, 1981
Inkjet print
20 × 30 in.
Private collection
page 14

Jackie's Mirror, 2000

Only God to Watch My Back, N.Y., 1987 (printed 2021)
Pigment print
24 × 32 in.
Courtesy Gallery Neptune & Brown, Washington, DC
page 39

The Clean Up (or *American Gothic*), 1988 (printed 2021)
Pigment print
32 × 42 in.
Collection of a Friend of the Memphis Brooks Museum of Art
page 38

Blues and Abstract Reality, 1990
Gelatin silver print
16 × 20 in.
Andre Kimo Stone Guess and Cheryl Peterson Guess Family Collection, Louisville, KY
page 41

The Bow, Modena, Italy, 1996
Inkjet print
58 × 83 1/4 in.
Andre Kimo Stone Guess and Cheryl Peterson Guess Family Collection, Louisville, KY
page 10

THE CULTURE: SOUND, TASTE, TOUCH

Youth in Harlem Series: Man Dancing with Two Girls, 1976
Inkjet print
16 ×20 in.
Collection of Sing Lathan and Bining Taylor
page 44

Beer Garden, Yonkers, 1982
Gelatin silver print
20 × 16 in.
Collection of Corrine Jennings, Kenkeleba House, New York
page 43

Smoke and the Lovers, Memphis (or *Smoke and the Lovers, Hawkins Grill*), 1992 (printed 2009)
Gelatin silver print
12 3/8 × 18 1/2 in.
The Museum of Modern Art, New York, David H. McAlpin Fund
page 102

Juneteenth '93, 19th of June Celebration, Mexia, Texas, 1993
Gelatin silver print
7 3/4 × 11 1/2 in.
Collection of the artist
page 106

J4YP (or *Wynton Marsalis at Jazz for Young People, New York City*), 1996
Gelatin silver print
14 × 11 in.
Collection of Robert G. O'Meally, New York
page 45

Warmdaddy in the House of Swing, New York, 1996
Inkjet print
34 × 49 in.
Collection of Sing Lathan and Bining Taylor
page 47

Stomping the Blues, 1997
Gelatin silver print
16 × 20 in.
Collection of Rob Gibson, Savannah
page 6

THE CULTURE: ARTISTS AND WORKPLACES

Alma W. Thomas (or *Alma Thomas, Painter*), 1976 (printed 2019)
Gelatin silver print
7 x 10 in. (image)
Bowdoin College Museum of Art, Brunswick, Maine, Museum Purchase, Gridley W. Tarbell II Fund
page 105

Romie in the Ocean, St. Martin, c. 1977
Gelatin silver print
20 × 16 in.
Collection of Gordon and Peggy Cooper Davis, New York
page 54

David C. Driskell (or *David C. Driskell, Painter*), 1978 (printed 2021)
Gelatin silver print
12 1/4 x 18 1/2 in. (image)
Bowdoin College Museum of Art, Brunswick, Maine, Museum Purchase, Gridley W. Tarbell II Fund
page 55

Endangered Species: David Hammons, 1981 (printed 2021)
Gelatin silver print
19 15/16 × 16 in.
Philadelphia Museum of Art, Purchased with the Lynne and Harold Honickman Fund for Photography, 2021, 2021-81-1
page 53

Keisha at Lola's, 1986
Gelatin silver print
20 × 16 in.
Collection of Sing Lathan and Bining Taylor
page 56

Boo and Humphrey, 1989
Gelatin silver print
16 × 20 in.
Andre Kimo Stone Guess and Cheryl Peterson Guess Family Collection, Louisville, KY
page 57

Skaine and Coopty, Palm Beach, Florida, 1992
Gelatin silver print
19 1/2 × 16 in.
Courtesy of Rodney M. Miller Collection
page 58

Cassandra Wilson, 1994
Gelatin silver print
16 × 20 in.
Andre Kimo Stone Guess and Cheryl Peterson Guess Family Collection, Louisville, KY
page 59

Marcus Roberts, 1994
Gelatin silver print
14 × 11 in.
Courtesy of Rodney M. Miller Collection
page 61

Roy Haynes, Alice Tully Hall, 2002
Gelatin silver print
14 × 11 in.
The Studio Museum in Harlem, New York; gift of Joy of Giving Something, Inc. 2018.47.28
page 60

ANCESTORS: AFRICA, THE CARIBBEAN, NEW ORLEANS

Call and Response, Abidjan, Côte d'Ivoire, 1974 (printed c. 2017)
Inkjet print
20 × 30 in.
Collection of George Nelson Preston, Museum of Art and Origins
page 140

Tailor Shop, Abidjan, Côte d'Ivoire, 1974
Gelatin silver print
11 × 14 in.
Collection of Sing Lathan and Bining Taylor
page 143

Untitled (from the *Second Line* series), 1976
Gelatin silver print
18 1/4 x 12 1/4 in. (image)
The Studio Museum in Harlem, New York, Gift of the artist, 1979.3.3
page 48

Homage to Cartier-Bresson, Camagüey, 1977
Gelatin silver print
16 × 20 in.
Collection of Beuford Smith, New York
page 98

One-Eyed Man, Santiago de Cuba, 1977 (printed 2017)
Gelatin silver print
20 × 16 in.
Collection of John-Conrad Ste Marthe, New York
page 92

Calling the Indians Out, 1978
Gelatin silver print
15 15/16 × 19 13/16 in.
National Museum of African American History and Culture, Washington, DC
page 144

Canal Street Shout, New Orleans, 1978 (printed 2017)
Gelatin silver print
11 × 14 in.
Collection of George Nelson Preston, Museum of Art and Origins
page 49

Number 1, 1978 (printed 2022)
Gelatin silver print
11 × 14 in.
Collection of Sing Lathan and Bining Taylor
page 93

Ellis and Wynton Marsalis, 1991
Gelatin silver print
16 × 20 in.
Private collection
page 99

I'm Still Here, New Orleans, 1991
Inkjet print
20 × 30 in.
Collection of Sing Lathan and Bining Taylor
page 101

Girl Reading, Mamfe, Ghana, 1997
Inkjet print
20 × 16 in.
Collection of John Simmons, Los Angeles
page 20

Clock of the Earth, Mamfe, Ghana, 1998
Inkjet print
30 × 30 in.
Andre Kimo Stone Guess and Cheryl Peterson Guess Family Collection, Louisville, KY
page 83

Getting the Spirit II, Mamfe, Ghana, 1998
Gelatin silver print
16 × 20 in.
Collection of Sing Lathan and Bining Taylor
page 84

Chief's Granddaughter, 1999
Gelatin silver print
19 7/8 × 15 5/16 in.
Philadelphia Museum of Art, Purchased with the Lynne and Harold Honickman Fund for Photography, 2021, 2021-81-14
page 85

Abena Pounding Fufu, Mamfe, Ghana (or *Pounding Fufu, Ghana*), 2000 (printed 2004)
Gelatin silver print
20 × 16 in.
Collection of George Nelson Preston, Museum of Art and Origins
page 87

Callejón de Hamel, Havana, 2002
Gelatin silver print
16 × 20 in.
Andre Kimo Stone Guess and Cheryl Peterson Guess Family Collection, Louisville, KY
page 97

Going for Salsa, Santiago de Cuba, 2003
Gelatin silver print
16 × 20 in.
Collection of Sing Lathan and Bining Taylor
page 91

Inside Out at La Conga, Santiago de Cuba, 2003
Gelatin silver print
16 × 20 in.
Collection of Sing Lathan and Bining Taylor
page 95

Santiago Carnival, 2003
Gelatin silver print
16 × 20 in.
Collection of Sing Lathan and Bining Taylor
page 96

Boy and Two Girls, Mamfe, Ghana, 2004
Gelatin silver print
16 × 20 in.
Collection of Sing Lathan and Bining Taylor
page 89

The Dead Man, Amanokrom, Ghana, 2004 (printed 2022)
Gelatin silver print
11 × 14 in.
Collection of Sing Lathan and Bining Taylor
page 86

Slave Castle, Cape Coast, Ghana, 2004 (printed 2022)
Gelatin silver print
20 × 16 in.
Collection of Sing Lathan and Bining Taylor
page 88

Bicycle II, Cienfuegos, c. 2004–5 (printed 2022)
Gelatin silver print
16 × 20 in.
Collection of Sing Lathan and Bining Taylor
page 94

George's Parlor, 2004
Inkjet print
19 7/8 x 15 7/8 in.
Collection of Dr. Walter O. Evans
page 90

AROUND THE WORLD: WINDOWS

Three Partitions, 1971
Inkjet print
27 1/2 × 39 in.
Collection of Sing Lathan and Bining Taylor
page 113

Communist Windows, Havana, 1977 (printed 2022)
Gelatin silver print
11 × 14 in.
Collection of Sing Lathan and Bining Taylor
page 147

Fulton Street, 1990
Gelatin silver print
11 × 14 in.
Collection of Sing Lathan and Bining Taylor
page 114

Perugia, 1996
Inkjet print on aluminum
19 3/4 × 19 3/4 in.
Collection of Sandra Grymes
page 115

Louisville, 1998
Inkjet print on aluminum
24 × 32 in.
Collection of Adam R. Rose and Peter R. McQuillan
page 117

AROUND THE WORLD: CHROMATIC MUSIC

Walter and Willie, 2004
Inkjet print
25 × 18 in.
Collection of Elizabeth Cooper Davis
page 121

Bone and Silhouette (or *Chris and Vincent*), 2009
Inkjet print
20 × 16 in.
Courtesy of Manny's Bistro, New York
page 122

Ahmad Jamal, 2013
Inkjet print
30 × 30 in.
Collection of Sing Lathan and Bining Taylor
page 145

Blood on the Fields, 2014
Inkjet print
33 × 49 in.
Collection of Greg Scholl
page 123

Cécile, New Year's Eve, 2016
Inkjet print
33 × 50 in.
Collection of Sing Lathan and Bining Taylor
page 126

Etienne, 2017 (printed 2022)
Inkjet print
22 × 17 in.
Collection of Sing Lathan and Bining Taylor
page 127

AROUND THE WORLD: CULTURES IN COLOR

Blue Car, Havana, 2002
Chromogenic print
33 × 48 in.
Private collection, Washington, DC
page 129

Watermelons, 2003
Inkjet print
30 × 40 in.
Collection of Sing Lathan and Bining Taylor
page 132

Yokohama, 2004
Pigment print
20 × 25 in.
Collection of Sing Lathan and Bining Taylor
page 130

Savannah Tour Bus, 2006
Chromogenic print
34 × 42 in.
Telfair Museums, funds provided by Ronald J. Strahan in honor of James McKenna, 2007.9
page 135

Three Young Camels, Mali, 2006
Inkjet print
33 × 40 ½ in.
Collection of George Nelson Preston, Museum of Art and Origins
page 137

Gorée Island Painter (or *Slave Castle Back*), 2006
Chromogenic print
35 × 42 ½ in.
Andre Kimo Stone Guess and Cheryl Peterson Guess Family Collection, Louisville, KY
page 138

Circle in the Square, Savannah, 2007
Chromogenic print
32 ½ × 39 in.
Telfair Museums, Ronald J. Strahan Art Acquisition Endowment Fund, 2018.12
page 2

God's Trombones, Harlem, New York, 2009 (printed 2022)
Inkjet print on aluminum
48 × 60 in.
Collection of Marquise Stillwell
page 111

St. Patrick's Day, Savannah, Ga., 2012 (printed 2021)
Chromogenic print
40 × 60 in.
Collection of Sing Lathan and Bining Taylor
page 134

Auckland, 2016 (printed 2021)
Pigment print
24 × 30 in.
Collection of Sing Lathan and Bining Taylor
page 131

Bean, Chicago, 2018 (printed 2022)
Inkjet print
30 × 40 in.
Collection of Sing Lathan and Bining Taylor
page 139

Cargo, England, 2020 (printed 2021)
Pigment print
25 × 30 in.
Collection of Fay and Blake Boswell
page 133

DRAWINGS: THE PHOTOGRAPHER'S SKETCHBOOK

Self-portrait, Dominican Republic, 1986
Gelatin silver print
16 × 20 in.
Collection of the artist
page 108

Lisbon, 1998 (printed 2021)
Gelatin silver print
16 × 20 in.
Collection of the artist
page 149 (top)

Seoul, 1998 (printed 2021)
Gelatin silver print
16 × 20 in.
Collection of the artist
page 149 (bottom)

Manchester, England, 2014
Inkjet print
11 × 14 in.
Collection of the artist
page 150 (top)

Swordsmen, New Iberia, LA, 2015
Inkjet print
11 × 14 in.
Collection of the artist
page 150 (bottom)

Cubism, Times Square, 2016
Inkjet print
16 × 20 in.
Collection of the artist
page 151 (top)

Cityscape, 2018
Inkjet print
20 × 16 in.
Collection of the artist
page 151 (bottom)

Amsterdam, 2019
Inkjet print
14 × 11 in.
Collection of the artist
page 152 (bottom)

China, 2019
Inkjet print
11 × 14 in.
Collection of the artist
page 152 (top)

Shanghai, 2019
Inkjet print
16 × 20 in.
Collection of the artist
page 153 (bottom)

Wu Han, 2019
Inkjet print
11 × 14 in.
Collection of the artist
page 153 (top)

ENVIRONMENTAL CATASTROPHE

Katrina: Clouds and Railroad Tracks, 2005
Chromogenic print
16 × 20 in.
Collection of George Nelson Preston, Museum of Art and Origins
page 155

Katrina's Houses I, 2005
Chromogenic print
16 5⁄16 × 22 in.
National Museum of African American History and Culture, Washington, DC
page 157

Katrina's Parlor, 2006
Chromogenic print
16 × 20 in.
Collection of George Nelson Preston, Museum of Art and Origins
page 19

Katrina: Hammond B-3, 9th Ward, New Orleans, 2007
Inkjet print
30 × 40 in.
The Medium Group, LLC, courtesy of Larry Ossei-Mensah
page 159

L'Isle Jean Charles, 2017
Inkjet print
11 × 14 in.
Collection of the artist
page 162

L'Isle Jean Charles: Man-made Reefs, 2017
Inkjet print
11 × 14 in.
Collection of the artist
page 163

California Fires Series, Camp Fire, 2018
Inkjet print
16 × 20 in.
Collection of the artist
page 165

California Fires Series, St. Helena, 2020
Inkjet print
16 × 20 in.
Collection of the artist
page 164

SELECT BIBLIOGRAPHY

Institutional restrictions due to the Covid pandemic have limited research access for this bibliography. Additionally, it was not within its intended scope to record all of Frank Stewart's commercially published photographs. Examples are included to provide a fuller account of his work.

BOOKS OF FRANK STEWART'S WORK

Elie, Lolis Eric. Photographs by Frank Stewart. *Smokestack Lightning: Adventures in the Heart of Barbecue Country.* New York: Farrar, Straus and Giroux, 1996.

Fine, Ruth. Foreword by David C. Driskell. *Romare Bearden: Photographs by Frank Stewart.* Petaluma, CA: Pomegranate Books, 2004.

Fine, Ruth. *Jazz: Frank Stewart.* Southport, UK: Café Royal Books, 2020.

Marsalis, Wynton, ed. *In the Spirit of Swing: The First 25 Years of Jazz at Lincoln Center.* San Francisco: Chronicle Books, 2012.

Marsalis, Wynton, et al. *Jazz at Lincoln Center: House of Swing.* New York: Nazraeli Press in association with Jazz at Lincoln Center, 2004.

Marsalis, Wynton, and Frank Stewart. *Sweet Swing Blues on the Road.* New York: Thunder's Mouth Press, 1994.

EDITED BY FRANK STEWART

Shange, Ntozake, and Frank Stewart, eds. Photographs by Kamoinge. *The Sweet Breath of Life: A Poetic Narrative of the African-American Family.* New York: Atria, 2004.

CATALOGUES AND BROCHURES ACCOMPANYING STEWART'S SOLO AND GROUP EXHIBITIONS

Childs, Adrienne L. et al. *Riffs and Relations: African American Artists and the European Modernist Tradition.* Washington, D.C. and New York: The Phillips Collection and Rizzoli Electa, 2019.

DeCarava, Roy. *Jules Allen, Beuford Smith, Frank Stewart: Photographs.* New York: National Urban League, Gallery 62, 1980.

Deutsch, Rose, and Jay Deutsch. *Frank Stewart: Blues People.* New York: Leica Gallery, 2015.

Fine, Ruth. *The Sound of My Soul: Frank Stewart's Life in Jazz.* Cambridge, MA: Harvard University Hutchins Center, Ethelbert Cooper Gallery of African and African American Art, 2019.

Jennings, Corrine, and Deborah Willis, eds., Frank Stewart, curator. *Two Schools, New York and Chicago—Contemporary African-American Photography of the 60s and 70s.* New York: Kenkeleba Gallery, 1986.

Millstein, Barbara Head, ed. Essays by Clyde Taylor and Deba P. Patnaik. *Committed to the Image: Contemporary Black Photographers.* Brooklyn: Brooklyn Museum, 2001.

Olander, William, Introduction. *Contemporary Afro-American Photography: Jules Allen, Anthony Barboza, Albert V. Chong, Adger W. Cowans, Louis Draper, Roland L. Freeman, John Pinderhughes, Wayne Providence, Coreen Simpson, Lorna Simpson, Ming Smith, Frank Stewart, Shawn Walker, Daniel S. Williams.* Oberlin, OH: Allen Memorial Art Museum, Oberlin College, 1983.

O'Meally, Robert G. *Traveling Full Circle: Frank Stewart's Visual Music.* New York: Jazz at Lincoln Center, 2011.

Parks, Gordon. *Still Photographs: Recent Photographs by Frank Stewart and Jeanne Moutoussamy-Ashe.* Chicago: The Chicago Public Library Cultural Center, 1980.

Powell, Richard. *The Blues Aesthetic: Black Culture and Modernism.* Washington, D.C.: Washington Project for the Arts, 1989.

Ruud, Brandon K., ed. *Photography from the Sheldon Museum of Art.* Lincoln: University of Nebraska Press, 2013.

Schjeldahl, Peter. *10 Photographers, Olympic Images: Louis Carlos Bernal, Robert Buitron, Jo Ann Callis, Jack Carnell, Robert Cumming, Bonnie Donohue, Jim Dow, Peter Reiss, Frank Stewart, Charles Traub.* Los Angeles: Los Angeles Center for Photographic Studies, The Museum of Contemporary Art, Olympic Arts Festival, 1984.

INTERVIEWS, ARTICLES, AND REVIEWS

"Benin Exhibits Three Photogs," *New Amsterdam News,* June 5, 1976.

The Black Photographers Annual, vol. 1, 1973, 138–42.

The Black Photographers Annual 2, 1974, 37.

The Black Photographers Annual 4, 1974, 21.

Booker, Bobbi. "Lifestyles: Romare Bearden Captured in Photos in Exhibit." *The Philadelphia Tribune,* November 20, 2015.

DeCarava, Sherry Turner. "Black Eyes/Light: Photos by Frank Stewart and Jules Allen." *New Amsterdam News,* February 17, 1979.

Fabricant, Florence. "Kitchen Bookshelf: For Summer, Outdoor and Indoor Adventures in Cooking. *Smokestack Lightning* by Lolis Eric Elie, with Photographs by Frank Stewart." *New York Times,* May 22, 1996.

"'Impressions of Cuba,' Photo Display, to Open," *New York Times,* July 6, 1977.

Jackson, David Earl. "Lifestyle: Call and Response, Books, Marsalis and Stewart Create a Beautiful Portrait in Jazz, Sweet Swing Blues on the Road." *Tri-State Defender,* December 10–14, 1994.

Jenkins, Mark. "Frank Stewart," *The Washington Post,* November 12, 2021.

Jenkins, Mark. "In the Galleries: The Influence of Jazz Resonates in Some of Frank Stewart's Photographs," *The Washington Post,* December 22, 2019.

Kaplan, Richard. "Frank Stewart: Photographer." In *Artist and Influence* 15 (1996): 250–62.

Murphy, Catherine, and George Luna. "Jazz and Rumba in Black and White: An Interview with Photographer Frank Stewart," *CUBANOW – The Digital Magazine of Cuban Arts and Culture*, June 13, 2004.

Reyes, Damaso. "Black photographers come into focus," *New York Amsterdam News*, February 25, 2010.

"Style: Seen," *Essence,* February 1997, 90.

Tate, Greg. "Jazz Crusader," *Vibe*, February 1996, Photographs by Frank Stewart, 54–57.

"Winners of *Black Creation* Photography Contest." *Black Creation: A Quarterly Review of Black Arts and Letters* 4, no. 3 (Summer 1973).

GENERAL REFERENCES (includes catalogues that do not feature Frank Stewart's work)

* Indicates publications known to be in Stewart's personal library

Alabiso, Vincent. *Timeless: Photographs by Kamoinge*. Atglen, PA: Schiffer Publishing, 2015.

* Ashe, Arthur R., Jr. *A Hard Road to Glory: A History of the African–American Athlete Since 1946*. New York: Warner Books, 1988.

* Baal-Teshuva, Jacob. *Mark Rothko, 1903–1970, Pictures as Drama.* Cologne: TASCHEN, 2012.

Bajac, Quentin, et al. *Photography at MoMA, 1960–Now.* New York: Museum of Modern Art, 2015.

* Baraka, Amiri, and Fundi. *In Our Terribleness (Some elements and meaning in black style)*. Indianapolis and New York: Bobbs-Merrill, 1970.

* Barker, Danny. *A Life in Jazz.* New York: Oxford University Press, 1986.

* Barnwell, Andrea D., et al. *The Walter O. Evans Collection of African American Art.* Seattle: The Walter O. Evans Foundation for Art and Literature, 1999.

Berger, John. *Ways of Seeing*. London: British Broadcasting Corporation and Penguin Books, 1977.

Berger, Maurice. *For all the World to See: Visual Culture and the Struggle for Civil Rights.* New Haven: Yale University Press, 2010.

* Borham, Pierre, et al. *André Kertész: His Life and Work*. Boston: Little Brown & Company, 1997.

* Campbell, Mary Schmidt. *An American Odyssey: The Life and Work of Romare Bearden.* New York: Oxford University Press, 2018.

Cartier-Bresson, Henri. *The Decisive Moment: Photographs by Henri Cartier-Bresson.* New York: Simon & Schuster, 1952.

Coar, Valencia Hollins. *A Century of Black Photographers: 1840–1960*. Providence: Museum of Art, Rhode Island School of Design, 1983.

Cole, Ernest. *House of Bondage: A South African Black Man Exposes in His Own Pictures and Words the Bitter Life of his Homeland Today.* New York: Random House, 1967.

Coleman, A. D. *Depth of Field: Essays on Photography, Mass Media, and Lens Culture.* Albuquerque: University of New Mexico Press, 1998.

* Cotton, Charlotte. *The Photograph as Contemporary Art.* London: Thames and Hudson, 2016 (reprint).

* Davis, Susan O'Connor. *Chicago's Historic Hyde Park.* Chicago: University of Chicago Press, 2013.

* Deacon, Terrence W. *The Symbolic Species: The Co-Evolution of Language and the Brain.* New York: Norton, 1997.

* Dodson, Howard, Foreword. *Black New York Artists of the 20th Century: Selections from the Schomburg Center Collections.* New York: New York Public Library, 1998.

* Driskell, David, et al. "The Dianne Whitfield-Locke and Carnell Locke Collection: Building on Tradition." *International Review of African American Art* 24, no. 4 (Fall 2013).

Eckhardt, Sarah L., et al. *Working Together: Louis Draper and the Kamoinge Workshop.* Richmond: Virginia Museum of Fine Arts, 2020.

Frank, Robert. *The Americans.* New York: Grove Press, 1959.

Frank, Robert. *Robert Frank: The Lines of My Hand.* New York: Pantheon Books, 1989.

* Friedlander, Lee. *The Jazz People of New Orleans.* New York: Random House/Pantheon Books, 1992.

Gibson, Ann Eden. *Abstract Expressionism: Other Politics.* New Haven: Yale University Press, 1997.

* Golden, Thelma, Foreword, et al. *The Bearden Project.* New York: The Studio Museum in Harlem, 2012.

* Graham, Alistair. Photographs by Peter Beard. *Eyelids of Morning: The Mingled Destinies of Crocodiles and Men.* San Francisco: A & W Visual Library, 1973.

Grundberg, Andy. *How Photography Became Contemporary Art: Inside an Artistic Revolution from Pop to the Digital Age.* New Haven: Yale University Press, 2021.

* Hanzal, Carla M., et al. *Romare Bearden: Southern Recollections.* Charlotte, NC: The Mint Museum, 2011.

Harris, Jessica B. *High on the Hog: A Culinary Journey from Africa to America.* New York: Bloomsbury Books, 2011.

* Hughes, Langston, and Roy DeCarava. *The Sweet Flypaper of Life.* New York: Simon & Schuster, 1955.

* Kaufman, Frederick. *Manuel Alvarez Bravo: Photographs and Memories.* New York: Aperture, 1997.

* Kelley, Robin D. G. *Thelonious Monk: The Life and Times of an American Original.* New York: Free Press, 2009

* Kismaric, Susan. *Manuel Alvarez Bravo.* New York: Museum of Modern Art, 1997.

* Kitchen Guild of the Tullie Smith House Restoration. *Tullie's Receipts: Nineteenth Century Plantation Plain Style Southern Cooking and Living.* Atlanta: Atlanta Historical Society, 1976.

* Kitto, Svetlana. *Sara Penn's Knobkerry: An Oral History Sourcebook.* Long Island City and New York: Sculpture Center and New York Consolidated, 2021.

* Lewis, Sarah Elizabeth, ed. *Vision and Justice: A Civic Curriculum.* New York: Aperture, 2019.

* Maddow, Ben. *Let Truth Be the Prejudice, W. Eugene Smith: His Life and Photographs.* Philadelphia: Philadelphia Museum of Art, 1985.

* Marsalis, Simeon. *As Lie Is to Grin.* New York: Catapult, 2017.

* Marsalis, Wynton and Carl Vigeland. *Jazz in the Bittersweet Blues of Life.* New York: Da Capo Books, 2001.

* Michaeli, Ethan. *The Defender: How the Legendary Black Newspaper Changed America, From the Age of the Pullman Porters to the Age of Obama.* New York: Houghton Mifflin Harcourt, 2016.

* *Mindfulness: HBR Emotional Intelligence Series.* Boston: Harvard Business School Review Press, 2017.

* Murray, Albert. *The Omni-Americans: Some Alternatives to the Folklore of White Supremacy.* New York: Random House, 1983.

Murray, Albert. *Stomping the Blues.* New York: McGraw-Hill, 1976.

* Parks, Gordon, et al. *Personal Vision: Photographs, Adger Cowans.* New York: Glitterati Incorporated, 2017

* Payne, Les. *A Report from South Africa: White Power/ Black Revolt.* Privately printed by Les Payne. Pulitzer Prize-winning author spent two and a half months in South Africa, as an "honorary White," to produce this eleven-part series first published in *Newsday* from January 30–February 9, 1977.

* Pollitzer, William S. *The Gullah People and their African Heritage.* Athens: University of Georgia Press, 2005. (reprint).

* Pogolotti, Graziella. *Wifredo Lam.* Havana: José Martí, 1997.

Rexer, Lyle. *The Edge of Vision: The Rise of Abstraction in Photography.* New York: Aperture, 2009.

* Rubinfien, Leo, ed. *Garry Winogrand.* San Francisco: San Francisco Museum of Art, 2013.

* Shange, Ntozake. *Wild Beauty/Belleza Salvaje: New and Selected Poems of Ntozake Shange.* Translated by Alejandro Álvarez Nieves. New York: Atria, 2017.

* Shu'aib, Tajuddin B. *The Prescribed Prayer Made Simple.* Los Angeles: Da'awah Enterprises International, 1983.

Taha, Halima. *Collecting African American Art: Works on Paper and Canvas.* New York: Crown, 1998.

Tanner, Lee. *The Jazz Image: Masters of Jazz Photography.* New York: Abrams, 2006.

* Walther, Ingo F. *Van Gogh.* Cologne: TASCHEN, 2000.

Willis, Deborah, ed. *Picturing Us: African American Identity in Photography.* New York: New Press, 1994.

INDEX

Note: Page numbers in *italic* type indicate illustrations.

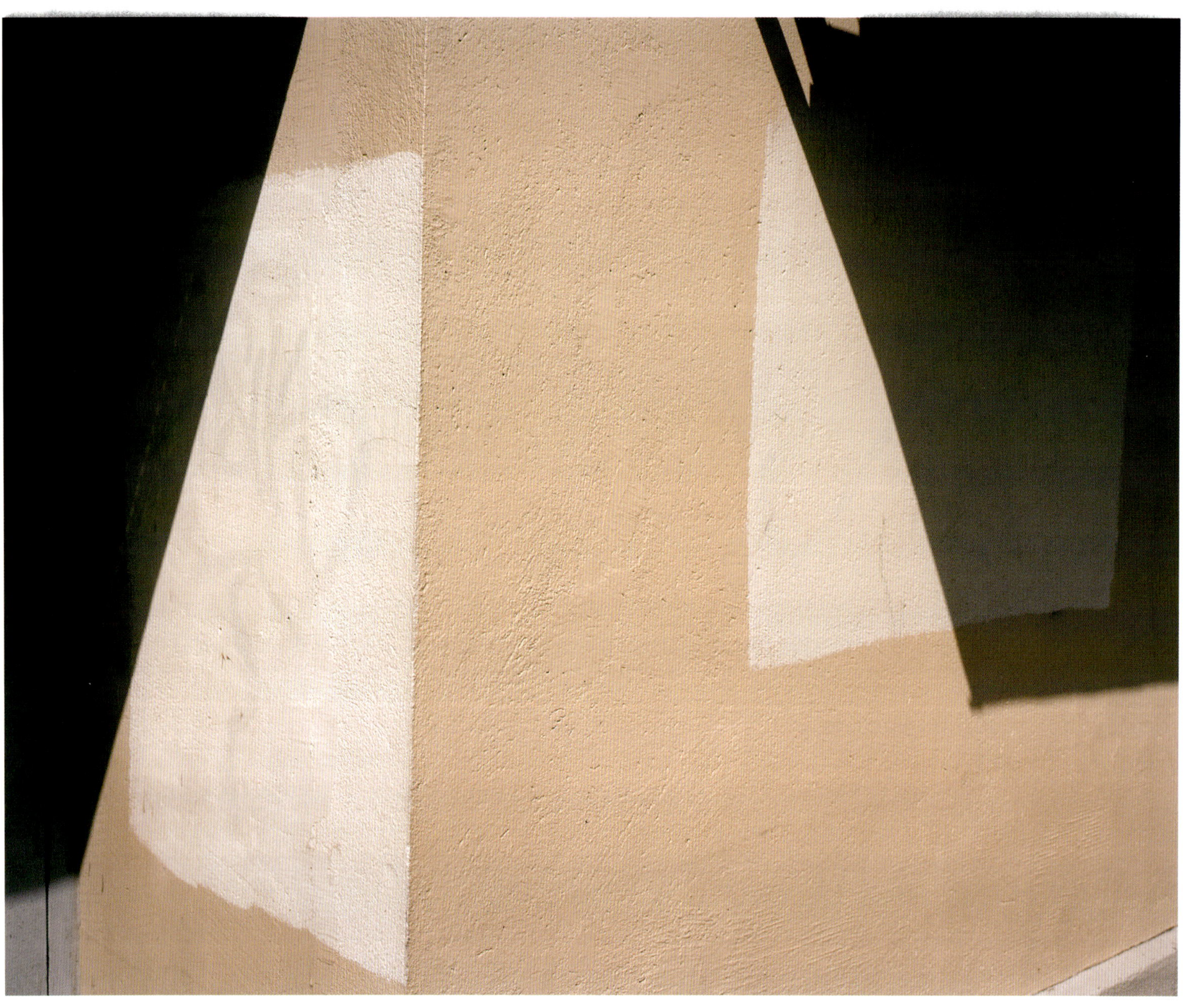

ACKNOWLEDGMENTS

All exhibitions are multifaceted group efforts. During the Covid pandemic, at a time of immense political unrest and expansive social and moral questioning of how society works, this has been especially true. Museum staff members, and other colleagues on hybrid schedules doing remote work, have needed to invent new ways to successfully communicate. We are extremely grateful to all who have contributed to *Frank Stewart's Nexus: An American Photographer's Journey, 1960s to the Present* as well as this catalogue and programming. The project overall is marked by the collective creativity that characterizes its subject, whose roots in the riffs and responses of the music he loves become more evident as the variety of data grows, often in contradiction, with each new piece discovered. The beat goes on.

Greatest appreciation goes to Frank Stewart for his generosity in sharing his time, life's stories, and unique photographic vision. Stewart's elder daughter, Sing Lathan, and grandchildren William, Malaya, Lyra, and Luke welcomed us into their home, with good humor and offers of family expertise. His younger daughter, Bining Taylor, and her children, Boaz and Kay Ling, have likewise been supportive from their home in Austin, Texas, with occasional trips east. Both daughters are important lenders to the exhibition.

Photographer Jeanne Moutoussamy-Ashe, whose friendship with Lee, the name by which Stewart is called by many longtime friends, has been of inspiration and support throughout the exhibition's development. She is also a lender to the exhibition.

To other generous lenders, listed elsewhere, we offer great appreciation for their parting with their treasures for the duration of the exhibition. Several lenders know Stewart personally, and their memorable stories about encounters with him, often over many decades, have immensely aided our research. They include Gordon and Peggy Cooper Davis, Walter O. Evans, Rob Gibson, Sandra Grymes, Andre Kimo Stone Guess and Cheryl Peterson Guess, Corrine Jennings, Wynton Marsalis, Robert O'Meally, George Nelson Preston, John Simmons, Beuford Smith, John-Conrad Ste Marthe, and Marquise Stillwell.

We are also appreciative of a wide range of assistance provided and memories conveyed by many others—gallerists, collectors, friends, and professional associates. The late Edwin "Beauregarde" Phillips provided a multi-day tour of Chicago's South Side, filled with sights, sounds, and tastes, and great memories of his shared childhood with Frank Stewart. Susan Sillins shared her extensive archives about the photographer, as did Halima Taha. Petra Richterová kindly shared many photographs of him. Others to whom we are grateful for a wide variety of assistance are Peg Alston, William Banks, Jonathan Bober, Mel Bochner, Nelson E. Breen, Robert Brown and Christine Neptune, Karen Bucky, Rodríguez Calero, Dana Cranmer, C. Daniel Dawson, Allan Edmunds, Julia Leigh Engel, Laura Frautschi and Ted Smoot, Jeffrey Hoone, Susan John, Jolie Jones, Zooey T. Jones, June Kelly, Sandra Levenson, Daniel Manso, Emma McNally, Michael Lobel, Ted Panken, Greg Scholl, Dalia Scruggs, Jordan Thomas, Kay Wolff, and Pamela Vander Zwan. Sarah Escarrez and Tessa

Two Shapes, c. 2008

Bachi Haas have given immense research and organizational support, and Adrianna Brusie has recently joined that team. Gustavo Garcia and Gabriella Grimaldo have helped with technical matters.

For their enthusiastic support of this catalogue, we thank Charles Miers, publisher of Rizzoli International Publications. At Rizzoli Electa, we are appreciative of critical contributions from Margaret Rennolds Chace, associate publisher; Andrea Danese, senior editor; Alyn Evans, production manager; and Natalie Danford, copyeditor. Phil Kovacevich's elegant design gracefully enhances the subtlety of Frank Stewart's art.

At The Phillips Collection and Telfair Museums, we are appreciative of the support of directors Dorothy Kosinski and Benjamin T. Simons and their enthusiastic staff, especially curators Renée Maurer and Erin Dunn, respectively, and other staff members thanked by the directors in their introductory remarks.

We also join the directors in their thanks to the exhibition's lenders, funders, and other supporters, especially our colleagues whose writing for this catalogue enhance our understanding of *Frank Stewart's Nexus: An American Photographer's Journey, 1960s to the Present*.

RUTH FINE
FRED MOTEN

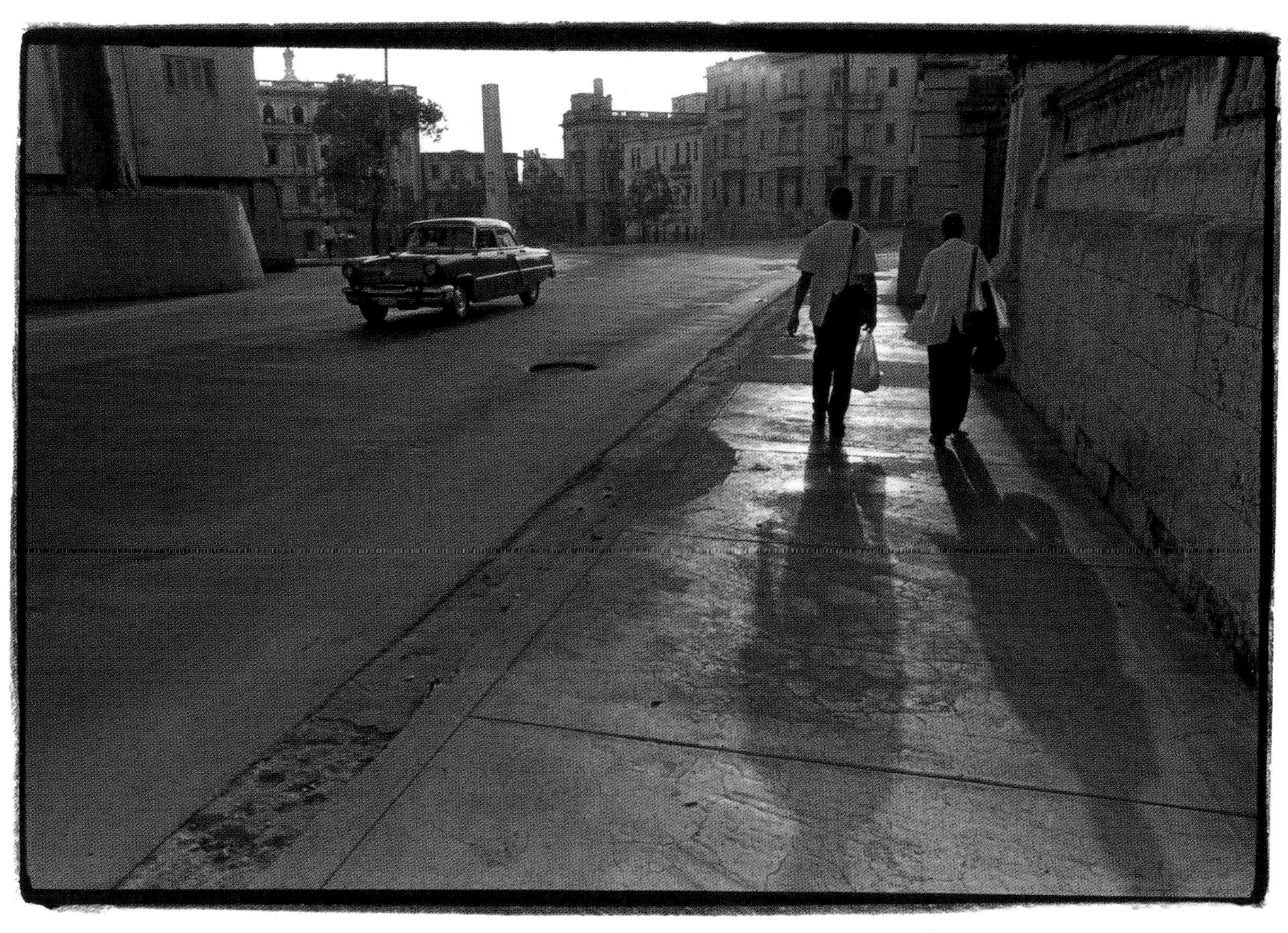

Two Shadows, 1977

This book is published on the occasion of the exhibition
Frank Stewart's Nexus: An American Photographer's Journey, 1960s to the Present

Exhibition Schedule
The Phillips Collection: June 10–September 3, 2023
Artis—Naples, The Baker Museum: October 14, 2023–January 7, 2024
Telfair Museums: February 9–May 12, 2024

All images on the following pages are courtesy Frank Stewart: 72, 73, 77, 78, 81, 168, 169, 170, 171, 173, 175, 177, 178, 179, 180, 181, 183, 184, 185, 186, 187, 188, 189, 190, 204, 207

George's Parlor (page 90), photograph for reproduction courtesy Andrew Gatti.

First published in the United States of America in 2023 by
Rizzoli Electa, A Division of
Rizzoli International Publications, Inc.
300 Park Avenue South
New York, NY 10010
www.rizzoliusa.com

in association with

The Phillips Collection
1600 21st Street, NW
Washington, DC 20009
www.phillipscollection.org

and

Telfair Museums
207 West York Street
Savannah, GA 31401
www.telfair.org

Copyright © 2023 by Telfair Museum of Art

For Rizzoli Electa:
Publisher: Charles Miers
Associate Publisher: Margaret Rennolds Chace
Editor: Andrea Danese
Design: Phil Kovacevich
Copyeditor: Natalie Danford
Proofreader: Kelli Rae Patton
Production Manager: Alyn Evans

All rights reserved. No part of this publication may be reproduced, stored in a retrieval system, or transmitted in any form or by any means, electronic, mechanical, photocopying, recording, or otherwise, without prior consent of the publishers.

Printed in Hong Kong

2023 2024 2025 2026 / 10 9 8 7 6 5 4 3 2 1

ISBN: 978-0-8478-9935-7

Library of Congress Control Number: 2022949899

Visit us online:
Facebook.com/RizzoliNewYork
Twitter: @Rizzoli_Books
Instagram.com/RizzoliBooks
Pinterest.com/RizzoliBooks
Youtube.com/user/RizzoliNY
Issuu.com/Rizzoli